Rereading Women in Latin America and the Caribbean

Latin American Perspectives
in the Classroom
Series Editor: Ronald Chilcote

Transnational Latina/o Communities: Politics, Processes, and Cultures
Edited by Carlos G. Vélez-Ibáñez and Anna Sampaio, with Manolo
González-Estay

Forthcoming

The Zapatista Movement in Chiapas: Indigenous Peoples and the State
Edited by Jan Rus, Rosalva Aída Hernández, and Shannan L. Mattiace

Rereading Women in Latin America and the Caribbean

The Political Economy of Gender

Edited by Jennifer Abbassi
and Sheryl L. Lutjens

ROWMAN & LITTLEFIELD PUBLISHERS, INC.
Lanham • *Boulder* • *New York* • *Oxford*

ROWMAN & LITTLEFIELD PUBLISHERS, INC.

Published in the United States of America
by Rowman & Littlefield Publishers, Inc.
An Imprint of Rowman & Littlefield Publishing Group
4720 Boston Way, Lanham, Maryland 20706
www.rowmanlittlefield.com

12 Hid's Copse Road, Cumnor Hill, Oxford OX2 9JJ, England

British Library Cataloguing in Publication Information Available

Library of Congress Cataloging-in-Publication Data

Rereading women in Latin America and the Caribbean : the political economy of gender
/ edited by Jennifer Abbassi and Sheryl L. Lutjens
    p. cm.
    Includes bibliographical references and index.
    ISBN 0-7425-1074-3 (cloth : alk. paper) — ISBN 0-7425-1075-1 (pbk. : alk. paper)
    1. Women—Latin America—Economic conditions. 2. Women—Caribbean
Area—Economic conditions. 3. Women—Latin America—Social conditions. 4.
Women—Caribbean Area—Social conditions. 5. Women in politics—Latin America. 6.
Women in politics—Caribbean Area. I. Abbassi, Jennifer, 1961– II. Lutjens, Sheryl.

HQ1460.5 .R46 2001
305.42'098—dc21

2001044219

Printed in the United States of America

♾ ™ The paper used in this publication meets the minimum requirements of American
National Standard for Information Sciences—Permanence of Paper for Printed Library
Materials, ANSI/NISO Z39.48-1992.

Contents

Series Introduction   ix
   Ronald H. Chilcote

Acknowledgments   xi

Introduction: Theory, Themes, and the Realities of Gender
in Latin America   1
   Jennifer Abbassi and Sheryl L. Lutjens

Part I: Women, Work, and Development

1   Introduction to Part I   19
   Selection from "Women, Development, and Anthropological
      Facts and Fictions," by *Eleanor Leacock*   20
   Selection from "Approaches to Understanding the Position of
      Women in the Informal Sector," by *Tamar Diana Wilson*   29

2   Economic Restructuring and Gender Subordination   43
   Helen I. Safa

3   The Urban Family and Poverty in Latin America   61
   Mercedes González de la Rocha

4   The Myth of Being "Like a Daughter"   78
   Grace Esther Young

5 Women in Mexico's Popular Movements: Survival Strategies against Ecological and Economic Impoverishment   91
Lynn Stephen

6 Caribbean Transnationalism As a Gendered Process   112
Christine G. T. Ho

Part II: Politics, Policies, and the State

7 Introduction to Part II   131
Selection from "Mobilizing Women: Revolution in the Revolution," by *Norma Stoltz Chinchilla*   132
Selection from "Gender Equality in the Salvadoran Transition," by *Ilja A. Luciak*   142

8 Chilean Women's Organizations and Their Potential for Change   157
Rosa M. Cañadell

9 *El Comité de Amas de Casa de Siglo XX:* An Organizational Experience of Bolivian Women   172
Moema Viezzer

10 The Mother of the Nicaraguans: Doña Violeta and the UNO's Gender Agenda   179
Karen Kampwirth

11 Constructing and Negotiating Gender in Women's Police Stations in Brazil   197
Sara Nelson

12 Reading between the Lines: Women, the State, and Rectification in Cuba   213
Sheryl L. Lutjens

13 Seeking Our Own Food: Indigenous Women's Power and Autonomy in San Pedro, Chenalhó, Chiapas (1980–1998)   231
Christine E. Eber

Part III: Culture, History, and Feminisms

14 Introduction to Part III   249

Selection from "Women, Class, and Education in Mexico,
  1880–1928," by *Mary K. Vaughan*   251
Selection from "Reclaiming Voices: Notes on a New Female
  Practice in Journalism," by *Margaret Randall*   261
Selection from "If Truth Be Told," by *Jan Rus*   264

15 Story without Words: Women and the Creation of a *Mestizo*
  People in Guayaquil, 1820–1835   278
  Camilla Townsend

16 Brazilian Women in Exile: The Quest for an Identity   294
  Angela Xavier de Brito

17 Remembering the Dead: Latin American Women's
  "Testimonial" Discourse   311
  Nancy Saporta Sternbach

18 Róger Sánchez's "Humor Erótico" and the *Semana Cómica*:
  A Sexual Revolution in Sandinista Nicaragua?   323
  David Kunzle

19 *Evita*: The Globalization of a National Myth   344
  Marta E. Savigliano

Annotated Index of Articles on Women and Gender in
  Latin American Perspectives   361

Index   375

About the Contributors   389

Series Introduction

Since its inception, *Latin American Perspectives* has worked to make its material available for classroom use. Our goal has been to introduce students to some of the important themes and issues about Latin America that have appeared in the journal and make them accessible to students. Our pedagogical plan has been to trim individual articles to their essential core, reorganize them into teachable groups—each preceded by a contextualizing commentary, and add a general introductory essay. To ensure that our material is effectively oriented for classroom use, all articles have been reviewed by three to four *LAP* editors, including the volume editors and myself.

The chapters in this volume all have been drawn from the journal, generally from several issues published during the past few years, but they have been reorganized, trimmed, and edited by Jennifer Abbassi and Sheryl L. Lutjens, with substantive introductions to guide students into issues and content. Relevant source material has been identified to encourage students to delve further into this dynamic subject.

All this would not have been possible without the enthusiasm and commitment of Rowman & Littlefield and its editor, Susan McEachern, who adopted the series and pushed it forward quickly. We are hopeful that the series will be different than past efforts of publishers to develop textbook anthologies as we strive to be relevant to a broad range of student interests in the social sciences and particularly in Latin America.

Ronald H. Chilcote
Series Editor

Acknowledgments

This book has been a labor of love, as well as of learning. We are grateful to Susan McEachern and others at Rowman & Littlefield for their concern that such a textbook be available to students, to the *Latin American Perspectives* Collective—and especially Ron Chilcote—for trusting us to carry out this project, and to the many authors whose writings are gathered here for the research that has forwarded the study of women in Latin America and the Caribbean.

We acknowledge the support of the College of Social and Behavioral Sciences, and Dean Susanna Maxwell, of Northern Arizona University. We have not been alone in the work of editing this collection of essays. For invaluable research and editorial assistance—from scanning to proofreading to searches in the library—thanks are due to Jessica L. Urban, Ph.D. candidate at Northern Arizona University, and T. Mark Montoya, Ph.D. student at Northern Arizona University. Finally, for her keen eye, quick mind, and willingness to work on weekends, much appreciation goes to Kudrat Virk, Randolph-Macon Woman's College alumna and Oxford University graduate student.

Introduction

Theory, Themes, and the Realities of Gender in Latin America

Jennifer Abbassi and Sheryl L. Lutjens

The study of women offers a special lens on the realities of contemporary Latin America, one that makes women visible as active historical subjects and invites a feminist rereading of the economic, political, and cultural construction of their lives and power. Though not entirely absent from historical narratives and other scholarship, research on women in recent decades has opened Latin America's past, legitimized new analytical tools, and created important scholarly space for the increasingly demanding examination of women's subordination, struggles for change, and possible futures. Women have been recovered and researched in different ways; the interplay of different theoretical traditions with women's actions, demands, and ideas—past and present—has fomented multiple, and often competing, frameworks for including women. Choices must be made about how to focus the lens that the study of women can provide. A feminist rereading shows why our choices are crucial for recovering women in practice and for theory; it explores the significance of their gains and struggles over time; and it reveals the contributions that feminist theorizing has made in promoting gender as a relevant—indeed necessary—concept in a critical political economy analysis of Latin America and the Caribbean.

"WOMEN" IN "LATIN AMERICA AND THE CARIBBEAN"

Viewed from afar, "Latin America" is a geopolitical division, a region whose colonial and postcolonial economic development, despite substantial and important variations, charts a historically defined, shared location within the capitalist world economy. A regional heritage of centralization and exclusionary

1

class politics traces striking similarities in state formation, including recent experiences with military rule that reflect ongoing problems in the pursuit of democracy. How is it possible to study the realities of women in the thirty-three different societies that comprise Latin America and the Caribbean? People are not normally analyzed as regional beings. In what ways does the category of Latin American women make sense? Women in Latin America and the Caribbean share with women everywhere basic inequalities in relation to men, and classifying women in regional terms may thus make common sense. Often disaggregated into the Caribbean, Central American, and South American subregions for statistical purposes, there are indeed patterned regional conditions that differentiate Latin American and Caribbean women from women in developed countries and other still-developing regions in what has been—and is still—called the Third World.

A broad-brushed portrait of the region's women might begin with some statistics, such as those published in the U.N. report on the status of women worldwide in 2000 (United Nations, 2000). Latin American and Caribbean women are distinguished by the rapid rise in their participation in waged work after 1950, for example. U.N. statistics report that between 1980 and 1997, women's economic activity rate rose from 38 percent to 43 percent in the Caribbean, from 27 percent to 33 percent in Central America, and from 27 percent to 38 percent in South America; in 1997, 53 percent of Caribbean women worked outside the home (compared to 44 percent in 1980), 39 percent of Central American women worked outside the home (compared to 31 percent in 1980), and 45 percent of South American women did (compared to 29 percent in 1980) (United Nations, 2000: 110). Statistics document additional changes that are widely assumed to be positive. Women's access to education has expanded tremendously in the Latin American and Caribbean region. Female illiteracy has declined, and gross combined primary and secondary school enrollment ratios for the 1994–1996 period are 93 for girls in the Caribbean, 80 in Central America, and 91 in South America, higher than for boys in both the Caribbean and South American subregions (United Nations, 2000: 86). Girls drop out of school at rates equivalent to boys, a significant gain when compared to other regions of the world, and women have moved in great numbers into higher education. And in the early twenty-first century, more women than ever are found in elected positions in local and national governments in the region.

Other measures of the conditions of women's lives offer more detail about what is specific to them, as women. Women's life expectancy has risen and is higher than men's in all subregions, for example. Women-as-mothers now demonstrate lower fertility rates; in the 1995–2000 period the fertility rate was 2.3 children per woman in the Caribbean, 3.7 children per woman in Central America, and 2.9 children per woman in South America, lower than in the 1990–1995 period and significantly lower than in the 1950s and 1960s. The percentage of married women using contraceptives in the 1993–1997 period was 56 percent in Central America and 62 percent in South America, a slight rise over the 1985–1992 period (percentages in the Caribbean were not reported; United Nations, 2000: 32). The percentage of births in health care facilities was 86 percent in the Caribbean, 62 percent in Central America, and 76 percent in South America (United Nations, 2000: 61), and infant mortality rates range from 6 per 1,000 live births in Cuba, 10 in Jamaica, and 11 in Chile to 45 in Guatemala, 56 in Guyana, 64 in Bolivia, and 83 in Haiti (UNICEF, 2000). The percentage of household heads who are women was 36 percent in the Caribbean, 22 percent in Central America, and 22 percent in South America (United Nations, 2000: 42).

Determining what a quantitative portrait of regional and subregional women provides, however, requires explicit awareness of what it is we wish to know about them. It is the task of theory to provide the ends and the means for analyzing women; theory catalyzes our questions and determines how they are answered. In 2001, the questions about women in Latin America are many, provocative, and intimately related to those asked about the region as a whole. Contemporary globalization, for example, provides a backdrop of striking international, regional, and national inequalities, and an extensive and deepening poverty that affects women and their children. The richest fifth of the world population has a 74-times greater share of global income than the poorest fifth, and while daily exchange averages more than $1 trillion on world currency markets, 1.3 billion people live on $1 each day (Wichterich, 2000: 126; "Special Report," 2000: 74). More than 600 million of these poorest of the poor are children (UNICEF, n.d.: 22). The neoliberal strategies that have reoriented Latin American and Caribbean economies to globalization's demands are celebrated for spurring the successful recovery of regional growth. Yet, income in Latin America rose but 6 percent in the past twenty years ("Special Report," 2000: 74), and two of the four countries that had the greatest internal inequalities in 1996 were in Latin America—Brazil and Guatemala (the others are Guinea-Bissau and the United States, Wichterich, 2000: 126). Nearly 40 percent of the population in Guatemala lives on less than $1 a day. How should we reconcile statistics that demonstrate women's gains with these indicators of misery and pain?

STUDYING WOMEN

Research on women has proliferated in past decades, reflecting the growing legitimacy of the category of "women" as a focus of scholarship in many disciplines, as well as the evolution and revolutions in feminist theorizing. Theory that has roots in feminism is quite diverse, though it is useful to note that feminism-as-ideology spotlights shared assumptions that the oppression or subordination of women exists, is wrong, and can be remedied (Jaggar, 1983). Feminist theorizing has attached variously to liberalism, Marxism, psychological theory, environmentalism, and "post"-thinking of all sorts, accepting foundational assumptions, recasting questions and methodologies in significant ways, and sometimes producing new answers (see the surveys in Humm, 1992; Tong, 1998; and Kemp and Squires, 1998). Feminist theorizing has also cultivated some distinctive insights, and can claim originality in pursuing the experiential "truth" of woman/women as a unique epistemology. The often-heated debates in feminism have pushed theorizing forward, both in terms of feminist adaptations of other theories and in the interior of a now distinctively feminist philosophical or epistemological field.

Signal points in the theoretical movements surrounding the study of women are several. One is choosing the concept of gender, rather than the category of women, to focus analysis. Gender, writes Scott, "is the social organization of sexual difference" (1998: 2); in contrast to the biologically based category of women, gender is the social construction that prescribes and proscribes behaviors, places, and their power as masculine and feminine. The use of gender in thinking about the dynamics of oppression(s) reflects feminisms' attempts to avoid "essentialism." Essentialism, according to Jackson, is "thinking that treats social phenomena (like gender and sexuality) as if they exist prior to and outside the social and cultural discourses, practices, and structures which give rise to them" (1998: 133). The gendering of individuals—biological as women and men may be—varies from society to society, though few dispute that the feminine is everywhere subordinated to the privileged masculine, or that gender hierarchies find an enduring expression in the distinction between the masculine public and the feminine private spheres. Feminist theorizing is thus keen to find and know the differences among women, liberating them from the power of a category (women) that universalizes experiences in sometimes dangerous ways (Fuss, 1989; Gunew and Yeats, 1993; Bulbeck, 1998).

A second point of reference is the political relocation that characterized the emergence of contemporary feminist theories. Key breakthroughs associated with dramatically new claims by 1970s feminists are typically identified in historical relation to Second Wave Feminism—the movements that began in the United States and Europe in the 1960s and 1970s. Though strong liberal currents were and still are found in feminist activism and scholarship, the issue of location invokes the specific relationship of feminism to New Left movements. Women reacted to the organizational sexism of the New Left, claiming the "personal as political" in several ways. On the one hand, those who became "radical" feminists redefined politics to bring it into the personal/private sphere, critiquing the personal sexism of New Left activists and identifying patriarchy as a primordial and universal system of power and domination (Daly, 1978). On the other hand, feminists also directed radical feminist insights to a reworking of some of the foundational assumptions of Marxism. What became socialist feminism still pursued transformation from the left, sustaining the critique of capitalism, including a concern with patriarchy as a system more or less "marriageable" to Marxism, and among other shifts, expanding the concept of labor to encompass the private sphere where women worked (Eisenstein, 1979; Barrett, 1980). Male (or gender) power versus capitalism and class power have in important ways delimited the terrain of debate as feminists retheorized their own and others' consciousness, practices, and power.

The celebration in the 1990s of an apparent consensus in feminist perspectives is a third point of reference. Feminisms now have an array of new labels to name themselves and their debates, including sameness versus difference feminism, rights versus cultural feminism, gynocentric versus postmodern feminism, and more (Bulbeck, 1998). In these debates, a victory has been proclaimed for difference/cultural/postmodern perspectives, a victory of "words" over "things," according to Barrett, one that reflects feminist engagements with "post"-thinking. Writing at the start of the 1990s, Barrett explained that humanities, arts, and philosophy were the fertile node of feminist theorizing, displacing social sciences.

> Within this general shift we can see a marked interest in analysing processes of symbolization and representation—the field of "culture"—and attempts to develop a better understanding of subjectivity, the psyche, and the self. The type of feminist sociology that has a wider audience, for example, has shifted away from a determinist model of "social structure" (be it capitalism, or patriarchy, or a gender-segmented labour market or whatever) and deals with questions of culture, sexuality, or political agency—obvious counterbalances to an emphasis on social structure. (Barrett, 1992: 204)

Barrett accepts that the paradigmatic shift and issues placed thereby on feminist agendas, such as sexuality, subjectivity, and textuality, may best reflect U.S. and European tendencies (1992: 204, 215). The shift—and tendencies—effect the rejections accomplished by postmodern theorizing in its various expressions (post-Marxist, poststructural, and postfeminist, among others) (Hollinger, 1994; Nicholson, 1990). The essentialized or naturalized subjects of modernist theory—liberalism's individual and Marxism's class—are no longer presumed to be self-determining, nor are meaning and experience authenticated by appeals to consciousness, universality, or metanarratives of any sort. In this way, the materialist foundations of Marxist and socialist feminisms have been abandoned by many; discourse, not structures, is the focus for understanding and analysis—of women, gender, and power. Materialism has been redefined as cultural or discursive materialism, and class, too, is undergoing a post-rethinking (Ebert, 1995; Gibson-Graham, Resnick, and Wolff, 2000).

THE GENDER OF POLITICAL ECONOMY

The "post" impulses also affect the political economy perspectives that have oriented the scholarship on and from Latin America. Old debates about the adequacy—and orthodoxy—of dependency and underdevelopment theories that issued from Latin America as original contributions to a Marxist political economy, already sidelined perhaps, have been displaced from center stage. Globalization's multiple logics—economic, political, and cultural—orient current discussions that are variously influenced by the older and newer "posts"—postdevelopment, postcolonialism—as well as cultural studies and subaltern studies (for example, Jameson, 1991; Williams and Chrisman, 1994; Rahnema, 1997; Sachs, 1992; During, 1993). Traditional approaches centered in class, structural analysis, and imperialism seem outmoded in the face of the internationalized production of the 2000s, associated with an unprecedented speed in the movement of commodities, finance capital, information, services, and labor. Serious discussion of the relevance of Marxism continues, however (Wood and Foster, 1997; Landry, 2000), and Latin American debates about postmodernism themselves encourage careful consideration of the realities—and materialities—of the old and the new in globalization (Beverley, Oviedo, and Aronna, 1995).

The gendering of political economy has been integral in the reorientation of the critics of capitalism in several ways. Feminists have interrogated the assumed gender-neutrality of political economy and international political economy, assailing and emending the masculine biases discovered (Chowdhry, 1994). Production is now quite commonly understood to include women, the domestic sphere, and reproduction, while the gendering of public and private is used to parse the place of women in the new global division of labor, as well as the differential impacts of internationalized production on women (Wichterich, 2000; Marchand and Runyan, 2000; Sassen, 1996). Indeed, these days the "private is global," according to Steans (1999) and others. The retheorizing that has got under way also implicates feminist theory in the move away from class and a critical, Marxist structuralism. As Post writes in offering a "reformulation" of Marxism,

> Both at the centre and on the periphery, if Marxism does not come to terms with the growing demand of women for their special liberation, by theorising it properly and thus giving a basis for appropriate action in alliance with non-Marxist feminists, it

will also have finally failed. This must form a major part of our task of reconstruction, demanding what will be termed here a "gendered reading" of any theoretical proposition. (Post, 1996: 21)

Munck agrees, noting "how capitalocentric" radical political economy is and commenting that "perhaps the most exciting and far-reaching interaction between theory and practice has been between feminism, postmodernism, and development" (2000: 153, 151).

Nevertheless, women are still omitted altogether in some scholarly writings on globalization, neoliberal capitalist strategies, and development, and radical political economy does not always acknowledge gender.

THIRD WORLD FEMINISM(S) AND LATIN AMERICA

The scholarship on women in Latin America and the Caribbean reflects these consequential currents in both feminist theories and radical political economy. This scholarship has grown enormously since the since the 1970s, both inside and outside the region (see Stoner, 1989); it addresses issues defined by old and new scholarly agendas, while posing intriguingly different questions about power relationships in feminist theories and practices. Have Latin American feminists written and acted separate from, underneath, or with the "center" feminisms in their academic production and preoccupations? From conquest and colonialism to the turbo capitalism of present-day globalization, regional history reflects its incorporation into international dynamics. The ideas of Third World feminism are especially relevant in seeing the ways in which writing by and about Latin America's women has been calibrated with, rather than by, the scholarship of researchers and feminists, inside and outside the United States.

Some center feminists still profess socialist feminist commitments or call for rethinking feminism in materialist terms (Segal, 1999; Ebert, 1995; Hennessy and Ingraham, 1997; Tinsman, 2000; also, see the radical feminist views in Bell and Klein, 1996). The tendency to claim the materiality of class relations and anticapitalist positions in the study of women and gender is particularly strong in the writing of the women of color and Third World feminists. Charging Second Wave U.S. feminists with middle-class, white prejudices that damaged their feminist theory and its practices (hooks, 1984, for example), an emergent Third World feminism forced attention to the intersection of gender, race, class, and sexuality, and the subsequent transformation of political strategies (Sandoval, 1995). The perception of multiple hierarchies of domination—and differences—now characterizes theorizing by and of Third World women elsewhere, with the addition of the domination enacted through global (postcolonial) capitalism (Mohanty, 1997). Care is needed, then, in theorizing the experience of Third World women, including women in Latin America and the Caribbean. As Johnson-Odim and Strobel warn, calling upon the path-breaking work of Chandra Mohanty (1991), women must not be assumed to be anomalies, victims, or "exotics" (1999: xxxiv).

The careful recovery of both extraordinary women and their more ordinary counterparts in Latin American and Caribbean history has advanced noticeably. Histories have been compiled for both students and scholars (Hahner, 1976; Lavrín, 1978; Miller, 1991; Socolow, 2000; and Navarro and Sánchez Korrol, 1999), studying women in their preconquest societal contexts, as slaves or workers under colonial rule, as colonialists, as wives and mothers, and as workers, activists, feminists. Thus, many more names join the ranks of such women as Malinche/Malinal/Malintzin, the Tabascan slave woman who participated in Cortés's conquest of the Aztec kingdom, and Mexican nun Sor Juana Inés de la Cruz (1648–1695), one of the greatest lyric poets ever to write in Spanish, according to Miller (1991: 24–27). Others, more contemporary, can include Alaide Foppe de Solórzano, an exile in Mexico who helped create the feminist journal *fem* (Mexico) and later was "disappeared" in her native Guatemala; the *Madres de la Plaza de Mayo* (Mothers of the Plaza de Mayo) in Buenos Aires; or Guatemalan Nobel Prize recipient Rigoberta Menchú Tum. Social science research also gathered momentum (for example, Pescatello, 1973).

Jaquette (1995) argues that the foment in center feminisms in the early 1970s was not mirrored in Latin American women's scholarship. Instead, the new research on women and work that began in the 1970s reflected the radical political economy perspective of capitalist development in Latin America. According to Nash's account, a first conference on "feminine perspectives" was held in Buenos Aires in 1974 (1986: 3), prompted by the need for empirical research to remedy the neglect of women's economic contributions (Aguiar, 1986). Four more conferences occurred in Latin America in the 1970s, followed by further regional and international gatherings in the 1980s (Nash, 1986: 3). Economic research produced needed empirical data and studies explored a number of issues, including labor market segmentation, the position of women in different modes of production, and changes in the international division of labor (Nash, 1986: 4). The scholarship appearing in English during the 1970s included pathbreaking collections, ranging from books (for example, Nash and Safa, 1976) to the special double issue "Women and Class Struggle" published in *Latin American Perspectives* in winter/spring 1977 followed by another issue in the fall.

The empirical methodological bent and embrace of Marxism, in Jaquette's view, allowed a radical critique that focused on women "without risking the label of 'feminist'" (1995: 113). Studies of women and economic development have continued, building on the pioneering work of the early feminist scholars inside and outside the region (Acevedo, 1995). The scholarship in Latin America has over time, however, created a distinctively feminist agenda. In the decades that followed the 1959 Cuban revolution, leftist politics included many women in regional struggles for social transformation, drawing them into armed struggle and pushing them into exile as military terror escalated. With the U.N. decade for women from 1975 to 1985, the repatriation of women from exile, and the return to democracy, explains Jaquette (1995), researchers could more safely identify as "feminist." The new democracies of the 1980s were in other ways propitious for expanding beyond economics to do more and deeper research on politics (Chancy, 1979). Jacquette asserts that women could draw on their own movements against dictatorship, using the unconventional politics of protest to advance political analysis of a feminist sort. The research on women's movements during and after military dictatorship has burgeoned (Jelin, 1990; León, 1994). Both within and outside the region, feminist scholars have crossed traditional boundaries to contend with the dilemmas of power and politics, exploring history, language, and culture (Dore, 1997), and the state (Dore and Molyneux, 2000).

The feminist agenda, both scholarly and political, reflects the complexities of regional history. Machismo and marianismo, the distinctive gender ideologies that have inflected women's lives with iberic traditions of family, church, and state (Stevens, 1973), are durable. Formal feminisms have found roots at different times and rates, in different geographical and cultural locations, as Lavrín points out in her history of turn-of-the-century feminisms in Chile, Argentina, and Uruguay (1995), and others have explored in recent studies (Alvarez, 1998; Vargas, 1992). These early Southern Cone feminisms had two "nuances," according to Lavrín: socialist and liberal (1995: 5). Much as the modern U.S. women's movement emerged in critical dialogue with the left, so have the Latin American feminisms long responded to, and engaged with, the region's left. That engagement continues (Castro, 1997), though it reflects myriad changes in feminists, feminisms, and the left inside and outside Latin America and the Caribbean, rather than the imposition or mimicking of other feminists' feminisms.

The study of women can indeed provide a special lens on contemporary Latin America, though we must focus it carefully if we are to achieve a gendered rereading of the puzzles of political economy in the 2000s. Lynne Segal writes, in defending her ongoing position as a socialist feminist:

> Fearful of totalizing generalizations we may be, and cautious we must be, but the most central global axes of economic exploitation and cultural oppression continue

to construct and reconstruct themselves in the interrelated terms of "gender" (tied in with sexual orientation), "class" (tied in with nationality and ethnicity) and "race" (tied in with nationality, ethnicity, and religion) within what is the currently *ever more* totalizing control of a transnational capitalist market. The invocation of specific differences can serve broadly based transformative ends, but only as part of *some wider political project* seeking to dismantle these basic structures of domination. (1999: 35)

THE BOOK

The writings gathered in this volume explore questions about women, their place and power, including how to theorize them into the past and future of a region that has long faced great economic and political challenges. The political economy of development in Latin America is thus the backdrop for thinking about women and gender. All the essays included here[1] have been published previously in *Latin American Perspectives*, founded in 1974 as a "theoretical and scholarly journal for discussion and debate on the political economy of capitalism, imperialism, and socialism in the Americas." The first special issues on women in Latin America and the Caribbean were published in the late 1970s; over time, the journal has included empirical studies of women's place in capitalist and socialist development, advanced socialist feminist theorizing as part of a critical political economy, and engaged directly the cultural turns that have so profoundly challenged Marxism and Marxist perspectives. As the annotated bibliography of articles that have appeared in the past twenty-seven years reveals, the presence of women in the pages of *Latin American Perspectives* tells an important story about the possibilities—and need—for gendering political economy, about the relevance of materialist feminisms, and about the political context of our choices for the study of Latin America.

The book offers a broad survey of women in Latin America, organizing the chapters into three sections to focus on work, politics, and culture. Certainly not a new thematic scheme, this organization presses attention to old and newer questions about women. The essays focus on women in a variety of countries in the region—from Cuba to Argentina, Mexico, Peru, Brazil, and Puerto Rico, among others. They also demonstrate a range of research strategies, including case studies, participant-observer methods, content analysis, as well as historical and comparative approaches and a vibrant concern for the "local." Together, the essays should promote critical thinking about methodological choices in studying women and gender, as well as about the structural dynamics of Latin American economies, contemporary forms of politics, and the significance of international and local cultural movements in twenty-first-century global capitalism. Each of the three sections begins with an excerpt that highlights a signal moment in feminist theorizing, as well as a brief introductory discussion of the state of the region's women and key issues in theory and research in the early twenty-first century. Inserts provide additional opportunities to reconsider specific women's lives. In this way, a rereading of political economy is encouraged, one that can explore critically the material and ideational conditions of women's lives and struggles, discovering their past and present contributions to development, and furthering our own understanding of Latin America and the Caribbean.

NOTE

1. Most of the essays appear here in an edited version.

SUGGESTED READINGS

Michèle Barrett, "Words and things: Materialism and method in contemporary feminist analysis," pp. 201–219 in Michèle Barrett and Anne Phillips (eds.), *Destabilizing Theory: Contemporary Feminist Debates*. Stanford, CA: Stanford University Press, 1992.

Teresa L. Ebert, "(Untimely) critiques for a red feminism," pp. 113–149 in Mas'ud Zavarzadeh, Teresa L. Ebert, and Donald Morton (eds.), *Post-ality: Marxism and Postmodernism*. Washington, DC: Marxist Boundary Work in Theory, Economics, Politics and Culture, vol. 1, Maisonneuve Press, 1995.

Jane Jaquette, "Rewriting the scripts: Gender in the comparative study of Latin American politics," pp. 111–133 in Peter H. Smith (ed.), *Latin America in Comparative Perspective: New Approaches to Methods and Analysis*. Boulder, CO: Westview Press, 1995.

Elizabeth Jelin (ed.), *Women and Social Change in Latin America*. London: Zed Books. 1990.

Francesca Miller, *Latin American Women and the Search for Social Justice*. Hanover, NH: University Press of New England, 1991.

Chandra Talpade Mohanty, "Under Western eyes: Feminist scholars and colonial discourses," pp. 51–80 in Chandra Talpade, Ann Russo, and Lourdes Torres (eds.), *Third World Women and the Politics of Feminism*. Bloomington: Indiana University Press, 1991.

Marysa Navarro and Virginia Sánchez Korrol, with Kecia Ali, *Women in Latin America and the Caribbean: Restoring Women to History*. Bloomington: Indiana University Press, 1999.

REFERENCES

Acevedo, Luz del Alba

1995 "Feminist inroads in the study of women's work and development," pp. 65–98 in Christine E. Bose and Edna Acosta-Belén (eds.), *Women in the Latin American Development Process*. Philadelphia: Temple University Press.

Aguiar, Neuma
1986 "Research guidelines: How to study women's work in Latin America," pp. 22–33 in June Nash and Helen I. Safa (eds.), *Women and Change in Latin America*. South Hadley, MA: Bergin & Garvey.

Alvarez, Sonia E.
1998 "Latin American feminisms 'go global': Trends of the 1990s and challenges for the new millennium," pp. 293–324 in Sonia E. Alvarez, Evelina Dagnino, and Arturo Escobar (eds.), *Cultures of Politics, Politics of Cultures: Re-Visioning Latin American Social Movements*. Boulder, CO: Westview Press.

Barrett, Michèle
1980 *Women's Oppression Today: Problems in Marxist Feminist Analysis*. London: Verso.
1992 "Words and things: Materialism and method in contemporary feminist analysis," pp. 201–219 in Michèle Barrett and Anne Phillips (eds.), *Destabilizing Theory: Contemporary Feminist Debates*. Stanford, CA: Stanford University Press.

Bell, Diane and Renate Klein
1996 *Radically Speaking: Feminism Reclaimed*. North Melbourne: Spinifex.

Beverley, John, José Oviedo, and Michael Aronna (eds.)
1995 *The Postmodernism Debate in Latin America*. Durham, NC: Duke University Press.

Bulbeck, Chilla
1998 *Re-Orienting Western Feminisms: Women's Diversity in a Postcolonial World*. Cambridge: Cambridge University Press.

Campioni, Mia and Elizabeth Grosz
1991 "Love's labours lost: Marxism and feminism," pp. 366–397 in Sneja Gunew (ed.), *A Reader in Feminist Knowledge*. London: Routledge.

Castro, Mary Garcia
1997 "Feminismos y feminismo: Reflexoes à esquerda." *Presença da Mulher* 11 (August).

Chaney, Elsa M.
1979 *Supermadre: Women in Politics in Latin America*. Austin: Institute of Latin American Studies, University of Texas Press.

Chowdhry, Geeta
1994 "Women and the international political economy," pp. 155–171 in Peter R. Beckman and Francine D'Amico (eds.), *Women, Gender, and World Politics: Perspectives, Policies, and Prospects*. Westport, CT: Bergin & Garvey.

Daly, Mary
1978 *Gyn/Ecology: The Metaethics of Radical Feminism*. Boston: Beacon Press.

Dore, Elizabeth (ed.)
1997 *Gender Politics in Latin America: Debates in Theory and Practice*. New York: Monthly Review Press.

Dore, Elizabeth and Maxine Molyneux (eds.)
2000 *Hidden Histories of Gender and the State in Latin America*. Durham, NC: Duke University Press.

During, Simon
1993 *The Cultural Studies Reader*. London: Routledge.

Ebert, Teresa L.
1995 "(Untimely) critiques for a red feminism," pp. 113–149 in Mas'ud Zavarzadeh, Teresa L. Ebert, and Donald Morton (eds.), *Post-ality: Marxism and Postmodernism*.

Washington, DC: Marxist Boundary Work in Theory, Economics, Politics and Culture, vol. 1, Maisonneuve Press.
Eisenstein, Zillah R. (ed.)
1979 *Capitalist Patriarchy and the Case for Socialist Feminism*. New York: Monthly Review Press.
Fuss, Diana
1989 *Essentially Speaking: Feminism, Nature, and Difference*. New York: Routledge.
Gibson-Graham, J. K., Stephen Resnick, and Richard D. Wolff (eds.)
2000 *Class and Its Others*. Minneapolis: University of Minnesota Press.
Gunew, Sneja and Anna Yeats (eds.)
1993 *Feminism and the Politics of Difference*. Boulder, CO: Westview Press.
Hahner, June E.
1976 *Women in Latin American History: Their Lives and Views*. Los Angeles: Latin American Center Publications, University of California.
Hennessy, Rosemary and Chrys Ingraham (eds.)
1997 *Materialist Feminism: A Reader in Class, Difference, and Women's Lives*. New York: Routledge.
Hollinger, Robert
1994 *Postmodernism and the Social Sciences: A Thematic Approach*. Thousand Oaks, CA: Sage Publications.
hooks, bell
1984 *Feminist Theory from Margin to Center*. Boston: South End Press.
Humm, Maggie (ed.)
1992 *Modern Feminisms: Political, Literary, Cultural*. New York: Columbia University Press.
Jackson, Stevi
1998 "Feminist social theory," pp. 12–33 in Stevi Jackson and Sherry Jones (eds.), *Contemporary Feminist Theories*. New York: New York University Press.
Jaggar, Alison M.
1983 *Feminist Politics and Human Nature*. Totowa, NJ: Rowman and Allen.
Jameson, Frederic
1991 *Postmodernism: The Cultural Logic of Late Capitalism*. Durham, NC: Duke University Press.
Jaquette, Jane
1995 "Rewriting the scripts: Gender in the comparative study of Latin American politics," pp. 111–133 in Peter H. Smith (ed.), *Latin America in Comparative Perspective: New Approaches to Methods and Analysis*. Boulder, CO: Westview Press.
Jelin, Elizabeth (ed.)
1990 *Women and Social Change in Latin America*. London: Zed Books.
Johnson-Odim, Cheryl and Margaret Strobel
1999 "Series editors' introduction: Conceptualizing the history of women in Africa, Asia, Latin America and the Caribbean, and the Middle East and North Africa," pp. xxxiii–lxvii in Marysa Navarro and Virginia Sánchez Korrol, with Kecia Ali, *Women in Latin America and the Caribbean: Restoring Women to History*. Bloomington: University of Indiana Press.
Kemp, Sandra and Judith Squires (eds.)
1998 *Feminisms*. Oxford: Oxford University Press.

Landry, Lorraine Y.
2000 *Marx and the Postmodernism Debates: An Agenda for Critical Theory.* Westport, CT: Praeger Publishers.
Lavrín, Asunción (ed.)
1978 *Latin American Women: Historical Perspectives.* Westport, CT: Greenwood Press.
Lavrín, Asunción
1995 *Women, Feminism, and Social Change in Argentina, Chile, and Uruguay, 1890–1940.* Lincoln: University of Nebraska Press.
León, Magdalena
1994 *Mujeres y participación política: Avances y desafíos en América Latina.* Bogotá: Tercer Mundo Editores.
Marchand, Marianne H. and Anne Sisson Runyan (eds.)
2000 *Gender and Global Restructuring: Sightings, Sites and Resistances.* London: Routledge.
Miller, Francesca
1991 *Latin American Women and the Search for Social Justice.* Hanover, NH: University Press of New England.
Mohanty, Chandra Talpade
1991 "Under Western eyes: Feminist scholars and colonial discourses," pp. 51–80 in Chandra Talpade, Ann Russo, and Lourdes Torres (eds.), *Third World Women and the Politics of Feminism.* Bloomington: Indiana University Press.
1997 "Women workers and capitalist scripts: Ideologies of domination, common interests, and the politics of solidarity," pp. 3–29 in M. Jacqui Alexander and Chandra Talpade Mohanty (eds.), *Feminist Genealogies, Colonial Legacies, Democratic Futures.* New York: Routledge.
Munck, Ronald
2000. "Dependency and imperialism in Latin America: New horizons," pp. 141–154 in Ronald H. Chilcote (ed.), *The Political-Economy of Imperialism: Critical Appraisals.* Lanham, MD: Rowman & Littlefield.
Nash, June
1986 "A decade of research on women in Latin America," pp. 3–21 in June Nash and Helen I. Safa (eds.), *Women and Change in Latin America.* South Hadley, MA: Bergin & Garvey.
Nash, June and Helen I. Safa (eds.)
1976 *Sex and Class in Latin America.* New York: Praeger Publishers.
1986 *Women and Change in Latin America.* South Hadley, MA: Bergin & Garvey.
Navarro, Marysa and Virginia Sánchez Korrol, with Kecia Ali
1999 *Women in Latin America and the Caribbean: Restoring Women to History.* Bloomington: Indiana University Press.
Nicholson, Linda J.
1990 *Feminism/Postmodernism.* New York: Routledge.
Pescatello, Ann (ed.)
1973 *Female and Male in Latin America.* Pittsburgh, PA: University of Pittsburgh Press.
Post, Ken
1996 *Regaining Marxism.* Hampshire and New York: MacMillan Press Ltd. and St. Martin's Press.
Rahnema, Majid (ed.), with Victoria Bawtree
1997 *The Post-Development Reader.* London: Zed Books.

Sachs, Wolfgang (ed.)
1992 *The Development Dictionary: A Guide to Knowledge As Power*. London: Zed Books.
Sandoval, Chéla
1995 "Feminist forms of agency and oppositional consciousness: U.S. Third World feminist criticism," pp. 208–226 in Judith Kegan Gardner (ed.), *Provoking Agents: Gender and Agency in Theory and Practice*. Urbana: University of Illinois Press.
Sassen, Saskia
1996 "Toward a feminist analysis of the global economy." *Indiana Journal of Global Legal Studies* 4(7): 7–41.
Scott, Joan Wallach
1998 *Gender and the Politics of History*, rev. ed. New York: Columbia University Press.
Segal, Lynne
1999 *Why Feminism?: Gender, Psychology, Politics*. New York: Columbia University Press.
Shelton, Beth Anne and Ben Agger
1993 "Shotgun wedding, unhappy marriage, no-fault divorce? Rethinking the Marxism-feminism relationship," in Paula England (ed.), *Theory on Gender/Feminism on Theory*. New York: Aldine De Gruyter.
Socolow, Susan Migden
2000 *The Women of Colonial Latin America*. Cambridge and NY: Cambridge University Press.
"Special Report"
2000 "Global capitalism: Can it be made to work better?" *BusinessWeek* (November 8): 73–100.
Steans, Jill
1999 "The private is global: Feminist politics and global political economy." *New Political Economy* 4 (March): 113–128.
Stevens, Evelyn P.
1973 "*Marianismo*: The Other Face of Machismo in Latin America," pp. 89–101 in Ann Pescatello (ed.), *Female and Male in Latin America: Essays*. Pittsburgh, PA: University of Pittsburgh Press.
Stoner, K. Lynn
1989 *Latinas of the Americas: A Sourcebook*. New York: Garland Publishing.
Tinsman, Heidi
· 2000 "Reviving feminist materialism: Gender and neoliberalism in Pinochet's Chile." *Signs: Journal of Women in Culture and Society* 26 (Autumn): 145–188.
Tong, Rosemary Putnam
1998 *Feminist Thought: A More Comprehensive Introduction*, 2nd ed. Boulder, CO: Westview Press.
UNICEF (United Nation's Children's Fund)
n.d. *The State of the World's Children, 2000*. New York: UNICEF.
2000 www.unicef.org.statis/Country_1Page45.html.
United Nations
2000 *The World's Women 2000: Trends and Statistics*. New York: Social Statistics and Indicators, Series K, no. 16, United Nations.
Vargas, Virginia
1992 "The feminist movement in Latin America: Between hope and disenchantment." *Development and Change* 23(3): 195–214.

Wichterich, Christa
   2000 *The Globalized Woman: Reports from a Future of Inequality*, translated by Patrick Camiller. North Melbourne and London: Spinifex Press and Zed Books.
Williams, Patrick and Laura Chrisman (eds.)
   1994 *Colonial Discourse and Post-colonial Theory: A Reader.* New York: Columbia University Press.
Wood, Ellen Meiksins and John Bellamy Foster (eds.)
   1997 *In Defense of History: Marxism and the Postmodern Agenda.* New York: Monthly Review Press.

I

WOMEN, WORK, AND DEVELOPMENT

1

Introduction to Part I

Work is an important dimension of women's historical and contemporary experiences, in Latin America, the Caribbean, and everywhere. How this work is defined and studied matters. Despite significant increases in women's participation in productive activities outside the home in the past thirty years and greater attention to gender issues within international development institutions and programs, women are not always accorded status as economic actors equivalent to men. Because it is often unwaged, women's work is not always counted; women contributed $11 trillion of the $16 trillion of global output identified as "invisible"—unwaged or underwaged work—in the 1995 *Human Development Report* (O'Connell, 1996: 36). Women and domestic labor are overlooked in other ways by scholars, and with the exception of feminists, gender analysis is still far from common.[1] The study of Latin American and Caribbean women has provided vital empirical evidence of the work that women do, contributing in important ways to theoretical debates about women's labor, development, and the gendered dynamics of local, national, and international economies in the 2000s. For feminists and other scholars, development practitioners, and activists interested in economic and social justice, making women's labor count remains a challenge.

In Latin America and the Caribbean, the number of women who work outside the home has grown markedly in recent decades, rising from an average of 28 percent in the 1970s to 38 percent in the early 1990s. Explanations of why women work and what their participation in the formal labor market means for them have not always focused carefully on women. In the orthodox—or liberal—modernization theory popular in the 1960s, and now again in the neomodernization approaches of the 1990s and 2000s, the meaning of work is embedded in assumptions about capitalism and economic growth; the value of work is simply presumed by such measures of development as rising gross national product (GNP), urbanization, expanding market trade, and an attendant individual modernization defined with GNP per capita, literacy rates, life expectancy, fertility, and attitudes. Dependency theorists and other critics attacked such thinking on many fronts, using and reformulating Marxist categories to explain imperialism's role in the distorted capitalist dynamics of development in the societies on the periphery of the international economy; both agricultural and industrial work were analyzed in terms of Third World production that served the advanced center economies' accumulation processes. Neither the liberal nor the Marxist approaches to development devoted explicit attention to women, though both suppose women's entrance into the public world of work as vital in the pursuit of their equality—or emancipation. The apparent "gender neutrality" of such conflicting understandings of capitalist development has been criticized. Feminists have called attention to male bias and "gender blindness," seeking in various ways to explain women's access to—and benefits from—participation in the formal labor market, the nature of domestic labor, and as Eleanor Leacock explains so vividly, the dynamics of exploitation that produce and naturalize women's oppression.

<hr />

REAL DEVELOPMENT

Eleanor Leacock

Selection from "Women, development, and anthropological facts and fictions," *Latin American Perspectives* 12/13, 4:1/2 (Winter/Spring 1977), pp. 8–17.

The view is commonly held that women have traditionally been oppressed in Third World societies, and that "development" is the key to changing their situation. The opposing view is that women's status was good in many (not all) Third World societies in the past, and that the structure and ideology of male dominance were introduced as corollaries of colonialism. Furthermore, accumulating evidence shows that, although contemporary development may afford political and professional roles for a few token women, given its imperialist context it continues to undermine the status and autonomy of the vast majority (Boserup, 1970; Bossen, 1975; Nash, 1975; Remy, 1975; Rubbo, 1975). To discuss the impact of development on women's status in society, therefore, means to confront the reality that women's oppression is inextricably bound up with a world system of exploitation. To analyze the status of women in order to change it, is to analyze the need for and possibility of the most fundamental social transformation.

Real development would mean bringing an end to the system whereby the multinational corporations continue to "underdevelop" Third World nations by consuming huge proportions of their resources and grossly underpaying their workers. (The United States makes up less than 10 percent of the world population, yet consumes some two-thirds of the world's irreplaceable resources.) To talk of development also means facing the reality that "underdeveloped" national groups exist in the heart of the "developed" industrial world—Black, Chicano, Hispanic, and Native American minorities in the United States, and immigrant workers from Third World nations in Europe. To talk of development means to talk of bringing an end to the present system of profit-making with its ever-present threat of war. It means talking about the desperate need for a peaceful and economically secure world in which people, not profits, are the central social value.

Third World women suffer manifold forms of oppression: as virtual slave labor in households, unpaid for their work as mothers who create new generations of workers, and as wives or sisters who succor the present one; as workers, often in marginal jobs and more underpaid than men; and as members of racial minorities, or of semi-colonial nations, subject to various economic, legal, and social disabilities. All the while, women bear the brunt, psychologically and sometimes physically, of the frustration and anger of their menfolk, who, in miserable complicity with an exploitative system, take advantage of the petty power they have been given over the women close to them. Perhaps the most bitter reality lies with the family, which is idealized as a retreat and sanctuary in a difficult world. Women fight hard to make it this, yet what could be a center of preparation for resistance by both sexes is so often instead a confused personal battleground, in which women have little recourse but to help recreate the conditions of their own oppression.

Although women bear the heaviest burden of national and of class oppression, they are often told that they must subvert their own cause at this time in the interest of the "larger" goals of national, racial, and class liberation from exploitation. To pit one form of oppression against another in this way is shortsighted and pernicious. The problem of ultimately transforming world capitalist society is so vast, so enormous, that to consider it seriously calls for the recognition of the need to combine the special drive for liberation of half of humanity, women as women, with the drive of women and men as workers and as members of oppressed races and nations.

Precisely because women's oppression is so deeply embedded in the entire economic, political, and social structure of capitalist society, to the extent that women organize around the problems they face, they can unify diverse struggles for class, race, and national liberation. Third World women in both "developed" and "developing" nations have a central role to play. The very totality of their oppression means that when they move to change their situation, they move against the entire structure of exploitation.

As women continue to seek effective forms of organization against oppression, anthropologists who study cultural evolution and cross-cultural comparisons have the choice: either to document the autonomous roles women played in egalitarian societies, for the perspectives they lend to organizational strategies and socialist goals; or to spin out ever more elegant rationales for exploitation.

REFERENCES

Boserup, Ester
    1970 *Woman's Role in Economic Development.* London: Allen and Unwin.
Bossen, Laurel
    1975 "Women in modernizing societies." *American Ethnologist* 2 (November): 587–601.
Nash, June
    1975 "Certain aspects of the integration of women in the development process: A point of view." United Nations World Conference of the International Women's Year.
Remy, Dorothy
    1975 "Underdevelopment and the experience of women: A Nigerian case study," pp. 358–371 in Rayna R. Reiter (ed.), *Toward an Anthropology of Women.* New York: Monthly Review Press.
Rubbo, Anna
    1975 "The spread of capitalism in rural Colombia: Effects on poor women," pp. 333–357 in Rayna R. Reiter (ed.), *Toward an Anthropology of Women.* New York: Monthly Review Press.

A gendered reading of women, work, and development raises a number of crucial questions about women's lives, desires, and power. The traditional distinction of public and private is important in the very definition of "work." The private world of domestic labor has been excluded from the "economy" as such; a patriarchal division of labor assigns and enforces the properly feminine activities of women, including the ideological and cultural constructions of home and family that support what Safa (in her chapter, "Economic Restructuring and Gender Subordination") labels "the myth of the male breadwinner." Feminist engagement with the puzzles of women's economic power have created new insights into the dilemmas of development and the changing international division of labor.

WORKING WOMEN AND WOMEN'S WORK

By most accounts, it matters that women can and do participate in the public world of work. Work has traditionally been defined in terms of the formal labor market, with women's presence in it serving as an indicator of the extent and possibilities of their equality with men. An examination of Latin American and Caribbean women's labor force participation reveals significant and meaningful progress, as well as problems. Feminists have explored a number of issues associated with women's movement in the public world of work, ranging from their access to the labor market, the conditions that define women's work, and the complex interface of waged work with the roles and responsibilities of the private sphere.

Women's share of the economically active population in Latin America and the Caribbean has risen dramatically in past decades. Between 1950 and 1980, the female labor force tripled; 17.9 percent of working-age women were active in 1950, rising to 19.2 percent in 1960, 21.7 percent in 1970, and 26.1 percent in 1980 (Bonilla, 1990: 223). In 1990, 34.0 percent of women worked and in 1998 44.7 percent did (OIT, 1999a: Cuadro 8). In terms of subregions,[2] U.N. figures report increases from 1980 to 1997, with women's activity rate growing from 44 percent to 53 percent in the Caribbean, 31 percent to 39 percent in Central America, and 39 percent to 45 percent in South America (United Nations, 2000: 110). As table 1.1 shows, rates of economic activity vary substantially among countries and between women and men.

Educational achievements and fertility rates are typically associated with the movement of more women into the workforce. Women's access to education has increased in Latin America and the Caribbean, the region where the highest enrollment levels of the developing world are found. Illiteracy has been reduced markedly (though with less dramatic change in rural areas, and men are still more literate). More than 90 percent of the region's school-aged girls are enrolled and women's percentage of enrollments in third-level education is high (United Nations, 2000: 85). The more education a woman has, the more likely is she to work. In 1998, 33.9 percent of women with five or fewer years of education were active in the labor force, compared to 72.1 percent of those with thirteen or more years (OIT, 1999a: Cuadro 5). More education is also associated with lower fertility rates. The regional fertility rate dropped from an average six children per woman in 1950 to 3.4 by 1985–1990 (FAO, 1995: Capítulo 4). Other factors are important in the education-fertility-work relationship, including urbanization, family planning or population policies, access to education, and employment opportunities for women. In Latin America and the Caribbean, urbanization has proceeded rapidly; in 1930, 68 percent of the

Table 1.1   Economic Activity: Latin American and Caribbean Women (W = women, M = men)

| Country | Adult (15+) Economic Activity Rate (%) | | | | Women in Labor Force (%) |
| | 1990 | | 1995–1997 | | 1995–1997 |
	W	M	W	M	
Argentina	29	79	41	76	37
Bahamas	65	81	67	81	47
Barbados	60	76	62	73	49
Belize	24	86	34	79	31
Bolivia	46	84	56	74	46
Brazil	44	85	51	82	40
Chile	32	75	35	75	33
Colombia	46	80	52	78	44
Costa Rica	33	83	36	81	32
Cuba	42	75	47	77	38
Dominican Republic	34	86	38	86	30
Ecuador	28	85	49	81	39
El Salvador	51	80	41	79	37
Guadeloupe	53	71	55	72	44
Guatemala	28	90	32	88	27
Guyana	37	84	40	85	33
Haiti	58	82	57	82	43
Honduras	34	87	41	88	34
Jamaica	62	77	69	81	46
Martinique	55	69	57	70	47
Mexico	34	84	39	84	34
Netherlands Antilles	51	74	52	68	48
Nicaragua	40	87	44	86	35
Panama	39	79	43	80	36
Paraguay	51	83	35	87	29
Peru	29	80	55	78	44
Puerto Rico	31	61	35	62	40
Suriname	30	74	33	64	35
Trinidad and Tobago	38	74	47	74	39
Uruguay	44	75	47	74	43
Venezuela	38	82	41	81	33

Source: United Nations, *The World's Women 2000: Trends and Statistics*. New York: Social Statistics and Indicators, Series K, no. 16, United Nations, 2000, Table 5.D, pp. 145–146.
Note: No information is available for Antigua and Barbuda, Aruba, Dominica, French Guyana, Grenada, St. Kitts and Nevis, St. Lucia, St. Vincent and the Grenadines, and U.S. Virgin Islands.

population was rural while in 1990 only 28.8 percent was (FAO, 1995: Capítulo 1). In 1980 3.8 million women were active in the agricultural workforce in Latin America and 4.4 million in 1994, an increase from 13.3 percent to 18 percent (Buvinič, 1997).

Turning to occupations, pay, and other conditions of women's work, a sexual division of labor emerges. The labor market is segmented; it segregates women into lower-status and lower-paying jobs that often appear to be extensions of domestic work. The sexual division of labor is also found within occupational categories, where a hierarchy of prestige, resources, and power finds women below men. Women have made progress in occupational terms, advancing into traditionally male work. For example, in the 1985–1997 period women in the three subregions were at least 49 percent of professional and technical workers; compared to the 1975–1984 period, their share of administrative and managerial workers rose 7 percent in the Caribbean (to 39 percent), 15 percent in Central America (to 29 percent), and 7 percent in South America (to 24 percent) (United Nations, 2000: 130). Women's fields of study in higher education may contribute to change; women equaled or exceeded men in enrollments in law and business in all three subregions in the mid-1990s, and they were well represented in science and engineering (United Nations, 2000: 93). Yet women remain overrepresented in some occupations, and underrepresented in others. Table 1.2 presents the distribution of working women by occupational category. Despite some subregional differences, women in Latin America and the Caribbean share relationships relative to men: a substantially higher percentage of men work in production and agricultural occupations, while fewer are found in sales, clerical, and professional and technical occupations.

The sexual division of labor establishes some daunting limits on equality and change. According to the United Nations, at the current rate of progress, the world's women will have to wait some 445 years (until 2465) to have equal representation with men at the top (United Nations, 1995: 41), and women in Latin America and the Caribbean are as scarce at the highest "echelons of economic power" as they are elsewhere. In Chile, for example, 2 percent of decision-making positions in the 500 biggest companies are filled by women (Htun, 1999: 546). Women, in general and on average, earn less than men—only 64 percent of what men earn, according to the International Labor Organization (OIT, 1999b). The gender wage gap is actually greater as women's educational levels rise, although wage discrimination weighs more harshly on the poorest women, whose average earnings are 17.5 percent of men's (ECLA, 2000: 28). Domestic work provides a good example of low status employment (see Chaney and Castro, 1989). In 1998, this category included 16 percent of women workers and accounts for 22 percent of new employment for women in the 1990s; in terms of pay, a female domestic worker receives 23 percent of the income of formal sector workers (although men in the same occupation receive 31 percent) (OIT, 1999b). Unemployment also falls more heavily on women than men, especially women in the poorest

Table 1.2 Percentage Distribution of Labor Force by Major Occupational Groups, 1985–1997 (W = women, M = men)

Subregion	Professional, Technical, and Related		Administrative and Managerial		Clerical and Related		Sales		Service		Agricultural and Other		Production and Related	
	W	M	W	M	W	M	W	M	W	M	W	M	W	M
Caribbean	12	8	5	5	15	5	15	7	18	10	7	17	18	38
Central America	14	7	3	3	13	4	21	9	23	8	6	33	20	34
South America	15	8	3	5	15	8	18	12	26	7	7	16	11	35

Source: United Nations, *The World's Women 2000: Trends and Statistics.* New York: Social Statistics and Indicators, Series K, no. 16, United Nations, 2000, Table 5.21, p. 129.

homes. Despite significant variations among subregions, countries, and age groups, unemployment for women was 5.5 percent in 1990 and 9.1 percent in 1998 (OIT, 1999a: Cuadro 8).

THE GENDERED DIVISION OF LABOR

Women's work outside the home is only partially mapped by traditional measures and the sexual division of labor, however, and feminists have pushed for a broader understanding of a gendered division of labor. Historical evidence reveals that women in Latin America and the Caribbean have always been present in the public sphere of production. Socolow's (2000) review of women in colonial Latin America uses race, class, and geography to describe incursions into the masculine public sphere. Despite cultural proscriptions, elite women managed property and businesses; other and differently "classed" women worked as slaves, artisans, shop owners, market women, and laborers in the "proto-industrial" textile work called *obraje* or in tobacco factories. Domestic work was a particularly female occupation with "low-prestige" after the sixteenth century; others included wet nurse, midwife, and prostitute. The marriage and family relations that defined proper work for women are reflected in—and deflected by—the actions of Spanish, Afro-Latina, mestiza, or Indian women of the colonial period, and they continue to construct "work," as Young's exploration of domestic workers in Peru reveals in the chapter "The Myth of Being 'Like a Daughter.'"

The interface of public and private spheres is complex, historical, and important for understanding women's labor. Gender ideologies, cultural practices, and material realities construct family life and women's roles and possibilities. It is estimated that women headed 21 percent of Latin American households in 1995 (some 19.7 million households) and 35 percent (3.1 million households) in the Caribbean (Marcoux, 1997; also, see ECLA, 2000: 41). Households are formed by marriage, as well as consensual unions; households headed by women may or may not include children or dependents; and women sometimes live alone. The "home" thus varies and families, moreover, are not always nuclear. Women's work outside the home is conditioned by the labor market, as well as their life-cycle stage, marital status and number of children, where they live, their educational level, and class (women in higher income households tend to work at higher rates) (Arriagada, 1995). With regard to women's access to economic power, the benefits of work are in no way automatic, as Safa's chapter suggests. The gendered division of labor involves husbands, children, and homes in the conditions and the consequences of women's work.

Reading gender dynamics out from the home and the conditions of private life, it is possible to see several notable "feminizations" of the workforce in recent decades, changes that raise questions about the inferior status of women's labor. One is the rapid growth of *maquila* production through the creation of export processing zones (EPZs) where foreign capital takes advantage of cheap and often female labor (Fernández-Kelly, 1983). Low-waged *maquila* manufacturing has flourished along the U.S.-Mexican border, though NAFTA has facilitated the creation of *maquilas* throughout Mexico. *Maquilas* and EPZs exist elsewhere, including Central America (Corporate Watch, 1998; MacEoin, 1999). Other export-oriented production also relies on cheap female labor, including fruit and vegetable packing and flower farming. As many have noted, over time and with technological change there has been an influx of men into the predominantly female *maquila* production (McClenaghan, 1997; ECLA, 2000: 25).

Feminization is also observed in the changing sectoral distribution of employment. The service sector's share of employment has increased. In 1998, 57.5 percent of employment was in the tertiary sector, where 85.6 percent of women's employment was concentrated (OIT, 1999c, 1999b). There is an even more dramatic—and significant—expansion of informality in the "public economy." Indeed, the formal sector's share of nonagricultural employment declined from 59.8 percent in 1980 to 42.3 percent (estimated) in 1998, while the informal sector's share rose from 40.2 percent to 57.7 percent (estimated) (OIT, 1999c: Cuadro 9-A). In the 1990s, the informal sector has created most of the new jobs, 84 of 100 (Franko, 1999: 260). Table 1.3 reports U.N. figures

Table 1.3   Activity in the Informal Sector, Selected Countries, 1991–1997

Country	Percentage of Nonagricultural Labor Force in Informal Sector		Women's Share of Informal Sector (Nonagricultural)
	Women	Men	
Bolivia	74	55	51
Brazil	67	55	47
Chile	44	31	46
Colombia	44	42	50
Costa Rica	48	46	40
El Salvador	69	47	58
Honduras	65	51	56
Mexico	55	44	44
Panama	41	35	44
Venezuela	47	47	38

Source: United Nations, *The World's Women 2000: Trends and Statistics.* New York: Social Statistics and Indicators, Series K, no. 16, United Nations, 2000, Chart 5.13, p. 122.

for women's share of the informal sector employment (nonagricultural) in selected Latin American countries, as well as the percentage of working women
active in the informal sector. Ranging from 74 percent in Bolivia to 41 percent
in Panama, in all cases women's percentage was higher than men's.

What is the informal sector? Tiano (1997) sees the informal sector as the
intersection of the public and the private. The informal sector is recognized
by low income and low productivity; by self-employment or small enterprises
with few employees, limited capital, and access to credit; and by instability
and a lack of protections afforded to formal sector workers. Franko identifies
three categories of informal sector activity: domestic work, own-account employment, and microenterprises (1999: 261). Women, found primarily in domestic work in the past, are now also engaged in personal services, production
of some manufactured products, and such work as washing clothes, food
preparation, sewing and tailoring, and, more recently, used-clothing sales. Re-
tailing of bodies might also be included. As Wilson explains, women may
make bricks, be street vendors, or pick garbage with their husbands and children, recycling cardboard, metals, or clothing.

❦

GARBAGE PICKERS

Tamar Diana Wilson

Selection from "Approaches to understanding the position of women workers in the
informal sector" Latin American Perspectives 99, 25:2 (March 1998), pp. 105–119.

In essence, the garbage pickers subsidize core capitalist enterprises through
self-exploitation and exploitation of family labor. Their work enables the paper companies to make higher profits. Women contribute to this subsidy
mainly as members of family labor forces engaged in full-time cardboard collection.

Women garbage pickers may be female heads of households for which
pepinando (gleaning, here of garbage) is the primary or a supplementary source
of income, members of nuclear or extended families whose garbage-picking activities provide only use values and/or supplementary income to the household,
or members of male-headed family labor forces for which most of household income comes from garbage picking. Women who work in the dump collect useful items, including clothing, irregularly cut diapers left by factory trucks,
slightly damaged toys, cutlery, mattresses and other household implements, furniture, and items destined for sale. Both for women heads of household with
children too young to be hired as formal- or informal-sector workers and for

garbage-picker families, the majority of household income may come from the dump. Money is earned mainly from collecting cardboard and metals or clothing for resale.

One female head of household with working-aged children in Mexicali sent bags of this recovered clothing to a daughter in Mexico City, where secondhand clothing is much in demand. The daughter sold the clothing in a local *tianguis* (market), returning half of the money to her mother. Another young woman with two children under the age of three went almost daily to the garbage dump to collect diapers of all sizes. Those that she could not use for her children she gave to a sister-in-law. Others she sold to women in the *colonia* where she lived to supplement the family income. The supply of such second- and thirdhand clothing also lowers pressures for wages high enough to pay for new clothing produced in the formal sector. While this may reduce markets for the garment industry, it protects the majority of formal-sector enterprises from organized pressure for a family-maintenance wage.

It is obvious that this segment of the disguised proletariat is functional for capitalist enterprise and for the profit-making capacities of the capitalist system as a whole. Women are a central part of this disguised proletariat, whether as recyclers of cardboard and metals or as bearers of supplements to another source of income.

Between 30 percent and 60 percent of microenterprises are operated by women (ECLA, 2000: 27). Banco Sol, the first commercial bank in the world created to service microenterprises, was founded in Bolivia in 1991; 78 percent of its clients are women, though it has no policy for promoting loans to women (González Vega et al., 1996). Where it contrasts with higher status, more secure formal sector employment that is "masculine," the informal sector reflects a significant feminization of Latin American and Caribbean economies.

THEORIZING WORK AND DEVELOPMENT

Debates about the significance of women's presence in the formal—and informal—labor force in Latin America and the Caribbean have changed since the earliest feminist rethinkings of women's work. Women's paid work may be a "measure of economic status and well-being," as Acevedo explains (1995: 65), inasmuch as income can improve family well-being and women's own bargaining

Street vendor's stall (with candies, herbs, and aborted llama fetuses), La Paz, Bolivia, 1979. *Photo courtesy of Roslyn A. Mickelson*

power in the home. The household is indeed an increasingly important unit of analysis for feminist scholars, and critical perspectives of the historical, political, and cultural dynamics of capitalist development have refined and deepened with the inclusion of gender. Suspicions about the exploitation of women continue to be important. Acosta-Belén and Bose propose that postcolonial conditions are an essential background for analyzing women and work.

> Understanding the development of Latin America, the Caribbean, and other Third World societies requires recognizing the fundamental differences in their processes of incorporation into a global system of capital accumulation. In this complex system of economic and social relations, the subordination of women has been ideologically conceived as an integral part of the natural order of things and perpetuated by cultural praxis, religion, education, and other social institutions. Thus, understanding development also entails drawing on the continuities of power relations and ideologies rooted and molded in the era of European imperial and colonial expansion and examining the set of socioeconomic and political practices that the dominant Western nations developed for their acquired overseas territories during the colonial era. (Acosta-Belén and Bose, 1995: 15)

The definition and discourse of development have evolved since the 1960s and 1970s. From modernization as capitalist industrialization and alternatives that counted on states to remedy underdevelopment or on a socialist development, to postmodern critiques and the concept of postdevelopment (Sachs,

1992; Crush, 1995; Escobar, 1995), the possibilities for including women as economic subjects have expanded (see Chowdhry, 1994; Wright, 1997). Beginning with Ester Boserup's classic 1970 text *Woman's Role in Economic Development*, the relationship of women to development has been studied critically, with various calls for correcting theory and international practices (Benería and Sen, 1986; Tinker, 1990; Sassen, 2000). Were women marginalized in development efforts, especially agricultural projects, as planners and projects ignored the work they did? Or were they exploited as an especially valuable and vulnerable source of new labor for capitalism's Third World programs? Strong criticisms of capitalism oriented the pioneering scholarship on women and work in Latin America (Nash and Safa, 1976, 1986; Nash and Fernández-Kelly, 1983; Leacock and Safa, 1986). Some research focused on rural women (Flora and Santos, 1986; Deere and León, 1987), and questions about the causes and consequences of women's rapid entry into waged work pushed thinking forward (Tiano, 1984).

The study of women in Latin America and the Caribbean has refined and enriched theory in different directions, as the essays in this section attest. In one direction, feminists' attention turned sharply to the micro level with an emphasis on women's private, family, home life as crucial in understanding the "push" of women into formal labor force, as well as the deeper "pull" of capitalist economic dynamics. Women's domestic activities have been recast as productive, expanding the concept of labor to encompass biological, familial, and social reproduction (Benería and Sen, 1986; Benería and Roldan, 1987; Acevedo, 1995). The gendered division of labor is thus seen as encompassing both home and workplace, and the state, too, is included in analysis of the ways in which patriarchal ideologies are enforced. The refining of structuralist explanations has looked in another direction to pursue a critical feminist reexamination of the international political economy. Thus, the new-international-division-of-labor paradigm that flourished in the 1980s (Nash and Fernández-Kelly, 1983; Fernández-Kelly and Sassen, 1995) has been extended. Women and Third World workers, in one view, have been seen as the "new pillars of accumulation"; exploited as workers, women are more deeply colonized through "housewifization"—isolation in the domestic sphere and devaluation of activities there (Mies, 1986; Mies, Bennholdt-Thomsen, and Von Werlhof, 1988). Women's work has, in another view, been refocused in ecofeminist terms (Mies and Shiva, 1993). Recent innovations in international relations theory disclose how gendered hierarchies link the micro and the macro in myriad ways (Peterson, 1996; Marchand and Runyan, 2000; Wichterich, 2000).

Women's work inside and outside the home may offer a particularly valuable vantage on the developmental difficulties of Latin American and

Caribbean societies. Beginning with the "Lost Decade" of the 1980s, a decade marked by the crisis provoked when debtor countries could no longer service their loans, austerity policies and subsequent structural adjustments reoriented regional economies. Externally sanctioned adjustments included opening the economy to foreign finance and investment capital, export-led growth strategies, a reduction of the state's role in managing the economy and providing social services, and the end of debate about alternatives to capitalism, markets, and individualism. Called neoliberalism, the policy consensus is supported by neomodernization theory and the larger shifts in the world system of production. The current phase of capitalism is defined—and debated as— globalization (Busch, 2000; Marchand and Runyan, 2000), and issues of women's place and power may be more relevant than ever.

GLOBALIZATION AND GENDER

Globalization is often assumed to be qualitatively different from earlier phases of capitalism. Its manifestations are economic, political, cultural, and ideological. According to Mittelman, globalization includes

> spatial reorganization of production, the interpenetrating of industries across borders, the spread of financial markets, the diffusion of identical consumer goods to distant countries, massive transfers of population within the South as well as from the South and East to the West, resultant conflicts between immigrant and established communities . . . and the emerging world wide preference for democracy. (1996: 2)

Space and time are altered, both cause and consequence of new technological dynamics that blur borders and seemingly shrink the world with instantaneous transfer of information and movement of capital; the nation-state cedes its sovereignty to the institutional regime of flexible production, including international financial institutions and the transnational corporations that organize the global economy. Not all agree that globalization is qualitatively different, however (Veltmeyer and Petras, 2000). Adjustment has been judged as successful in many cases of export-led recovery—though not in the same way or at the same rate in all cases. The outcomes of adjustment also include increased poverty, higher rates of unemployment, and a Darwinian assault on the weak, including women (Sparr, 1994).

Three points about globalization suggest how critical questions about women, work, and neoliberal development can be. First is the matter of global inequalities. The world is richer, though many note a shocking spread of poverty, as well as its feminization. World income increased dramatically from 1950 to 1992, from $4 trillion to $23 trillion (O'Connell, 1996: 27); yet in

1994, the richest fifth of the world population received 86 percent—and the bottom fifth 1.1 percent—and women count for 70 percent of the poorest people (Wichterich, 2000: 125, 124). The number of people living in poverty grew to 1.3 billion by 1993. In 1990, the poverty category encompassed 41 percent of all households in Latin America (48 percent of the population), and in 1997, 36 percent (44 percent of the population) (CEPAL, 2000: Cuadro 1–2, 40). Poverty rates vary among countries and among female- and male-headed households (Marcoux, 1997), and the recent downward trend belies the absolute number of people in poverty. Though seldom visible in statistics of women and work, Latin America's indigenous peoples are overrepresented in poverty categories (ECLA, 2000: 35–36). In Brazil, 24 percent of the population lives in poverty; in Peru, 49 percent; Chile, 15 percent; Ecuador, 30 percent; Nicaragua, 44 percent (UNICEF, n.d.: 76). Poverty affects women and families in cities throughout Latin America, as González de la Rocha explores in "The Urban Family and Poverty in Latin America," with obvious and less obvious effects. Nearly a million children younger than five died in 1990, three-quarters of them from preventable illness, and some 17.5 million of the region's 5–14 year old children work, with an estimated 80 percent of that unpaid work for their families (Green, 1998: 142, 33, 36).

A second point about globalization is the feminization of resistance to the dislocations of adjustment and the new demands of globalized production. Women have responded to globalization's costly consequences in expected and unexpected ways. The feminization of resistance thus finds women pursuing the survival of their families, augmenting their work inside and outside the home as they stretch scarce resources and seek more through additional labor. As Stephen's chapter, "Women in Mexico's Popular Movements: Survival Strategies against Ecological and Economic Impoverishment" explores, women have also organized collectively to fulfill community needs. They created *comedores populares* or *ollas comunes* [people's cafeterias or collective kitchens], labored in the community to provide services that the state has renounced, and moved to protect the environment (Radcliffe and Westwood, 1993; Küppers, 1994; Campfens, 1990; Fisher, 1993; Boggio Carillo, 1993). Women have also protested austerity, ranging from the looting of stores in Sao Paulo in 1983, which spawned the women-dominated Brazilian unemployed movement, to the boycotting of supermarkets organized by the *Amas de Casa Populares* in Argentina (Lievesley, 1999: 138–139). They participate in anti-International Monetary Fund (IMF) actions, and have organized as workers in Nicaragua, on the U.S.-Mexico border, and elsewhere, fighting the antiunion strategies that help maintain sources of cheap, flexible, and feminized—though not always female—labor.

Finally, the organizational power of globalization reflects the feminization of production internationally (Standing, 1989), as well as an international division of labor that is gendered in new ways. Although Özler notes (1999: 223) that the growing literature on the relationship between globalization and labor markets in developing countries shows a "surprising" neglect of gender (see also Grown, Elston, and Cagatay, 2000), gender has become a resilient category of analysis for United Nations and other international women and development specialists. Indeed, in addition to the new globalization index to measure economic activity, a Gender-Related Development Index and Gender Empowerment Measure were created to organize thinking about development in the mid-1990s. International financial institutions that manage neoliberal adjustments, the IMF and World Bank, have also professed awareness of the human costs of contemporary capitalism. Yet gendering goes deeper. It connects the household and private life to supranational processes that are frequently cast as inevitable, immutable, and impervious to the nation-states that have historically organized economic and political power. At countless points, Latin American and Caribbean women labor in old and new ways, pushed and pulled by manufacturing jobs in export processing zones, by the informal economy that accommodates a new "jobless" growth, by access to professional/managerial positions or to tourism and its exploitation of women's bodies. Where labor markets themselves are transnationalized in new ways, they are regendered. In her chapter "Caribbean Transnationalism As a Gendered Process," Ho examines these processes in the Caribbean. Women now migrate to global urban centers in the United States and Europe to labor as domestics, prostitutes, field hands, and service workers (Portes, 2000).

Capitalism is still the central reality of globalization, and feminist analysis of women and their work problematizes that fact in new ways. The kaleidoscopic array of activities pursued by women to sustain selves and families reveals new combinations of productive and reproductive labor that navigate the still-strong ideological and cultural boundaries of public and private spheres. Assumptions about women's exploitation by capitalism and/or patriarchy, long debated in the scholarship, are still at issue as scholars continue to examine the dual-spheres dichotomy and the victimization it might mistakenly prescribe by refusing women's agency or the possibility that work outside the home may benefit women in ways that matter to them (Mohanty, 1997; Tinsman, 2000; Fernández-Kelly, 2000). Perhaps the "newness" and inevitability of globalization are naturalizing claims, akin to those that have constructed the gendered division of labor and obscured the meaning of women's work—in theory and in practice.

NOTES

1. For example, in one recent collection of 330 pages of writing on Latin American political economy, only twelve pages were indexed to women: one six-page chapter and another six pages in a chapter on inequalities in Latin America (Frieden, Pastor Jr., and Tomz, 2000).

2. The subregions used in U.N. statistics group countries as follows: Central America includes Belize, Costa Rica, El Salvador, Guatemala, Honduras, Panama, Mexico, and Nicaragua; South America includes Argentina, Bolivia, Brazil, Chile, Colombia, Ecuador, French Guyana, Guiana, Paraguay, Peru, Suriname, Uruguay, and Venezuela; and the Caribbean includes Antigua and Barbudos, Aruba, Bahamas, Barbados, Cuba, Dominica, Dominican Republic, Grenada, Guadeloupe, Haiti, Jamaica, Martinique, Netherlands Antilles, Puerto Rico, St. Kitts and Nevis, St. Vincente and Grenadines, Trinidad and Tobago, U.S. Virgin Islands (United Nations, 2000: 178).

SUGGESTED READINGS

Christine E. Bose and Edna Acosta-Belén (eds.), *Women in the Latin American Development Process.* Philadelphia, PA: Temple University Press. 1995.

Elsa M. Chaney and Mary Garcia Castro (eds.), *Muchachas No More: Household Workers in Latin America and the Caribbean.* Philadelphia, PA: Temple University Press, 1989.

Geeta Chowdhry, "Women and the international political economy," pp. 155–171 in Peter R. Beckman and Francine D'Amico (eds.), *Women, Gender, and World Politics: Perspectives, Policies, and Prospects.* Westport, CT: Bergin & Garvey, 1994.

Jo Fisher, *Out of the Shadows: Women, Resistance and Politics in South America.* London: Latin American Bureau, 1993.

Patrice Franko, *The Puzzle of Latin American Economic Development.* Lanham, MD: Rowman & Littlefield, 1999.

Duncan Green, *Hidden Lives: Voices of Children in Latin America and the Caribbean.* London: Cassell, 1998.

Marianne H. Marchand and Anne Sisson Runyan, "Introduction: Feminist sightings of global restructuring: Conceptualizations and reconceptualizations," pp. 1–22 in Marianne H. Marchand and Anne Sisson Runyan (eds.), *Gender and Global Restructuring: Sightings, Sites and Resistances.* London: Routledge, 2000.

Heidi Tinsman, "Reviving feminist materialism: Gender and neoliberalism in Pinochet's Chile." *Signs: Journal of Women in Culture and Society* 26 (Autumn 2000): 145–188.

REFERENCES

Acevedo, Luz del Alba
1995 "Feminist inroads in the study of women's work and development," pp. 65–98 in Christine E. Bose and Edna Acosta-Belén (eds.), *Women in the Latin American Development Process.* Philadelphia, PA: Temple University Press.

Acosta-Belén, Edna and Christine E. Bose
1995 "Colonialism, structural subordination, and empowerment: Women in the development process in Latin America and the Caribbean," pp. 15–37 in Christine E. Bose and Edna Acosta-Belén (eds.), *Women in the Latin American Development Process*. Philadelphia, PA: Temple University Press.

Arriagada, Irma
1995 "Unequal participation by women in the workforce [reprinted abridged from CEPAL *Review*, April 1990]," pp. 333–349 in James L. Dietz (ed.), *Latin America's Economic Development: Confronting Crisis*, 2nd ed. Boulder, CO: Lynne Rienner.

Benería, Lourdes and Martha Roldan
1987 *The Crossroads of Class and Gender: Industrial Homework, Subcontracting, and Household Dynamics in Mexico City*. Chicago: University of Chicago Press.

Benería, Lourdes and Gita Sen
1986 "Accumulation, reproduction, and women's role in economic development: Boserup revisited," pp. 141–157 in Eleanor Leacock and Helen I. Safa (eds.), *Women's Work: Development and the Division of Labor*. South Hadley, MA: Bergin & Garvey.

Boggio Carrillo, Zoila
1993 "Autogestión y movimiento social: Organización de las mujeres en comedores populares en Perú," pp. 63–119 in Maria del Carmen Feijoó (ed.), *Tiempo y espacio: Las luchas sociales de las mujeres latinoamericanas*. Buenos Aires: Consejo Latinoamericano de Ciencias Sociales.

Bonilla, Elssy
1990 "Working women in Latin America," special section, pp. 207–256 in Interamerican Development Bank, *Economic and Social Progress in Latin America, Annual Report*. Washington, DC: Johns Hopkins University.

Bose, Christine E. and Edna Acosta-Belén (eds.)
1995 *Women in the Latin American Development Process*. Philadelphia, PA: Temple University Press.

Boserup, Ester
1970 *Woman's Role in Economic Development*. London: Allen and Unwin.

Busch, Andreas
2000 "Unpacking the globalization debate: Approaches, evidence and data," pp. 21–45 in Colin Hay and David Marsh (eds.), *Demystifying Globalization*. London and New York: Macmillan Press and St. Martin's.

Buvinič, Mayra
1997 "Women in poverty: A new global underclass." *Foreign Policy*, no. 108 (Fall): 38–53.

Campfens, Hubert
1990 "Issues in organizing impoverished women in Latin America." *Social Development Issues* 13 (Fall): 20–43.

CEPAL (Comisión Económica para América Latina y el Caribe)
2000 *Panorama social de América Latina, 1999–2000*. Santiago: United Nations, August. www.eclac.org/egi-bin/getProd.asp?...es/xml/2/4422/P4422.xml&xsl=/tpl/a16f.xsl.

Chaney, Elsa M. and Mary Garcia Castro (eds.)
1989 *Muchachas No More: Household Workers in Latin America and the Caribbean*. Philadelphia: Temple University Press.

Chowdhry, Geeta
   1994 "Women and the international political economy," pp. 155–171 in Peter R.
   Beckman and Francine D'Amico (eds.), Women, Gender, and World Politics: Perspectives, Policies, and Prospects. Westport, CT: Bergin & Garvey.
Crush, Jonath (ed.)
   1995 The Power of Development. London: Routledge.
Deere, Carmen Diana and Magdalena León (eds.)
   1987 Rural Women and State Policy. Boulder, CO: Westview Press.
ECLA (Economic Commission for Latin America and the Caribbean), Women and Development Unit
   2000 The Challenge of Gender Equity and Human Rights on the Threshold of the Twenty-First Century. Santiago: ECLA.
Escobar, Arturo
   1995 Encountering Development: The Making and Unmaking of the Third World. Princeton, NJ: Princeton University Press.
FAO (Organización de las Naciones Unidas para la Agricultura y la Alimentación), Oficina Regional para América Latina y el Caribe
   1995 Mirando hacia Beijing 95—mujeres rurales en América Latina y el Caribe; situación, perspectivas, propuestas. Santiago: FAO.
Fernández-Kelly, María Patricia
   1983 For We Are Sold, I and My People: Women and Industry in Mexico's Frontier. Albany, NY: State University of New York Press.
   2000 "Reading the signs: The economics of gender twenty-five years later." Signs: Journal of Women in Society and Culture 25 (Summer): 1107–1112.
Fernández-Kelly, M. Patricia and Saskia Sassen
   1995 "Recasting women in the global economy: Internationalization and changing definitions of gender," pp. 99–124 in Christine E. Bose and Edna Acosta-Belén (eds.), Women in the Latin American Development Process. Philadelphia, PA: Temple University Press.
Fisher, Jo
   1993 Out of the Shadows: Women, Resistance and Politics in South America. London: Latin American Bureau.
Flora, Cornelia Butler and Blas Santos
   1986 "Women in farming systems in Latin America," pp. 208–228 in June Nash and Helen I. Safa (eds.), Women and Change in Latin America. South Hadley, MA: Bergin & Garvey.
Franko, Patrice
   1999 The Puzzle of Latin American Economic Development. Lanham, MD: Rowman & Littlefield.
Frieden, Jeffry, Manuel Pastor Jr., and Michael Tomz
   2000 Modern Political Economy and Latin America: Theory and Policy. Boulder, CO: Westview Press.
González Vega, Claudia et al.
   1996 "Banco Sol: El reto del crecimiento en organizaciones de microfinanzas," Economics and Sociology Occasional Paper No. 2345, Rural Finance Program, Department of Agricultural Economics, Ohio State University (May).

Green, Duncan
1998 Hidden Lives: Voices of Children in Latin America and the Caribbean. London: Cassell.
Grown, Caren, Diane Elson, and Nilufer Cagatay
2000 "Introduction." World Development, special issue, 28 (July): 1145–1156.
Htun, Mala N.
1999 "Women's rights and opportunities in Latin America: Problems and prospects," pp. 535–551 in Richard E. Feinberg and Robin L. Rosenberg (eds.), Civil Society and the Summit of the Americas: The 1998 Santiago Summit. Miami, FL: North-South Center Press, University of Miami.
Kempadoo, Kamala
1999 "Continuities and change: Five centuries of prostitution in the Caribbean," pp. 3–33 in Kamala Kempadoo (ed.), Sun, Sex, and Gold: Tourism and Sex Work in the Caribbean. Lanham, MD: Rowman & Littlefield.
Küppers, Gaby (ed.)
1994 Compañeras: Voices from the Latin American Women's Movement. London: Latin American Bureau.
Leacock, Eleanor and Helen I. Safa (eds.)
1986 Women's Work: Development and the Division of Labor by Gender. South Hadley, MA: Bergin & Garvey.
Lievesley, Geraldine
1999 Democracy in Latin America; Mobilization, Power and the Search for a New Politics. Manchester: Manchester University Press.
MacEoin, Gary
1999 "Maquila neoslavery, under conditions from bad to inhuman." National Catholic Reporter (August 13) www.natcath.com/NCR_Online/archives/0813990081399i.htm.
Marchand, Marianne H. and Anne Sisson Runyan
2000 "Introduction: Feminist sightings of global restructuring: Conceptualizations and reconceptualizations," pp. 1–22 in Marianne H. Marchand and Anne Sisson Runyan (eds.), Gender and Global Restructuring: Sightings, Sites and Resistances. London: Routledge.
Marcoux, Alain
1997 "The feminization of poverty: Facts, hypotheses and the art of advocacy." Food and Agricultural Organization (FAO), Women and Population Division, Population Programme Service (June).
McClenaghan, Sharon
1997 "Women, work, and empowerment: Romanticizing the reality," pp. 19–35 in Elizabeth A. Dore (ed.), Gender Politics in Latin America: Debates in Theory and Practice. New York: Monthly Review Press.
Mies, Maria
1986 Patriarchy and Accumulation on a World Scale: Women in the International Division of Labor. London: Zed Books.
Mies, Maria, Veronika Bennholdt-Thomsen, and Claudia Von Werlhof
1988 Women: The Last Colony. London: Zed Books.
Mies, Maria and Vandana Shiva
1993 Ecofeminism. London: Zed Books.

Mittelman, James H. (ed.)
1996 *Globalization: Critical Reflections.* Boulder, CO: Lynne Rienner.
Mohanty, Chandra Talpade
1991 "Under Western eyes: Feminist scholars and colonial discourses," pp. 51–80 in Chandra Talpade Mohanty, Ann Russo, and Lourdes Torres (eds.), *Third World Women and the Politics of Feminism.* Bloomington: Indiana University Press.
1997 "Women workers and capitalist scripts: Ideologies of domination, common interests, and the politics of solidarity," pp. 3–29 in M. Jacqui Alexander and Chandra Talpade Mohanty (eds.), *Feminist Genealogies, Colonial Legacies, Democratic Futures.* New York: Routledge.
Molyneux, Maxine
1985 "Mobilization without emancipation: Women's interests and the state in Nicaragua." *Feminist Studies* 11(2): 227–254.
Moser, Caroline
1989 "Gender planning in the Third World: Meeting practical and strategic gender needs." *World Development* 17(11): 1799–1825.
Nash, June
1986 "A decade of research on women in Latin America," pp. 3–21 in June Nash and Helen I. Safa (eds.), *Women and Change in Latin America.* South Hadley, MA: Bergin & Garvey.
Nash, June and María Patricia Fernández-Kelly (eds.)
1983 *Women, Men, and the International Division of Labor.* Albany: State University of New York Press.
Nash, June and Helen Icken Safa (eds.)
1976 *Sex and Class in Latin America.* New York: Praeger Publishers.
1986 *Women and Change in Latin America: New Directions in Sex and Class.* South Hadley, MA: Bergin & Garvey.
O'Connell, Helen
1996 "Going global: Women and economic globalisation," pp. 27–38 in Mary Van Lieshout (ed.), *A Woman's World: Beyond the Headlines.* Dublin and Oxford: Attic Press and Oxfam.
OIT (Organización Internacional del Trabajo), Oficina Regional para América Latina y el Caribe
1999a "Indicadores de la situación laboral de las mujeres 1990–1998," in *Panorama laboral nro. 6, 1999.* Lima: OIT. www.ilolim.org.pe/spanish/260ameri/info/estadis/estadais.shtml
1999b "Temas especiales, mejora la situación laboral de las mujeres, pero aún persisten fuertes desigualdades respecto a los hombres," in *Panorama laboral 1999.* Lima: OIT. www.ilolim.org.pe/spanish/260ameri/publi/panorama/1999/temasespe.shtml
1999c "Decent work and protection for all: Priority of the Americas," Report of the Director General, XIV Regional Meeting, Lima, Peru (August 14–27).
Özler, Süle
1999 "Globalization, employment and gender," pp. 223–234 in *Globalization with a Human Face; Background Papers, vol. 1, Human Development Report 1999.* New York: Human Development Report Office, U.N. Development Program.
Peterson, V. Spike
1996 "The politics of identification in the context of globalization." *Women's Studies*

International Forum 19 (January–April): 5–15

Portes, Alejandro
   2000 "Globalization from below: The rise of transnational communities," pp. 253–270
   in Don Kalb et al. (eds.), *The Ends of Globalization: Bringing Society Back In*. Lanham,
   MD: Rowman and Littlefield.

Public Citizen. Global Trade Watch.
   1998 "NAFTA at five: A report card," *Global Trade Watch* (December), www.corpwatch
   .org/trac/feature/humanrts/globalization/nafta/html.

Radcliffe, Sarah A. and Sallie Westwood (eds.)
   1993 *"Viva": Women and Popular Protest in Latin America*. London: Routledge.

Sachs, Wolfgang (ed.)
   1992 *The Development Dictionary: A Guide to Knowledge As Power*. London: Zed
   Books.

Sassen, Saskia
   2000 "The state and the new geography of power," pp. 49–65 in Don Kalb et al. (eds.),
   The Ends of Globalization: Bringing Society Back In. Lanham, MD: Rowman & Littlefield.

Shiva, Vandana
   1988 *Staying Alive: Women, Ecology, and Development*. London: Zed Books.

Socolow, Susan Migden
   2000 *The Women of Colonial Latin America*. Cambridge: Cambridge University Press.

Sparr, Pamela (ed.)
   1994 *Mortgaging Women's Lives: Feminist Critiques of Structural Adjustment*. London:
   Zed Books.

Standing, Guy
   1989 "Global feminization through flexible labor." *World Development* 17 (July):
   1077–1096.

Tiano, Susan
   1984 "The public-private dichotomy: Theoretical perspectives on 'women in development.'" *Social Science Journal* 21(4): 11–28.
   1997 "The role of women," pp. 237–269 in Richard S. Hillman (ed.), *Understanding
   Contemporary Latin America*. Boulder, CO: Lynne Rienner.

Tickner, J. Ann
   1992 *Gender in International Relations: Feminist Perspectives on Achieving Global Security*. New York: Columbia University Press.

Tinker, Irene
   1990 "The making of a field: Advocates, practitioners, and scholars," pp. 27–53 in
   Irene Tinker (ed.), *Persistent Inequalities: Women and World Development*. Oxford: Oxford University Press.

Tinsman, Heidi
   2000 "Reviving feminist materialism: Gender and neoliberalism in Pinochet's Chile."
   Signs: Journal of Women in Culture and Society 26 (Autumn): 145–188.

UNICEF (United Nations Children's Fund)
   n.d. *The State of the World's Children, 2000*. New York: UNICEF.

United Nations
   1995 *Women: Looking Beyond 2000*. New York: United Nations.
   2000 *The World's Women 2000: Trends and Statistics*. New York: Social Statistics and

Indicators, Series K, no. 16, United Nations.

United Nations, Department of Economic and Social Affairs
    2000 *World Economy and Social Survey 2000: Trends and Policies in the World Economy.* New York: United Nations.

Veltmeyer, Henry and James Petras
    2000 *The Dynamics of Social Change in Latin America.* London and New York: Macmillan and St. Martin's Press.

de Villota, Paloma (ed.)
    1999 *Globalización y género.* Madrid: Editorial Síntesis.

Wichterich, Christa
    2000 *The Globalized Woman: Reports from a Future of Inequality,* trans. Patrick Camiller. North Melbourne and London: Spinifex Press and Zed Books.

Wright, Joanne
    1997 "Deconstructing development theory: Feminism, the public/private dichotomy and the Mexican maquiladoras." *The Canadian Review of Sociology and Anthropology* 34 (February): 71–93.

2

Economic Restructuring and Gender Subordination

Helen I. Safa

Although there were variations by country, the period from 1950 to 1980 in Latin America and the Caribbean was characterized by considerable economic growth. Total production increased five-fold and per capita production doubled. Industry expanded and diversified, with manufacturing output increasing six-fold between 1950 and 1987. The tertiary sector grew at an even faster rate, together with a decline in agricultural employment. Population more than doubled from 1950 to 1980, and there was a marked shift toward urban areas, where the percentage of total population increased from 40.9 percent to 63.3 percent in the same period. Urban growth, concentrated in large cities, was due largely to internal migration, particularly of women and young adults, and contributed to sharp declines in fertility as well as mortality and infant mortality. As a result, life expectancy increased to over 60 years in most countries, with a growing percentage of aged, especially women. Household size fell, particularly after 1960, and the percentage of households headed by women grew to about 20 percent. Educational levels and employment rates increased for both sexes during this period but at a faster rate for women than for men. From 1950 to 1980, the size of the female labor force in Latin America and the Caribbean increased three-fold, with participation rates for women growing from 18 to 26 percent. This increase reflected both a growth in the supply of women workers due to higher educational levels, lower fertility, and heavy rural-urban migration and increasing demand for women in the growing service sector and export processing (ECLAC, 1988a: 7–9; 1988b: 1–3).

This chapter first appeared in *Latin American Perspectives* 85, 22:2 (Spring 1995), pp. 32–50.

The economic crisis that hit most of Latin America and the Caribbean in the 1980s threatened to overturn the progress of the previous three decades and to halt all attempts at income redistribution. The crisis was brought on by rising prices of imports, particularly oil; a decline in both the quantity and the price of exports, particularly agricultural products and minerals such as bauxite and nickel; and a steep rise in interest rates on the foreign debt, which totaled US$410 billion in 1987 (ECLAC, 1988a: 11). The proportion living in poverty grew during the crisis while unemployment increased by 48 percent between 1980 and 1985; real wages declined between 12 and 18 percent in the same period (ECLAC, 1988b: 16). In desperation, several countries were forced to implement structural adjustment programs designed by the International Monetary Fund (IMF) and the World Bank to cut government expenditures, improve the balance of trade, and reduce the foreign debt. These policies, however, often resulted in greater hardship for the poor, because they included devaluation of the currency, accelerating the rate of inflation and cost of living; the elimination of government subsidies for basic foods and subsidized credits to farmers; cuts in government expenditures, particularly for social services; and a freeze on real wages (Cornia, Jolly, and Stewart, 1987: 27). The philosophy behind structural adjustment policies is to shift all responsibility for survival from the state to the individual and the family, forcing families to absorb a greater share of the cost of living by reducing government policies aimed at redistribution.

The impact of the economic crisis has been particularly severe on women in Latin America and the Caribbean and threatens to undermine their newly won gains. Most analysts agree that women (along with children and the elderly) constitute a more vulnerable group than men because their occupational distribution and access to resources is more limited (Cornia, Jolly, and Stewart, 1987; ECLAC, 1988a). At the same time, the crisis is increasing the importance and visibility of women's contribution to the household economy as additional women enter the labor force to meet the rising cost of living and the decreased wage-earning capacity of men. The share of women in the labor force rose from 32 percent in 1980 to 38 percent in 1988 (ECLAC, 1992: 59). The economic crisis also increased the demand for female labor in the new *maquiladora* or export-led industries promoted by the shift away from import substitution and the domestic economy toward export promotion in the international economy. The increased economic importance of women, coupled with the rise of female-headed households, is challenging the myth of the man as the principal breadwinner in Latin American and Caribbean households.

Economic restructuring is not confined to Latin America and the Caribbean; it extends to other developing areas such as Africa, where the effects of the crisis and structural adjustment policies have been even more devastating. Women are not only increasing their involvement in paid wage labor but seeking alternative sources of income through the informal sector, migration, and domestic production (Benería and Roldán, 1987; Grasmuck and Pessar, 1991; Nash, 1993). Even in advanced industrial countries, the loss of jobs due to de-industrialization and the decline of real wages have forced more women into the labor force and replaced the concept of the family wage (based on the male breadwinner) with that of the two-wage-earner family (Nash, 1989; Lamphere et al., 1993). This massive increase in women's wage labor as a result of economic restructuring has generated intense debate over its effects on women's status. Does wage labor merely exploit women as a source of cheap labor and add to the burden of their domestic chores? Or does it give women greater autonomy and raise their consciousness regarding gender subordination?

This article will attempt to answer these questions by examining the factors affecting the impact of paid labor on women's status in three countries of the Hispanic Caribbean—Cuba, Puerto Rico, and the Dominican Republic—in which I have conducted extensive research on women industrial workers since 1980. These countries share cultural and historical patterns rooted in Spanish colonialism, plantation slavery, and U.S. hegemony but differ radically in terms of state policy.

Women bicycle-taxi drivers, Havana, Cuba, December 1999. *Photo courtesy of Robert Neustadt*

Puerto Rico and the Dominican Republic have followed export-led industrialization policies, which began in Puerto Rico as early as the 1950s under Operation Bootstrap and served as a model for other developing countries, even in Asia. Despite its current decline, the Puerto Rican model can offer important lessons on the limitations of this model for self-sustaining growth. The Dominican Republic, by contrast, is a classic case of recently initiated export manufacturing, with a total of 135,000 workers in 385 firms in free-trade zones in 1991 (FUNDAPEC, 1992: 30), and has become the leading source of exports under the Caribbean Basin Initiative (CBI) in the Caribbean. Its success is directly attributable to currency devaluations mandated by the IMF, which made the cost of labor and other expenses in the Dominican Republic among the lowest in the Caribbean.

The Cuban revolution in 1959 led to a radical transformation into a socialist economy whereby the state took over most forms of production and focused primarily on sugar exports and import-substitution industrialization. Import-substitution industrialization, sugar production, and other policies provided full male employment in Cuba until the economic crisis in 1990 resulting from the collapse of Cuba's trade with the former socialist countries of Eastern Europe and the Soviet Union (which occurred after this research was conducted). As we shall see, the redistributive policies of the Cuban socialist state also led to a decline in dependence on the male breadwinner, even within a context of full male employment.

Differences in state policy have had differential impacts on male and female participation rates in Cuba, Puerto Rico, and the Dominican Republic, with profound implications for the gender composition of the labor force in each country. While all three countries have experienced rapid increases in female labor force participation rates, most of the Cuban women studied here are not replacing men as principal breadwinners as are many of the women workers studied in Puerto Rico and the Dominican Republic. In the Dominican Republic and Puerto Rico, male labor force participation rates have declined or stagnated as a result of the disintegration of the sugar economy and the emphasis on labor-intensive export manufacturing and the growth of the service sector, which employs largely women. The more gradual decline in agricultural employment in Cuba and the absorption of men into import-substitution industrialization provided a stable source of male employment at the same time that the wage and consumer policies of the Cuban state instituted in the 1970s promoted women's incorporation into paid employment. In addition, the redistributive mechanisms of the Cuban socialist state made the household less dependent on purchasing power to assure it of basic needs, also lessening women's dependence on male wages. The increased importance of women's contribution to the household economy in all three countries eroded male authority and led women to redefine their domestic role and challenge the myth of the male breadwinner.

The key to understanding the impact of paid wage labor on women's status is the importance of their contribution to the household economy, particularly among married women. As long as women work but still depend primarily on male wage earners, they are defined as supplementary wage earners. Most women continue to be seen as supplementary wage earners in the workplace, where they are confined to poorly paid, unstable jobs, and by the state, which emphasizes their domestic responsibilities as wives and mothers over their rights as workers or citizens. However, women themselves are becoming more aware of their critical contribution to the household economy, and this has led many to challenge male dominance, at least within the home, where women have always had more legitimacy than in the public sphere of the workplace and the state. This helps explain why, in my study, women have gained more negotiating power in the household than at the levels of the workplace and the state, still considered the domains of men. It suggests that there are various levels of gender subordination and that these different levels, while linked, need to be kept analytically separate.

My analysis of women industrial workers in Puerto Rico, the Dominican Republic, and Cuba reveals four fundamental factors that condition the impact of paid wage labor on women's status: (1) state policy, particularly regarding development strategy, which affects the demand for female and male labor and also affects supply through the provision of educational resources and other state services; (2) access to income-producing resources, including the level of wages, working conditions, and other job-related factors, as well as alternative income sources such as transfer payments, the informal sector, and migration; (3) the structure of the household, including the life cycle of the women employed, the number of contributors to the household economy, and support from kin, and (4) gender ideology, which is governed by cultural and structural factors and affects the way in which women define their role, whether as supplementary wage earners or as major providers. Traditional gender ideology that is rooted in separate spheres for men and women (the private/public dichotomy) may obfuscate the contribution women make to the household and maintain the myth of the male breadwinner, but, as we shall see, this ideology is breaking down in each of the countries studied.

In addition to secondary data, this study is based on household surveys and in-depth interviews conducted in all three countries at various time periods. In 1980 I supervised a survey of 157 women workers in three Puerto Rican garment plants of the same manufacturer, while in 1981 the *Centro de Investigación para la Acción Femenina* (CIPAF), a private Dominican women's research center, conducted a survey of 231 women workers in the three oldest export-processing zones of the Dominican Republic and allowed me to analyze these data. In 1986 I conducted in-depth interviews with a sub-sample of working women in these surveys in both countries that enabled me to examine the effects of the economic crisis in the intervening period, particularly in the Dominican Republic. In 1986, under my supervision, a team of researchers from the Federation of Cuban Women carried out a survey of 168 women workers in a large textile factory in Cuba, and I returned in 1987 to conduct in-depth interviews with a sub-sample of these women. Although there are considerable differences between the garment and textile industries, my analysis focuses less on the labor process than on the impact of different development strategies on rates of male and female labor force participation and on changing gender roles in the household.

STATE POLICY

In Puerto Rico and the Dominican Republic, the state's principal role in export manufacturing is to create a favorable climate for foreign investment through investment incentives and the control of wages and labor. Most garment export manufacturing firms are direct subsidiaries of multinationals rather than domestic producers subcontracted to these foreign investors. Workers in export-processing zones are generally entitled to the minimum wage, provided they can meet their production quotas, since production workers generally operate on a piece-rate basis.

Labor control can be achieved through outright repression or prohibition of unions in free-trade zones, as in the Dominican Republic, or through co-optation of labor, as in Puerto Rico. Both repression and co-optation lead to a weak and fragmented labor movement that increases the vulnerability of women (and men) workers in both countries. Labor is also weakened by structural adjustment measures that have resulted in higher levels of unemployment and lower real wages. For example, the real hourly minimum wage in the Dominican Republic declined 62.3 percent between 1984 and 1990, at the height of the crisis, while unemployment in the same period never went below 26 percent and continues to be higher for women than for men. In Puerto Rico, however, since 1950 unemployment rates have been higher for men than for women, and in our sample survey of garment workers 90 percent say that it is easier for a woman than for a man to find a job.

Increased demand for female labor in export manufacturing and the tertiary sector has contributed to rising female participation rates in both countries, particularly in the Dominican Republic, where female labor force participation increased from 9.3 percent in 1960 to 38 percent in 1991 (Ramírez et al., 1988; Baez, 1991). This rapid increase also reflects the economic crisis, which forced women to compensate for the declining employment opportunities and real wages of men. As a result, working women are becoming major economic contributors to the household, and in our sample of women workers in export manufacturing 38 percent consider themselves to be the major economic providers. In Puerto Rico as well, the working woman's salary is never less than 40 percent of the total household income and for married women and female heads of household is often much higher.

In Cuba, the state is committed to a policy of full employment for men and has actively promoted women's incorporation into the labor force as a means of promoting greater gender equality. In addition, the Cuban state has instituted several measures to encourage women to seek gainful employment, including (1) greater educational opportunities, which eliminated illiteracy and led to a significant increase in the number of women professionals and technicians; (2) special support services to alleviate women's domestic load, such as day care centers, lunchrooms for students and workers, laundries, housing, transportation to workplaces, and special shopping plans; (3) *puestos preferentes* (positions in which women have preference), a kind of affirmative-action plan; and (4) the Family Code, enacted in 1975 to encourage couples to share household responsibilities and child rearing. Mass organizations such as the *Federación de Mujeres Cubanas* (Federation of Cuban Women—FMC) and the Frente Femenino or Feminine Front of the *Confederación de Trabajadores Cubanos* (Confederation of Cuban Workers—CTC) were also instructed to promote the incorporation of women into the labor force. These policies' real impact was not felt until the 1970s, when wage and consumer policies reinforced women's desire to earn additional income. At this point women's share of the labor force began to climb steadily, from 15.9 percent in 1970 to 34.8 percent in 1990 (Valdés and Gomaríz, 1992: 38).

In short, in all three countries women are assuming greater economic responsibility in the household, but in Puerto Rico and the Dominican Republic it is partly because of a decline in real wages and male employment opportunities. Dominican and Puerto Rican women not only are challenging the man's role as principal breadwinner but in some cases are being asked to assume that role, which may add to their burdens in the household.

ACCESS TO RESOURCES

State policy also plays an important role in determining women workers' access to resources, since it can influence wages and working conditions (through the minimum wage and other regulations), provide social services such as education and day care centers, and redistribute income through transfer payments and redistributive mechanisms such as rent control or agrarian reform. In socialist Cuba, where almost all workers are employed by the state and virtually all sectors of the economy have been nationalized, state power is clearly stronger than in capitalist societies such as Puerto Rico and the Dominican Republic, where the state is often at the mercy of the private sector in defending workers' rights.

In Cuba, women workers are guaranteed equal pay for equal work, paid vacations and generous maternity benefits, and a much wider array of support services than is found in capitalist societies. In fact, in our sample, 68 percent of the women earn 200 pesos or more a month, compared with 45 percent of their husbands (not all of whom work in the factory). However, wage differentials still exist because of occupational segregation both within the workplace and between different sectors, with more women found in social service sectors such as education and public health, where pay is lower than in industry or other productive activities.

The new Cuban economic and management system instituted in 1976 may have increased occupational segregation by putting pressure on industry to reduce costs and increase productivity, which made factory management give top priority to highly skilled workers, generally male. In the textile mill studied, women production workers are recruited primarily for lower-level jobs and are not given certain positions (e.g., as mechanics) that offer the best salaries and the most possibilities for advancement. At the intermediate level, women technicians constituted half of the factory labor force while a third of the engineers were women, but at the top level of management there were again only a few women. Women textile workers apparently experience higher rates of turnover and absenteeism because of their family responsibilities, especially in production jobs that demand rotating shifts. The women textile workers we interviewed complain that they do not have the same opportunities for advancement as men and that their need for support services, especially day care centers and housing, is not adequately addressed.

Women are relatively recent recruits to the labor force in the factory, which has a strong male worker tradition. This may have led union and management to undervalue women workers in comparison with men. Male workers are also threatened by the continued increase in women workers in the factory and may try to defend their superior status by barring women from the more prestigious jobs and by devaluing the work women do. As in recent studies of the textile industry in other Latin American countries such as Brazil, Chile, and Nicaragua, gender is integrated into the hierarchical structure of production (cf. Humphrey, 1987; Gálvez and Todaro, 1988; Pérez Alemán, Martínez, and Widmair, 1989). Occupational segregation in socialist or capitalist countries keeps women in inferior job positions and defends the role of the male breadwinner.

The changes in the composition of the female labor force in all three countries suggest some weakening of occupational segregation as growing numbers of women enter the professions, clerical work, and the public sector. These changes again reflect state policies that increased the supply of qualified women workers through increased educational opportunities and lower fertility levels made possible by public access to birth control, though abortion is legal only in Cuba. However, as in Cuba, in Puerto Rico and the Dominican Republic women are primarily concentrated in certain feminized professions, especially the social services and clerical work.

It is harder to document occupational segregation within the workplace in the garment plants studied in Puerto Rico and the Dominican Republic because virtually all production workers are women whereas management is entirely men. In Puerto Rico this makes for a very paternalistic setting, in which older women are treated as girls and loyalty to the company is promoted over workers' solidarity. The Puerto Rican plants are unionized, but most women workers in our sample regard the International Ladies' Garment Workers' Union (ILGWU) as a company union that does little to defend their interests or invite rank-and-file participation. The union's primary interest is in containing worker demands to retard the flight of garment plants to cheaper wage areas elsewhere, but in this it has not been very successful. In addition, the proportion of unionized workers in Puerto Rico as a whole dropped from 20 percent in 1970 to 6 percent in 1988, partly because of unions' neglect of women workers (Santiago Rivera, 1989: 93).

Despite migration and the growing employment of women, poor families in Puerto Rico became increasingly dependent on transfer payments such as social security or food assistance to support themselves. While seen as subsidies to workers, these transfer payments are also aids to low-wage industries such as the apparel industry that do not pay an adequate wage and might otherwise leave the island because of wage increases or a shortage of cheap labor. By providing alternative or supplementary sources of income, transfer payments further reduce a woman's dependence on a male wage but increase her dependence on the state. Transfer payments combined with slow job growth also contributed to an overall shrinkage in the total population in the labor force, which stood at 45.4 percent in 1990; in 1983 over half of all families were without wage earners (Amott and Matthaei, 1991: 278).

Wages and working conditions are much worse in the Dominican export-manufacturing plants, where brutal discipline, long working hours, and forced overtime are practiced. Workers are subject to the intense pressure of high production quotas and to the constant threat of dismissal. Discontent is expressed in turnover or eventual withdrawal rather than labor organizing. Unions have only recently begun operating legally in the Dominican free-trade zones; previously workers were fired and blacklisted with other firms for

participating in union organizing. Dominican women workers in export manufacturing receive little support from the government in their struggle for better wages and working conditions, and those who have tried to take complaints of mistreatment or unjust dismissal to the Ministry of Labor have
generally been rejected in favor of management.

Why don't workers protest? Many factors contribute to the lack of worker
solidarity in Dominican and Puerto Rican export-manufacturing plants, including the youth of and constant turnover among workers, their recent entry into industrial employment, family responsibilities, and lack of job alternatives. In addition, the enclave pattern of export-led industrialization in the
Caribbean, combined with low investment in research and development and
tariff regulations requiring the use of U.S. materials, results in little skill or
technology transfer to these developing countries and dampens rather than
stimulates domestic production. This heavy dependence of the garment industry on U.S. capital, technology, and markets and the lack of linkages to the
domestic economy in any area but labor significantly reduce the country's
ability to generate capital and more indigenous and capital-intensive forms of
industrial production, either in export processing or in the domestic economy,
as occurred in Asia. They also limit the growth of male employment and further erode the man's role as economic provider.

In no country, then, do women have equal access to income-producing resources with men, who still dominate the more highly skilled, better-paid jobs
and enjoy greater possibilities of advancement. This cannot be explained by
gender differences in educational levels, since in all three countries women's
educational levels are superior or equal to those of men. Occupational segregation and wage differentials would again appear to reflect the myth of the
male breadwinner, although Cuba has gone farthest in combating this myth.
Women are no longer used as a cheap labor reserve, as in Puerto Rico and especially the Dominican Republic, and the array of support services provided
to Cuban women may actually make them more expensive to employ than
men. In part this stems from the fact that Cuba attempted to reduce working
women's double day through services provided by the state rather than giving
priority to the more equitable gender division of labor in the home advocated
by feminists in capitalist countries.

THE HOUSEHOLD ECONOMY

While they are relatively weak at the level of the workplace and the state,
where power must be exercised collectively, Dominican and Puerto Rican
women workers in export processing have begun to assume more authority in

the family. In both countries the majority of married women now maintain that they share household decisions with their partners and that men no longer have exclusive budgetary control. Their authority in the home is derived from their increased economic contribution to the household, which has taken on major significance in the light of increased male unemployment and its debilitating impact on a man's ability to be the sole breadwinner. In short, it is not simply a question of whether women are employed but one of the importance of their contribution to the household economy, which gives women a basis of resistance to male dominance in the family.

Most women workers agree that paid employment has given them greater legitimacy in negotiating with their husbands. In general, more egalitarian relationships in all three countries seem to be found among stably married couples in which both members work and are better educated. Most of the changes in household authority patterns have come about through a gradual process of negotiation in which women use their increased economic contribution to the household to bargain for greater autonomy and authority, although the changes are less marked in the Dominican Republic than in Puerto Rico or Cuba. Eighty percent of the married Dominican women workers interviewed still consider the husband the head of the household, and husbands tend to dominate financial decisions such as making major purchases and paying the bills.

Compared with the Puerto Rican sample, the Dominican women workers sampled are younger (three fourths are under 30), with young children to support, and they also have more children, which increases their dependence on male wages. Households with young children to support are in the most critical stage economically, and this is the period when women are the most dependent on men. The rate of consensual unions is also much higher than among Puerto Rican women, increasing the rate of marital instability. Dominican women have not been working as long and enjoy less protection on the job. They are not entitled to transfer payments, which offer another buffer to the unemployed and poorly paid workers in Puerto Rico. Even some of the health services to which Dominican and Cuban workers are entitled have been crippled by lack of funds, medicine, and equipment. These factors, coupled with the pressures of the economic crisis, heighten women's insecurity and their fear of challenging male dominance.

Female heads of household carry the heaviest financial responsibility and constitute 27 percent of our Dominican sample compared with 16 percent of the Puerto Rican, reflecting the higher rate of marital instability generally among Dominican women. Most Dominican female heads of household are younger women separated from one or more consensual unions, often initiated when they were very young. Many of these women are reluctant to remarry and cite the independence their work has given them as one of the reasons for remaining alone.

Female heads of household are generally poorer, in part because they have fewer wage earners in the household. The age of the female head of household also makes a difference. Many of the Puerto Rican heads of household are older and live alone or with an older child or sister, so they do not have young children to support, as in the Dominican Republic and Cuba. They can manage on the low salaries paid in the garment industry, particularly if they own a home.

In addition, rural Puerto Rican households have a particularly tightly knit network of kin and neighbors who help each other out in child care, house building, and shopping; they may even ride to work together. Sixty percent of the younger women sampled have relatives working in the same plant.

In the Dominican Republic, because of the cost of housing and child care, women workers often leave their children with their mothers or other relatives in the rural area and visit them once a week or less. They often live alone and send money regularly to their children and parents. However, since their relatives live at some distance and are also very poor, they cannot offer the same level of support as the relatives of Puerto Rican or Cuban women workers, many of whom live in the same neighborhood.

The households of the Cuban women workers are the largest in the sample, with 38 percent consisting of five or more members. This is partly due to the housing shortage in Cuba, which forces families to double up, so that 41 percent of the Cuban households contain three or more generations compared with only 17.8 percent of the Puerto Rican households, most of which are nuclear families with two generations. Extended families in Cuba often have the highest incomes because of the large number of wage earners per household. In the Cuban sample as a whole, nearly half of the households have three or more wage earners, compared with 16.5 percent in the Puerto Rican sample.

Many of these extended families consist of teenage single mothers or recently married couples who continue to live with their parents or in-laws, to whom they are clearly subordinate. There is a high rate of teenage pregnancy in Cuba, despite the availability of contraceptives and abortions, and nearly half of the women in our sample had had a child before they were 20. This figure is even higher among female heads of household, suggesting that teenage pregnancies contribute to the problem of marital instability in Cuba, which has also increased since the revolution. When teenage single mothers live with their parents, the older generation continues to make the decisions and administer expenses, and the mother often takes care of the children while the daughter works. While this provides assistance to young working mothers, it also perpetuates traditional gender roles and discourages any challenge to male dominance. Crowded living quarters also contribute to marital instability.

Three-generation households are even more frequent among female-headed households, which are almost equally divided between these young single mothers and older women who have their daughters living with them. Female-headed households constitute 35 percent of the Cuban sample, higher than for the samples in Puerto Rico or the Dominican Republic, even though the national percentage in Cuba is lower than in either of the other two countries.[1] Contrary to the norm for larger extended families, 62 percent of female heads of household have only one or two wage earners in the household and, except for some priority in obtaining employment, receive no assistance from the government. The fathers of these children are supposed to contribute to their support, but few do, and several young single mothers say that they do not want to press claims for support because this would give the fathers more authority over their children. For example, Odalys receives no assistance from the father of her three-year-old twins and wants none "because now they are only mine and he has no rights at all." Here we can see a clear correlation between economic support and authority patterns.

As in Puerto Rico and the Dominican Republic, paid employment in Cuba has had an impact on authority patterns, since more than half of the married women interviewed maintain that they make decisions jointly with their husbands and also administer expenses together. Both husband and wife contribute heavily to the household, and married women often have the best-equipped households, with washing machines, refrigerators, radios, and televisions. However, despite the Family Code and the massive incorporation of women into the labor force, men's household responsibilities have changed little. While men accept the idea that their wives work and probably also welcome the added income, most of them do not share in the housework or child care, nor do their wives appear to encourage them to do so. The extended-family pattern found in Cuba tends to perpetuate this traditional division of labor, but it is also prevalent in Puerto Rican and Dominican households, where nuclear families predominate. In none of the households in our study do men do much of the housework or child care, except for occasional chores like shopping or paying the bills. This suggests that authority patterns have changed more than the gender division of labor and can be partly explained by the perpetuation of traditional gender ideology.

GENDER IDEOLOGY

Traditional gender ideology is more difficult to document than many of the structural changes analyzed thus far, because it is rooted in women's dual productive/reproductive role. Traditionally, women are charged with primary responsibility for domestic chores and child care, whereas men are designated as the primary breadwinners. Designating men as primary breadwinners maintains male control over female labor and creates separate spheres in which women are confined to the private sphere while men control the public one of work and politics.

The public-private split in Western industrial society is even stronger in Latin America and the Hispanic Caribbean and dates back to the Spanish colonial *casa/calle* distinction, fostered by Catholicism, whereby women were relegated to the home and men to the street as a way of maintaining family honor and female virginity. This distinction was never fully followed by the poor and subordinated ethnic groups such as African slaves and indigenes, among whom women had to work to contribute to the family's survival, but it was upheld as the norm, and women's wage work came to be even more stigmatized than in more ethnically homogeneous industrializing countries because of its close association with these subordinated groups. For example, in Cuba in 1899, one year after U.S. occupation, nearly three quarters of all women wage earners, most employed in domestic service, were colored, although people of color composed only a third of the population (Pérez, 1988).

As more women began to enter the labor force and elite women were educated for professions such as teaching and nursing, the stigma of women's wage labor began to fade, but the boundaries between *casa* and *calle* or private and public spheres have not been eroded to the same extent as in advanced industrial societies, despite variation with class and race. The norm of the male breadwinner is so strong that even among the working class it remains the ideal, relegating women to the role of supplementary wage earners. This reflects socioeconomic differences such as the limited and more recent incorporation of women, particularly married women, into the labor force in Latin America as compared with the advanced industrial countries. It also reflects cultural differences rooted in gender ideology. Patriarchal laws championing the man as provider and protector still prevail in many Latin American countries, whereas the rights of women to divorce or equality before the law and to family planning or abortion are very limited. The patriarchal family is upheld by the patriarchal state, which is committed to the maintenance of certain gender, racial, and class hierarchies.

Even in Cuba, the Latin American country where the most radical measures have been undertaken to establish gender equality, women's domestic or reproductive role continues to be emphasized. For example, women are still barred from certain hazardous jobs for fear that the work will endanger their reproductive capacity, and until recently only women could take leave from their jobs to tend to hospitalized family members. The Family Code, though mandating the sharing of responsibility within the household, is also aimed at strengthening the family, which is threatened by rising divorce rates and teenage pregnancies. Socialist support for the family is partly due to the state's recognition of the family's importance to social reproduction and of its limited ability to perform the family's functions in this regard (Bengelsdorf, 1985). In socialist as well as capitalist societies, the contribution that the family makes to social reproduction greatly alleviates the role of the state. This is particularly evident in times of crisis, when the state's resources are limited in the extreme, placing additional burdens on the household to meet basic needs. This has been most evident in Cuba during the special period since 1990, but in Puerto Rico and especially the Dominican Republic structural adjustment policies have also shifted more responsibilities from the state back to the household.

CONCLUSION

Has the casa/calle distinction been eroded through the massive incorporation of women into the labor force? Certainly working women in Cuba, Puerto Rico, and the Dominican Republic now have a more visible presence in the public sphere, but, as we have seen, they are still clearly subordinated in the workplace and in the polity. In part, the confinement of women to the home has been replaced by occupational segregation, which allows women a limited representation in the workplace in selected female occupations that are often extensions of their female roles, even in professions such as teaching and nursing. Wage differentials between genders at all class levels also reinforce the notion of women as supplementary wage earners dependent on primary male breadwinners.

The lack of change in the household division of labor for most of the women studied here is also evidence of the maintenance of the casa/calle distinction. The fault lies not only with men but with women themselves, who continue to define household chores and child care as their primary responsibility even if they are working full-time and making a major contribution to the household economy. As Stolcke (1984) notes, the family provides women with a social identity that proletarianization as wage workers has not diminished. In fact, most of these women now consider paid employment part of their domestic role, because they are working to contribute to the household economy rather than for their own self-esteem or personal autonomy. Among female heads of household, paid employment is critical to the family's survival, and the extreme poverty of these households, particularly in the Dominican Republic, makes all women realize how difficult it is to get along without a male provider.

However, many Dominican and Puerto Rican women are being forced to support their families without much help from men, because high rates of labor force participation for women have coincided with declining job opportunities

for men due to the disintegration of the domestic economy with the shift toward export-led industrialization. Export manufacturers prefer women workers
because they are cheaper to employ and less likely to unionize and seem to have
more patience with the tedious, monotonous work in assembly operations.
Cuba succeeded in integrating women into the labor force without displacing
men, but its economy is also in crisis now that its trade and aid links with the
socialist bloc have collapsed. All three countries suffer from a high rate of marital instability and female-headed households, but these have been alleviated
through transfer payments in Puerto Rico and through redistributive mechanisms such as rationing that ensure "relative equality amidst austerity" in Cuba
(Pérez-Stable, 1993). Dominican women are undoubtedly the most exploited
at every level and suffer the greatest pain.

Standing (1989) suggests that this pattern of "global feminization of labor,"
with increased female labor force participation and declining male participation, extends far beyond the Caribbean region to developing countries in Asia
and Africa and is due to increased international competition and the growth
of export manufacturing, labor deregulation, and structural adjustment measures that have weakened workers' bargaining power in advanced industrial as
well as developing countries. The primary beneficiaries of this form of economic restructuring are advanced industrial countries such as the United
States, which have promoted this strategy in order to remain competitive
within an increasingly global market. Even in these advanced industrial countries, workers, many of whom are women, suffer from a loss of jobs due to relocation of production to other areas of the country and abroad (see, e.g.,
Safa, 1981; Nash, 1989). Thus, economic restructuring weakens labor and
strengthens capital. By placing additional burdens on women and marginalizing men, it may be of little benefit to either gender.

However, the lack of recognition of women as breadwinners is also due to
women themselves, who still define themselves in terms of the *casa/calle* distinction. Men are seen as workers with family responsibilities, while women
view themselves and are viewed as wives and mothers with economic responsibilities. Women continue to identify primarily with the family, whereas men
are more closely identified with their economic role. This is why women can
be roused to collective action more easily by threats to their families' survival
than by threats to their rights as workers (Safa, 1990).

Gender consciousness is growing as the contradiction between women's increasingly important economic contribution to the household and their subordination in the family, in the workplace, and in the polity becomes more apparent. But the myth of the male breadwinner is preserved by public forms of
patriarchy embedded in the state and the workplace, which continue to profit
from women's subordination.

NOTES

The book on which this article is based, *The Myth of the Male Breadwinner: Women and Industrialization in the Caribbean*, was published by Westview Press. The author thanks Magaly Pineda, director of the Centro de Investigación para la Acción Femenina, for providing data and Lorraine Catanzaro, Quintina Reyes, and Milagros Ricourt for their assistance in analysis. She also thanks the Federation of Cuban Women, Francis Pou and Carmen A. Pérez for their assistance in fieldwork in Cuba, the Dominican Republic and Puerto Rico, respectively.

1. One reason for this discrepancy may be the failure of national census figures to capture female heads of household who continue to live with their parents.

REFERENCES

Amott, Teresa and Julie Matthaei
   1991 *Race, Gender, and Work: A Multicultural Economic History of Women in the United States.* Boston: South End Press.
Baez, Clara
   1991 *Mujer y desarrollo en la República Dominicana: 1981–1991.* Report prepared for Inter-American Development Bank, Santo Domingo, Dominican Republic.
Benería, Lourdes and Martha Roldán
   1987 *The Crossroads of Class and Gender: Industrial Homework, Subcontracting, and Household Dynamics in Mexico City.* Chicago: University of Chicago Press.
Bengelsdorf, Carollee
   1985 "On the problem of studying women in Cuba." *Race and Class* 2 (Fall): 35–50.
Cornia, Giovanni A., Richard Jolly, and Frances Stewart
   1987 *Adjustment with a Human Face.* Vol. 1. New York: UNICEF/Oxford: Clarendon Press.
ECLAC (Economic Commission for Latin America and the Caribbean)
   1988a *Latin American and Caribbean Women: Between Change and Crisis.* LC/L.464 (CRM.4/2).
   1988b *Women, Work, and Crisis.* LC/L.458 (CRM.4.6).
   1992 *Economic Survey of Latin America and the Caribbean 1990.* Vol. 1. Santiago de Chile.
FUNDAPEC (Fundación APEC de Crédito Educativo, Inc.)
   1992 *Encuesta nacional de mano de obra.* Report prepared for Inter-American Development Bank, Santo Domingo, Dominican Republic.
Gálvez, Thelma and Rosalba Todaro
   1988 "La segregación sexual en la industria," pp. 281–319 in *Mundo de mujer: Continuidad y cambio.* Santiago: Centra de Estudios de la Mujer.
Grasmuck, Sherri and Patricia Pessar
   1991 *Between Two Islands: Dominican International Migration.* Berkeley: University of California Press.
Humphrey, John
   1987 *Gender and Work in the Third World: Sexual Divisions in Brazilian Industry.* London: Tavistock.

Lamphere, Louise, Patricia Zavella, Felipe Gonzáles, with Peter Evans
1993 *Sunbelt Working Mothers: Reconciling Family and Factory.* Ithaca: Cornell University Press.
Nash, June
1989 *From Tank Town to High Tech: The Clash of Community and Corporate Cycles.* New York: Columbia University Press.
Nash, June (ed.)
1993 *Crafts in the World Market: The Impact of International Exchange on Middle American Artisans.* Albany: State University of New York Press.
Pérez, Louis A.
1988 *Cuba: Between Reform and Revolution.* New York: Oxford University Press.
Pérez Alemán, Paola, Diana Martínez, and Christa Widmair
1989 *Industria, género y mujer en Nicaragua.* Managua: Instituto Nicaragüense de la Mujer.
Pérez-Stable, Marifeli
1993 *The Cuban Revolution: Origins, Course, and Legacy.* New York: Oxford University Press.
Ramírez, Nelson, Isidoro Santana, Francisco de Moya, and Pablo Tactuk
1988 *República Dominicana: Población y desarrollo 1950–1985.* San Jose: Centro Latinoamericano de Demografía.
Safa, Helen I.
1981 "Runaway shops and female employment: The search for cheap labor." *Signs* 7 (2): 418–433.
1990 "Women's social movements in Latin America." *Gender and Society* 4 (3): 354–369.
Santiago Rivera, Carlos
1989 "Industrial reconversion and economic restructuring: The challenge for the Puerto Rican labor movement." *Radical America* 23 (1): 91–100.
Standing, Guy
1989 "Global feminization through flexible labor." *World Development* 17 (7): 1077–1096.
Stolcke, Verena
1984 "The exploitation of family morality: Labor systems and family structure on São Paulo coffee plantations, 1850–1979," pp. 264–296 in R. T. Smith (ed.), *Kinship Ideology and Practice in Latin America.* Durham: University of North Carolina Press.
Valdés, Teresa and Enrique Gomaríz (eds.)
1992 *Mujeres latinoamericanas en cifras: Cuba.* Madrid: Instituto de la Mujer, Ministerio de Asuntos Sociales de España/Santiago de Chile: Facultad Latinoamericana de Ciencias Sociales (FLACSO).

3

The Urban Family and Poverty in Latin America

Mercedes González de la Rocha

Translated by Barbara B. Gantt

DOMESTIC STRATEGIES IN RESPONSE TO ADJUSTMENT AND REORGANIZATION

After two decades of more or less sustained economic growth,[1] Latin America was characterized in the 1980s by economic recession and the consequences of crisis. Both economic prosperity and recession have a strong impact on the organization and economies of domestic groups because of the constraints and opportunities they engender. In situations of economic growth, the domestic group's dependence for survival and reproduction on external factors increases. The opposite occurs in situations of recession and scarcity, when households are forced to intensify the salaried work of working-age and other members,[2] extend the workday, and partially withdraw from the marketplace of goods and services through reduced consumption and intensification of domestic work by women and children. Although growth had opened up external options for the domestic group, especially in employment, the crisis and the extent of adjustment and reorganization have closed the door to these options to the point that workers and their families have had to emphasize internal resources: work by adult males as well as women, children, and youth, underconsumption, and transformations in family budgets, the use of individuals' time, and the division of labor within households. Although domestic arrangements and modifications have their own dynamic, they are shaped and conditioned by the external context. Yet not all households in the popular urban sector are equally well equipped to react to situations of prosperity and adversity. There are households whose vulnerability—in terms of

This chapter first appeared in *Latin American Perspectives* 85, 22:2 (Spring 1995), pp. 12–31.

their structure and composition and the availability of labor—makes them less able both to take advantage of the options in the workplace that open up in an era of prosperity and expanding employment and to defend themselves against a decline in salaries and economic deterioration.[3]

The economic crisis erupted during a process of economic growth and accentuated the already precarious living conditions of the urban majority. It is not my objective here to delve into the characteristics of the economic crisis or the international pressures that led Latin American governments to restructure their economies. An important part of the reordering is the change from a model based on economies that were to a certain extent self-contained[4] (promoting import-substitution industrialization) (Buvinič et al., 1991) to an "open" model oriented to the international market. In this new model, the control of salaries is a powerful instrument for achieving market competitiveness and attracting international capital. Urban workers and their households have been severely hit by the deterioration of real wages, unemployment, stagnation of formal employment, and reduced government social spending. The middle sectors that benefited from the previous era of growth have also suffered the negative effects of the crisis, and the levels of income and patterns of consumption of middle-class households have undergone modification (CEPAL, 1991; Escobar and Roberts, 1991).[5] Although incomes in middle-sector households have diminished proportionally more than those of the popular sectors (manual laborers), it is the latter that have found themselves in the more disadvantageous situation.

Contemporary Latin America is fundamentally urban and is characterized by higher indexes of absolute poverty in urban contexts than in rural ones. The situation is different in terms of relative poverty: 53 percent of rural households and 61 percent of the rural population were considered poor in 1990 while 34 percent of urban households and 39 percent of the urban population were in this situation (CEPAL, 1992b). Without diminishing the importance of the greater relative poverty of the rural population, it is clear that more of the poor reside in cities and in this sense poverty in Latin America in the 1990s is primarily urban.[6] The increase in poverty in the cities is doubtless related to the impoverishment of the rural population and rural-urban migration. Some analysts have proposed that because of the increasing integration of labor markets and the greater dependence of peasants on alternative sources of income, the boundary between urban and rural contexts has become fluid and difficult to identify. Although the Latin American peasantry persists as a reserve of extensive poverty, de Janvry, Sadoulet, and Young (1989) argue that the symptoms of the failure of development are transferred daily to urban economies, increasingly informal. At the same time, information on various countries in the region reveals an increase in the concentration of income in the 1980s.[7]

Structural adjustment has included a reduction of subsidies and funds allocated to social welfare. These measures have had a strong impact on households in three principal ways. First, the decrease in public social spending has meant the reduction in number and, on occasion, the disappearance of jobs previously provided by government agencies. Secondly, public services have been weakened in quantity and quality, and if they were insufficient prior to the economic crisis they have now become very limited indeed and very difficult to acquire. Lastly, the government subsidies that once lowered the cost of basic food items have also been reduced and in some cases eliminated altogether, with the result that the costs of production are reflected in increased prices paid by consumers.[8] The impact, then, has been felt in employment, access to public services, and the availability of consumption goods in the market.

Urban employment has been strongly affected by the crisis and the policies of adjustment. Employment has diminished in manufacturing and in the public sector and increased in services—especially personal services, since social services have suffered severe budget cuts.[9] Through its link to work-related health insurance, the decrease in public employment and in large-scale business has affected access to public health services. Formal employment has stagnated or declined, and the numbers of part-time workers without benefits or legal protection (informal workers) and of the self-employed have increased (CEPAL, 1991). In addition to the low wages earned by workers, this decline in employment constitutes the setting in which individuals organized in domestic units have found themselves in their daily struggle to survive. As a consequence, there has been restructuring of lifestyles and family organization, and a series of transformations has taken place in households with limited resources (Benería, 1992; Pérez Alemán, 1992; McFarren, 1992; Chant, 1994; González de la Rocha, 1991). The worsening of poverty and the scarcity produced by the economic crisis have been mediated by the capacity for response in the private sphere. I will discuss some of the most important strategies that have been developed within households to cushion and mediate the effects of the crisis. Although these changes may also be related to the aging of households—that is to say, to the changes in composition produced by the domestic cycle—it is clear that households have responded with important modifications to the external processes of economic change and the deterioration of living standards as well.

INTENSIFICATION OF WORK

In the first place, the increase in unemployment of male heads of household and the decline in wages have affected the rate of participation by other members of domestic groups. One of the most important changes is the increase in women's participation in the workforce in the majority of Latin American cities.[10] Although men continue to be the majority in urban labor markets, the increase in recent years in the number of women who work has been verified by both quantitative analyses and ethnographic studies. Oliveira and García (1990) have asserted that the determinants of women's participation in the labor market have changed in such a way that increasing numbers of married or once-coupled women with children and low levels of education are entering the labor markets in Mexican cities. Prior to the crisis and restructuring, the increase in women's employment had involved better-educated women who were single and without domestic responsibilities. Longitudinal studies conducted throughout the 1980s show that the crisis forced housewives—mothers with heavy responsibilities in domestic work and low levels of education—into the workplace (González de la Rocha, 1988; Barrig, 1993; Moser, 1989), and it has been observed that they are being forced into informal and poorly remunerated jobs or self-employment.

In five of the six countries for which comparable data are available from the beginning to the end of the 1980s there was a reduction in the proportion of the hours worked by heads of households as a proportion of hours worked by household members. No doubt this is related to the increase in unemployment of heads of households and the growing importance of other household members as workers. According to information provided by the *Comisión Económica para América Latina y el Caribe* (CEPAL), the contribution of heads of urban households is less than 80 percent and, in the majority of countries, less than 60 percent of income in these households (CEPAL, 1991: Table 17). All the indicators point to the growing importance of income earned by other members of the household in recent years.[11] The increase in the number of workers has been through their entry into insecure jobs in small businesses and in the informal sector. For seven countries that include 80 percent of the total economically active population of the region, employment in the informal sector and in small business grew during the decade (1980–1989) at a rate equivalent to double the growth in the working-age population and triple the growth in population (CEPAL, 1992a: Table 3).

Qualitative analyses undertaken in various Latin American countries have shown that, in effect, the urban household has increased both its number of workers and its sources of income. As salaried work has become unstable and difficult to find, domestic groups have broadened their sources of income with the aim of not having to depend solely or primarily on anyone. The structure of household incomes has also shown important changes. In general terms, the proportion of total earnings represented by salaries and wages has declined in the majority of urban households in the region. Conversely, the proportion of earnings represented by wages for independent work and pensions has increased. These changes are especially noticeable in the poorest households (CEPAL, 1991: Table 16). As much as possible, families have tended to send a larger number of members into the labor market. The intensification of work—what Pastore, Zylberstajn, and Pagotto (1983) have called "overload"—has fallen above all to women, although children and teenagers are also involved either directly or indirectly.[12] This has made it possible for total household incomes to decline at a lower rate than individual earnings. In Venezuela the total income of urban households decreased by 22 percent from 1981 to 1986 despite the fact that individual income fell 34 percent. The same was observed in urban areas in Uruguay and Costa Rica, where total household incomes decreased by 14 percent from 1981 to 1988 while individual income was reduced by 22 percent (CEPAL, 1991: 23, 41). The difference was about 10 percent in the majority of cases. A study carried out at different time periods during the decade in Guadalajara, Mexico, demonstrated that total household income had decreased by 11 percent (deflated according to rates of inflation in the period) between 1982 and 1985. Bearing in mind that individual income lost 35 percent of its purchasing power, we can appreciate the true importance of the family and the domestic group in mediating poverty and cushioning the effects of the crisis. From 1985 to the end of the decade there was a decrease in the number of workers per household while levels of employment remained the same as in 1982 (González de la Rocha, 1988; 1991). This is the reason that ECLAC's records from the beginning and the end of the decade do not reflect a significant increase in the number of workers. This decline may be because in the majority of countries the impact of the crisis was most intense during the early 1980s. It may also be because the costs of sending household members into the labor market exceeded the benefits obtained, especially in urban contexts of increasingly precarious employment (very low salaries and minimum benefits). What is certain is that the testimonies compiled through ethnographic methods offer evidence of the intensification of work, remunerated or not, and of increasing interdependence among members of households.

Urban households in the 1980s were characterized by an increase in the number of workers per household, intensification of non-remunerated domestic work, and the growing importance of extended-family households as a strategy for saving on housing costs and incorporating more able-bodied members. Sending more household members into salaried work was not, however, sufficient to palliate the effects of inflation and deteriorating wages.

CHANGING PATTERNS OF CONSUMPTION

Patterns of consumption, culturally and historically defined, are not a mechanical result of level of income, but income level does establish the framework within which choices of certain products take place. As level of income increases, individuals have broader access to the market in goods and services. The growth in income during economic boom times was accompanied by an increase in the consumption of food, clothing, and other more durable consumer goods.[13] With the deterioration in real income in the majority of Latin American cities during the 1980s, households allocated a larger proportion of their incomes to food, with a consequent decline in other areas of consumption such as education, health, and clothing. Furthermore, there was a withdrawal from the marketplace of goods and services, with housewives taking on the tasks of mending more clothes, preparing lunches for workers to take to their workplaces, etc. Women were forced to intensify their domestic work in order to save and to devote the savings to basic consumption (food) while reducing spending on recreation, clothing, education, and even health. Thus, a domestic strategy could be identified in which some areas of consumption were sacrificed in order to protect others that were considered more important.[14] In spite of these protective actions, however, the pattern of food consumption was transformed.

Food consumption by the urban poor was already deficient in the period of prosperity, especially with regard to the products and quantities consumed. In Mexico, for example, poor families in the cities had a diet made up mostly of carbohydrates and sugars that provided a source of almost immediate energy. Nevertheless, families did include products that varied the diet, although in small amounts, as well as other types of nutrients, such as animal protein.[15] When the means of protecting consumption proved insufficient, the urban poor were forced to consume less. In Chile from 1970 to 1985, the consumption of wheat, sugar, rice, meat, and milk products decreased to such a degree that their levels of per capita consumption by the mid-1980s were lower than the levels of the 1960s. The only products that seem to have been an exception were cooking oil and corn (Ortega and Tironi, 1988: 44). Studies of patterns of consumption by people of limited resources in Mexico reveal a situation very similar to the one in Chile. Among the most important changes in the patterns of food consumption are a marked decrease in the consumption of expensive products of animal origin and their replacement by less expensive ones such as eggs and organ meats, the consumption of which increased. During the years of the crisis meat was almost completely absent from the tables of the urban poor ("They have turned us into vegetarians"). In the case of Mexico, the cost of the basic food basket as a percentage of the minimum wage increased from 34.78 percent in 1980 to 49.5 percent in 1987. As a result of the difficulties that housewives faced in trying to make their money stretch, national per capita consumption of meat decreased by 5 kilograms between 1982 and 1985 (from 16.7 to 12.1 kilograms), and the consumption of milk reached its lowest point in 1987. In addition, the consumption of products such as rice, beans, and corn, elements of the traditional Mexican diet, was reduced in those years (Cordera and González Tiburcio, 1991: 33; see also Moser, 1989, for Ecuador and Gutiérrez, 1992, for Venezuela). The result of this, as might be expected, was a nutritional deficit for the urban population.

The evidence from Mexico indicates that not all households were able to maintain their patterns of consumption at the same level or were affected in the same way. Extended households, which had more workers and were at the stage of consolidation or stability,[16] were more successful in protecting their consumption patterns, although they did modify those patterns. Young households, frequently nuclear and with fewer workers, were more vulnerable, and in the Mexican study they modified their patterns of consumption more than other households. Households headed by women, although poorer than male-headed households, tended to be more equitable in the distribution of resources and of the goods acquired for consumption and to have more balanced patterns of food consumption, with greater consumption of vegetables and fruits in the daily diet, in large part because of the allocation of a higher percentage of income to food. Thus, the per capita consumption of food tended to be greater in these households. These alternative patterns were facilitated by the fact that in these households women had greater control over income and the material bases of survival (González de la Rocha, 1994a).

CHANGES IN THE COMPOSITION OF HOUSEHOLDS

During the era of economic growth the majority of households were nuclear. Qualitative studies have shown one aspect of the strategies adopted by urban inhabitants during the years of the crisis: the number of extended households increased as a mechanism for saving on housing costs and conserving and/or adding able-bodied members for salaried and domestic work. Although nuclear households continued to predominate, the importance of extended and female-headed households increased. In fact, it has been calculated that although extended households are not as numerous as nuclear ones, they shelter a greater number of persons because of their larger size (CEPAL, 1992a). We must remember, however, that these distinct types of domestic structures are not mutually exclusive; the same household may display characteristics of both the nuclear and the extended structure over time, and the extended structure offers the household more flexibility, especially if the added members are able-bodied and can participate in the income-generation strategy and in domestic work.[17] The legality of unions, on the other hand, is not homogeneous; there is great diversity in the various countries of the region. Even when there has been an increase in legal unions, common-law marriage remains very important, especially at certain stages in the lives of women (e.g., for the group from 15 to 24 years of age) and in the poorest and least-educated sectors (CEPAL, 1992a).

PARTICIPATION IN NETWORKS OF MUTUAL ASSISTANCE

The social responses that we have been discussing are private, produced and taking place within households. Although these are of great importance, survival and reproduction depend on relationships that extend beyond the domestic sphere. The emergence of "collective kitchens" in Peru and the "collective kettles," the "glass of milk," and the "march for life" in La Paz, Bolivia, were indications of the enormous capacity for extra-domestic response there. In other countries, such as Mexico, the responses were more private (Benería, 1992; González de la Rocha, 1988; 1991), the population being focused on survival at the household level and much more silent and overwhelmed than in previous years. It has been shown that during the years of crisis a surprising social calm prevailed in Mexico[18] and that it was grounded in the intensification of work and of conflict and negotiation within the household. Stressing the "private" character of these strategies does not, however, diminish the importance of the networks of mutual assistance maintained by relatives and neighbors, godparents, friends, and fellow workers that have formed part of the sources of income and resources of the urban poor in Latin America. In fact, I have had the opportunity to test the relevance of reciprocal exchange and mutual assistance through the analysis of deviant cases in which bonds among equals are lacking, and this analysis reveals that social isolation creates greater difficulty in obtaining employment, confronting emergencies, and even managing to avoid obstacles in the daily struggle for survival (González de la Rocha, 1994c).

UNEQUAL DISTRIBUTION OF RESOURCES: HOUSEHOLDS HEADED BY MEN AND WOMEN

Reference has already been made to the vulnerability of households headed by women and to the increase in the number of households of this type in the past decade. The perspective that highlights the vulnerability of these house-holds has recently been contrasted with another that—without losing sight of the factors that lead to reduced levels of income—also underscores a more eq-uitable distribution of work, resources, income, less differentiated patterns of consumption, and a greater emphasis on the consumption of food (Buvinič, 1990; Chant, 1988; Folbre, 1991; González de la Rocha, 1994a). Therefore, although it can be said that the absence of a male head of household increases the chances of permanent poverty, it is important to keep in mind these households' more balanced pattern of consumption, with less income devoted to alcohol and cigarettes and more to food, clothing, health, and education, as well as a tendency towards a more equitable allocation of household work. The vulnerability of these women and their children should be evaluated through analysis of levels of per capita consumption and of the other elements that constitute, make possible, or preclude well-being: diet, health, education, and power relationships within the household. It is a fact that households headed by women are concentrated at the lowest levels of income[19] and that they have increased in numbers among the poorest, but, as I have suggested, women and children in households headed by men in the context of urban poverty may be equally vulnerable because of relationships of domination and subordination permeated by gender and generation (González de la Rocha, 1994a). These relationships surface in unequal distribution of shares of food among the members of the household and differential access to educational and health services. Power and relationships of gender and generation are re-flected in differential levels of well-being observable among the members of a single domestic group. Thus the fact that a household has a level of income that places it slightly above the poverty line does not mean that all its mem-bers enjoy a homogeneous or equitable state of well-being. At the same time, being part of a male-headed household does not guarantee greater well-being because of differential consumption and similarly differential access to re-sources. Asymmetrical consumption practices in contexts of poverty lead to high levels of malnutrition for some members of the household (women and children) that translate into reduced physical and intellectual capacity. Mal-nourished children will have a low success rate at school that will translate into fewer work possibilities in the long run. The few systematic studies on in-fant malnutrition have shown an increase in the percentage of children under two years of age who are seriously malnourished. This may be related to the fact that small children predominate in very young households, which have had difficulty in defending their previous levels of food consumption in the crisis. It may also be related to the shorter period of breastfeeding brought about by women's greater participation in the labor market or, again, to chil-dren's lack of power and increasingly neglected position.

It is important to keep in mind in designing future research that the special circumstances of consensual unions have implications for the life expectancies of children. The notable increase in this type of union throughout the 1980s, its concentration in the poorest households, and the evidence of lower scholastic performance by children of these unions make it imperative to delve deeper into the different types of marriages and their relationships to distinct family structures, patterns of distribution of income and access to resources, and the well-being of different members of households.

FINAL REFLECTIONS:
ECONOMIC DEPENDENCE ON FAMILY LABOR

As we have seen, the survival and reproduction of households in the context of urban poverty is based on an organization of mutual dependence and on the use of internal resources of which labor is the most important. The model of the nuclear family living on the salary of the male head of household applies only to a limited number of cases. The large majority of poor households requires a combination of diverse sources of income and participation by more than one member in the labor market. Work by women, youth, and children is a resource that is used in cases of necessity (more frequent every day), although the amount they earn may be small. Intradomestic-group economic dependence increases as individual survival becomes more difficult, not without consequences for the well-being of individuals and their families in the medium and long term. The social cost of the economic crisis and policies of adjustment has yet to be fully appraised, and it is found not only in the economic sector but in others. Negotiation over the use of resources has turned into confrontation. Domestic violence and conflict between individual and collective interests have increased as a consequence of the increased tensions generated by the use and control of income (González de la Rocha, 1988; González de la Rocha, Escobar, and Martínez, 1990; Barrig, 1993). Moser (1989) documents this phenomenon in her study in Guayaquil, Ecuador, arguing that there has been a parallel increase in alcoholism and drug addiction—male consumption practices that exacerbate the problem of domestic violence.[20] Some of the consequences of the intensification of work include school desertion, a double shift for women, and a work overload for family members. The limits of this strategy are seen in the increase in the number of young males (between 15 and 25 years of age) who are neither studying nor working. Upon leaving school to supplement household incomes, they face a labor market that is difficult to enter. Going to work at an early age undoubtedly has consequences for their level of schooling, the type of incorporation into the labor market, both at entry and later, and medium- and long-range levels of remuneration. This is only one example of the profound contradiction between short- and long-term survival. The elements of a short-term strategy limit individuals' possibilities in the long term.

The greater vulnerability of certain types of households, including young households, those of advanced age, and households headed by women, all characterized by low income, is related to their limited possibilities of sending a larger contingent of individuals into the labor market and to the precariousness of the types of employment in which their members participate. Not only are they less capable of increasing their number of workers but also they confront greater difficulties in defending their levels of consumption in a deteriorating economy. The vulnerability of young households is particularly alarming because they constitute the social units that contain the majority of the infant population, but households headed by the elderly are also extremely poor; the growing numbers of the elderly will experience a greater need for medical attention and economic assistance and greatly diminished possibilities for the generation of income. Poverty in households headed by women is clearly related to the gendered income differentials that prevail in the workplace.

Yet the identification of at-risk groups should be sensitive to the differences within households, the differential burdens of the strategies of intensification of work, and the benefits—also unequal—of these efforts. Women and children are the most vulnerable members. Concretely, it is important to recognize that throughout these years of deterioration in standards of living and in real wages women have been the artisans of survival and reproduction and that the main burden of the social cost of neoliberal-style policies has fallen on their shoulders. This unequal burden contrasts with the limited control that women still have over their incomes in the domestic environment. Moreover, the income differentials according to sex that are characteristic of labor markets in our countries have not only persisted but increased. Women's wages are not secondary income but instead have become important pillars of family and domestic support, despite the fact that they are meager and invisible (Benería and Roldán, 1987). Women's wages and the control that women may have over them are crucial to the analysis of poverty and family well-being, since women's control of income, when it exists, translates into substantial improvement in the well-being of children in terms of nutrition, health, and education (Blumberg, 1991). Increasing the salaries and wages of women would have direct and immediate repercussions on diet, access to doctors and medicines, and the living conditions of the urban population. We need to rethink the criteria for granting subsidies and credit in light of the primordial role of women in the generation and management of well-being.

The difficulties that men confront in fulfilling their traditional role of provider in a context in which there are no alternative normative and ideological models is part of a complex intensification of the contradictions that have developed within households (Kaztman, 1992). On the one hand, the crisis has forced women to participate in remunerated work, although it has not liberated them from their domestic responsibilities; on the other hand, the norms and values that are attributed to men and women have not changed. The conflict between men's and women's expectations and everyday responsibilities has worsened, and it is a conflict that must be resolved through solidarity and consensus rather than through confrontation and violence.

NOTES

A first version of this article, entitled "Poverty and the Urban Family in Latin America," was prepared for the Economic Commission for Latin America and the Caribbean and presented at the preliminary meeting for the International Year of the Family in Cartagena de las Indias, Colombia, in August 1993. The text was discussed with Bryan Roberts, Rubén Kaztman, Elizabeth Jelin, Manuel Chiriboga, and Barry Chevannes, whom the author thanks for their suggestions. This revised version has benefited from the comments of Juan Feres, Carmen Diana Deere, M. Gandásegui, and a fourth evaluator who remains anonymous.

1. This growth was clearly reflected in the level of well-being of the population. From 1970 to 1976 the extent of poverty decreased considerably. The proportion of families with middle and high incomes increased notably, to the point that the middle sectors expanded and developed higher and more sophisticated patterns of consumption. Non-manual labor expanded, and rates of occupational mobility increased. Poverty continued, however, to be one of the principal characteristics of the region. At the beginning of the 1970s, 40 percent of the total Latin American population was in a situation of poverty, while in 1980 the poor constituted 35 percent of the population. The extent of urban poverty also declined, although insignificantly; 26 percent of urban households were poor in 1970 and 25 percent of them were poor in 1980 (CEPAL, 1991).

2. Non-working-age members are the elderly and those less than 15 years of age. For a more precise and elaborate definition of members available and unavailable for work, see Pastore, Zylberstajn, and Pagotto (1983: 18).

3. Young households in the expansion phase of the domestic cycle, households headed by the elderly, in which the children have already left to form their own households, and households headed by women are generally more vulnerable because of the difficulty of increasing the number of workers (González de la Rocha, 1991). The increase in the number of households headed by women in Latin American countries, especially in the poorest sectors, and their vulnerability have been the inspiration for many studies of the factors underlying their consistently lower incomes in comparison with male-headed households (Bolles, 1985; Buvinič, 1990; Folbre, 1991; Engle, 1988). Without denying their vulnerability, other studies have emphasized elements of well-being existing in households headed by women such as the lower incidence of domestic violence, per-capita income equal to or

higher than in male-headed households, and greater emphasis on food and reduced spending on alcohol (Chant, 1985; González de la Rocha, 1991; 1994a).

4. Only to a certain extent, since we are dealing with a model of an internal market with strong flows of capital from international banks.

5. Groups that had not been part of the urban poor before the crisis became part of that contingent in the 1980s. The impoverishment of the middle sectors has inspired analyses showing that in the case of Mexico the first half of the 1980s was characterized by "equity in impoverishment" (Cortés and Rubalcava, 1991; see also González de la Rocha, 1994b).

6. In 1990 almost 23 million urban households versus 15 million rural households (116 versus 81 million individuals) were poor (CEPAL, 1992b). The CEPAL studies are based on the relationship between per-capita income of the household and the value of the poverty line. In the case of urban zones the poverty line was calculated by doubling the value of the line of indigence, which corresponds to the cost of the basic food basket that would cover the needs of all household members. To the value of this food basket, CEPAL added an estimate of the resources required by households to satisfy the basic food necessities.

7. In Chile, for example, during the period from 1970 to 1973, the richest 20 percent of the population earned 50 percent of the income and the poorest 40 percent earned 12.9 percent. From 1982 to 1984, however, the rich earned 60 percent and the poor earned only 9.8 percent (Ortega and Tironi, 1988). In Brazil, where real product fell 3.8 percent between 1980 and 1983 and per capita real product diminished 10.6 percent in the same period, a decrease of 8.8 percent was observed in the minimum real wage. In 1982, 46.2 percent of families found themselves below the poverty line (defined in this study as family income of two minimum wages) (Singer, 1985).

8. Social spending in Mexico as a percentage of the gross national product diminished from 7.6 percent in 1981–1982 to 5.6 percent in 1987–1988 (Cordera and González Tiburcio, 1991). This decrease in governmental spending for social services took place in all the countries of the region. Fortuna and Prates (1989) mention that in Uruguay there was a reduction in government social spending and a withdrawal of the state from providing public housing; the responsibility for the reproduction and survival of workers fell almost exclusively to families and domestic groups.

9. Only in Costa Rica was there no change in the levels of paid labor in the public sector; in the rest of the countries the decline in employment in this sector was sharper than in the private sector (CEPAL, 1991).

10. In non-metropolitan urban zones in Brazil the economic participation of women heads of household increased by 16 percent and that of women who were not heads of household by 25 percent between 1979 and 1987. Both of these increases were greater than the increase in the rate of participation by the population 15 years and older, which was 9 percent. The rest of the countries showed the same tendency with slight variations. In Argentina, for example, the economic participation of women heads of household and those who were not heads of household increased to the same degree (10 percent from 1980 to 1986) and more than that of the population 15 years and older. In non-metropolitan Colombian cities, the economic participation of women heads of household increased more than that of women who were not heads of household, and the same occurred in metropolitan and urban Costa Rica and in the non-metropolitan cities of Venezuela (CEPAL, 1991: Table 3).

11. The percentage of unemployed heads of household increased by more than half in countries such as Argentina, Colombia, Brazil, and Venezuela (CEPAL, 1991).

12. Women who perform domestic work, for example, require the help of their children when they return from school and on weekends in doing errands and caring for younger siblings (usually the work of young girls). Indeed, housewives who find themselves required to undertake paid labor generally delegate greater responsibility and workloads to their children.

13. According to Singer, in Brazil a considerable increase was observed in the purchase of appliances for the home (refrigerators, radios, televisions), and this seems to have been a common element in the rest of the countries in the region. The manufacturing industry of these goods required the expansion and consolidation of an internal market for their products. According to Singer's data (1985: 36), from 1960 to 1970 the proportion of urban homes with refrigerators increased from 23.3 percent to 42.5 percent, while the number of television sets also increased: 9.5 percent of urban homes in 1960 had a television, and in 1970 that figure had increased to 40.2 percent.

14. Two studies of these strategies are those of Ortega and Tironi (1988) and Schkolnik and Teitelboim (1988); see also González de la Rocha (1991). The testimonies from Chile presented by Schkolnik and Teitelboim recognize such mechanisms as abstaining from buying gas for heating and food preparation, instead substituting more economical combustibles or none at all; ceasing to pay for lights or water in order to protect their ability to pay for food; and changing the schedule of meals from three to two daily. See also Moser (1989) and Gutiérrez (1992).

15. Efforts to obtain a more complete and nutritious diet are not the same as equitable consumption; great differences exist in what is consumed by different members of households. Qualitative studies have shown that portions and types of food are distributed according to the individuals' positions in the household. Thus, the hierarchical relationships by gender and age that are dominant in our societies mean that women and children receive what remains in the cooking pots after males who work, especially adult males, have been fed (González de la Rocha, 1986).

16. This stage of the domestic cycle is characterized by the greatest degree of equilibrium or balance between consumers and generators of income and by higher levels of total per capita income. Furthermore, a large number of households in this stage are extended households (González de la Rocha, 1986).

17. The emphasis on the economic benefits of extended households should not be allowed to obscure the fact that the extension frequently implies the intensification of conflict between members of the household. It is common for married sons living with their parents to continue to hand over their economic contributions to their mothers, not without profound effects on their wives. Control of resources and the education of children/grandchildren in households that combine several generations are among the areas of greatest conflict among members of extended households.

18. This calm has been severely disturbed since the last year of the Salinas presidency (1994), when poverty and the long-standing subordination of Indians were evidenced in the uprising of the National Liberation Zapatista Army. Multiple instances of violence have disturbed the social order in Mexico at various points during the 1990s.

19. Their per capita income is frequently equal to that found in households headed by men and in some cases higher, given their smaller size (González de la Rocha, 1994a).

20. The increase in tensions is also related to the presence in the household of persons who are not members of the conjugal unit or direct descendants. Although the extended

household offers greater flexibility and is associated with higher domestic income, greater participation by women in employment, and greater capacity to defend levels of consumption (González de la Rocha, 1991), it also fosters conflict, especially between in-laws. Chant (1994), from another perspective, proposes that extended households are more democratic, masculine authority being subject to pressures that arise from the fact that their wives are not alone in negotiating for the control of domestic resources.

REFERENCES

Barrig, Maruja
   1993 Seis familias en la crisis. Lima: ADEC-ATC, Asociación Laboral para el Desarrollo.
Benería, Lourdes
   1992 "The Mexican debt crisis: Restructuring the economy and the household," in Lourdes Benería and Shelley Feldman (eds.), Economic Crises, Persistent Poverty, and Women's Work. Boulder, CO: Westview Press.
Benería, Lourdes and Martha Roldán
   1987 The Crossroads of Class and Gender: Industrial Homework, Subcontracting, and Household Dynamics in Mexico City. Chicago: University of Chicago Press.
Blumberg, Rae L.
   1991 "Introduction: The 'triple overlap' of gender stratification economy and the family," in Rae L. Blumberg (ed.), Gender; Family, and Economy. Newbury Park, CA: Sage.
Bolles, Lynn
   1985 "Economic crisis and female-headed households in urban Jamaica," in June Nash and Helen Safa (eds.), Women and Change in Latin America. South Hadley, MA: Bergin and Garvey.
Buvinič, Mayra
   1990 "The vulnerability of woman-headed households: Policy questions and options for Latin America and the Caribbean." Paper delivered at the Economic Commission for Latin America and the Caribbean conference "Vulnerable Women," Vienna, Austria, November 26–30.
Buvinic, Mayra et al.
   1991 La suerte de las madres adolescentes y sus hijos: Un estudio de caso sobre la transmisión de la pobreza en Santiago de Chile. (CEPAL LC/R.1038). Santiago.
CEPAL (Comisión Económica para América Latina y el Caribe)
   1991 La equidad en el panorama social de América Latina durante los años ochenta. LC/R.1686.
   1992a Hacia un perfil de la familia actual en Latinoamérica y el Caribe. LC/R. 1208.
   1992b El perfil de la pobreza en América Latina a comienzos de los años 90. LC/L.716 (Conf. 82/6).
Chant, Sylvia
   1985 "Single-parent families: Choice or constraint? The formation of female-headed house-holds in Mexican shanty towns." Development and Change 16: 635–656.
   1988 "Mitos y realidades de la formación de familias encabezadas por mujeres: El caso de Querétaro, México," in L. Gabayet, P. García, M. González de la Rocha, S. Lailson, and A. Escobar (eds.), Mujeres y sociedad. Salario, hogar y acción social en la occidente de México. Guadalajara: El Colegio de Jalisco/CIESAS.

1994 "Women and poverty in urban Latin America: Mexican and Costa Rican experiences," in Fatima Meer (ed.), *Poverty in the 1990s: The Responses of Urban Women.* Tours, France: UNESCO/International Social Science Council.

Cordera, Rolando and Enrique González Tiburcio
1991 "Crisis and transition in the Mexican economy," in Mercedes González de la Rocha and Agustín Escobar Latapí (eds.), *Social Responses to Mexico's Economic Crisis of the 1980s.* La Jolla: Center for U.S.-Mexican Studies, University of California, San Diego.

Cortés, Fernando and Rosa Marla Rubalcava
1991 *Autoexplotación forzada o equidad por empobrecimento.* Mexico City: El Colegio de México.

Deere, Carmen Diana, Peggy Antrobus, Lynn Bolles, Edwin Melendez, Peter Phillips, Marcia Rivera, and Helen Safa
1990 *In the Shadows of the Sun: Caribbean Development Alternatives and U.S. Policy.* Boulder, CO: Westview Press.

de Janvry, Alain, Elisabeth Sadoulet, and Linda Wilcox Young
1989 "Land and labour in Latin American agriculture from the 1950s to the 1980s." *Journal of Peasant Studies* 16 (3): 396–424.

Engle, Patricia
1988 "Women-headed families in Guatemala: Consequences for children." Paper delivered at the conference "Consequences of Female Headship and Female Maintenance," Population Council/International Center for Research on Women, Washington, DC, February 27–28.

Escobar, Agustín and Bryan Roberts
1991 "Urban stratification, the middle classes, and economic change in Mexico," in Mercedes González de la Rocha and Agustín Escobar Latapí (eds.), *Social Responses to Mexico's Economic Crisis of the 1980s.* La Jolla: Center for U.S.-Mexican Studies, University of California, San Diego.

Folbre, Nancy
1991 "Women on their own: Global patterns of female headship," in Rita Gallin and Ann Ferguson (eds.), *Women and International Development Annual,* vol. 2. Boulder, CO: Westview Press.

Fortuna, Juan Carlos and Suzana Prates
1989 "Informal sector versus informalized labor relations in Uruguay," in Alejandro Portes, Manuel Castells, and Lauren A. Benton (eds.), *The Informal Economy: Studies in Advanced and Less Developed Countries.* Baltimore: Johns Hopkins University Press.

González de la Rocha, Mercedes
1986 *Los recursos de la pobreza: Familias de bajos ingresos de Guadalajara.* Guadalajara: El Colegio de Jalisco/CIESAS/SPP.
1988 "Economic crisis, domestic reorganization, and women's work in Guadalajara, Mexico." *Bulletin of Latin American Research* 7 (2): 207–223.
1991 "Family well-being, food consumption, and survival strategies during Mexico's economic crisis," in Mercedes González de la Rocha and Agustín Escobar Latapí (eds.), *Social Responses to Mexico's Economic Crisis of the 1980s.* La Jolla: Center for U.S.-Mexican Studies, University of California, San Diego.
1994a "Household headship and occupational position in Mexico," in *Poverty and Well-Being in the Household: Case Studies of the Developing World.* Center for Iberian and Latin Studies, University of California, San Diego, Working Paper 5.

1994b "Reestructuración social en dos ciudades metropolitanas: Un análisis de grupos domésticos en Guadalajara y Monterrey." Paper delivered at 18th International Congress of the Latin American Studies Association, Atlanta, GA, March 10–12.

1994c *The Resources of Poverty: Women and Survival in a Mexican City.* Oxford: Basil Blackwell.

González de la Rocha, Mercedes, Agustín Escobar, and M. Martínez

1990 "Estrategias vs. conflicto: Reflexiones para el estudio del grupo doméstico en época de crisis," in Guillermo de la Peña et al. (eds.), *Crisis, conflicto y sobrevivencia: Estudios sobre la sociedad urbana en México.* Guadalajara: Universidad de Guadalajara/CIESAS.

Gutiérrez, Ana Teresa

1992 "¿Vivir para comer? El consumo de los sectores populares urbanos," in Cecilia Cariola (ed.), *Sobrevivir en la pobreza: El fin de una ilusión.* Caracas: CENDES/Nueva Sociedad.

Kaztman, Rubén

1992 "¿Por qué los hombres son tan irresponsables?" *Revista de la CEPAL* 46: 87–95.

McFarren, Wendy

1992 "The politics of Bolivia's economic crisis: Survival strategies of displaced tin-mining households," in Lourdes Benería and Shelley Feldman (eds.), *Unequal Burden: Economic Crises, Persistent Poverty, and Women's Work.* Boulder, CO: Westview Press.

Moser, Caroline

1989 "The impact of recession and adjustment policies at the micro-level: Low-income women and their households in Guayaquil, Ecuador," in *The Invisible Adjustment: Poor Women and the Economic Crisis.* Santiago: UNICEF.

Oliveira, Orlandina and Brígida García

1990 "Cambios en los determinantes del trabajo femenino en México." Manuscript, El Colegio de México.

Ortega, Eugenio R. and Ernesto B. Tironi

1988 *Pobreza en Chile.* Santiago: Centro de Estudios del Desarrollo.

Pastore, José, Helio Zylberstajn, and Carmen Silvia Pagotto

1983 *Mudança social e pobreza no Brasil, 1970–1980: O que ocorreu com a família brasileira?* São Paulo: Fundação Instituto de Pesquisas Econômicas/Livraria Pioneira Editora.

Pérez Alemán, Paola

1992 "Economic crisis and women in Nicaragua, " in Lourdes Benería and Shelley Feldman (eds), *Unequal Burden. Economic Crises, Persistent Poverty and Women's Work.* Boulder, CO: Westview.

Schkolnik, Mariana and Berta Teitelboim

1988 *Pobreza y desempleo en poblaciones: La otra cara del modelo neoliberal.* Santiago: Programa Economía del Trabajo, Colección Temas Sociales 2.

Singer, Paul

1985 *Repartição da renda: Pobres e ricos o regime militar.* Rio de Janeiro: Jorge Zahar.

4

The Myth of Being "Like a Daughter"

Grace Esther Young

A small group of dedicated women is organizing domestic servants in Lima, Peru. Like the maids they organize, these women migrated at a young age from their rural, poor families to work in moderate- and upper-income, urban families. Their efforts to organize the sector are frustrated both by structural aspects of the relationship of the domestic servant to her family, as well as by the pervasive ideology of the family sphere, which is sanctioned through collective institutions.

The journey young women make from the rural to urban context is facilitated through the medium of the family as a socioeconomic and ideological form. The family has seemingly universal characteristics as well as aspects that are specific to particular class and cultural contexts. I shall argue that the idiom of the family as inclusive, just, and as a "natural" age-based division of labor and power, serves to structure a relationship of inequality—indeed, exploitation—one powerfully legitimized by the church and the state. But, the metaphor of the family is itself contradictory at least in its application to the conditions of domestic service, something that emerges in the experience of the domestic servants themselves.

Efforts to organize the domestic servant sector began in the early 1970s, during a period of sustained economic growth and stability of the Peruvian economy. The macroeconomic changes occurring in Peru serve to restructure the nature of the domestic domain, thereby changing the character of the domestic servant's position. As these changes occur, creative strategies for organizing the sector are demanded.

Having moved from their families of origin, domestic servants walk a fine line in their new patron families. They find themselves both members and nonmem-

This chapter first appeared in *Latin American Perspectives* 54, 14:3 (Summer 1987), pp. 365–380.

Fourteen-year-old live-in domestic, Managua, Nicaragua, 1993. *Photo courtesy of Cynthia Chavez Metoyer*

bers, standing simultaneously within the familial boundaries yet outside them. Their case exemplifies the linkage of domestic and collective institutions that are bonded by an ideology of paternalism and dependency. This article demonstrates that the contour of familial boundaries and the changes occurring on the macroeconomic level in Latin America maintain domestic servants in a marginal position, the nature of which is revealed in the reality of their life cycles.

The first part of this article provides a discussion of the family's socioeconomic and ideological characteristics, with a particular focus on its inherent ideology, which masks the true relations of production therein. The second part demonstrates the changes apparent in the domestic servant sector as a result of the recession in Peru. The recession's effects on middle-income earners coupled with the growth of a vendor sector interact to bring new definition to the position of the domestic servant. As it is redefined, the cultural conception of the domestic servant's position takes on a new form.

FROM FAMILY OF ORIGIN TO PATRON FAMILY: SOCIALIZATION AND MARGINALIZATION

Central to feminist analysis of the subordination of women is the relationship of the public, or politicoeconomic, sphere and the family. While the analysis is varied and expansive, raising issues of the origin and the universality of the dichotomy, its relevance with regard to the domestic servant is in framing a discussion of the interdependence of the two realms. Sacks (1975) and Rapp (1978) suggest that the dichotomy of the public and the private spheres is specific to class-stratified, state-organized societies. With the transformation of pre-state societies, the domestic sphere developed as the heart of the reproduction, socialization, and the maintenance of new generations, while the public sphere became the center for law-making, political administration, and economic production and regulation (Sacks, 1975). Women's subordinate status is directly tied to their location in the domestic and marginal sphere. Integral to these analyses is the dominance of ideology in maintaining the dichotomy (Rapp, 1978).

These formulations provide a framework for analyzing the interplay of the constructs of class and gender with the dominant ideology of the family. However, they lack an analysis of the relations of authority within the domestic sphere that would bring insight to the particular location of the domestic servant as a worker in the private domain. Such insight into the internal structure of the family is necessary to understand the transition the domestic servant makes between families, and her situation in the patron family. It is the apparent continuity between "family" of origin and "family" of employment that shores her position. Therefore, it is necessary to demonstrate those aspects of the family that seem to stretch cross-culturally and across class, as well as those that are specific to the context from which she comes and into which she moves.

Many rural, young women migrating to Lima have traditionally found work in middle-income homes. The growth in demand for servants has come primarily from this sector. As in much of Latin America, the middle-income strata in Peru developed during the stage of steady economic growth from the post–World War II period until the mid-1970s. The service sector grew concomitantly as the middle-income groups grew. The growth in demand for domestic servants in Lima from 1940 to the mid-1970s was in part due to the growing number of middle-income women entering white-collar service jobs, such as government work, nursing, secretarial work, teaching, and the like. The development process in Lima took on a disparate nature, bringing employment opportunities for women in white-collar service jobs while manual work, usually filled by lower-income women, increasingly disappeared. Growth in the number of these jobs, though small, disproportionately favored men. Lower-income women found employment in the unskilled end of the service sector, such as domestic service (Scott, 1984).

The urban families that young women enter are framed by boundaries that separate them from the public sphere. Whereas boundaries of upper-class, urban families are extremely secure in Peru,[1] middle-class, urban families tend to be flexible. Such flexibility is responsive to macroeconomic changes, as can be seen in the particular situation of domestic servants (see next section). The boundaries that separate the poor, rural family from the public sphere, in contrast, are very penetrable. Though many parents prefer that their girls stay at home, they cannot support them, and domestic service is one of the few opportunities available to young, poor women. Their poverty encourages them to leave their own familial confines in search of work.

In Peru, as in modern Western society, the family is heavily imbued with an ideology that crosses class and cultural boundaries and is reinforced by the cultural forms of church and state. It is a sphere characterized by love and devotion and respect. In modern Western society it is defined as an antithesis of the public sphere. Whereas in the private sphere one's work is of a voluntary nature, given in love and devotion, the public sphere is ruled by economic laws of wage labor, business cycles, and profit motives. An ambiguous overlap of these notions provides a conduit for the incorporation of the young, rural girl into the arms of the urban middle- or upper-income family. Once inside the private sphere, with its stress on duty and respect, and on work as a voluntary contribution, the young woman becomes "like a daughter" in the patron family.

The family's hierarchical and patriarchal nature, which itself varies somewhat across class and cultural lines, also facilitates the domestic servant's transition. The nature of the hierarchy, the amount of authority vested in the father, and the division of labor by sex varies among families depending in part on the economic status and on individual family member's economic roles outside the familial sphere.[2] The status of women in the domestic sphere often varies also. In many of the Peruvian highland peasant communities boy babies are preferred to girls (Bourque and Warren, 1981). Cases of fathers selling their daughters to wealthy *patrones* (the married couple considered the active head of the household) for a burro are not unknown in this context (CERA, 1982). Like the domestic servant's siblings, she is expected to contribute economically to the family from a young age, whereas middle- and upper class children are removed from these demands. Variations in the familial hierarchy are apparent in the type of relationship the servant develops in the patron family. Whereas in the upper-class family distance is maintained between the domestic servant and her *patrones*, the middle-class family tends to incorporate her and, in particular, to encourage her to further her education (Figueroa Galup, 1977). However, as a paternal institution and as the locus for enculturating appropriate gender roles, the family spans class and cultural barriers. In the Peruvian context, girls and women are identified with the domestic sphere and men are "in the street."

The young woman passes from the paternalism of her own familial environment to the paternalism of her new working environment. From the time she is very young, she has been directed to fulfill the prescribed role of mother and wife in the domestic setting. Like the woman for whom she works, she has learned to serve and work in the home, to enact those roles as part of her own personal identity.[3] Though she may have difficulty adjusting to her new patron family,[4] the acculturation of the female gender role coupled with her own economic insecurity are important factors propelling the transition between families.

The domestic servant's entrance into her new family is through the señora (the Mrs., mistress, or acting female head of the household). It is the señora's role to bring her into the paternalistic arms of the patron family. The patron family functions ostensibly as a civilizing agent to transform her rural customs into appropriate urban ones. The señora is the primary person guiding her, and it is she who directs and teaches the domestic servant the nature of service in her particular family.

Her youth and background make the domestic servant particularly sensitive to the images she meets in the new context. She enters the family at a very young age,[5] unfamiliar with urban life in middle- and upper-income families. She moves into an environment that is foreign to her. Here she is met with entirely new concepts of appropriate family life. Apart from a very romanticized notion, rural life and all its images are devalued in Peruvian society. Though all Peruvians may be proud of Peru's Incan heritage (indeed, everyone from all socioeconomic and cultural backgrounds was adamant that I visit the famous Incan ruins of Machu Picchu), rural Indians today are a marginalized group in society and are considered culturally inferior. A woman with more than three or four children and who straps an infant to her back is not a dominant, positive image of a mother in Peruvian society. Domestic servants' own families are not viewed as acceptable role models. Their families are rooted in peasant relations of production and organization, whereas the urban families for whom most domestic servants work are patterned after the family structure of the middle-class, industrial West.

Within the patron family, the servant often becomes like one of the children. There may exist an ambiguous division between the "real" children and the domestic servant. A study of middle-class families in Lima states, "A domestic servant might be treated very affectionately, and she often seemed to take on a status of step-daughter or god-child in the family where she worked" (Anderson, 1978: 81). As a child, she often develops a filial relationship with the señora, which is set within a frame of duty and respect. The domestic servant who defines herself within the boundaries of obedience and respect that are delineated for her may stay with a family for many years. Indeed, she is the ideal maid, and her devotion provides her some protection; certainly her basic needs are met, and she may develop intimate relationships with family members.

However, the ideology of the family, with its stress on the commitment of close kin, as well as on duty and devotion within the protected boundaries, conceals the marginal position the domestic servant occupies in the private sphere. The definition of the domestic servant as "like a daughter" is part of the effort to secure her dependence and continual devotion to the family. Though her work is cloaked in terms of love and respect, the domestic servant's labor provides important material benefits for the members of the family, particularly the señora. Although the domestic servant and the señora may be united by the duty to serve well the family's needs, it is the domestic servant's labor that removes the señora from the laborious chores of cooking, cleaning, washing, and ironing. The domestic servant is an important status symbol for the señora, as she provides for her leisure.

Though she may be told she is a member, the domestic servant will not be allowed to follow the cyclical development of "real" children. She will never realize the full adult benefits of family membership. Inherent to the relationship of the domestic with the patron family is that, as she entered as a child, she remain as a child. To define herself within the boundaries of the patron family means she must negate her own needs as an adult woman. She cannot expect to live in a place apart from the patron family, because most señoras prefer a live-in maid who is available to them both early in the morning and late at night. If she has children, she will not be retained. Statistics show that domestic servants continue to be overwhelmingly single, young women without responsibilities of children and who live in the families in which they work.

The nature of the family with its diffuse and fluid relationships conceals the hierarchy contained within it. A strict division of labor between the "real" children and the domestic servant brings clarity to the ambiguous relationship. As Anderson (1978: 81) points out,

> What was not ambiguous was who actually cooked, cleaned, and picked up after whom. The "real" children had exceedingly light duties in the household. Their duty was to do as well as they could in school. The *empleada* (employee), in stark contrast, fit whatever preparation for school she could manage around the demands that were made on her for running special errands besides her scheduled daily responsibilities.

Her labor provides the real children the privilege of undivided attention to their education. Her liminal membership in the patron family does not give her access to the cultural or material capital of the middle- or upper-class family to which the real children are admitted. The progression of her own life cycle (see next section) is a living testimony of her exclusion from it.

An often-repeated comment by domestic servants when asked what it is like working in their patron families is, "I'm like a part of the family. They treat me like I was their daughter." Key to their explanations is a paternalistic notion embedded in the words, *el trato* (the treatment). Because she is in a vulnerable position in the patron family and is left unprotected by institutions outside the familial sphere, the aspect of treatment is almost as important as the wage she may or may not receive.[6]

The dependent, paternalistic relationship the domestic servant develops in the patron family is reinforced by the church, which sanctifies the protected familial environment. The Catholic church plays an important role in legitimating the idiom of duty and devotion to the family. Schools that recruit and train young women to become domestic servants are administered by the Catholic church. It is an important mediator in the transition of young women from their rural to their new urban families. Although it instills an important sense of pride in domestic work, its fundamental message guides domestics to be agents of harmony and unity within their patron families.[7] Within a framework of duty and obedience to God, these young women are taught service and respect to their patron families to be.

As a means of confronting their dependent and insecure position, domestic servants began to meet informally, and in some cases clandestinely, in the early 1970s. They gathered in neighborhood parks during their free hours on Sundays to talk about their situation. Some maids who went to school began to meet after class. Through sharing information, a slow process of consciousness-raising began as they discovered that, while each girl's situation had its specified characteristics, they all were subject to very similar conditions in their patron families. They began to identify with one another; as workers in homes, and as rural, Indian people.

Structural aspects of the relationship of the domestic servant with her family, such as the amount of time she must be at their service, as well as the ideology of the family which seeks to keep maids from identifying with other *cholas* (derogatory term for Indian) in the street impedes maids' organizing efforts. Their work directly challenges the fundamental nature of the servant's position. As long as she remains ignorant of the implications of her position as a domestic servant, she will not question her marginal position. In essence, she is restricted to the lowest rung of the patron family, almost excluded from the familial boundaries, a marginal area, unprotected by outside institutions. And as the Peruvian economic reality changes, so too does the nature of her position.

DOMESTIC SERVICE VERSUS VENDING:
NEW OPTION OR LAST RESORT

For those girls and young women who continue to migrate to Lima, domestic service remains one of the few available employment options. For a variety of reasons, the vendor sector is not an attractive alternative. First, they must have their own accommodation, which is rare among these young women. The majority of girls seeking domestic servant work migrate alone or with distant family members (Young, 1986) who are anxious for them to find work in homes. Their own families, whether in rural or urban areas, are unable to support them. Second, in order to enter the vendor sector, the servant must have a certain amount of capital, which is a deterrent.

Independent studies profiling the domestic-service sector and the vending sector indicate that, although the women who work in both sectors are migrants from the rural, highland areas of Peru, their age, educational level, and familial status are different. Vendors in Lima tend to be older, less educated women with the responsibilities of children (Smith, 1980). The attraction of the vendor sector to a mother with children, who can keep them near her while she works and can choose her own hours (Arizpe, 1975), is not paralleled in the case of the domestic servant.

While young women continue to look to domestic service for employment, fewer jobs are available. Increasing numbers of families are unable to hire them. The recession has negatively affected the earning power of the middle-income sector, which accounted for the growth in demand for domestics' services until the crisis (Figueroa, 1982; Suárez et al., 1982). A random sample of the middle-income housing development "Residencial San Felipe" in 1970 showed 51 percent of the families with at least one domestic servant (Anderson, 1978). My random sample of the same area in 1981 showed only 25 percent with servants. This evidence is substantiated by a report that compares the type of families in urban areas in 1974, before the crisis, and in 1978, during the crisis. It found an approximate 50 percent decrease in the number of families with domestic servants and an increase in the number of extended families (Chueca and Vargas, 1982).

The decrease in demand for the services of domestics has precipitated a drop in their wages. A comparison of their real wages in 1974 with the real value of their wages in 1984 demonstrates that their wages have fallen by nearly half. While domestic servants' wages are falling, they are not falling at the fast rate of those of minimum wage earners. Despite its unattractiveness, the decrease in demand and concomitant decrease in wages is forcing some women to look to other employment alternatives. As fewer domestics' services are demanded, those women seeking employment in the sector who do not have the characteristics señoras demand[8] must look to other income-generating sources. Few opportunities are available to them apart from the vendor sector. The absorption of these women into the vendor sector, then, is a result of their expulsion from the domestic-service sector.

The decrease in demand for domestic servants as a result of the recession has come particularly from middle-income earners, which has meant a restructuring of domestic chores, in some cases by the use of extended family members, such as aunts or grandmothers. The growth of the informal labor market is in part due to the decrease in demand for domestic servants, as those women who enter into service do not meet the prescriptions of the ever-shrinking demand. However, in large measure, the informal labor market is composed of women entering later in their life cycle as a response to the recession in hopes of supporting their own families. The economic history of the majority of these women was to begin working as domestic servants for a number of years before having families, and to then enter the vendor sector since the crisis.

The changing nature of the patron families as they restructure ways to complete domestic responsibilities has a parallel changing ideological component that acts to reaffirm the traditional conception of the private sphere. Domestic servants are increasingly viewed within the context of the very visible vendor sector, removed entirely from the private realm of the patron family.

The vendor sector has had great impact on the cultural conception of the domestic servant sector. While there are fewer migrants coming to Lima, many of those migrants who have already made their homes in Lima are a very visible and vocal force in the life of the capital. Throughout Lima, people line the streets selling their wares on the black market. There are daily newspaper and radio reports that tell of vendors' attempts to protect their illegal business from police relocation.

Señoras tell of increasing numbers of maids leaving the servant sector to become vendors. They state that maids now seek their freedom in the street. Labor officials and economists report that the informal labor market is the cause of a decrease in the supply of maids, despite a high demand for their services.

Though *muchachas* (maids) continue to be "an incomparable theme for a lively first conversation" between señoras (Anderson, 1978: 56), the nature of their conversation has changed. Whereas before "the women laughed at the girls' bumpkin ways without fear that anybody would be offended" (Anderson, 1978: 56), now conversation centers on a perceived change in the maids. Señoras relate that it is no longer possible to find a "good" maid. The claim that maids no longer act like family, lacking respect for those for whom they work. It is said that the maid will inherently steal from her patron family. Señoras relate that maids now make excessive demands on them for higher wages, for meat every day, for the use of the color television, and so on.

Once viewed as a status symbol, the domestic servant is now increasingly depreciated by potential *patrón* families. As increasing numbers of families go without their services, they become defined as a group that cannot be brought into the paternalistic arms of the patron family. Instead, in every maid is seen the seed of a vendor, according to those who relate that maids inherently want to work in the street to be free from their señoras.

Señoras' discussions centering on the departure by maids from the strict lines of obedience and respect to their patron families serve to reaffirm the idiom of duty and respect within the family. In addition, the focus on duty and respect reasserts the notion of the family as a sphere removed from the exigencies of the public one. As the flexible boundaries of the patron family place the domestic servant outside their borders, they are re-secured.

Whether she is included within the arms of the patron family on its lowest rung, or excluded from it as a vendor, her marginalization merely takes on a new form. Though crucial to both the patron family's as well as to society's maintenance, her position retains her as a marginal member of the social totality.

As a result of the recession and its negative impact on domestic servants wages, women organizing the sector have begun to focus on petitioning the government for minimum wages and minimum working hours, as well as for recognition of their union. Laws governing the sector of domestic servants support her isolation by legitimizing the separation of the family from the public sphere. This is apparent in the laws that relate to the working conditions of minors as well as in the recent government legislation for minimum wages and working hours.

Although a law governing minors who work in formal settings states, for example, that they cannot work more than six hours a day, domestic servants, a large percentage of whom are underage, are exempt from such coverage. The legislation governing servants places their labor in a separate category, arguing that because their work is restricted to the domestic sphere, it should be excluded from laws governing the sphere of business and profit. The only law governing length of their working day states that they must have eight hours of rest daily.[9]

The efforts to petition the government for such rights as a minimum wage and minimum working hours have been met by the following governmental response: "The relation of dependence between the employer and the domestic servant is eminently one of trust which implies a sense of familiarity and adhesion that should exist between the dependent worker and the family" (Cámara de Diputados, 1980,1981). By defining her labor apart from labor for profit, and by stating that the relationship with those who benefit from her labor is one of trust, the government legitimates the paternalistic ideology of domestic service. The domestic servant is left in a marginal and unprotected position.

CONCLUSION

The dependent, paternalistic relationship the domestic servant develops in the patron family has characteristics of feudal economic forms as well as those of the modern capitalist world. Collective institutions, both the church and the government, enhance a dependent paternalism, and seem to impede the entrance into the familial sphere of such aspects of market labor relations as wage contracts or minimum working hours. These institutions promote an ideology of two separate, independent, and secure realms, the public and private; they render the position of the domestic servant, the patron family's least powerful member, insecure and vulnerable.

As the Peruvian socioeconomic reality changes, the domestic servant is increasingly placed outside the patron family and is becoming part of an ever-growing urban underclass. While in the patron family, her position is concealed by the familial ideology of dependence and paternalism—an ideology strengthened by the church and government regulations. Whether she is within its boundaries or outside them, her situation is one of dependence and economic insecurity. The contradiction inherent in the idiom of the family, an idiom that promises protection and familial security, is apparent in the reality of the domestic servant's life cycle. As a poor, Indian, migrant woman, she has few opportunities for securing her own economic independence and stability. Should she have a family, her situation, exacerbated by Peru's recession, becomes more difficult as her opportunities narrow even more.

Domestic servants' organizing efforts continue to focus on a slow and steady process of education and consciousness-raising as a means of finding a collective solution to their situation, and of providing support to one another. These efforts indicate that domestic servants are confronting the fundamental nature of their situation in a manner that seeks to change the underlying causes of their exploitation; however, implications of this for their future remain uncertain.

NOTES

This article is based on five months of field research carried out in Lima, Peru, from May to October 1984, and was made possible by a grant from the Inter-American Foundation.

1. Such boundedness is very literal in its implications. Census officials reported that the most difficult data to obtain were from the very wealthy strata, which had their elaborate system of gates, intercoms, and multiple domestic servants to deter any census official.

2. Scott (1984) suggests that the dependence of wives on husbands in the "bourgeois" family form, where women are not expected to work outside the home, is more prominent

than in the "popular" family form. But Rubbo and Taussig (1982) argue that "peasant household authoritarianism" is pronounced in the rural Colombian context.

3. See Ann Oakley for a discussion of the "female's preparation for domesticity," which acts "as a common denominator in the socialization of women" (1974: 113).

4. See Rutté Garcia (1973) for personal testimonies of domestic servants' difficulties during their first few months.

5. Whereas men tend to migrate when they are between the ages of 20 and 24, the majority of women moving to the urban centers are between the ages of 15 and 19 (Ferrando de Velásquez, 1984). Contrary to the opinion of some researchers, who theorize that girls' younger age at migration is because they migrate as spouses and are therefore often younger than their male counterparts (Aramburú, 1981), the young female migrants are single and migrate with distant family members (Young, 1986).

6. Domestic servants' wages vary greatly. In 1984 they ranged from 0 to 150,000 *soles* ($42 per month), with an average of 78,000 soles ($22 per month; based on dollar-to-sol exchange rate of August 22, 1984).

7. See, for example, *La República,* September 3, 1984, for proclamations by leading Catholic bishops to a gathering of approximately 1,500 domestic servants regarding their role in their patron families.

8. Señoras' demands are very explicit. A labor office of the state that places domestic servants states, "The available information permits us to affirm that the wishes of the employers are very defined with respect to the characteristics of the labor in the home that they are seeking; i.e., they prefer young or younger, adult, single women with some degree of education (primary school completed), one to three years of experience, not attending school, who do not have familial responsibilities (young children), and who can be a live-in servant in the home of the employer" (DGE, 1981).

9. See Velazco Caro (1982) for a more complete discussion of the contrast in legislation governing the sector of domestic service with that governing minors.

REFERENCES

Anderson, Jeanine
1978 "The middle class woman in the family and the community: Lima, Peru." Ph.D. dissertation, Cornell University.
Aramburú, Carlos Eduardo
1981 *Migración interna en el Perú.* Lima: AMIDEP.
Arizpe, Lourdes
1975 *Indígenes en la ciudad de México: El caso de las "Marías."* Mexico City: Sep/Setentas.
Bourque, Susan C. and Kay Warren
1981 *Women of the Andes.* Ann Arbor: University of Michigan.
Cámara de Diputados
1980 1981 Dictamen de la Comisión de Trabajo y Servicio Civil, en los proyectos de ley no.117 y 787; en virtud del que proposen que se reconoscan para las trabajadores del hogar, los obreros de la actividad privada. Reg. No. 1017-IP, Proy 117 y 787.

CERA (Centro de Estudios Rurales Andinos)
1982 Basta: Testimonios. Cusco: "Bartólome de las Casas" y Sindicato de Trabajadoras del Hogar del Cusco.

Chueca, Marcela and Vilma Vargas
1982 "Estrategias de sobrevivencia de la mujer en la actual crisis de la economía peruana." Paper presented at the Congreso de investigación acerca de la mujer en la región andina. Asociación Perú-Mujer, Universidad Católica del Perú, AMIDEP.

DGE (Dirección General de Empleo, Ministerio de Trabajo y Promoción Social)
1981 Situación ocupacional del Perú. Informe 1980. Lima (October).

Ferrando de Valásquez, Delicia
1984 Participación económica de la mujer en el Perú: Análisis censal 1940–1981. INE, USAID.

Figueroa, Adolfo
1982 "El problema distributivo en diferentes contextos socio-políticos y económicos: Perú, 1950–1980." Lima: CISEPA, Pontificía Universidad Católica del Perú.

Figueroa Galup, Blanca
1977 "La doméstica en Lima metropolitana." Lima: AMIDEP .

Oakley, Ann
1974 The Sociology of Housework. Bath, England: Pitman Press.

Rapp, Rayna
1978 "Family and class in contemporary America: Notes toward an understanding of ideology." Science and Society 42 (3): 278–300.

Rubbo, Anna and Michael Taussig
1982 "Up off their knees, servanthood in southwest Colombia." Latin American Perspectives 10 (Fall): 5–23.

Rutte García, Alberto
1973 Simplemente explotadas. Lima: DESCO.

Sacks, Karen
1975 "Engels revisited: Women, the organization of production and private property," in R. R. Reiter (ed.), Toward an Anthropology of Women. New York: Monthly Review Press.

Scott, Alison MacEwen
1984 "Economic development and urban women's work: The case of Lima, Peru," in Richard Anker and Catherine Rein (eds.), Sex Discrimination and Sex Segregation in Urban Labour Markets in the Third World. ILO.

Smith, Margo Lane
1980 "Women's careers in Lima, Peru: Domestic service and street vending." Paper presented to the Annual Meeting of the American Anthropological Association.

Suárez, Flor, Vilma Vargas, and Joel Jurado
1982 "Cambio en la economía peruana y evolución de la situación de empleo de la mujer." Paper presented at the seminar "Análisis y promoción de la participación de la mujer en la actividad económica," Lima.

Velazco Caro, Elena
1982 "La problemática del menor trabajador doméstico en el Cuzco." Tésis para optar el grado de asistenta social, Universidad San Marcos, Lima.

Young, Grace Esther
1986 "Incorporating an analysis of gender to the study of migration: The case of Peruvian migration patterns." Migration News 2 (April–June).

5

Women in Mexico's Popular Movements: Survival Strategies against Ecological and Economic Impoverishment

Lynn Stephen

The Mexican economy, along with those of other dependent capitalist countries of Latin America, has often been described as characterized by "functional dualism" (Cockcroft, 1983; de Janvry, 1981; Faber, 1992). In many parts of Mexico, a dominant capitalist export sector acquires a cheap labor supply by perpetuating and maintaining impoverished subsistence and informal sectors. Broadening the concept of dependent development allows us to see impoverishment in environmental as well as economic terms. For example, as Faber (1992) and Millikan (1992) point out, it highlights the impact that poor semiproletarianized peasants can have on their environment in their struggles to survive without land (Faber, 1988). It also reveals the social movements focused on the ecological and communal conditions for the reproduction of labor-power as class-based opposition to the ecological conditions of capitalist production (O'Connor, 1988). Although the demands of such movements are often phrased in terms of consumption needs and access to resources and services instead of specific conditions of work (as within a factory), they are nevertheless an aspect of class conflict. The basis of this conflict is not a capital/labor split in the industrial division of labor, but an unequal distribution of the ecological and economic hardships at the level of both the household and the gendered division of labor resulting from dependent capitalist development.

The economic crisis of dependent capitalist development in Mexico has exacerbated the hardships faced by women in both the urban informal sector and the rural subsistence and wage-labor sectors.[1] Impoverishment in the form of lack of access to water, shortages of firewood, landlessness, under- and unemployment, deteriorating health conditions, a general lack of urban and

This chapter first appeared in *Latin American Perspectives* 72, 19:1 (Winter 1992), pp. 73–96.

Hortensia Hernández Mendoza, leader and founding member of Poblado Maclovio Rojas Márquez, created in 1988 (from a squatters' movement) southeast of Tijuana; she's been under house arrest since April 2001, due to legal disputes over the land—purchased in 1994 with assistance from the federal government and now surrounded by *maquiladoras* and condominiums. *Photo courtesy of Sheryl L. Lutjens*

rural infrastructure, and cutbacks in social services has forced women to develop survival strategies related to their traditional gender roles in reproducing the labor force.[2] These roles include providing food, clothing, and education for children and often housing as well. While ethnic and class background strongly affects the specifics of female gender roles in Mexico, heavy responsibility for the reproduction of labor-power is shared by most women, particularly among the poor.

A gendered division of labor that gives women the primary responsibility for reproducing labor-power with extremely limited resources has encouraged them to participate in popular movements against the hardships imposed by dependent capitalist development and shrinking social services. Three case studies examined here suggest that this participation does not necessarily result in changes in traditional gender roles or in an increase in women's power in the household or in popular organizations. If women are allowed to organize semiautonomously, succeed in achieving true integration in mixed organizations, and receive encouragement to raise questions about traditional domestic divisions of labor and domestic violence, oppressive gender roles may be questioned and possibly begin to change.

BACKGROUND: MEXICO'S ECONOMIC CRISIS

Once touted as the country in Latin America most likely to become a "developed nation," Mexico saw its star decline in 1982 with the fall of oil prices (see also Goldrich and Carruthers, 1992). Its debt increased from $10 billion in 1973 to $108 billion in 1989, and during the de la Madrid administration (1982–1988) inflation reached nearly 90 percent and the economy averaged an annual growth rate in real gross domestic product of −4 percent (Pool and Stamos, 1989: 101). The human costs of a chronically ill economy are apparent in a 50 percent drop in real minimum wages since 1982 and a 30 percent drop in the internal consumption of basic grains during the 1980s (Carlsen, 1988: 36). These numbers add up to no work, little income, and tremendous pressure on households to compensate for services and resources not provided by the government or obtainable through employment. Mexico's poor majority bears the brunt of a malfunctioning economy by eating less, working more, and engaging in a creative variety of activities to generate income and find food.

In urban areas, the unemployed, underemployed, and poorly paid engage in petty trade and services that are labeled "the informal economy." In 1985 it was estimated that the informal sector generated over 38 percent of Mexico's gross domestic product (Vera, 1987: 81). The booming informal sector in Mexico's cities is directly connected to the countryside. Migration to large urban areas, the border, or the United States is a popular survival strategy for the rural and provincial poor. In 1970 it was estimated that over 50 percent of those living in Mexico City over 20 years of age had not been born in the city (Muñoz, de Oliveira, and Stern, 1971). The flow of migrants to Mexico City beginning in the 1960s reached an average of 270,000 people per year in the 1980s (Nuccio and Ornelas, 1990: 39). This migration has contributed to the industrial labor force and a transfer from the countryside to the city of surplus labor, a reserve labor force that constitutes the rank and file of the informal sector (Benería and Roldán, 1987: 19). The rapid growth of Mexico City has been repeated in other major urban areas including Monterrey, Tijuana, Ciudad Juárez, and Guadalajara. In fact, by 1987, Mexico's population was 69.6 percent urban (Inter-American Development Bank, 1988).

Those who arrive in Mexico City are faced with few formal job opportunities, little infrastructure, and some of the worst health conditions imaginable. As a result of extreme centralization of population, industry, manufacture, and government functions, Mexico City has become pollution central, with a wide range of polluters spewing "approximately 6,000 tons of contaminants into the atmosphere daily" (Nuccio and Ornelas, 1990: 40). Thermal inversions in the 1980s and record air-pollution levels in December of 1990 have left many Mexico City inhabitants, particularly the elderly and children, with permanent respiratory problems. One of the worst effects of pollution is linked to leaded gasoline. A recent study of 102 newborns found that 50 percent had lead levels in their blood similar to those that in children in other countries resulted in slower rates of mental development (Brannigan, 1988).

The environmental degradation and growth of the informal sector in Mexico's cities were accompanied by transformations in the agrarian economy. While during the 1930s, 1940s, and the early 1950s the far-reaching agrarian reform carried out under Lázaro Cárdenas allowed large numbers of agricultural wage-earners to become peasants with access to land, the tide turned when capitalist development intensified in the countryside beginning in the mid-1950s. The increasing dominance of large capitalist farms in Mexico was in part tied to policies designed to stimulate import-substitution industrialization. Until the discovery of 72 billion barrels of oil reserves in 1977, agricultural products were the primary source of foreign exchange for Mexico's industrialization program. Cárdenas's land reform had encouraged some collective forms of production in *ejidos* (agrarian reform communities) in the 1930s, but after 1940 capital improvements and investments were primarily directed toward private property, particularly in the northwest and northeast (Paré, 1989: 99). The southern portion of Mexico, including the states of Oaxaca, Chiapas, and Quintana Roo, has very little capitalist investment and remains a source of migrant labor for other parts of the country.

The strategy of exporting basic grains and luxury crops has had a major impact on Mexican patterns of food production. In 1975 Mexico was importing 10 percent of the grain it consumed; by 1983 it was importing half of it (Cornelius, Gentleman, and Smith, 1989: 5). Although the establishment of the *Sistema Alimentaria Mexicana* (Mexican Alimentation System—SAM) in 1982 and a 1980 Law of Agricultural Development attempted to shift policy emphasis from livestock and irrigated production of luxury crops to rain-fed subsistence crops produced by peasants, the goal of food self-sufficiency was never reached. Corn imports decreased between 1980 and 1982, but bean imports declined only slightly, soybean imports doubled, and other food imports also increased (Cockcroft, 1983: 198).

Women were not formally singled out in the original agrarian reform law. They acquired specific use-rights (only as widows and single mothers) in *ejido* plots and in the communal land of indigenous communities only when the law was modified in 1971. In spite of their invisibility in the original law and in official employment statistics, they have been active in both subsistence and commercial sectors. From 1940 through the 1970s, many rural women stayed home and carried on subsistence work in addition to their normal work while men migrated (Crummet, 1987: 252–254; Stephen, 1991). Some engaged in wage labor as well. In some parts of Mexico this pattern expanded and inten sified in the 1980s. In other parts, women became part of the migrant stream and worked as wage laborers in commercial production.

Mexico's agrarian structure today is characterized by both proletarianization and the continuation of a subsistence-oriented agricultural sector. The process of depeasantization has never been completed in Mexico precisely because of the dynamics of commercialized agriculture oriented toward export. More often than not, subsistence farming supplements wage labor (Cockcroft, 1983: 191; Flores Lúa, Paré, and Sarmiento, 1988). A definite trend toward proletarianization can be seen, however, since the 1940s. This is indicated not only by increased rates of landlessness but also by the numbers of rural people who must earn part of their living through wage labor even if they do own land privately or have access to *ejido* land.

The absolute number of privately held small farms declined 39 percent between 1950 and 1970, and smallholding peasants controlled only 3 percent of the cultivated land and contributed 4 percent of agricultural production in 1970 (de Janvry, 1981: 129). For those holding land in agrarian reform or *ejido* communities, access to land has not been a guarantee of survival. In 1950 about 85 percent of those working on *ejidos* earned more than half their income from farming, whereas in 1985 less than 40 percent did (Cockcroft, 1983: 191).

By the early 1980s, the expansion of capitalist agriculture had resulted in the marginalization of a vast portion of the rural subsistence sector. Cockcroft (1983: 191) estimates that nearly 80 percent of Mexico's 25,000 *ejidos* and Indian communities could "no longer support themselves on farming alone, even though 'legally' they account for 43 percent of cultivatable land." In 1980, the economically active population in agriculture was over 5,699,971 (*Instituto Nacional de Estadística, Geografía e Informática*, 1984: 146) of whom approximately 54 percent were landless wage earners and 46 percent were direct producers (Paré, 1989: 100).

POOR WOMEN'S STRATEGIES FOR CRISIS MANAGEMENT

The long-term effects of the economic crisis and current plans to offer cheap Mexican labor and markets as enticements for foreign investment are distributed unevenly. The economic and ecological hardships of dependent capitalist development have fallen most heavily on women who work in the so-called informal sector and on landless and land-poor rural women. As the material resources, social services, and real income they have to maintain their families dwindles, women develop survival strategies that place them under increasing stress.

Studies conducted on marginalized urban women during the 1980s indicate several major trends, including increasing entry into the informal wage-labor force, self-provisioning of goods and services formerly purchased, and heavy domestic work loads (Arizpe, 1977; Benería and Roldán, 1987; González de la Rocha, 1989; Sánchez Gómez, 1989). Women are receiving little help from husbands and children with the most time-consuming domestic duties, and ecological impoverishment creates a harsh living and working environment. Deteriorating health conditions cause increasing physical strain on women as they care for themselves and often permanently sick children. Lack of access to drinking water, transportation, and food markets in peripheral city areas often further increases the time required to perform their unpaid domestic chores.

One of the reasons women enter into poorly paid industrial home work is so that they can continue their duties as wives and mothers. A number of studies (Sánchez Gómez, 1989; Sánchez Gómez and Martini Escobar, 1987; Arizpe, 1977) demonstrate that women tend to engage in paid activities that facilitate their domestic work. Many women are conscious of their exploitation in the underpaid, informal wage-labor force, but they still feel a strong commitment to carrying out their socialized roles as wives and mothers.

When urban marginal women enter the paid labor force, they receive some help from their husbands and children but still work long hours. Benería and Roldán found that although a high proportion of husbands helped their working wives, this help was concentrated almost exclusively in "activities outside of the home. . . . There was no instance of collaboration in house-cleaning or food preparation" (1987: 130). Despite their status as wage earners, women continued to be responsible for procuring and preparing food, obtaining water, providing clothing, taking care of household needs, and often covering at least part of their children's educational and medical costs. As urban ecological conditions deteriorate, these costs become ever higher.

The survival strategies that women have developed in urban areas are mirrored in the countryside. In fact, many of the young women who are working in the informal sector in urban areas are part of an increasing rural exodus that is primarily female. Official statistics indicate that the percentage of rural women in the wage-labor force jumped from 5.6 percent in 1975 to 20 percent in 1985 (Arizpe et al., 1989: 254). That number is believed to be 10 percent higher in 1990. This mass entry into the paid labor force is a response to an overall decline in real wages, decreases in guaranteed prices for basic crops, cutbacks in rural services, and increasing commoditization of goods such as firewood, medicine, and basic foods that were formerly collected free or produced through subsistence agriculture.

While few studies have counted the hours rural women work, this has hardly been necessary. Most ethnographic accounts describe their day as beginning at

5 a.m. and finishing at 9 or 10 p.m. When they are participating in community, ceremonial, and political life, the hours can be even longer (Stephen, 1991). Peasant women are in charge of all the unpaid labor of reproduction, which in agrarian societies is much heavier and more strenuous than that performed by most urban women (Arizpe and Botey, 1987: 75). They also participate in agricultural production, the degree of this participation varying by region, ethnicity, and type of production unit. In many instances, women will take on so-called men's work both in agriculture and in some types of artisan production when men migrate (Arizpe and Botey, 1987; Stephen, 1991).

Women's reproductive work includes preserving, processing, and preparing food, washing, repairing and often producing clothing, socializing and educating children, participating in kin networks on ceremonial occasions, cleaning houses and courtyards, hauling water and firewood (often from a long distance), transporting food to market to be sold, maintaining the household's ties with the church, providing medical and psychological care, and mediating family disputes and conflicts. The production of use-values related to domestic reproductive work is also reflected in their agricultural roles. Many women raise vegetables and care for animals including chickens, ducks, pigs, goats, and sheep. They often participate in planting, weeding, and harvesting of both subsistence and cash crops and may also engage in plowing if local tradition permits or if the males who traditionally do the work are absent (Arizpe and Botey, 1987; Stephen, 1991).

When they seek wage work, these women may find it in their own communities in agriculture or in putting-out systems for craft production (see Stephen, 1991; Cook and Binford, 1986) or they may migrate to work in commercial agriculture or as domestic servants. Expanding agribusiness, particularly in tomatoes, strawberries, tobacco, pineapple, and citrus is absorbing increasing numbers of young peasant women. Using the "natural dexterity" rationale adopted by maquiladora managers and home-based industry entrepreneurs to justify an underpaid, young female labor force (Fernández Kelly, 1983), agro-industrialists, along with their urban counterparts, pay sub-minimum wages. Arizpe and Aranda (1986: 177) found that in 1980, female strawberry packers were being paid from U.S.$.63 to U.S.$.66 per hour. A majority of the workers who ranged from 15 to 24 years of age earned 74 percent less than the legal minimum wage of U.S. $193.63 per month (Arizpe and Aranda, 1986: 186). These wage levels would not even support a single person, let alone a family with children.

Women working in fruit and vegetable production for export expose themselves to many hazardous working conditions. A 1980 investigative report in the *Los Angeles Times* stated that in Culiacán, Sinaloa, government doctors saw two or three pesticide poisonings every week (cited in Weir and Shapiro,

1981: 12). Angus Wright (cited in Nuccio and Ornelas, 1990: 36) reports that pesticides can cause "symptoms ranging from dermatitis to death, severe respiratory diseases, long-term nerve damage, blindness, mental disturbances, birth defects, abortions, leukemia, aplastic anemia, liver cancer, kidney cancer, and a variety of other serious disease syndromes." Wright (1986, 1990) documents a wide range of worker poisoning by pesticides throughout Mexico.

FEMALE CONSCIOUSNESS AMONG POOR URBAN AND RURAL WOMEN

As their responsibilities for reproducing the urban and rural labor force have intensified under conditions of economic and environmental impoverishment, women have increasingly begun to participate in grass-roots popular organizations. This participation is often initially motivated by what Kaplan (1982) calls "female consciousness." Within a particular class and culture, a particular gendered division of labor results in certain rights and obligations for women. When women accept the gender system and the division of labor that goes with it, they have female consciousness in Kaplan's sense. For example, in Zapotec indigenous peasant communities, female consciousness revolves around women's roles in maintaining ritual, raising children, processing food, maintaining labor exchanges and networks of kin and *compadres*, and working in weaving and agricultural production (Stephen, 1991). The way in which this consciousness is expressed in daily life varies according to class and age. In urban areas female consciousness revolves around food procurement and food preparation, administration of household budgets, production of household necessities, and providing for children. When social disorder endangers or disrupts daily routines or access to resources or limits the rights and obligations that they perceive that they have as women, women will work to reestablish order. Women's routines, access to resources, and therefore ability to carry out their social roles have been undercut throughout the marginal populations of Mexico, and women are taking action in accordance with their roles in the gendered division of labor to confront institutions and individuals that are limiting their ability to carry out their traditional roles (Kaplan, 1982: 550).

POPULAR VERSUS SOCIAL MOVEMENTS

The importance of being poor, marginal, and female is common to the majority of participants in Mexico's mobilizations. For this reason, they are more appropriately called "popular" than "social." Jelin (1986: 22, cited in Escobar,

1989) defines social movements as "forms of collective action with a high degree of popular participation, which use non-institutional channels, and which, at the same time that they formulate their demands, also find forms of action to advance those demands and to establish themselves as collective subjects, that is, as a group or a social category" (p. 28). Highlighting the meaning of popular participation underscores the centrality of the relations of production and distribution of material goods in the popular movements of Mexico as contrasted with the non-class nature and largely symbolic stakes identified with the "new social movements" of Europe. "Popular" connotes common economic marginalization; whether referring to culture or class, it is used to link a wide range of disenfranchised groups. These groups include disinherited indigenous populations, landless and land-poor peasants, participants in the urban informal sector, and the under- and unemployed (Stephen and Logan, 1990)—all those who populate the contradictory categories and identities created by the process of dependent capitalist development in Latin America (Escobar, 1989: 38). Three specific examples of women's participation as organized groups in broader popular movements offer insights into the types of demands and forms of participation they bring to these movements, their struggles to politicize what have been seen as "women's domestic" issues, and the circumstances under which they may move from being the foot soldiers of a popular movement to being leaders.

WOMEN IN POPULAR MOVEMENTS: THREE EXAMPLES

Coordinadora Regional de Mujeres, CONAMUP

By the late 1970s, a significant proportion of Mexico's marginal urban population had at least a decade of history struggling together for land, housing, and public services. In October 1979, regional popular organizations from 13 states met in Monterrey to form the Coordinadora Nacional del Movimiento Urbano Popular (National Council of the Urban Popular Movement—CONAMUP).[3] A majority of the participants in CONAMUP activities were women, but they were not represented in the leadership. Women were often on the front lines when police arrived to evict people from land occupations. They relentlessly confronted officials in trying to obtain roads, running water, and sewage services. Yet in discussions of internal democracy the issue of equal participation by women in organizational decision making was seldom discussed. After several years of internal struggle, several seasoned organizers succeeded in pulling together a national meeting of women from CONAMUP in 1983. In that same year, the Women's Regional Council of the CONAMUP was formed. Its objective was to provide women a forum for demands that were specifically female, generally arising from the difficult conditions under which women had to perform their domestic work. Some 25 neighborhood-based organizations came together as a unit in the Women's Regional Council of the CONAMUP and about 15 of them have ongoing projects today.

The council's work has focused on obtaining services such as running water, health centers, and schools, and title to land for housing. It has formed consumer cooperatives and collective kitchens, and held workshops on health, sexuality, and domestic relations (Stephen, 1989; Brugada and Ortega, 1987: 97–102). More recent programs have focused on subsidized tortillas, school lunches, and cooking gas. One of its most successful projects has been the distribution of over 16,000 government-subsidized breakfasts to children each day.

In short, much of its work has involved improving the urban economic and environmental conditions for social reproduction. The council is also represented in the national leadership of the CONAMUP, funneling issues and projects into the national organization. In addition, it has worked to pressure specific Mexico City bureaucracies and state agencies for resources and services. In the process of *concertación social* (social concertation) begun by President Carlos Salinas de Gortari, in which organized sectors of the population were invited to participate in government programs, CONAMUP was a target organization.

Coordinadora de Mujeres, Unión de Ejidos "Lázaro Cárdenas"

The economic crisis and the political events of the 1980s were experienced in Mexico's countryside against the historical backdrop of agrarian reform and the government policies of the 1980s. One of the most important developments during the 1970s was the emergence of regional peasant organizations (Paré, 1990: 84). The *Unión de Ejidos "Lázaro Cárdenas"* (Lázaro Cárdenas Union of *Ejidos*—UELC) emerged in 1975 with the assistance of a dynamic team of community organizers working under the federal government's *Programa para Inversiones en Desarollo Rural* (Program for Investment in Rural Development—PIDER). As did many government offices, it contained committed young organizers, many of whom had been active in the student movement in the late 1960s. The issue around which the UELC organized in 1975 was winning the rights to a major government fertilizer distributorship. This victory laid the basis for a peasant-managed, regional development organization with projects such as community food councils, community-managed housing, and crop price mobilizations (Fox and Hernández, 1989; 11–13; Hernández, 1990).

Three of the UELC's member *ejidos* were the sites of special agricultural or small industrial projects for women who did not have access to *ejido* land. These projects were called *Unidades Agroindustrias de la Mujer* (Agro-industrial Units for Women—UAIMs). UAIMs were built into the 1971 modification of the agrarian reform law and allowed women as a group to receive communal land from indigenous communities and plots from *ejidos*. They also gave the group of women who formed the UAIM one vote in the *ejido* organization or the indigenous-community meeting. This program did not give women equality with men in terms of access to land or voting rights, but it was the first agrarian program to offer all women a chance to use land and be represented in *ejido* and indigenous-community politics.

In Nayarit, three UAIMs served as the basis for further organizing of women. At the urging of male leaders of the UELC, two female organizers began to discuss organizational options with women in these UAIMs. They decided that the best way to mobilize women would be through a strategy designed to increase household and community production of basic goods to combat the impact of inflation. This strategy was also seen as a way to begin to integrate women into the UELC, where they had no representation, voice, or vote. While women were formally a part of the UAIMs, they were not included in the daily life of their *ejidos* or in the UELC. When they attempted to speak in the general assembly of the UELC and began to agitate for a formal women's presence within the union, they met opposition from the male directorate. In addition to being denied a platform, they were also denied use of the resources for their projects (Camarena, 1988: 7–20).

In 1987, with help from the government's *Distribuidora Conasup. S.A.* (Distributor for National Food Program—DICONSA), the two organizers and women from the UAIMs began to set up projects that would regenerate the backyard economy by raising animals, vegetables, and fruit that women could sell on the market. In conjunction with these projects, an effort was made to expand the formal organization of women. The participants chose a female promoter from each community to form a women's organization. Major impetus was provided by the women of one indigenous community, who had had 15 years' experience as a women's group. In 1987 a formal women's council was constituted of the three original UAIMs and women from one other community. In 1988, the women managed to form a total of 15 UAIMs that were integrated into the women's council. These UAIMs met about once a month as a group, with each community sending representatives. In these meetings they would compare notes on their respective projects and plan future projects and organizing strategies.

In 1989, with the help of a grant of over U.S.$119,000 from several government agencies arranged by President Salinas, 11 of the UAIMs of the women's council began construction on a wide range of productive projects including corn mills, vegetable plots, orchards, chicken and turkey hatcheries, bakeries, and sewing workshops. By January 1991, many of these projects were near completion. Another 3–4 UAIMs now meet as a separate block and are involved in health training of indigenous women in remote mountain communities as well as in local projects. Almost all of the women's projects focus on recuperating conditions for subsistence and communal production which have been lost with increasing commodification of basic grains, fruits, vegetables, animals, and medicines. The women's council has a representative in all of the general assemblies of the UELC and is struggling to increase its influence beyond one vote.

Women's Meetings within the *Coordinadora Nacional "Plan de Ayala"*

The 1970s produced several alternative national peasant unions and coalitions. *Coordinadora Nacional "Plan de Ayala"* (Plan de Ayala National Council—CNPA), which takes its name from Emiliano Zapata's 1911 plan for land redistribution, was founded in 1979 by 10 regional peasant organizations. Their principal demands included "the legal recognition in longstanding indigenous land rights; the distribution of land exceeding the legal limits for private property; community control over and defense of natural resources; agricultural production, marketing, and consumption subsidies; rural unionization; and the preservation of popular culture" (Paré, 1990: 85). CNPA participants included indigenous peoples with communal land or no land, minifundia peasants, peasants who were soliciting land, and small producers and agrarian wage workers. At its height in the early 1980s, it had 21 member organizations. Because it operates at a national level and pulls together a tremendous diversity of groups, its unity has always been fragile, and it now has 12 to 16 members.

The first effort to organize a women's presence within the CNPA came in 1981. The national organization decided, however, that an autonomous women's group would be divisive. A second attempt in 1984 during the second CNPA congress resulted in the creation of a women's commission whose charge was to organize a national meeting of peasant women in 1986. The commission tried to establish a direct relationship with women in all of the CNPA's constituent organizations (CONAMUP, CNPA, et al., 1987: 119). This work was extremely difficult because the women associated with the CNPA were not formally members of local and regional peasant organizations and had little or no political experience. Further, the communities they came from were politically marginalized, often under the control of regional political bosses. The few discussions that exist of women's participation in member organizations of the CNPA create a picture of women doing a great deal of work but receiving no formal recognition. As described by Carbajal Rios (1988: 426–427, my translation): "When the fight is in its most intense moments, women go to the occupations of lands and offices, to marches and meetings. They confront the police and armed guards of the *caciques* [political bosses] because it is often argued that such guards are more violent with men. As a consequence women are beaten and mistreated. . . . Women are absent in decision making in local and regional meetings and also in training and educational meetings."

Women in the CNPA organized to create jobs, obtain social services, lower the cost of basic goods, and explore health and educational issues. CNPA's participation in national coalitions such as the primarily urban *Frente Nacional en Defensa del Salario y Contra la Austeridad y la Carestía Nacional* (National Front in Defense of Wages against Austerity and the High Cost of Living— FNSDSCAC) and the *Comité en Defensa de la Economía Popular* (National Committee for the Defense of the Popular Economy—CNDEP) provided natural links for poor rural women with their urban counterparts.

The official report from the 1984 CNPA meeting reflects considerable dissatisfaction on the part of the women's commission about the role of women in the organization. It states that women have had little participation in official negotiations with the state, have received little political training, and they never participated in choosing authorities within the CNPA or achieved positions of authority themselves. The commission enumerated problems related to women and asked for financial support, child care, and other resources which would help them to participate more fully in the CNPA. It also encouraged the inclusion of women's specific demands in the demands adopted by the organization, requested that women be given *ejido* plots regardless of their marital status, and urged that the CNPA include at least one woman in its directorate (*Documentos del Movimiento Campesino*, 1984: 123–126).

In preparation for a national meeting of peasant women in 1986, the women's commission held four regional meetings—in Jalisco, Morelos, México, and Sonora. In these meetings there was little emphasis on formal public speaking; instead, women spoke with each other about the problems they had in trying to organize production cooperatives and their roles within the CNPA (Canabal Cristiani, 1985; Stephen, 1991).

In 1986, 150 women from 11 states came to a national meeting of CNPA women with the intention of establishing a national council of women. They concluded, however, that they were not ready to do so. Instead, they decided that they needed to continue to build regional women's organizations before uniting at the national level (CONAMUP, CNPA, et al., 1987: 120). The meeting did, however, result in the incipient integration of a few women from

CNPA into wider women's coalitions. In 1987, several women from the CNPA went to the third national meeting of the Women's Regional Council of the CONAMUP, where they compared organizing experiences, demands, and strategies (*Las mujeres tenemos la palabra*, 1988).

THE GENDERED DYNAMICS OF GRASS-ROOTS ORGANIZING AMONG THE IMPOVERISHED

Women's motivation to participate in popular movements is related to their specific roles as wives and mothers in the reproduction of the labor force. The most common agendas for women are strategies for overcoming the hardships resulting from economic and ecological impoverishment. The increased domestic burden placed on poor women through their increased subsistence duties and participation in the labor force clearly sets their initial political agendas. This view is corroborated by studies of women's participation in popular organizations in other Latin American countries (Jelin, 1990; CEPAL, 1984). As Jelin (1990: 188) points out, when women's political involvement centers on their responsibility for the reproduction and maintenance of the domestic unit, their collective action seems to reinforce their traditional roles. She then asks a critical question: "Is it relevant to ask whether the conditions under which women leave their traditional role rooted in daily life to enter the public domain constitute a significant departure with regard to social changes in women's subordination, helping to form gender identities that put in doubt the current system of domination?"

While women often have difficulty obtaining permission from their husbands to participate in productive projects, ultimately many will be successful in convincing their husbands and families of the importance of projects that increase household income or result in subsistence goods. When their organizing demands move outside of material production into the sexual and social dimensions of reproduction, they experience a much higher level of resistance on the part of men and sometimes other women as well. As women spend more time organizing and begin to ask for help with their domestic responsibilities, they encounter conflict at home and within their organizations. Many women in the CONAMUP report physical intimidation on the part of their husbands as they become increasingly involved in the organization. According to one organizer (Elvia, age 38), "To leave the house and go to a demonstration causes husbands to get angry. Women being active causes problems which can even result in beatings. . . . For example, a woman who took on a leadership position and could speak very clearly often later had problems with her husband. That would be it. She would have to leave the organization."

An organizer from the women's council of the UELC also reported many domestic confrontations. When the council and its constituent UAIMs began to receive funds from the Inter-American Foundation and from the Ministry of Agrarian Reform, the male leadership of the UELC blocked those funds and selectively distributed them (Camarena, 1988). When the women began to pressure for formal representation within the UELC and looked to the Ministry to back them up, domestic confrontations, between men and women were daily occurrences. According to an organizer of the council (María, age 35) "This was a very difficult time for women. At home men and women were arguing; there were physical confrontations, and some marriages even split up. It was rough." Women interviewed from 9 UAIMs also reported consistent threats of physical violence and occasional beatings that resulted from their husbands' perceptions that they were neglecting their domestic duties to engage in politics.

When the process of women's organizing itself results in possible violence and increased domestic stress for women, it is understandably difficult to organize around the issue of domestic violence. The Women's Regional Council of the CONAMUP is one of the few popular women's organizations that has begun to take on this issue. It holds workshops on women's health, sexuality, and judicial rights in a few neighborhood organizations. A neighborhood CONAMUP activist (Angela, age 24) describes the problem: "Women are considered inferior and because of this we are denied rights—the right to walk freely on the street without being attacked, the right to leave our homes without our husbands' permissions. . . . A lot of times we are treated like humans without rights of our own." In some neighborhoods women carry whistles, and when a woman is beaten, others blow their whistles and go en masse to confront the batterer. In one rare instance, women punished a man who raped his granddaughter by stripping him naked and locking him up overnight in their headquarters (Stephen and Logan, 1990). Organizing around domestic violence seems to work best where people in a neighborhood have a long history together.

When viewed from a distance, it seems predictable that the difference between the positions of poor men and women in the domestic division of labor will result in conflict when both genders participate in the same popular organization. Women's domestic responsibilities lead to particular demands, and their efforts to organize around these demands disrupt the domestic routine in their households. Their experience of domestic difficulties once they begin to organize often results in either reversion to silence within the larger mixed organizations of which they are part or the creation of autonomous meeting spaces for women.

The establishment of women's groups within larger organizations allows women of varying ages and types of political skills to discuss their ideas and problems. There will of course be power differences within them based on age and specific class and ethnic experience, but these groups nonetheless provide a more open space for political participation than larger mixed organizations or rural communities that have only allowed women to act as supporters and informal participants. Once such groups become established, women are better prepared to participate as a group in mixed-gender organizations. Autonomous women's groups within regional organizations can provide opportunities for women to learn how to organize on the national level. Links between women's groups are important for preparing women to assume leadership in their own organizations. In contrast to the situation in other Latin American countries such as Brazil and Chile, where women are starting to be courted by independent unions in an attempt to broaden their membership, in Mexico the struggle to participate equally with men in the same organization is still fundamental. Autonomous women's groups are critically important in providing an organizational space for women who want to move beyond being the support network for male activists.

CONCLUSION

The increasing economic and ecological pressure felt by poor Mexican women is directly related to their traditional roles in maintaining and reproducing the labor force. As deficiencies in urban areas characteristic of functional dualism such as lack of public housing, electricity, running water, drainage, security, paved roads, access to markets, and transportation become normal living conditions, women become responsible for finding solutions. In rural areas, increasing landlessness, loss of communal forest resources, lack of social services and basic infrastructure, erosion of natural resources, use of pesticides leading to health problems, and high prices call on women to develop survival strategies for maintaining the working population. The initial inclination of poor women to defend their rights to resources and services that permit them to carry out their role in reproduction reinforces a gendered division of labor that indirectly maintains dependent capitalism. Thus the role of the gendered division of labor in maintaining functional dualism is reflected in the structure and demands of popular movements.

When women begin to organize around ecological, consumer, and service demands, they are changing from individual survival strategies to collective ones that place pressure on political parties and government bureaucrats. Such organizing does not, however, necessarily change the gendered division of labor or alter women's responsibility for family maintenance under conditions of scarcity. In some cases it may simply result in a triple work load for women as they work in the wage-labor force, engage in domestic work, and are also political activists. Under certain circumstances, when women form autonomous political spaces within larger popular organizations and when there is public recognition of the conflict between women's traditional roles in the household division of labor and their roles as public activists, gender roles may begin to change.

When popular movements respond to pressure to allow women to participate, they themselves may begin to provide alternative models of the division of labor, slowly changing the subordinate roles of women and providing them with positions of leadership and power in mixed organizations as well as at home. Often, however, the continued pressure on women to feed, clothe, educate, and socialize the next generation under conditions of ecological impoverishment and exploitation of cheap labor can prevent many from becoming activists. Without a questioning and reordering of gender roles that place women at the center of reproduction, the larger reproduction of peripheral capitalism and the kinds of marginal living conditions it produces for the urban and rural poor of Mexico will remain.

NOTES

Research for this article was supported by The Inter-American Foundation and by the Whiting Foundation.

1. On the relationship between women's increased burdens in the informal and subsistence sectors see Rao (1989), Jelin (1990), and Dankelman and Davidson (1989).

2. Women's responsibility here extends far beyond the material and biological to "the reproduction of an entire set of social relations, including a division of labor, means of socialization and preparation for production, means of recruiting or creating future group members" (Gailey, 1987: 271).

3. Analysis of the CONAMUP is based on interviews with activists, observation, and movement documents. Analysis of the Women's Union of the UELC is based on participant observation, attendance at meetings, and extensive interviews in nine communities. Analysis of the CNPA is based on movement documents, secondary literature, and interviews with activists from non-governmental agencies who have worked with CNPA.

REFERENCES

Arizpe, Lourdes
    1977 "Women in the informal sector: The case of Mexico City." Signs: Journal of Women in Culture and Society 3 (1): 24–37.
Arizpe, Lourdes et al.
    1989 "Efectos de la crisis económica 1980–1985 sobre la condición de vida de las mujeres campesinas en Mexico," in El ajuste invisible: los efectos de la crisis económica en las mujeres pobres. Bogotá: UNICEF.

Arizpe, Lourdes and Josefina Aranda
   1986 "Women workers in the strawberry agribusiness in Mexico," pp. 174–193 in Eleanor Leacock and Helen Safa (eds.), *Women's Work: Development and the Division of Labor by Gender.* South Hadley, MA: Bergin & Garvey.
Arizpe, Lourdes and Carlota Botey
   1987 "Mexican agricultural development policy and its impact on rural women," pp. 67–83 in Carmen Diana Deere and Magdalena León de Leal (eds.), *Rural Women and State Policy: Feminist Perspectives on Latin American Agricultural Development.* Boulder, CO: Westview.
Benería, Lourdes and Martha Roldán
   1987 *The Crossroads of Class and Gender: Industrial Homework, Subcontracting, and Household Dynamics in Mexico City.* Chicago: University of Chicago Press.
Brannigan, William
   1988 "Bracing for pollution disaster." *The Washington Post* (November 28): A 14.
Brugada, Clara and Zenaida Ortega
   1987 "Regional de Mujeres del Valle de México de la Coordinadora Nacional del Movimiento Urbano Popular (CONAMUP)," pp. 97–102 in Alejandra Massolo y Martha Schteingart (eds.), *Participación social, reconstrucción y mujer: El sismo de 1985.* Mexico City: Reproducción de Documentos de El Colegio de México.
Camarena, Milagros
   1988 "Cronología del proceso organizativo de las mujeres en el sur del estado de Nayarit." Unpublished manuscript, Inter-American Foundation.
Canabal Cristiani, Beatriz
   1985 "Un grito de rebeldía." *Que sí, que no México* (November).
Carbajal Rios, Carola
   1988 "Una experiencia de participación de las campesinas en el movimiento popular," pp. 424–430 in Josefina Aranda Bezaury (ed.), *Las mujeres en el campo.* Oaxaca: Instituto de Investigaciones Sociológicas de la Universidad Autónoma Benito Juárez de Oaxaca.
Carlsen, Laura
   1988 "Grassroots social movements in Mexico." *Radical America* 22 (July–August): 35–52.
CEPAL (Comisión Económica para América Latina)
   1984 *La mujer en el sector popular urbano: América Latina y el Caribe.* Santiago: Author.
Cockcroft, James
   1983 *Mexico: Class Formation, Capital Accumulation, and the State.* New York: Monthly Review Press.
CONAMUP (Coordinadora Nacional del Movimiento Urbano), CNPA (Coordinadora Nacional "Plan de Ayala") et al.
   1987 "Mexico: La situación del país y la organización de la mujer del pueblo," pp. 89–131 in Comisión Organizadora del Encentro de Mujeres de los Sectores Populares de México, Centroamérica y el Caribe (eds.), *Las mujeres del pueblo avanzan hacia la unidad.* Mexico City: Comisión Organizadora del Encuentro de Mujeres de los Sectores Populares de México, Centroamérica y el Caribe.
Cook, Scott and Leigh Binford
   1986 "Petty commodity production, capital accumulation, and peasant differentiation: Lenin vs. Chayanov in rural Mexico." *Review of Radical Political Economics* 18 (4): 1–31.

Cornelius, Wayne, Judith Gentleman, and Peter Smith
    1989 "Overview: The dynamics of political change in Mexico," pp. 1–54 in Wayne Cornelius, Judith Gentleman, and Peter Smith (eds.), *Mexico's Alternative Political Futures*. University of California, San Diego, Center for U.S.-Mexican Studies, Monograph 30.
Crummet, María de los Angeles
    1987 "Rural women and migration in Latin America," pp. 239–260 in Carmen Diana Deere and Magdalena Léon de Leal (eds.), *Rural Women and State Policy*. Boulder, CO: Westview.
Dankelman, Irene and Joan Davidson
    1989 *Women and Environment in the Third World: Alliance for the Future*. London: Earthscan Publications/International Union for Conservation of Nature and Natural Resources.
de Janvry, Alain
    1981 *The Agrarian Question and Reformism in Latin America*. Baltimore: Johns Hopkins University Press.
Documentos del Movimiento Campesino
    1984 " Acuerdos y resoluciones del II Congreso Nacional Ordinario de la CNPA." *Textual* 5 (17): 115–127.
Escobar, Arturo
    1989 "Social science discourse and new social movements research in Latin America: Trends and debates." Paper presented at the 15th International Congress of the Latin American Studies Association, December, Miami, FL.
Faber, Daniel
    1988 "Imperialism and the crisis of nature in Central America." *Capitalism, Nature, Socialism: A Journal of Socialist Ecology* 1 Fall: 39–46.
    1992 "Imperialism, revolution, and the ecological crisis of Central America." *Latin American Perspectives* 19 (1): 17–44.
Fernández Kelly, María Patricia
    1983 *For We Are Sold, I and My People: Women and Industry in Mexico's Frontier*. Albany: State University of New York Press.
Flores Lúa, Graciela, Luisa Paré, and Sergio Sarmiento Silva
    1988 *Las voces del campo: Movimiento campesino y política agraria 1976–1984*. Mexico City: Siglo XXI.
Fox, Jonathan
    Forthcoming "Democratic rural development: Leadership accountability in state-structured peasant organizations." *Development and Change*.
Fox, Jonathan and Luis Hernández
    1989 "Offsetting the iron law of oligarchy: The ebb and flow of leadership accountability in a regional peasant organization." *Grassroots Development* 13 (2): 8–15.
Gailey, Christine
    1987 *Kinship to Kingship: Gender Hierarchy and State Formation in the Tongan Islands*. Austin: University of Texas Press.
Goldrich, Daniel and David B. Carruthers
    1992 "Sustainable development in Mexico? The international politics of crisis or opportunity." *Latin American Perspectives* 19 (1): 97–122.
González de la Rocha, Mercedes
    1989 "Crisis, economía doméstica y trabajo femenino en Guadalajara, " pp. 159–176

in Orlandina de Oliveira (ed.), *Trabajo, poder y sexualidad*. Mexico City: El Colegio de México.

Hernández, Luis
1990 "Autonomia y liderazgo en una organización campesina regional," pp. 9–113 in Arturo Cano (ed.), *La Unión de Ejidos Lázaro Cárdenas*. Mexico City: Cuadernos de Base.

Instituto Nacional de Estadística, Geografía e Informática
1984 *Agenda estadística 1984*. Mexico City: Instituto Nacional de Estadística, Geografía e Informática.

Inter-American Development Bank
1988 *Economic and Social Progress in Latin America: 1988 Report*. Washington, DC: Inter-American Development Bank.

Jelin, Elizabeth
1986 "Otros silencios, otras voces: El tiempo de la democratización en Argentina," in F. Calderón (ed.), *Los movimientos sociales ante la crisis*. Buenos Aires: CLACSO/UNO.
1990 "Citizenship and identity: Final reflections," pp. 27–42 in Elizabeth Jelin (ed.), *Women and Social Change in Latin America*. London: Zed Books.

Kaplan, Temma
1982 "Female consciousness and collective action: The case of Barcelona, 1910–1918." *Signs: Journal of Women in Culture and Society* 7 (3): 545–560.

Las Mujeres Tenemos la Palabra
1988 *III Encuentro Nacional de Mujeres de la CONAMUP 20, 21 y 22 de Noviembre de 1987, Zacatecas*. Mexico City: Ediciones Pueblo.

Millikan, Brent H.
1992 "Tropical deforestation, land degradation, and society: Lessons from Rondônia, Brazil." *Latin American Perspectives* 19 (1): 45–72.

Muñoz, Humberto, Orlandina de Oliveira, and Claudio Stern
1971 "Categorías de emigrantes y nativos y algunas de sus características socioeconómicas: Comparación entre las ciudades de Monterrey y Mexico," in *Migración y desigualdad social en la ciudad de México*. Mexico City: Universidad Nacional Autónoma de México and Colegio de México.

Nuccio, Richard A. and Angelina M. Ornelas
1990 "Mexico's environment and the United States," pp. 19–57 in Janet Welsh Brown (ed.), *In the U.S. Interest: Resources, Growth, and Security in the Developing World*. Boulder, CO: Westview.

O'Connor, James
1988 "Capitalism, socialism, and nature: A theoretical introduction." *Capitalism, Nature, and Socialism: A Journal of Socialist Ecology* 1 (Fall): 11–38.

Paré, Luisa
1989 "The development of capitalism in Mexican agriculture and the proletarianization of the peasantry," pp. 96–107 in R. Boyd, R. Cohen, and P. Gutkind (eds.), *International Labor and the Third World: The Making of a New Working Class*. Aldershot: Avebury.
1990 "The challenge of rural democratization in Mexico." *Journal of Development Studies* 26 (July): 79–96.

Pool, John Charles and Steve Stamos
1989 *The ABCs of International Finance: Understanding the Trade and Debt Crisis*. Lexington, MA: Lexington Books.

Rao, Brinda
1989 "Struggling for production conditions and production conditions for emancipation: Women and water in rural Maharashtra." *Capitalism, Nature, Socialism: A Journal of Socialist Ecology* 1 (Summer): 65–82.

Sánchez Gómez, Martha Judith
1989 "Consideraciones teórico-metodológicas en el estudio del trabajo doméstico en México," pp. 59–80 in Orlandina de Oliveria (ed.), *Trabajo, poder y sexualidad*. Mexico City: El Colegio de Mexico.

Sánchez Gómez, Martha Judith, and M. F. Martini Escobar.
1987 "Trabajo doméstico y reproducción social: Un estudio de caso en la Colonia Santa Ursula Xitla." Unpublished master's thesis, Escuela Nacional de Antropología e Historia, Mexico City.

Stephen, Lynn
1989 "Popular feminism in Mexico." *Z Magazine* 2 (December): 102–106.
1991 *Zapotec Women*. Austin: University of Texas Press.

Stephen, Lynn and Kathleen Logan
1990 "Women in Mexican popular movements: A critical discussion of new social movements theory." Paper presented at the annual meeting of the American Anthropological Association, November 28–December 2, New Orleans, Louisiana.

Vera, Oscar
1987 *La economía subterránea en México*. Mexico City: editorial Diana.

Weir, David and Mark Shapiro
1981 *Circle of poison: Pesticides and People in a Hungry World*. San Francisco: Institute for Food and Development Policy.

Wright, Angus
1986 "Rethinking the circle of poison: The politics of pesticide poisoning among Mexican farm workers." *Latin American Perspectives* 13 (Fall): 26–60.
1990 *The Death of Ramón González: The Modern Agricultural Dilemma*. Austin: University of Texas Press.

6

Caribbean Transnationalism As a Gendered Process

Christine G. T. Ho

Migration is nothing new to the Caribbean, having begun five centuries ago when the region was absorbed into the orbit of global capital accumulation and became a crossroads of population movements. After the genocide of its native peoples in less than a hundred years, for three and a half centuries it was a crucible for blending, although not completely fusing, peoples from Africa, Asia, and Europe. For the past century and a half it has been a net exporter of people, mostly to North America and to a lesser extent to Europe (Palmer, 1995: 9–17). As a whole, the Caribbean exports more of its people than any other region of the world (Deere et al., 1990). Indeed, emigration is undertaken by so many to expand their life choices (Thomas-Hope, 1992: 5) that few Caribbean families have been untouched by the departure of at least one of their members. Migration is also fostered by a shortage of schools that drives pupils to seek schooling elsewhere and by the production of more skilled workers of certain kinds than can be absorbed into the local economy (Basch, Schiller, and Blanc, 1994: 72). In addition, postcolonial Caribbean governments contribute to the transnational traffic by treating migration as a safety valve for surplus labor and by emphasizing capital rather than human resources in their development plans (Basch, Schiller, and Blanc, 1994: 61). These governments are also turning more and more to foreign exchange derived from transmigrant remittances as a strategy to offset, if only partially, the unfavorable balance of payments caused by debt servicing and the high cost of imports in relation to the value of exports (Basch, Schiller, and Blanc, 1994:

This chapter first appeared in *Latin American Perspectives* 108, 26:5 (September 1999), pp. 34–54.

68). Moreover, the large civil services left behind by the European colonizers have turned into swollen state bureaucracies that are the principal employers of a large segment of the population, access to jobs being controlled by political patronage. The resulting expenditures for civil servant salaries are enormous and deflect resources from more productive sectors (Basch, Schiller, and Blanc, 1994: 70).

As Caribbean governments respond to the changing structure of global capital, the resulting eroded salaries and declining living standards provoke a mass exodus of all social classes in search of a better life (Basch, Schiller, and Blanc, 1994: 68). However, the impact of global capitalism not only varies from class to class but differs according to gender. For example, in contrast to the Caribbean elite, who tend to migrate as entire families and to settle permanently, working-class women in the Caribbean not only migrate independently but practice circular migration (Thomas-Hope, 1992: 4) and often pave the way for the eventual migration of others. In this essay I want, first, to locate gender within capitalist relations of production by examining the role of Caribbean women as workers and mothers and as key players in the construction and maintenance of social relationships that cross national boundaries. Second, I want to clarify the linkage between the family and the wider political economy by demonstrating how Caribbean family units are constantly being reshaped by the changing needs of global capitalism. Third, as a complement to political economic analyses of globalization (Watson, 1994), rather than treating Caribbean transmigrants as mere units of labor I want to stress the human dimension of these global processes by identifying the tremendous human costs entailed in transnationalism. Last, I want to make more explicit the relation of transnationalism to global capitalism and the implications of transnationalism for class reproduction and differentiation.

WOMEN IN THE CARIBBEAN AS MOTHERS

The West Indian kinship system has been the object not only of extensive research but of intense debate. Space does not permit me to revisit this decades-long controversy, but a brief excursion into Caribbean kinship is important for understanding Caribbean women as workers because the family is related to the capitalist economic system of which it is a part. Caribbean family structure has been characterized as matrifocal. This "mother-centered" dynamic of the domestic group is defined by close emotional ties between mothers and children and the emergence of strongly bonded clusters of female kin, mainly daughters and children of daughters (Smith, 1996: 42–45). Matrifocality should not be confused (as often happens) with the female-headedness of households. Rather, it refers to patterns of relationships within the household that have a matrilateral bias (Smith, 1996: 45), whether or not a husband-father is present. (Indeed, many mother-centered kinship units are male-headed.) Matrifocality exists because Caribbean kinship ideology valorizes the mother-child bond above all others (Smith, 1996: 55). It is not only the most important bond but expected to be the most enduring—a lifelong relationship that results in adult children's essentially becoming "old-age insurance" for elderly mothers. Another Caribbean cultural ideal is that child care is a collective responsibility rather than the sole obligation of biological parents; whoever is in the best position to accept responsibility for a child does so. In practice, this obligation usually devolves to groups of female (sometimes fictive) kin. In this way, it is common for children to be shifted between households and live with kin other than their biological parents (Smith, 1996: 53).

Scholars observing brittle conjugal relationships, low frequencies of early legal marriage and its corollary, high illegitimacy rates, and matrifocality and child dispersal have characterized them all as "normlessness" (Smith, 1996: 35). Nuclear household structure, monogamous marriage, and egalitarian conjugal relations being assumed to be universal, the woman-centeredness of widely ramifying networks of extended kin and the lack of monogamy encountered in the Caribbean have been treated as "distorted" forms of nuclear family (Smith, 1996: 54). The fact that most of the world's population does not live in nuclear configurations is evidence that the nuclear family is not necessary for child rearing or the financial support of women and children, and indeed, it has been argued that it is a capitalist construction (Tong, 1989: 67). The nuclear assumption is flawed not only in projecting Eurocentric ideals onto Caribbean society but in obscuring the complex linkages between the family and the wider political economy and the status system based on color (McKenzie, 1993; Powell, 1986; Smith, 1996). Most family studies have been conducted among lower-class families and have attributed their unorthodox structure to poverty. This simplistic explanation fails to account for similar marriage and kinship behavior on the part of the middle and upper classes that suggests shared cultural imperatives.

Specifically, the poverty thesis overlooks the dual-union system practiced by all classes, which is intimately connected to the status system. Institutionalized centuries ago during slavery as a system of concubinage coupled with legal marriage, dual unions were practiced by the ruling class and aspired to as an ideal by other classes. The system, which reserves legal marriage for status equals and nonlegal unions for partners of lower status (Smith, 1996: 59–80), persists today, allowing young upper- and middle-class men to marry women of equal status while simultaneously having "outside" sexual relations with women of lower status and fathering children by them (Powell, 1986: 84–92). In contrast, most lower-class men practice nonlegal unions and refrain from legal marriage until later in life, partly because they lack the financial resources either to fully support their women or to exempt them from work outside the home but mainly because of the sharp separation in both ideology and practice between sexual relations and legal marriage, the latter symbolizing a rise in community status (Smith, 1996: 55, 86). Hence, polygynous tendencies among men of all classes are widespread and accepted by all. Such deviations from the Christian moral code by the upper and middle classes have been conveniently ignored by researchers and policy makers alike, permitting them to blame only the lower class for this "morally depraved" behavior. It should be obvious, however, that illegitimacy is not a monopoly of the lower class. Nevertheless, problems arise in this fluid mating system with respect to the economic support of women and children, where it remains unclear how the supportive roles of men may be linked to family structure (Smith, 1996: 16).

Clearly, the matrifocal relations described above are not the problem but the *solution* to the problem of the economic support of women and children under the capitalist mode of production in the Caribbean. That matrifocality is not the same thing as matriarchy must also be stressed. As "reluctant matriarchs," Caribbean women are of necessity strong and independent—which is not to be confused with being powerful and dominant (Reddock, 1993: 49). Many a strong Caribbean woman has allowed her man to rule and dominate her (Smith, 1996: 94). Indeed, conjugal roles form the foundation of the complex linkages between the domains of family and work because the family is not merely an economic unit but also an ideological one (Anderson, 1986: 314–320; Reddock, 1993: 49–52). In contrast to the "coupling" ideology and "joint" gender roles normative in nuclear family structure, Caribbean kinship permits, in both ideology and practice, multiple forms of union of which legal marriage is but one. More important, it sanctions "segregated" gender roles in which men and women lead more or less separate lives. Thus, matrifocality implies not only that conjugal unions are less solidary than bonds between mothers and children but that conjugal partners engage in separate spheres of activities both in the home and with kin and friends outside; mates are not expected to provide emotional support or to share in domestic chores, child care, or recreational activities (Smith, 1996: 44, 56).

Unfortunately, the result of this sharp gender cleavage has been the disproportionate burdening of Caribbean women with double workloads and the lack of male support, both emotional and financial. They succeed in juggling their many roles only with assistance from female kin, friends, and neighbors (Ho, 1991; 1993). To understand their situation, an explanation of why patriarchy has not perished under socialism provides a clue. Social-ist feminists argue that as long as an ideology of gender inequality persists, gender relations will remain unequal (Tong, 1989: 176). In other words, we cannot understand gender oppression in terms of class oppression alone. This is because patriarchy and capitalism are not Siamese twins but two separate monsters, although they function in partnership to produce both gender and class oppression (Tong, 1989: 177). Put differently, (material) changes in the mode of production may alter the family as an economic unit but do little to change it as an ideological (nonmaterial) one (Tong, 1989: 181). There is no question that women's oppression is founded on their economic dependence on men and men's control over their labor power and other economic resources as well as their reproductive capabil-ity and sexuality (Tong, 1989: 180). Nor is there any doubt that the insti-tution of the nuclear family is the instrument through which domination is exercised. However, as socialist feminists see it, patriarchy, being chiefly an ideological structure, can be destroyed only by nonmaterial means, which is to say by psychocultural revolution (Tong, 1989: 177).

WOMEN IN THE CARIBBEAN AS WORKERS AND AS MOTHERS

The dual roles performed by Caribbean women for centuries as workers and as mothers render fuzzy the Western feminist distinction between the public world of work and the private domain of the home (Anderson, 1986: 293). Caribbean women's participation in the public workplace has been necessi-tated by capitalist relations of production that have historically denied ade-quate earning power to a large segment of men, making it unrealistic to ex-pect them to be sole breadwinners. Thus, the historical construction of gender in the Caribbean has generated a structural contradiction. By denying women male financial support and protection, the system also demands of them eco-nomic independence and responsibility for their families (Anderson, 1986: 308–312; Green, 1994: 151; Senior, 1991: 104–128). However, because many are unskilled laborers, their wages are often not enough to make ends meet, and this forces them to appeal to men to supplement their incomes (Green, 1994: 154). The end result is that while women strongly aspire to economic independence, they are actually dependent on their men (Anderson, 1986: 319; Senior, 1991: 115). This gender paradox has rendered analysis of women's work difficult. What constitutes work is problematic partly because the income-earning activities of working-class women do not lend themselves easily to measurement and partly because they perform a wide range of eco-nomic activities. Imported definitions of work that include as "economically active" only those receiving wages for their labor are not very useful in a region where labor statistics seldom match women's livelihood activities. Such data mask the fact that many women work only intermittently, that their income is extremely low, and that they tend to work in the informal sector, many as "higglers" or vendors of farm produce or other items. Hence, "unrecognized work" such as that in the informal economy, on which many women depend for their livelihood, constitutes an analytical problem because the women performing it are invisible in labor statistics (Reddock, 1993: 55).

Today, capitalism continues to be responsible for the economic predicament in which many Caribbean women find themselves. For instance, with the shift from agriculture to industry in the post–World War II period, agricultural work for women declined without the development of alternatives for those displaced, forcing most into domestic labor (Green, 1994: 157; Senior, 1991: 119). Domestic work, either in private homes or in the hotel industry, which dates back to the postemancipation period, continues to be a common occupation because more than 88 percent of Caribbean women have no more than primary school education and are therefore not competitive in the job market; only one-third are working full-time, mainly in domestic work, and are paid a minimum wage (Senior, 1991: 125). Because of the lack of livelihood options, others accept low wages and inflexible working hours in assembly plants of export processing industries (EPZs) producing goods solely for export to advanced industrialized countries (Safa, 1995: 1–36; Senior, 1991: 121). There they are often hired for the short term or laid off to help employers escape the costs of fringe benefits (Senior, 1991: 121). Furthermore, women's participation in the labor force is more likely than men's to be affected by changes in domestic situations such as pregnancy, the birth of a baby, and the illness or death of a child-care provider (Anderson, 1986; Senior, 1991). While these female liabilities are not unique to the Caribbean, their impact there is more devastating because so many women are sole breadwinners for their families. Moreover, their lack of education and skills coupled with high unemployment rates ensure that they will remain marginalized as a reserve labor pool (Safa, 1995; Senior, 1991). And as long as Caribbean women merely constitute a labor reserve they will be unable to achieve the economic independence from men that, some feminists argue, women's emancipation requires.

Feminist explanations of the emergence of the private/public dichotomy are helpful in tracing the origins of women's economic dependence on men. Long ago, the extended family/household was the "primitive" seat of production in which an assortment of kin worked together (Tong, 1989: 39–69). In these joint economic activities, the labor of women was as crucial as that of men in reproducing themselves from generation to generation, as a result of which women enjoyed high status despite a division of labor based on sex. Industrial capitalism changed all that by shifting the locus of economic production away from the household into the public workplace. As men's productive activity outside the home became more highly valued than women's reproductive activity and as the work of women (childbearing, child rearing, preserving, cooking, cleaning) came to be regarded as nonproductive, women's status declined accordingly. Actually, women are producers of domestic simple use-values without which the *production of people*, particularly the reproduction of the labor force, would be impossible. In this way, men gained power over women and patriarchy was born. Moreover, in the early stages of industrial capitalism, working-class women and children also entered the public labor force to serve surplus extraction further. In the absence of socialization of domestic work and child care, however, there was no one left in the household for reproductive activities. Therefore, a bargain was struck between patriarchy and capitalism (the two distinct structures responsible for women's oppression, which intersect only partially). Instead of paying men, women, and children equal wages, capitalism capitulated to patriarchy by granting men a "family wage" sufficient to allow women and children to stay at home (Tong, 1989: 180–181). Ever since then, patriarchal ideology has rested on the material foundation of the family wage, keeping women and children out of the public workplace.

While very insightful, this conception of the trajectory of industrial capitalism, obviously based on the European and Euro-American experience, falls short of explaining Caribbean women's condition as workers and as mothers. This is not to deny the penetration of the region by industrial capitalism. Indeed, it has been argued that Caribbean sugar plantations practiced industrial relations of production centuries before the Industrial Revolution (Mintz, 1985: 48). Nevertheless, the capitalism of plantation slavery and later indenture has been an altogether different experience for Caribbean women. First, the majority of Caribbean men have never been paid a "family wage"; instead, they have been daily confronted with job insecurity, working mostly in low-skill, low-wage jobs. Second, most Caribbean women have not been excluded from the public workplace; rather, they have been forced to work outside the home, also in low-skill, low-wage occupations. Third, they have always been burdened with a double workload, as they have never been exempted from household responsibilities even though domestic work has been at least as devalued for them as it was for their European and Euro-American counterparts.

Therefore, Caribbean women's dilemma has been coercion into the public domain without the socialization of private housework and child care. Recognizing that men are necessary as providers even if they are unable to be sole providers, many Caribbean women strike up liaisons with higher-income/ higher-status men to supplement their own incomes (Barrow, 1986: 132; McKenzie, 1993: 84). Because they are seldom economically self-sufficient, their solution has been to manipulate their way around the capitalist system by appealing for support from a wide range of men in various statuses (e.g., lover, son, and sometimes husband) rather than relying on a single source of income that may be subject to the vagaries of an unstable economy (Barrow, 1986: 156–170). This strategy is indispensable to survival, given that men have multiple claims on their resources—in order of cultural importance, from their mothers, their legal wives, their common-law wives, mothers of their children with whom they have visiting relationships, and last, their current lovers (Smith, 1996: 94). In sum, Caribbean women's performance of their dual roles as workers and as mothers, while ensuring their survival and that of their children (Matthei, 1996: 44), challenges the reasoning of those who argue that labor force participation brings about gender equality.

GLOBALIZATION AND THE "WOMAN QUESTION" IN THE CARIBBEAN

Of the numerous consequences of global economic restructuring, perhaps the most profound for family life and conjugal relations has been the increased participation of women in the worldwide labor force, giving rise to the heated debate about whether participation in the labor force has enhanced the general status of women. The reasons for women's paid employment are many, chief among them being the greater unemployment, underemployment, and declining wages of men that make it necessary for women to be either substitute or supplementary wage earners. However, the "feminization" of the labor force has only been in the low-wage, low-skill sectors (Watson, personal communication, 1997), and it is not the result of forced displacement of high-wage, high-skill men. Rather, the level of skills and cost of social reproduction make it more profitable for capitalism to redefine certain types of assembly work as women's work (Watson, personal communication, 1997). Thus, the argument that wage work reduces female dependence on men, increasing their autonomy and decision-making power and raising their consciousness of gender subordination, seems misguided. Safa (1995: 4) points out that paid employment has restricted most women to menial, poorly paid work that does not free them from a "double day" or from the dominant ideology that they are merely supplementary wage earners.

In the Caribbean, the new international division of labor has intensified chronic poverty, widespread unemployment, and underemployment. This has forced Caribbean women either to work under more oppressive conditions than ever or to turn to emigration, which has increased steadily since the 1980s (Sutton, 1987: 15–29).

THE HUMAN COSTS OF GENDERED TRANSNATIONALISM

The story of one transnational family[1] illustrates well the gendered process of constructing kin units whose members are dispersed across national boundaries. The existence of Caribbean transnational families has gender implications because the web of connections is constructed mainly by women (Sutton, 1992: 246). Women are the protagonists in the drama of globalizing Caribbean kinship, which requires the active maintenance of circuits of exchange of goods, services, communication, travel, and personnel. This is not a new challenge for Caribbean women, who for centuries have been embedded in large kin-based support networks. Today's transnational structures are merely the postmodern versions of this tradition on a global scale.

Marilyn Price is the third of eight children, five sisters and two brothers. Marilyn left Trinidad at the age of 20, when her eldest sister, who had migrated to New York years before, decided to "send for" their mother, Pearl. Marilyn, who had graduated from secondary school two years earlier, and her youngest sister, Debbie, accompanied their mother, leaving behind three other sisters, two brothers, and their father. Several months later her older brother, Tyrone, also migrated to New York on the urging of their mother, who wanted a man around the house. For several years Marilyn, Pearl, Tyrone, and Debbie shared a household close to where her eldest sister and her husband and three children had settled in New York. Marilyn found a job as a loan officer in a bank, and 12-year-old Debbie started junior high school. Tyrone was too old to be sponsored by Pearl as her dependent, and so he had to do odd jobs (as a security guard and framing paintings in an art gallery) for three years until he became a legal resident and could train to be a machinist.

Although Marilyn and her siblings encountered Americans in their daily life on the job, in school, and so forth, their social life revolved mainly around Trinidadians but for the first time embraced people from other parts of the Caribbean region. For example, within a month of moving to New York Marilyn met a Jamaican, Ronnie, at a West Indian party. She later married him, and a couple of years after that they had a baby daughter, Gloria. Although Marilyn, Ronnie, and Gloria shared an apartment with Ronnie's mother, she stayed in close touch with Pearl and her siblings, especially when Ronnie, who was in the music industry, became involved with drugs. During this period, she went to Los Angeles to visit a friend she had known since childhood. She loved California and persuaded Ronnie to move there. Meanwhile, Tyrone got his green card after three years in New York and met and fell in love with a Trinidadian woman, Janet. They decided to live together in New Jersey, where he spent their first year together training to be a machinist. At the end of that year they had their first child, Angela. Although still committed to Janet, Tyrone decided in their second year to join the U.S. Army for a year, training to drive a big rig. When he rejoined Janet after he left the army, he decided to move to California (about the same time as Marilyn and Ronnie) because he had never liked the cold or the New York lifestyle and felt that the city was no place to raise a child. Andrew was born in California the following year, and Tyrone and Janet decided to get married.

Although they occupied separate households, Marilyn and Tyrone maintained close ties, moving into adjoining apartments in the same building with their respective mates and children and sharing many resources including child care. Two years later they were joined by their mother (who preferred the milder climate), Debbie (who had graduated from high school, married a Trinidadian, Michael, and was pregnant with their first child), and their sister Sharon, her husband Steve, and their two children. This three-generation extended family found two other apartments in the building where Marilyn and Tyrone lived with their families. Pearl took care of the youngest children while the adults were at work, and Marilyn and her siblings and their mates rotated responsibility for transporting the school-aged children to and from school. They also cooked and ate meals together and shared other resources. This arrangement was particularly beneficial to Marilyn and Debbie when both their marriages ended and they needed emotional and child-care support. Several years later Daniel, the brother who had remained in Trinidad, moved to Los Angeles and bought a home for himself, his mother, and his divorced sisters Marilyn and Debbie and their children. At that point Tyrone also bought a home for himself, Janet, and the two children a few miles away. Although Marilyn and Tyrone no longer lived next door to each other, they continued to have daily contact both face-to-face and on the telephone and continued to cooperate in terms of child care and transportation of children.

Miami has recently been added as another link in the Price network because it is a popular destination for Caribbean migrants. Debbie and Sharon, now also divorced, have both moved to Miami with their children. Their sisters Sheila, Rachel, and Joan migrated to New York a year or so before Marilyn and Tyrone moved to California and, having married and had children, continue to live there. They visit California from time to time and send their children to spend summers there with their cousins and aunts and uncles. Now living in Trinidad are Marilyn's father, Colin, and her brother Daniel, who returned a few years ago to go into business for himself and has married and had children there. All the Prices stay in close touch, mainly by tele-phone, daily for those in the same city, weekly for those in another city, and monthly for those out of the country. They also travel to Trinidad every few years and have family reunions from time to time, mainly in New York, where there are more of them than elsewhere. There they organize family cookouts involving 25 or more people. Pearl is trying to sell the house Daniel bought her, partly because he has stopped making the mortgage payments but partly because she shuttles back and forth between New York and Los Angeles to spend time with her children and grandchildren and prefers the medical care she receives from a particular Trinidadian doctor in New York. Clearly, the Price family is transnational in scope.

This vignette suggests that Caribbean transnationalism rests on the foun-dation of the family and the careful cultivation of kinship ties, a global drama in which women play the protagonists. The centrality of the Price women in launching the moves, first to New York from Trinidad and later to Los Ange-les and Miami, is apparent. A multilayered tapestry of complex kin networks spanning two countries has enabled the Price family as a whole to exploit re-sources in many locations, making it less vulnerable to any single national economy and allowing it to triumph over dependency. Sharing an apartment in New York, for example, and renting several apartments in the same build-ing in Los Angeles, eating their meals together, and sharing responsibility for the care of all the Price children facilitated the pooling of the resources of in-dividual Prices. When no single location offered enough in the way of re-sources to satisfy basic economic needs, as many family links as possible were activated at different times in different places. This can be seen in Pearl's moving from New York to Los Angeles to serve as the caretaker for all the Price children and assist with other household duties. The family strategy of activating multiple links not only built bases in several locations but also en-hanced the symbolic unity of the family. Indeed, it is this flexibility and plas-ticity, the hallmarks of Caribbean kinship systems for centuries, that allow the Prices to triumph over the contradictions of global capital.

In short, although they may not be conscious of it, Caribbean family units are constantly being reconfigured to suit the changing needs of global capitalism as it continually destroys forms of its own existence (Watson, personal communication, 1997). For instance, children constitute building blocks in transnational social systems. Because they lack child care support in the destination country, the working-class women who migrate from the Caribbean leave children behind (Matthei, 1996: 46). This practice amounts to transplanting overseas the centuries-old custom of child mind-ing, an arrangement whereby children are cared for by female kin or close friends, and it is unsurpassed in providing child care and peace of mind for young mothers who migrate (Ho, 1993: 36). It bears repeating, however, that it is the women who orchestrate the comings and goings of these children. The Price children spend summers alternately in New York and Los Angeles and occasionally in Trinidad. However, as a rule the movement of children is not simply one-way: whereas some young children are left behind, others who have already migrated are sent home to the Caribbean for schooling, where the schools are considered to be of a higher caliber and the children are thought to perform better away from the racial tensions and urban violence of North America. After they finish primary and secondary school they move back to North America or Europe for their higher education. Thus schooling is a bidirectional, transnational family project. Put differently, the exchange of children is a form of human currency on both a symbolic and a physical level that cements network relations between distant kin more solidly than other types of reciprocity.

In contrast to the rosy picture of the Price family acting in concert for the well-being of the entire network, according to Henry (1994: 63–73) all is not well in the Promised Land for the Caribbean diaspora in Toronto. Henry reports finding close to 25 percent of households being headed by single parents and few multigenerational matrifocal households, as well as network disintegration with successive generations. While the single-parent finding is by no means a radical departure from patterns observed in the Caribbean, what is problematic about it in Canada is the absence of female extended kin who might provide child care. The inability of women to find child care is a serious problem that has implications for the upward mobility that is the ultimate goal of migration. Without child care, these young single mothers cannot work, except at menial, low-wage jobs, nor can they continue interrupted schooling to improve their skill levels. The end result for them is either chronic poverty or dependence on public assistance.

The greatest toll exacted by Caribbean transnationalism is marriage and relationship breakdown. Within three years of migrating to Toronto, the marriages or relationships of 90 percent of Henry's sample had ended in either separation or divorce (Henry, 1994: 86). According to Henry, the long separations that result from the pattern of women's migrating first, to be reunited with mates and children only after they become settled, have seriously undermined conjugal relationships. Thus, North American immigration policy, in the service of capitalist restructuring, destabilizes and reshapes family units to reproduce needed labor and skills (Watson, personal communication, 1997). Even more destructive of marriages has been "double-lap" migration (moving first to Britain and then to Canada), particularly if the partners have disagreed about the second move. Marriages also collapse under the weight of new pressures encountered in the host society. For one thing, Caribbean women have had far greater access to employment than their male counterparts in Toronto, sometimes accepting menial jobs as domestics and nannies. For another, Caribbean men not only have encountered a job shortage but have been handicapped by their lack of skills and experience. To compound the problem, women continue to have expectations of their men as breadwinners, despite the latter's inability to find work. They are also the ones less likely to return home because their earning power is greater overseas and more flexible gender roles there allow them more personal freedom (Wiltshire, 1992: 184). Changing gender ideology in the new society also contributes to friction between spouses and mates as women begin to adopt the notion of marriage as an equal partnership; no longer tolerating male domination, they become financially independent, often being the main breadwinners (Bonnett, 1990). Few marriages are able to withstand the financial pressures, let alone the ideological shifts.

Another consequence of migration is strained parent-child relationships. As Caribbean mothers assert their authority and make decisions independent of Caribbean fathers, children also challenge their fathers, constantly forcing them to exercise their power (Bonnett, 1990: 143). This intergenerational conflict is often made worse as the children adopt the norms and values of the new society, causing the parents to disagree about how to cope with the problems of their children (Henry, 1994: 91). Furthermore, family dynamics also become strained when children are reunited with their parents after a long separation. Not only are the children still emotionally attached to their grandmothers, aunts, or other caretakers but their parents seem to them complete strangers. Things are particularly strained when children are reunited with one parent who has a new conjugal partner with whom the children do not get along or with stepsiblings whom they regard as rivals (Henry, 1994: 80–84). Indeed, while many of Henry's findings do not appear to be radical departures from Caribbean patterns past or present, that of intergenerational conflict seems to be a genuinely new development. The grief and suffering resulting from this are poignantly depicted in Cecil Foster's *Sleep On, Beloved* (1995). In this novel a young Jamaican woman moves to Canada under the auspices of a government program providing domestics for the Canadian middle class. Official policy prevents any dependents from migrating with her, so she has to leave her child behind to be cared for by her mother and struggle alone against racism and many other forms of social injustice. After many years she overcomes the bureaucratic obstacles and finally succeeds in bringing her daughter, by then an adolescent, to Canada. Unable to cope with the alienation and racism, the teenage daughter succumbs to peer pressure at school to rebel in a variety of ways, the most innocuous of which is working as a nude dancer in a bar. She also becomes a petty thief and gets into trouble with the law. Unable to cope with her daughter's delinquency in addition to her husband's infidelity and racist pressures at work, the migrant woman suffers a nervous breakdown. This novel articulates eloquently how the political economy of North America destabilizes the family structure of immigrants and how immigration policy, crafted to fulfill labor needs, makes life difficult for the immigrants.[2]

CONCLUSION: THE RECONSTITUTION OF CLASS AND RACE

Given the direction of global capitalist restructuring, the prospects for Caribbean migrants are not bright (Watson, personal communication, 1997). Despite its human costs, however, migration continues unabated because it is, as always, motivated by the desire of individuals and their families to renegotiate their class position. Migration is not merely a matter of geography but one of social mobility. Embedded within transnational family strategies are class projects, the goals of which are to transform advancement in one setting into economic, cultural, and symbolic capital in another (Basch, Schiller, and Blanc, 1994: 87). Indeed, class processes are embedded in the strategies of kin groups reproducing themselves in distant places (Lauria-Perricelli, 1992: 253). However, class mobility is no simple matter. Although collective kin efforts are necessary for individual mobility, transnational strategies do not benefit all equally, and at times they generate tension within kin groups. This tension is often masked by a strong kinship ideology but nevertheless results in class differentiation within families. Transnationalism is of paramount importance for class formation in the home society; the billions of dollars in remittances sent home from abroad foster the growth of a domestic middle class in ways otherwise unimaginable (Basch, Schiller, and Blanc, 1994: 88). The most profound implication of transnationalism for class reproduction, however, is that while transnational networks may facilitate easy movement along many dimensions (personal, psychological, cultural, social, political, and economic), they militate against serious challenge to postcolonial political systems because they channel energy into individual mobility, undermining class opposition and class-based activism (Basch, Schiller, and Blanc, 1994: 262).

The social construction of race in the host societies also undermines class solidarity and strengthens transnationalism (Basch, Schiller, and Blanc, 1994: 234). Despite their best efforts at bettering their educational credentials and avoiding stigmatized identities, Caribbean migrants face glass ceilings blocking their occupational advancement and racial discrimination in all spheres of life (Henry, 1994: 102–147). Through painful experience, they learn that race is linked to political and economic domination in North America and Europe, where they are classified in both official and folk taxonomies in essentialist racial categories that recognize neither class nor cultural difference. Paradoxically, the social rejection of Caribbean peoples has promoted intense overidentification with the home country to escape underclass categorization (Wiltshire, 1992: 184) and the cultivation of multiple layers of strong transnational connections and loyalties (Basch, Schiller, and Blanc, 1994: 234). Hence, migrants persist in retaining stronger Caribbean identities than at home, in part because they lack political and economic security and want to keep their options open but mainly because of a sense of loss, displacement, exile, and alienation resulting from the destabilizing effects of capitalism.

In summary, I have tried to reveal the centrality of gender in the building and maintenance of transnational networks. In underscoring the human dimension of transnational processes, I have also tried to draw attention to some of the costs of transnationalism for human relationships. In addition, I have tried to clarify the link between family and work by looking at Caribbean women as workers and as mothers and the impact of global restructuring on gender relations, particularly conjugal roles. In response to the limitations imposed by global capitalism, Caribbean women have resorted to a family strategy of base building in multiple locations. The meaning of these fluid and dynamic linkages and complex systems of exchange extends beyond material acts of mobility to symbolic acts of resistance. Caribbean transnationalism is at once reaction and resistance to the postcolonial region's peripheral economic position in the world system. As such, it grows and prospers by contesting global hegemonic processes.

NOTES

1. The research on which this story is based was carried out among Afro-Trinidadians in Los Angeles and was based on participant-observation and semistructured interviews to elicit genealogies, information about household membership, marriage/consensual and other types of union, children of their own, children of their mates, children living in the household, children living elsewhere, and child-care arrangements. Participants in the research were also questioned about where kin resided, degree of relatedness, type of contact, frequency of contact, and content of exchanges. Funding was provided partly by a grant from the Chancellor's Patent Fund at the University of California, Los Angeles, and partly by a Research and Creative Scholarship grant from the University of South Florida.

2. Many of the Caribbean women who migrated to Canada on their own did so under a government program designed to bring domestic workers to perform household duties in middle-class Canadian homes. They were prohibited from bringing dependents with them until they had achieved landed immigrant status, a process that took many years. Even then, they could afford to send only for their children and not for the adult caretakers of their children (who would not be self-supporting in Canada).

REFERENCES

Anderson, Patricia
   1986 "Conclusion: Women in the Caribbean." *Social and Economic Studies* 35(2): 291–324.
Barrow, Christine
   1986 "Finding the support: Strategies for survival." *Social and Economic Studies* 35(2): 131–176.
Basch, Linda, Nina Glick Schiller, and Cristina Szanton Blanc
   1994 *Nations Unbound: Transnational Projects, Postcolonial Predicaments, and Deterritorialized Nation-States.* Amsterdam: Gordon and Breach Science Publishers.
Bonnett, Aubrey
   1990 "The new female West Indian immigrant: Dilemmas of coping in the host society," pp. 139–149 in R. Palmer (ed.), *In Search of a Better Life.* New York: Praeger.
Deere, Carmen, Peggy Antrobus, Lynn Bolles, Edwin Melendez, Peter Phillips, Marcia Rivera, and Helen Safa
   1990 *In the Shadows of the Suit: Caribbean Development Alternatives and U.S. Policy.* Boulder, CO: Westview Press.
Foster, Cecil
   1995 *Sleep On, Beloved.* New York: Ballantine Books.
Green, Celia
   1994 "Historical and contemporary restructuring and women in production in the Caribbean," pp. 149–171 in H. Watson (ed.), *The Caribbean in the Global Political Economy.* Boulder, CO: Lynne Rienner.
Henry, Frances
   1994 *The Caribbean Diaspora in Toronto: Learning to Live with Racism.* Toronto: University of Toronto Press.
Ho, Christine G. T.
   1991 *Salt-Water Trinnies: Afro-Trinidadian Immigrant Networks and Non-Assimilation in Los Angeles.* New York: AMS Press.
   1993 "The internationalization of kinship and the feminization of Caribbean migration." *Human Organization* 52(I): 32–40.
Lauria-Perricelli, Antonio
   1992 "Towards a transnational perspective on migration: Closing remarks," pp. 251–258 in N. Glick Schiller, L. Basch, and C. Blanc-Szanton (eds.), *Towards a Transnational Perspective on Migration.* New York: New York Academy of Sciences.
McKenzie, Hermione
   1993 "The family, class, and ethnicity in the future of the Caribbean," pp. 75–89 in J. E. Greene (ed.), *Race, Class, and Gender in the Future of the Caribbean.* Kingston: Institute for Social and Economic Research, University of the West Indies.
Matthei, Linda Miller
   1996 "Gender and international labor migration." *Social Justice* 23(3): 38–53.
Mintz, Sidney W.
   1985 *Sweetness and Power: The Place of Sugar in Modern History.* New York: Penguin Books.
Palmer, Ransford
   1995 *Pilgrims from the Sun: West Indian Migration to America.* New York: Twayne.

Powell, Dorian
  1986 "Caribbean women and their response to familial experiences." *Social and Economic Studies* 35(2): 83–130.
Reddock, Rhoda
  1993 "The primacy of gender in race and class," pp. 43–73 in J. E. Greene (ed.), *Race, Class, and Gender in the Future of the Caribbean*. Kingston: Institute for Social and Economic Research, University of the West Indies.
Safa, Helen I.
  1995 *The Myth of the Male Breadwinner: Women and Industrialization in the Caribbean*. Boulder, CO: Westview Press.
Senior, Olive
  1991 *Working Miracles: Women's Lives in the English-Speaking Caribbean*. Bloomington: Indiana University Press.
Smith, Raymond T.
  1996 *The Matrifocal Family: Power, Pluralism, and Politics*. New York: Routledge.
Sutton, Constance
  1987 "The Caribbeanization of New York City and the emergence of a transnational sociocultural system," pp. 15–30 in C. Sutton and E. Chaney (eds.), *Caribbean Life in New York City: Sociocultural Dimensions*. New York: Center for Migration Studies.
  1992 "Some thoughts on gendering and internationalizing our thinking about transnational migrations," pp. 241–249 in N. Glick Schiller, L. Basch, and C. Blanc-Szanton (eds.), *Towards a Transnational Perspective on Migration*. New York: New York Academy of Sciences.
Thomas-Hope, Elizabeth
  1992 *Explanation in Caribbean Migration: Perception and the Image*. London: Macmillan Caribbean.
Tong, Rosemarie
  1989 *Feminist Thought: A Comprehensive Introduction*. Boulder, CO: Westview Press.
Watson, Hilbourne
  1994 "Global restructuring and the prospects for Caribbean competitiveness: With a case study from Jamaica," pp. 67–90 in H. Watson (ed.), *The Caribbean in the Global Political Economy*. Boulder, CO: Lynne Rienner.
Wiltshire, Rosina
  1992 "Implications of transnational migration for nationalism: The Caribbean example," pp. 175–187 in N. Glick Schiller, L. Basch, and C. Blanc-Szanton (eds.), *Towards a Transnational Perspective on Migration*. New York: New York Academy of Sciences.

II

POLITICS, POLICIES, AND THE STATE

7

Introduction to Part II

Much as globalization restructures the economic realities of women, the associated return to democracy in Latin America in the 1980s and 1990s has established a scholarly agenda for the study of women's political power. Long-lasting military authoritarianism plagued societies in the region, including Brazil (1964–1985), Uruguay (1973–1990), Argentina (1976–1983), Paraguay (1954–1989), Peru (1954–1989), and Chile (1973–1990). State terror and violence marked years of civil war in El Salvador and Guatemala, where peace accords were made in 1992 and 1996, respectively. And elsewhere people faced a dangerous low-intensity warfare, frequently sponsored by the United States. The transitions from military rule in Latin America helped to create a global trend—often called the third wave of democracy—that is charted in the sequential (re)establishment of liberal democracies, including the revitalization of individual rights and liberties, electoral competition for selection of decision-makers, and an accompanying revival—or creation—of the associational activity of civil society. The inclusion of Latin American women within new liberal democracies raises a number of significant—and feminist—issues (Jacquette, 1994; Foweraker, 1998).

Feminist political theory has identified the historical exclusion of women from politics everywhere, an exclusion rooted in the public/private divide that assumes its distinctive form in different societies over time and geographical space (Okin, 1998). From often quite different positions, feminists have uncovered the gender biases of liberal, Marxist, and other modern political theories, including the androcentric assumptions about power and agency that enforce the obvious and more subtle exclusion of women. The gendered dynamics of liberal democracies and their policies are seldom at issue for the scholars engaged in "transitology"—or redemocratization—studies, however (Waylen, 1993, 1994).

131

Feminist perspectives suggest how and why new democracies may marginalize women, directing attention to matters of power, the state, and women's agency.

The questions about women, new democracies, and power must be asked and answered in historical context. The recent experiences of the Latin American left are a crucial part of this context, offering important insights into the variously gendered engagements of women with and in the public sphere. Petras (1999) sees three periods in the contemporary Latin American left: the first in the 1960s and 1970s, consisting of the pursuit of socialism through both traditional communist parties and rural and urban armed struggles; the second coinciding with redemocratization and including the left's embrace of electoral politics; and the third identified with the reemergent militancy of contemporary rural struggles, including the Landless Peasant Movement in Brazil (also see Chilcote, 1994; Lievesley, 1999). Though Petras's periodization does not focus on women, women's relationships with the left have indeed been consequential in the development of feminist understandings of the oppression and empowerment of women. Women were active in the left parties and armed struggles of the first period—and before; they challenged traditional gender norms and political exclusion as they pursued nationalist goals, embraced the working class and its interests, and fought for an end to capitalist oppression. As feminists recognized the specificities of women's oppression, class interests and strategies that once oriented a Marxist left forced the difficult choices for them that Chinchilla explains in the excerpt below (also see J. Franco, 1998). In subsequent periods, women's bold movements against authoritarian states, often based on traditional gender roles, forced other choices in thinking about both the left and a feminist politics. How, why, and with what power, do women participate in the politics of Latin America's new democracies?

THEORETICAL CONSIDERATIONS: CLASS MOVEMENTS AND SEX MOVEMENTS

Norma Stoltz Chinchilla

Selection from "Mobilizing women: Revolution in the revolution,"
Latin American Perspectives 15, 4:4 (Fall 1977), pp. 83–102.

In the process of creating the revolution, the conditions for its success are also created. The transformation of social relationships can begin *even before* the complete transformation of material conditions in the period of socialist construction. The question of division of labor in the family can be raised as a point of struggle even before it is possible to fully socialize housework and childcare or fully incorporate women into social production. This is the conception that has prevailed in Cuba where the new Family Code provides for men sharing in the housework so that their wives can participate more fully, economically and politically, and where struggle over this policy has been encouraged at every level.

It is not divisive to raise such issues (as some comrades maintain), rather it is divisive not to. That is, when the questions are not addressed, the material divisions imposed by class society are simply taken for granted, re-enforced, and perpetuated. It is true that the inequalities of class society can never be fully overcome until classes themselves are liquidated (and this is a long process), but it is also true that in the process of overcoming class society examples of what socialism can mean must be created. This idea is expressed well in a report about the conference of Mozambican women in March 1973, chaired by the President of FRELIMO. The participants emphasized a need to engage women directly in all tasks of the revolution in Mozambique, saying:

> In this way . . . [women] will contribute directly to the victory of the revolution, that is, to hastening the day of their liberation. What is more, by joining the struggle at all levels, they are opening up new prospects for their future, *destroying in practice* the concepts which relegated them to a massive and voiceless role in society. In short, they are creating the conditions for participating in the exercise of power, taking their destiny into their own hands. (Liberation Support Movement Information Center, 1974: 21; emphasis mine)

The African and Asian liberation movements in their pre-revolutionary stages and the Cuban revolution in its post-revolutionary stage give us an idea of how social relationships are and can be transformed in the process of revolution. They give us examples of how the party can play a leading role in stimulating these transformations. This is true in spite of the fact that the parties and movements which have initiated and sometimes even lead the socialist women's movements have been male-dominated, a fact which has led some feminists to doubt their commitment to women's liberation or to deny their ability to transform the conditions of women. But the important fact, from our view, is not whether the initiating and guiding organizations are predominantly male (as are *most* political organizations in class society in advanced as well as backward countries) but whether they provide the *possibility* for the masses of women to take a direct part in their own liberation. Whether they provide this possibility is determined by whether they understand the basis of female oppression and are able to transform this understanding into a revolutionary program. It is also determined by the extent to which female membership and leadership is an explicit goal of the party. But most important of all, it is determined by the way the party understands its relationship to non-party mass organizations.

In the context of that history the call for an autonomous socialist women's movement is understandable. But what does autonomous really mean? Certainly not autonomous from social classes, for such a state of existence would be impossible in class society. If it means that the movement must always be autonomous from the leadership of Marxist-Leninist cadres, then under whose leadership will it be and what politics will it reflect? Would independent socialist-feminists be opposed to Leninists winning leadership of a mass women's organization, not through manipulation but through exemplary practice and demonstrated ability to guide successful struggles? If not, then the question becomes one of insuring that the relationship between the party and the mass organization is one that both advances class struggle and is influenced by the masses in its outcome.

Whether or not one argues that an independent women's movement should exist (as a matter of principle or as a strategic necessity at any particular historical moment), historically the relationships between women's movements and left movements have been close, with women's movements most often appearing in the course of general struggle of a class movement. In the United States in the 1960s the rebirth of feminist struggles appeared in the course of the civil rights and student movements and became a separate struggle only when the male leadership of those movements failed to respond to the very legitimate concerns about how women were treated in the movement and about the priority given to organizing women outside. In neo-colonial countries such as India, women's movements also occur in the course of general protests in which women become involved (such as the Anti-Price Rise Front of 1973–1975) and raise special "women's demands" together with general class demands in the course of a movement led by communist cadres.

There is a wide diversity of issues directly affecting women that socialist movements have transformed into short-range and long-range demands. In countries with strong feudal laws and customs, the effect of an attack on feudal conditions affecting women (dowry, child marriage, foot-binding, exclusion of widows, etc.) has been quite explosive (e.g., China, Vietnam, India). The very conditions that served in the past to keep women in backward conditions become those that propel them into militant action when the movement fights against them.

Feudal customs regarding women are not as strong in Latin America today as they were in pre-revolutionary China, Vietnam, or Mozambique. In most places the separation of household labor from social production (with the consequence of driving women into isolated labor in the home) has already taken place, especially in urban centers. Part of the "bourgeois-democratic" revolution affecting women has also taken place. Laws which provide for easier divorce, recognition of common-law marriages and illegitimate children, and protection of female workers have been passed in many (though not all) Latin American countries during periods of nationalist reform. Legal equality is far from complete in Latin America as it is even in the United States today. Thus, a socialist women's movement in Latin America would not be primarily a campaign against pre-capitalist laws and customs (although it would include that) but a campaign to complete the bourgeois-democratic revolution and establish the basis for liberation (i.e., full participation in all areas of production and political life with relief from housework and childcare, an end to subordinate relations in the family, or a change in the family itself, and a new egalitarian culture). Where pre-capitalists remnants are very strong, the pace of change would be much slower, and intermediate demands would be more important than in advanced countries where monopoly capitalism itself has radically transformed the relations of production and the functioning of the family.

It is necessary for socialists and communists to wage a struggle both in countries where women are excluded from social production in large numbers (i.e., in most neocolonial countries) *and* in the advanced countries where they have been re-incorporated in large numbers in production outside the home. To the extent that bourgeois ideology and relations of domination continue to exist for working women, they hold back the class struggle in many forms, as Dixon argues in the following passage:

> The principal definition of "respectable" women as wife-mothers has been the source of low class consciousness and the limited political development of working women because, while working, they identify more as wife and mother (or wife-to-be) than as wage worker. Consequently, women relate to husbands, not to capital; to their children, not to struggles with capital; to their sexuality and to the base world in which they see themselves as passive, dependent and excluded. The alienated and isolated housewife, the strike-breaking wife-mother, the apolitical, passive and submissive female workers in manufacturing are, in part, results of women's ideological submission to bourgeois morality, reinforced by complementary male prejudices and by the realities of female superexploitation. . . . Subjugation historically has produced low class-consciousness and a resistance to political development. Refusal to deal with the realities of female oppression serves only to perpetuate what capital wishes: *not to have to fear the militance of the female half of the proletariat.* (1977: 24)

Of course, bourgeois ideology is not always as successful in suppressing militance of women as the bourgeoisie would like. Given a choice between the bosses and their striking husbands, women in the most oppressive family relationships have fought militantly on the side of the workers. Working women saddled with heavy home responsibilities nevertheless have found the time and energy to wage struggles against capital, sometimes over the opposition of their families. And women who identify as mothers rather than members of a class have gone to battle against a bourgeois state on behalf of their children. But the spontaneous and isolated militance of individual or small groups of women is transformed into a permanent explosive power only when the forces that are holding it back are attacked (submissiveness, lack of confidence, lack of leadership experience, heavy household and child care responsibilities). Only when the desires of these women to participate equally in the struggle are supported sympathetically and concretely will their efforts be transformed into the sustained militance of many more.

The process of revolution, therefore, is a process of transformation of material conditions, social relationships, and ideas. It is a process which begins in the pre-revolutionary stage, intensifies with the taking of state power, and deepens in the period of socialist transformation. Where the taking of state power has been preceded by a long, protracted "people's war," the transformation of social relations (especially those between men and women) has advanced the furthest.

The greater the changes in the initial stages of revolution, the faster the gains thereafter. Changed relations based on sex become one yardstick of changed relations in general (between the proletariat and the bourgeoisie), a measure of the progress toward socialism. Two African liberation leaders have expressed this very well: "One of the principles of our fight is that our people will never be free until the women are free as well" (Amilcar Cabral, quoted in Liberation Support Movement Information Center, 1974: 7), and "The liberation of women is a basic requirement for the Revolution, the guarantee of its continuity and a precondition for its victory" (Samora Machel, quoted in Liberation Support Movement Information Center, 1974: 24).

REFERENCES

Dixon, Marlene
    1977 "The subjugation of women under capitalism: The bourgeois morality." *Synthesis* 1 (Spring): 18–30.
Liberation Support Movement Information Center
    1974 "The Mozambican woman in the revolution." Richmond, B.C., Canada: LSM Press.

DEMOCRACY AND PARTICIPATION

The restoration of democracy in Latin America focuses attention on the institutional arrangements that organize politics, including electoral processes, the rule of law, and individual rights and liberties. Citizenship, a gender-neutral category of political agency according to liberal democratic theory, defines political actors and their equality. Participation, a crucial feature of all models of democracy, reveals the place and power that women-as-citizens have. Women's participation has increased in the redemocratization process, and a critical reading of their inclusion might properly begin with the gender hierarchies that divide the public and private.

The exclusion of women from the public sphere in Latin America can be traced with the durable distinction of *la calle* (the streets) as masculine and *la casa* (the home) as the feminine place for mothers, wives, and daughters. This gender order is anchored in masculine practices widely recognized by the term machismo, described by Stevens (1973) as the "cult of virility"—masculinity defined in "exaggerated aggressiveness and intransigence in male-to-male interpersonal relationships and arrogance and sexual aggression in male-to-female relationships." The feminine becomes the distinctive counterpart of the masculine, according to Stevens. In Latin America, the "cult of feminine spiritual superiority," or *marianismo*, invokes the qualities of "Mary"; in this view, women are "semi-divine" and "spiritually stronger than men," not victims of machismo (Stevens, 1973: 90–91). The gendered division of labor inscribed in modern definitions of public and private may obscure the flexible boundaries of male and female worlds, however. From preconquest kingdoms through colonial and postcolonial societies, women were excluded from the public and its power but not completely and not always successfully. Women had access to economic power in pre-Inca Andean communities, for example, and high-ranking women may also have had some political control (Silverblatt, 1987; Socolow, 2000). Dore argues that pervasive as "male prerogatives" were in colonial society, "the extent of women's legal subordination has been greatly exaggerated"; the "Ibero-American colonial state did not deny women a legal existence" (2000: 11). Women owned property, for instance, and abundant examples of unusual women show that they took public roles reserved for men. Women led revolts in colonial times—including Micaela Bastidas, wife of Tupac Amaru; female slaves became "runaways" to Brazilian *quilombos* and Jamaican Maroons; and women were spies and soldiers, participating in wars for independence (Latin American and Caribbean Women's Collective, 1980: 23–24; Navarro, 1999; Miller, 1991).

Women's suffrage, a crucial element of citizenship, is a twentieth-century phenomenon in Latin America and the Caribbean. Women organized to pursue the right to vote and other demands, moving in new ways into the public sphere. Lavrín (1995) locates first-wave feminist organizing in Latin America in the early twentieth century, later than in the United States or England, though the seeds were sown in nineteenth-century philanthropy, crusades for women's education, labor organizing, and feminist ideas. Suffrage was the main objective of the Inter-American Commission of Women created in 1928, the first intergovernmental organization oriented to the civil and political rights of women. With or without full citizenship, women organized associations, collaborated with traditionally male political groupings, and sometimes created their own parties (Luna and Villarreal, 1994; Lavrín, 1995; Miller, 1991; Soto, 1990). Though the record again shows some highly visible individual women, such as Patricia Galvão (called Pagú), who became a Communist Party militant in Brazil in 1930, or Argentina's Evita Perón, the extension of the franchise to women is part of older and quite specific national histories that tell the story of women's imperfect relegation to the private realm as the public was itself a changing space. Table 7.1 shows the pre– and post–World

Table 7.1   Women's Suffrage in Latin America and the Caribbean Region

Year	Country
1929	Ecuador
1932	Brazil, Uruguay
1934	Cuba
1939	El Salvador
1942	Dominican Republic
1944	Jamaica
1945	Panama, Guatemala (limited)
1946	Trinidad and Tobago
1947	Venezuela, Argentina
1948	Suriname
1949	Chile, Costa Rica
1950	Haiti, Barbados
1951	Antigua and Barbuda, Dominica, Grenada, St. Lucia, St. Vincent and the Grenadines
1952	Bolivia, St. Kitts and Nevis
1953	Mexico, Guyana
1955	Honduras, Nicaragua, Peru
1957	Colombia
1961	Paraguay
1962	Bahamas
1964	Belize

Source: Organization of American States, *Inter-American Commission of Women, 2000,* www.oas.org/cim/English/history5.htm.

War II inclusion of women as voting citizens, beginning with Ecuador in 1929 and ending with Belize in 1964.

The return to democracy calls attention to the most recent phase of women's participation in electoral politics, after the interruptions of military rule and a longer period that Chilean feminist Julieta Kirkwood (1986, 1987) called the *silencio feminista* (feminist silence). Women have, in fact, made gains in their share of elected positions in the upper reaches of national political institutions. Some have been "high-flyers" (Lievesley, 1999: 146)—presidents or prime ministers, including Violeta de Chamorro in Nicaragua, Laura Gueller in Ecuador, Janet Jagan in Guyana, Pamela Gordon in Bermuda, and Mireya Moscoso in Panama. More women occupy seats in legislative bodies than before, though there is variation among countries and subregions. Table 7.2 shows the percentage of seats held by women in lower- or single-chamber bodies in the region between 1987 and 1999. Of the countries for which data are available, Cuba shares top ranking with Argentina in 1999, and Paraguay is at the bottom with 3 percent. Declines are noted in some countries, as well as relative lack of change in others. In upper houses, figures ranged from 14.8 percent in Mexico in 1997,

to 8.2 percent in Venezuela and 3.7 percent in Peru (Craske, 1999: 64, 66).
At the local level, Luis Erundina became mayor of São Paulo in 1988 and
Rosario Robles governed Mexico City after Cuáhtemoc Cárdenas joined the
race for the 2000 presidential election. The percentage of women heading

Table 7.2 Women in Politics

Country	Parliamentary Seats Single/Lower Chamber (% held)			Ministerial Positions (% held)	
	1987	1995	1999	1994	1998
Antigua and Barbuda	0	5	na	0	0
Argentina	5	22	28	0	8
Bahamas	4	8	15	23	17
Barbados	4	11	na	0	27
Belize	4	3	7	6	0
Bolivia	3	11	12	0	6
Brazil	5	7	6	5	4
Chile	na	8	11	13	13
Colombia	5	11	12	11	18
Costa Rica	11	14	19	10	15
Cuba	34	23	28	0	5
Dominica	10	9	9	9	20
Dominican Republic	8	12	16	4	10
Ecuador	1	4	17	6	20
El Salvador	7	11	17	10	6
Grenada	13	20	na	10	14
Guatemala	7	8	13	19	0
Guyana	37	20	18	12	15
Haiti	8	na	4	13	0
Honduras	8	7	9	11	11
Jamaica	12	12	13	5	12
Mexico	11	14	17	5	5
Nicaragua	15	16	10	10	5
Panama	6	8	na	13	6
Paraguay	2	3	3	0	7
Peru	6	10	11	6	10
St. Kitts and Nevis	7	0	13	na	0
St. Lucia	0	0	11	8	10
St. Vincent and the Grenadines	5	10	5	0	10
Suriname	8	6	16	0	5
Trinidad and Tobago	17	19	11	19	14
Uruguay	4	7	7	0	7
Venezuela	4	6	13	11	3

Source: United Nations, *The World's Women 2000: Trends and Statistics.* New York: Social Statistics and Indicators, Series K, no. 16, United Nations, 2000, Table 6.A, p. 172.
na = data not available

local governments was between 20 percent and 30 percent in Guyana, Dominica and the Bahamas in 1997, and less than 10 percent in Chile, Cuba, Costa Rica, Colombia, and others (ECLA, 2000: 48).

The global democratization under way since the 1980s does not reflect increases for women in national legislatures, however. In 1988 women held 14.8 percent of seats worldwide, falling to 11.6 percent in 1995 and rising slightly to 12.5 percent at the end of the decade. South and Central America's 12.1 percent is only slightly below this low figure (Reynolds, 1999: 558–559). Statistics do not explain why women's share of legislatures rose, fell, or stayed the same, however. In the case of the 1994 Chilean elections, for example, only three of forty-six senators and nine of 120 deputies (7.5 percent) were female, despite a campaign to elect more women (Dandavati, 1996). In Mexico, women's percentage of the chamber of deputies declined a percentage point in the 2000 elections (Fernández Poncela, 2001: 9). The adoption of quota systems may help explain increases in some countries. Quota laws—*leyes de cupos*—were adopted in Argentina in 1991, and in varying forms in Brazil in 1995; Costa Rica, 1996; Dominican Republic, Ecuador, Panama, Bolivia, and Peru, 1997; and Venezuela, 1998 (Htun, 1999: 539). The type of electoral system may be important in understanding the fate of women in elections, as are political parties and women's place in them (see Waylen, 2000). Women's presence is also facilitated by their appointment, rather than election, to leadership positions. As table 7.2 shows, the Caribbean states tend to include more women in the top levels of administration, though in Colombia 18 percent of positions were held by women in 1998, in Chile 13 percent, and in Costa Rica 15 percent.

Electoral politics reflect their gendering in several ways. Campaigning for office relies on gendered appeals, as Kampwirth's examination, in her chapter "The Mother of the Nicaraguans: Doña Violeta and the UNO's Gender Agenda," of the multiple images projected by Chamorro in the 1990 Nicaraguan elections reveals; male figures—husbands or fathers—may still be primary sources of legitimacy. Once elected or appointed, women may experience further the division of political labor through posts, activities, and the issues that define them. In her classic study of women officials in Chile and Peru in the late 1960s and early 1970s, Elsa Chaney advanced the image of the *supermadre*. Discussing the established "boundaries" that circumscribe "legitimate professional and political activity," Chaney argued that "the female public official often is forced to legitimize her role as that of a mother in the larger 'house' of the municipality or even the nation, a kind of *supermadre*" (1979: 5). Chaney reports that the women surveyed tended to be "intimidated" by their experience, and that "opposition and male prejudice" helped push women back out of politics (1979. 9), reconfirming the traditional division of masculine and feminine spheres of power. Though two women occupied posts as foreign ministers (Rosario Green in Mexico and Maria Emma Mejía Velez in Colombia) in 1999, women are still found more often in "feminine" areas of decision making, such as health, education, welfare, or women's affairs.

WOMEN AND GENDER INTERESTS

Liberal democracy presumes the representation of interests, and the inclusion of women is thus more than a matter of numbers. Disparities in access to formal positions raise issues of equality, as well as vital questions about decision making and the practices of power in the liberal democratic state. While researchers turn to examine the relationship of women officials to decision making (Archenti and Gómez, 1994), other issues have been raised. What, exactly, are women's interests? Who can represent them? Contemporary scholarship on women and politics has devoted considerable attention to these and related questions, pushing beyond a focus on electoral politics.

The motivations and outcomes of women's participation may be but poorly captured by universalizing claims about citizenship or the category of women. Feminist theorizing has argued that it mistaken to assume that "women" is a category—a container—that usefully reflects what women are, want, and do. Latin American women have carried their often different interests into the public sphere in different ways at different times. Women have joined men in union struggles, as in the case of Bolivia recounted by Viezzer, in the chapter "*El Comité de Amas de Casa de Siglo XX:* An Organizational Experience of Bolivian Women," and in the radical left political groups that are now widely criticized as authoritarian or patriarchal. They have participated in successful and unsuccessful revolutionary struggles in the Caribbean, Central America, and South America, moving into the masculine world of warfare and violence and sometimes as combatants (Lobao, 1990; Vázquez, 1996). Women were 30 percent of the 13,600 combatants documented in the demobilization process in the early 1990s in El Salvador, for example (*Las Dignas*, 1995: 13), a case explored by Luciak in the excerpt below. Women were victims of state terror during military rule—abducted, tortured, and murdered (Partnoy, 1986; Bunster, 1993; Hollander, 1996). Yet women were crucial participants and leaders in the new social movements that opposed military dictatorship, expressing their interests in protest and resistance and contributing to what some see as the ongoing enactment of subaltern counterpublics (Alvarez, 1998).

GENDER DISCRIMINATION
IN THE SALVADORAN TRANSITION

Ilja A. Luciak

Selection from "Gender equality in the Salvadoran transition,"
Latin American Perspectives 105, 26:2 (March 1999), pp. 43–67.

On January 16, 1992, the guerrilla forces, integrated into the *Frente Farabundo Martí para la Liberación Nacional* (Farabundo Martí National Liberal Front—FMLN), and the government of El Salvador signed the historic peace accords at Chapúltepec Castle in Mexico. This agreement ended a 12-year conflict (1979–1992) that had traumatized a whole nation. The war had ravaged the country, creating 1.5 million refugees and claiming the lives of more than 70,000 people, most of them civilians. In the wake of the accords, optimism regarding El Salvador's future was widespread.

The significant female participation in the Salvadoran guerrilla movement raises the question whether women continue to play an important role in the FMLN now that it has become a political party. It is common for female militants to express the fear that women have been demobilized as a result of the transition from the popular/revolutionary struggle of the 1970s and 1980s, which was characterized by mass participation, to the electoralism of the 1990s (interview with María Candelaria Navas, Blacksburg, VA, May 1, 1997). What are the consequences of the transition? Have women obtained significant representation in the party's political structures? What is the FMLN's record concerning gender equality?

Women's issues received scant or no attention in the peace negotiations, although Nidia Díaz, Lorena Peña, and Ana Guadalupe Martínez, all high-ranking female commanders, participated in this process. Peña, reelected to the Salvadoran parliament in 1997, reported that the special problematic of women was simply not discussed during the negotiations. Now a committed feminist, she recognized that women's emancipation had not been an issue during the war and that she had had no idea of gender theory at the time of demobilization (interviews, San Salvador, July 29, 1993, and May 4, 1995). Martínez expressed support for the inclusion of women in all party activities but considered the organized women's movement extremist and radical. Díaz strongly supported women's rights within the party but tended to keep a low public profile concerning women's emancipation (interviews, San Salvador, February 10 and March 18, 1997).

The lack of a gender perspective evident in the design of the reintegration programs translated into discrimination when female combatants initially did not receive equal treatment in the allocation of crucial resources such as land

(Romero, 1995: 370–371). The reasons were many, ranging from machismo to lack of support from the male-dominated leadership of the guerrilla movement. Peña claimed in 1993 that an estimated 70 to 80 percent of female combatants did not receive the benefits allocated to them (interviews, San Salvador, July 29, 1993, and April 25, 1996).

Male and female FMLN members alike faced enormous challenges in their efforts to reintegrate themselves into society. Yet FMLN Women were confronted with additional hurdles "due to their gender, since society in general restricts the opportunities for development of women as such and because of this there is greater discrimination toward FMLN women who did and do not conform totally with the stereotypical roles assigned to women" (*Fundación 16 de enero*, 1993: 11). For example, female ex-combatants seeking to rejoin their families were treated as outcasts by their own parents, siblings, and children for having chosen the revolutionary struggle over their families (Ana Gertrudis Méndez, interview, San Salvador, December 12, 1995). Not surprisingly, the feelings of guilt these women experienced were foreign to fathers in similar situations. Whereas women were seen as "having betrayed their families," men were recognized for "their heroic struggle." Salvadoran society, no different from any other, applies different standards to men and women.

REFERENCES

Fundación 16 de enero
1993 "Diagnóstico de la situación de la mujer ex-combatiente." San Salvador.
Romero, Irene
1995 "La reinserción de la mujer ex-combatiente: un legado de guerra." *Realidad* 44 (March–April: 369–383).

Women's activism reflects their different needs and interests. West and Blumberg (1990) identify four orientations in women's protest activities, ranging from economic survival to nationalist and race/ethnic demands, nurturing or humanistic ends, and pursuit of women's rights. All of these are present in the movement activity of women in Latin America and the Caribbean in recent decades. Women organized collectively and in massive numbers to pursue economic survival of selves and family in the difficult decades of neoliberal adjustment and women's press for human rights opposed military authoritarianism in critical ways. *Conavigua* in Guatemala, the *Comadres* in El Salvador, and the *Madres de la Plaza de Mayo* (the Mothers/Grandmothers of the Plaza de Mayo), homemakers who organized in Buenos Aires in 1977, have become a symbol of the "militant motherhood" of those whose children had been abducted and murdered by the military—perhaps 30,000 or more Argentines were "disappeared" in this way during the *"guerra sucia"* (dirty war) (Mellibovsky, 1997; Argentina, 1986). Whether motivated by economic, human rights, or other concerns, women defied prohibitions against any use of public space for protest, acting as mothers with responsibilities for reproduction of the family, the community, and the nation writ large. Contemporary feminisms have been joined by, and joined with, other movements, including the unconventional associational activity motivated by liberation theology (see Aquino, 1993), and the identity-based claims and demands of indigenous peoples, gays and lesbians, and Afro-Latin Americans.

Presuming that all women have the same interests means ignoring race, ethnicity, geography, age, sexual preference, and class in the shaping of subjectivity—or agency. Here, the provocative distinction between practical and strategic gender interests and needs has been useful for understanding the power of women's participation in a variety of public—and private—sites. Practical gender interests are those defined by material needs and interests rooted in the traditional gender order; these are the interests that motivate women to find solutions to the immediate problems of survival, for example, often in the traditional terms of mothers, daughters, wives, and neighbors. Strategic gender interests are distinguished by the consciousness they reflect; the pursuit of strategic gender interests means recognizing gendered inequalities and oppressions as the problem (Molyneux, 1985; Moser, 1989). Though the binary classification of interests has been criticized, numerous studies have demonstrated how participation rooted in practical gender interests—traditional maternal or motherist interests—could be and was subversive, contributing to redemocratization, the radicalization of women, and feminist rethinkings of politics (Jaquette, 1994; Radcliffe and Westwood, 1993; Fisher, 1993; Küppers, 1994; Taylor, 1996; León, 1994; Fowler-Salamini and Vaughan, 1994).

If women and feminists had an important place in initiating transitions, how have the interests they may share been included in the institutional dynamics of new democracies? Both conventional electoral politics and unconventional movement politics reflect that women are not always feminists, and are not always on the left in ideological terms. As in the past, women may be in the middle or on the right (Power, 1999). In the chapter "Chilean Women's Organizations and Their Potential for Change," Cañadell explores women's organizing in Chile; Chilean women did not uniformly support a return to democratic rule, and Evelyn Matthei, the daughter of a general who helped rule under Pinochet, emerged as a promising right-wing politician in transition politics (Boylan, 1997). Craske notes, moreover, "few of the women active in popular protest have secured entry into institutional politics" (1999: 65). The nature of the inclusion of "women's" issues—not simply women as decision-makers—is part of a changing problematic of representation and power.

Women's interests have a formal institutional expression in most governments in the region, though with different foundations, status, and dynamics. Institutions dedicated to women sometimes predate redemocratization, though expectations for them have been particularly high in the transition period. They include ministries created in Peru in 1974 and Haiti in 1988; the Costa Rican National Institute (1974) and Chilean National Service (1949), which have ministerial status; the commission created in Mexico in 1974 (now slated for change); and the National Women's Institute in Venezuela created in 1989 (ECLA, 2000: 17–19; Friedman, 2000). In Cuba, there is the Federation of Cuban Women, officially designated as a nongovernmental organization (NGO). The relationship of feminist and women's movements to these institutions has been questioned. In some cases, as in Brazil, there has been a strategic pursuit of inclusion through them (Alvarez, 1990; Macaulay, 2000); in other cases the state has appropriated the dynamism of women's and feminist associational activity and claims (Craske, 1999; Fitzsimmons, 2000). The proliferation of NGO's as problem-solving mediators between state and society has further complicated the realities of representation. In a mid-1990s list of 20,000 regional NGOs, half were identified as oriented to women (Miller, 1999).

STATES AND POLICY

The electoral politics of "redemocratization" directs attention to the problem of essentializing women and their interests, as well as to the policies and practices of liberal democratic states. Feminist theorizing inside and outside the region has explored how states constrain women's political power, offering alternative readings of the definition, purpose, and practices of democracy.

The problematic of the state may be crucial for feminist analysis of women and politics in Latin America, though according to Molyneux it is understudied (2000b; also, see essays in Dore and Molyneux, 2000). The state is more than government, and it is approached in different ways in feminist and other theories. The state may be viewed as coercive, to be feared and avoided, or as a facilitator of women's welfare (Rai, 1996). In Pettman's definition, the state is "an abstraction that refers to a set of relations, practices, and institutions.

States are not monolithic, uniform, or unitary. Each state consists of a variety of sites, institutions, operations and functions." (1996: 9). Modern states organize membership—citizenship—in the political community delimited by national boundaries, order and regulate productive power, and provide legitimations for their appearance and projects. From the feminist vantage, the historical and perhaps universal maleness of states is at issue. Not only have they excluded women from citizenship and leadership, but states and state policies organize the "power relations of gender" (Connell, 1990: 520, cited in Pettman, 1996: 9), representing and enforcing a division of public and private. As Dore writes:

> State politics normalizes a variety of gender relations . . . acceptable and unacceptable ways of being female and male may vary, depending on class and race. However, states establish a quasi-official gender regime by regulating as many aspects of life as they can reach, including sexual practices, prostitution, vagrancy, contraception, abortion, marriage, and the family. (2000: 8)

Studying the state thus seems as necessary for locating women and their power as it is difficult. Generalizations about patriarchal impositions must be unpacked, small changes appreciated for their contributions to transformations in the gender order, and electoral politics and policy making placed in their larger context. Legal reform, for example, has been consequential in altering patriarchal power. As Dore explains, extending *patria potestad* to women—making them equal with men as guardians of their children—was a crucial shift; women-specific initiatives such as legalization of divorce or birth control are also obviously beneficial (Dore, 2000), though even apparently gender-neutral state policy has gendered effects. The difficulties of studying states and their policies may be especially apparent in the case of Cuba. Cuba's socialist state, one of six twentieth-century state formations Molyneux identifies in Latin America (2000b), promotes policies that differ significantly from those of the region's liberal democracies, though as Lutjens explores in her study of women in the first half of the 1990s, in the chapter "Reading between the Lines: Women, the State, and Rectification in Cuba", their outcomes cannot be deduced from an ideological commitment or Marxism (also see Molyneux, 2000a). As feminists in the region are famed for claiming, and thinking about the state supports, democracy must be in the home and all the other places where women are and act.

State policies in Latin America and the Caribbean, and sometimes constitutional changes (Morgan, 2000), do reflect some women's interests. Though most countries in the region acted much earlier, by 1993 all had ratified the Convention on the Elimination of Discrimination against Women (CEDAW),

Women in Huehuetenango, Guatemala, late 1980s. *Photo courtesy of Miguel and Marina Vasquez*

an international yardstick for legislation that respects, extends, and protects women's human rights. As the Platform for Action of the Fourth World Conference for Women in Beijing reiterates, women's human rights have been defined to include, among other things, control over sexuality, including sexual and reproductive health, "free of coercion, discrimination and violence" (ECLA, 2000: 49). Positive policies for women include legislation that prohibits and punishes—to varying degrees—sexual harassment and domestic and other violence against them (Oré-Aguilar, 2000; Rivera, 2000). In this vein, Nelson, in her chapter "Constructing and Negotiating Gender in Women's Police Stations in Brazil," explores the creation of women's police stations in Brazil.

Legislation is not always effective, however, and some areas of law reflect obvious continuities in patriarchal authority. Agrarian policy provides good examples (Deere and León, 1987). The Catholic Church offers others, especially in its recent efforts to "demonize" feminism, according to Jean Franco (1996), in response to the "hundreds" of groups that define themselves as feminist. The doctrinal opposition to abortion and birth control continues to find expression in legal proscriptions throughout the region (J. Franco, 1996). Only three countries, including Cuba, permit unrestricted access to abortion, and in three, including Chile, it is illegal under any circumstances. Rayas

(1998) reports that in Chile there are an estimated 170,000 abortions each year, and that half of all pregnancies in Mexico and a third in Peru end in abortions. Less obvious, perhaps, are the effects that neoliberal and other apparently gender neutral policies have on women and their practical and strategic gender needs and interests.

POWER AND SOVEREIGNTY

The feminist questions that have been asked about women and politics in new democracies are not unique to the region, though the historical context invites a careful consideration of what Westwood and Radcliffe call the "internalities" of political protest. In contrast to "externalities" that consist of "pre-existing political organizations, socio-economic structures and reproductive responsibilities," internalities include "gender and political identities, images and practices that shape everyday behavior, symbolism and place in political culture" (Westwood and Radcliffe, 1993: 1). Definitions of politics and power are invoked in considering—and reconsidering—the internalities of women's participation. Wieringa writes:

> Women's acts of resistance, or self-affirmation, as social actors in their different historical and political contexts, are already in themselves subversive to existing power relations but women have been "sub-versive" also in another sense: in circumventing, uncoding and denying the various, distinct and multi-layered verses in which their subjugation is inscribed. (1995: 1)

Feminists everywhere have contended with definitions of power that inscribe it as male in multiple ways, rendering it unavailable to women. Replacing the masculinist "power over," a definition that inheres in liberal theory and an individualist epistemology, feminists have provided some radical alternatives. Townsend and her colleagues (1999), for example, explore multiple alternatives in the Mexican context: "power from within," "power with," "power to," "power as resistance," and "empowerment" (also see León, 1997). Whether women want the same power as men matters, and how we understand what constraints—externalities—exist may matter even more.

Recent scholarship has lamented the waning of the radical potential of Latin America's distinctive social movements. Beyond abstention and other signs of declining interest in conventional politics, concerns include the prospects for the "democratization of everyday life" that the new social movements incited. Jelin sees a danger in the networks of professionals and activists that have formalized around movement issues (1998: 411), a fear echoed in regional feminist debates about the NGO-ization of their own movements.

Schild warns of the negative effects of the "cultural-political project" of ne-oliberalism, a project that redefines citizenship with the imposition of an entrepreneurial individualism and drains issues from the domain of representative politics via privatization (1998: 94–96). Writing in reflection upon the Latin American *supermadre*, Chaney (1998) noted that women seemed less willing to be included in the formal politics of new democracies, a perception of the meaning of participation quite similar to what she observed in the late 1960s. All these suspicions have implications for women and the feminists who have already questioned women's inclusion, calling for autonomy from the state, its policies, and its enforcements of public and private power.

Excavating the internalities of women's participation requires coming to grips with the externalities created by globalization and its restructurings. If the sovereignty of the nation-state has been diminished, interests may no longer be either represented or well regulated by the state. Cross-border movements around shared issues, ranging from human rights to the environment, economic justice, children's well-being, and democracy, have forged an internationalized politics in which feminisms have an important place (Alvarez, 1998; Gabriel and Mcdonald, 1994; Stienstra, 2000). Such internationalization has been viewed positively, as it facilitates networks, mediations, and associations that reflect the multiplicity of organizational experiences that still escape the "fixities" of the state. The Zapatista movement in Chiapas has become a symbol of the possibilities of this new politics, one that expresses local resistance to globalization, replete with a postmodern electronic network of international support. The Zapatista Revolutionary Law for Women, published as the movement initiated its challenge to globalization on January 1, 1994, claimed women's right to fair wages, to choose sexual partners and numbers of children, to health care and education, to freedom from rape and violence, to participate in democracy and the revolutionary struggle, and to hold leadership positions (Rojas, 1996; Olivera, 1995; see also Glusker, 1998). Yet understanding of the internalities of the women included—by choice or geography—in the movement politics of the ELZN are not explained with e-mail messages. Such understanding, as Eber's ethnographic study, "Seeking Our Own Food: Indigenous Women's Power and Autonomy in San Pedro, Chenalhó, Chiapas (1980–1998)," attests, requires a careful look at the places and perceptions of women themselves.

Other leftist alternatives in the political landscape of Latin America and the Caribbean may be useful in mapping the power of women's participation in terms of the gendering of the public sphere. Elections do matter, and recent leftist leadership in Montevideo, Mexico City, and local government in Venezuela are sometimes cited as examples of opportunities for the left (Stolowicz, 1999). In Brazil, Workers' Party leadership at state and local levels is highlighted by the ongoing experience with participatory budgeting in Porto Alegre, a case that offers a compelling alternative for representation and policy making (Abers, 2000). And the sometimes-armed Landless Peasant Movement in Brazil is part of what Petras (1999) sees as third wave of the Latin American left. Petras defends a class-analytical understanding of the resurfacing left, rejecting identity politics and the pluralism that orients post-Marxist theorizing of interests and agency (1999: 100); women and feminists are mainly absent from his account, however. Essentializing class by ignoring gender may still be as misleading as essentializing women.

Indeed, the past and present actions of Latin America's political movements have reflected a range of interests and progressive, emancipatory aspirations; pluralism cannot be ignored. Leftist parties have in some ways included new feminist claims (N. Franco, n.d.). And class may still be a choice in women's struggles against "a multitude of oppressions," as Castro (1999) explains in analyzing the expansion of working class feminism in contemporary Brazil.

SUGGESTED READINGS

Sonia E. Alvarez, "Latin American feminisms 'go global': Trends of the 1990s and challenges for the new millennium," pp. 293–324 in Sonia E. Alvarez, Evelina Dagnino, and Arturo Escobar (eds.), *Cultures of Politics, Politics of Cultures: Re-Visioning Latin American Social Movements.* Boulder, CO: Westview Press, 1998.

Nikki Craske, *Women and Politics in Latin America.* New Brunswick, NJ: Rutgers University Press, 1999.

Elizabeth Dore (ed.), *Gender Politics in Latin America: Debates in Theory and Practice.* New York: Monthly Review Press, 1997.

Joe Foweraker, "Ten theses on women in the political life of Latin America," pp. 63–77 in Victoria E. Rodríguez (ed.), *Women's Participation in Mexican Political Life.* Boulder, CO: Westview Press, 1998.

Jane S. Jaquette (ed.), *The Women's Movement in Latin America: Participation and Democracy,* 2nd ed. Boulder, CO: Westview Press, 1994

Maxine Molyneux, "Mobilization without emancipation: Women's interests and the state in Nicaragua." *Feminist Studies* 11(2) 1985: 227–254.

REFERENCES

Abers, Rebecca Neaera
   2000 *Inventing Local Democracy: Grassroots Politics in Brazil.* Boulder, CO: Lynne Rienner.
Alvarez, Sonia E.
   1990 *Engendering Democracy in Brazil: Women's Movements in Transition Politics.* Princeton, NJ: Princeton University Press.

1998 "Latin American feminisms 'go global': Trends of the 1990s and challenges for the new millennium," pp. 293–324 in Sonia E. Alvarez, Evelina Dagnino, and Arturo Escobar (eds.), *Cultures of Politics, Politics of Cultures: Re-Visioning Latin American Social Movements*. Boulder, CO: Westview Press.

Aquino, María Pilar
1993 *Our Cry for Life: Feminist Theology from Latin America*. Maryknoll, NY: Orbis Books.

Archenti, Nélida and Patricia Laura Gómez
1994 "Las legisladoras argentinas. Estudio sobre la participación política de las mujeres." *América Latina Hoy; Revista de Ciencias Sociales*, segunda epoca, no. 9 (November): 60–69.

Argentina. Comisión Nacional sobre la Desaparición de Personas
1986 *Nunca más (Never Again): A Report*. London and Boston: Faber in association with Index on Censorship.

Boylan, Delia M.
1997 "The rise and fall (and rise?) of a technopol: The Evelyn Matthei story," pp. 195–227 in Jorge I. Domínguez (ed.), *Technopols: Freeing Politics and Markets in Latin America*. University Park: Pennsylvania State University Press.

Bunster, Ximena
1993 "Surviving beyond fear: Women and torture in Latin America," pp. 98–125 in Marjorie Agosín (ed.), *Surviving Beyond Fear: Women, Children and Human Rights in Latin America*. Fredonia, NY: White Pines Press.

Castro, Mary Garcia
1999 "The rise of working class feminism in Brazil." *NACLA: Report on the Americas* 32 (January–February): 28–31.

Chaney, Elsa M.
1979 *Supermadre: Women in Politics in Latin America*. Austin: Institute for Latin American Studies, University of Texas Press.
1998 "*Supermadre* revisited," pp. 78–83 in Victoria E. Rodríguez (ed.), *Women's Participation in Mexican Political Life*. Boulder, CO: Westview Press.

Chilcote, Ronald H.
1994 "Post-Marxism, the left, and democracy in Latin America," pp. 214–235 in Stuart S. Nagel (ed.), *Latin American Development and Public Policy*. New York: St. Martin's Press.

Connell, R. W.
1990 "The state, gender, and sexual politics: Theory and appraisal." *Theory and Society* 19(5): 507–544.

Craske, Nikki
1999 *Women and Politics in Latin America*. New Brunswick, NJ: Rutgers University Press.

Dandavati, Annie G.
1996 *The Women's Movement and the Transition to Democracy in Chile*. New York: Peter Lang.

Deere, Carmen Diana and Magdalena León (eds.)
1987 *Rural Women and State Policy*. Boulder, CO: Westview Press.

Las Dignas, Mujeres Por La Dignidad y La Vida
1995 *Las mujeres ante, con, contra, desde, sin, tras . . . el poder político*. San Salvador: Las Dignas.

Dore, Elizabeth
    2000 "One step forward, two steps back: Gender and the state in the long nineteenth century," pp. 3–32 in Elizabeth Dore and Maxine Molyneux (eds.), *Hidden Histories of Gender and the State in Latin America*. Durham, NC: Duke University Press.
Dore, Elizabeth and Maxine Molyneux (eds.)
    2000 *Hidden Histories of Gender and the State in Latin America*. Durham, NC: Duke University Press.
ECLA (Economic Commission for Latin America and the Caribbean), Women and Development Unit
    2000 *The Challenge of Gender Equity and Human Rights on the Threshold of the Twenty-First Century*. Santiago: ECLAC.
Fernández Poncela, Anna M.
    2001 "Las elegidas al Legislativo Federal, año 2000." *fem* 25 (January): 7–9.
Fisher, Jo
    1993 *Out of the Shadows: Women, Resistance and Politics in South America*. London: Latin American Bureau.
Fitzsimmons, Tracy
    2000 *Beyond the Barricades: Women, Civil Society, and Participation after Democratization in Latin America*. New York: Garland.
Foweraker, Joe
    1998 "Ten theses on women in the political life of Latin America," pp. 63–77 in Victoria E. Rodríguez (ed.), *Women's Participation in Mexican Political Life*. Boulder, CO: Westview Press.
Fowler-Salamini, Heather and Mary Kay Vaughan (eds.)
    1994 *Women of the Mexican Countryside, 1850–1990: Creating Spaces, Shaping Transitions*. Tucson: University of Arizona Press.
Franco, Jean
    1996 "The gender wars." *NACLA: Report on the Americas* 29 (January–February): 6–9.
    1998 "The long march of feminism." *NACLA: Report on the Americas* 31 (January–February): 10–15.
Franco, Nora
    n.d. "Debemos profundizar el debate sobre nuestra participación política." *Tendencias*, no. 5, separata.
Friedman, Elisabeth J.
    2000 "State-based advocacy for gender equality in the developing world: Assessing the Venezuelan National Women's Agency." *Women and Politics* 21(2): 47–80.
Gabriel, Christina and Laura Macdonald
    1994 "NAFTA, women and organising in Canada and Mexico: Forging a 'feminist internationality.'" *Millennium: Journal of International Studies* 13 (Winter): 535–562.
Glusker, Susannah
    1998 "Women networking for peace and survival in Chiapas: Militants, celebrities, academics, survivors, and the stiletto heel brigade." *Sex Roles* 39 (October): 539–557.
Hollander, Nancy Caro
    1996 "The gendering of human rights: Women and the Latin American terrorist state." *Feminist Studies* 22 (Spring): 41–81.
Htun, Mala N.
    1999 "Women's rights and opportunities in Latin America: Problems and prospects," pp. 535–551 in Richard E. Feinberg and Robin L. Rosenberg (eds.), *Civil Society and*

the Summit of the Americas: The 1998 Santiago Summit. Miami, FL: North-South Center Press, University of Miami.

Jaquette, Jane S. (ed.)
1994 The Women's Movement in Latin America: Participation and Democracy, 2nd ed.
Boulder, CO: Westview Press.

Jelin, Elizabeth
1998 "Toward a culture of participation and citizenship: Challenges for a more equitable world," pp. 405–414 in Sonia E. Alvarez, Evelina Dagnino, and Arturo Escobar
(eds.), Cultures of Politics, Politics of Cultures: Re-Visioning Latin American Social Movements. Boulder, CO: Westview Press.

Kirkwood, Julieta
1986 Ser política en Chile: las feministas y los partidos. Santiago: FLACSO.
1987 Tejiendo rebeldías, escritos feministas de Julieta Kirkwood. Santiago: Centro de Estudios de la Mujer, Casa de la Mujer La Morada.

Küppers, Gaby (ed.)
1994 Compañeras: Voices from the Latin American Women's Movement. London: Latin
American Bureau.

Latin American and Caribbean Women's Collective
1980 Slaves of Slaves: The Challenge of Latin American Women. London: Zed Press.

Lavrín, Asunción
1995 Women, Feminism, and Social Change in Argentina, Chile, and Uruguay, 1890–
1940. Lincoln: University of Nebraska Press.

León, Magdalena (ed.)
1994 Mujeres y participación política: avances y desafíos en América Latina. Bogotá: Tercer Mundo Editores.
1997 Poder y empoderamiento de las mujeres. Bogotá: Tercer Mundo Editores.

Lievesley, Geraldine
1999 Democracy in Latin America: Mobilization, Power, and the Search for a New Politics.
Manchester and New York: Manchester University Press.

Lobao, Linda
1990 "Women in revolutionary movements: Changing patterns of Latin American
guerrilla struggle," pp. 180–204 in Guida West and Rhoda Lois Blumberg (eds.),
Women and Social Protest. New York: Oxford University Press.

Luna, Lola G. and Norma Villarreal
1994 Movimientos de mujeres y participación política en Colombia 1930–1991. Barcelona:
Comisión Interministerial de Ciencia y Tecnología, CICYT

Macaulay, Fiona
2000 "Getting gender on the policy agenda: A study of a Brazilian feminist lobby
group," pp. 346–367 in Elizabeth Dore and Maxine Molyneux (eds.), Hidden Histories
of Gender and the State in Latin America. Durham, NC: Duke University Press.

Mellibovsky, Matilde
1997 Circle of Love over Death: Testimonies of the Mothers of the Plaza de Mayo. Willi-
mantic, CT: Curbstone Press.

Miller, Francesca
1991 Latin American Women and the Search for Social Justice. Hanover, NH: University
Press of New England.
1999 "Feminisms and transnationalism," pp. 225–336 in Mrinalini Sinha, Donna Guy,
and Angela Woollacott (eds.), Feminisms and Internationalism. Oxford: Blackwell.

Molyneux, Maxine
 1985 "Mobilization without emancipation: Women's interests and the state in Nicaragua." *Feminist Studies* 11(2): 227–254.
 2000a "State, gender, and institutional change: The Federación de Mujeres Cubanas," pp. 291–321 in Elizabeth Dore and Maxine Molyneux (eds.), *Hidden Histories of Gender and the State in Latin America*. Durham, NC: Duke University Press.
 2000b "Twentieth-century state formations in Latin America," pp. 33–81 in Elizabeth Dore and Maxine Molyneux (eds.), *Hidden Histories of Gender and the State in Latin America*. Durham, NC: Duke University Press.
Morgan, Martha with Mónica María Alzate Buitrago
 2000 "Founding mothers and contemporary Latin American constitutions," pp. 204–218 in Adrien Katherin Wing (ed.), *Global Critical Race Feminism: An International Reader*. New York: New York University Press.
Moser, Carolyn O.
 1989 "Gender planning in the third world: Meeting practical and strategic gender needs." *World Development* 17(11): 1799–1825.
Navarro, Marysa
 1999 "Women in pre-Columbian and colonial Latin America and the Caribbean," pp. 5–57 in Marysa Navarro and Sánchez Korrol with Kecia Ali, *Women in Latin America and the Caribbean: Restoring Women to History*. Bloomington: Indiana University Press.
Okin, Susan Moller
 1998 "Gender, the public, and the private," pp. 116–141 in Anne Phillips (ed.), *Feminism and Politics*. Oxford: Oxford University Press.
Olivera, Mercedes
 1995 "Práctica feminista en el *Movimiento Zapatista de Liberación Nacional*," pp. 168–184 in Rosa Rojas (ed.), *Chiapas ¿y las mujeres qué? II Tomo*. Mexico DF: Editorial La Correa Feminista.
Oré-Aguilar, Gaby
 2000 "Sexual harassment and human rights in Latin America," pp. 362–374 in Adrien Katherin Wing (ed.), *Global Critical Race Feminism: An International Reader*. New York: New York University Press.
Partnoy, Alicia
 1986 *The Little School: Tales of Disappearance & Survival in Argentina*. San Francisco: Cleis Press.
Payne, Leigh
 2000 *The Armed Right Wing and Democracy in Latin America*. Baltimore, MD: Johns Hopkins University Press.
Peterson, V. Spike
 1996 "The politics of identification in the context of globalization." *Women's Studies International Forum* 19 (January–April): 5–15
Petras, James with Todd Cavaluzzi, Morris Morley, and Steve Vieux
 1999 *The Left Strikes Back: Class Conflict in the Age of Neoliberalism*. Boulder, CO: Westview Press.
Pettman, Jan Jindy
 1996 *Worlding Women: A Feminist International Politics*. London: Routledge.
Power, Margaret
 1999 "Women on the right." *NACLA: Report on the Americas* 32 (March–April): 24–27.

Radcliffe, Sarah A. and Sallie Westwood (eds.)
1993 "Viva": Women and Popular Protest in Latin America. London: Routledge.

Rai, Shirin
1996 "Women and the state in the Third World," pp. 25–39 in Haleh Afshar (ed.), Women and Politics in the Third World. London: Routledge.

Rayas, Lucía
1998 "Criminalizing abortion: A crime against women." NACLA: Report on the Americas 31 (January–February): 22–26.

Reynolds, Andrew
1999 "Women in the legislatures and executives of the world: Knocking at the highest glass ceiling." World Politics 51 (July): 547–572.

Rivera, Jenny
2000 "Puerto Rico's domestic violence prevention and intervention law: The limitations of legislative responses," pp. 347–361 in Adrien Katherine Wing (ed.), Global Critical Race Feminism: An International Reader. New York: New York University Press.

Rojas, Rosa
1996 Del dicho al hecho . . . reflexiones sobre la ampliación de la Ley Revolucionaria de Mujeres del EZLN. Mexico DF: Editorial La Correa Feminista.

Schild, Veronica
1998 "New subjects of rights? Women's movements and the construction of citizenship in the 'new democracies,'" pp. 93–117 in Sonia E. Alvarez, Evelina Dagnino, and Arturo Escobar (eds.), Cultures of Politics, Politics of Cultures: Re-Visioning Latin American Social Movements. Boulder, CO: Westview Press.

Silverblatt, Irene
1987 Moon, Sun, and Witches: Gender Ideologies and Class in Inca and Colonial Peru. Princeton, NJ: Princeton University Press.

Socolow, Susan Migden
2000 The Women of Colonial Latin America. Cambridge: Cambridge University Press.

Soto, Shirlene
1990 Emergence of the Modern Mexican Woman: Her Participation in Revolution and Struggle for Equality, 1910–1940. Denver, CO: Arden Press.

Stevens, Evelyn P.
1973 "Marianismo: The other face of machismo in Latin America," pp. 89–101 in Ann Pescatello (ed.), Female and Male in Latin America: Essays. Pittsburgh, PA: University of Pittsburgh Press.

Stienstra, Deborah
2000 "Dancing resistance from Rio to Beijing: Transnational women's organizing and United Nations conferences, 1992–6," pp. 208–223 in Marianne H. Marchand and Anne Sisson Runyan (eds.), Gender and Global Restructuring: Sightings, Sites and Resistances. London: Routledge

Stolowicz, Beatriz (ed.)
1999 Gobiernos de izquierda en América Latina: El desafío del cambio. Mexico, DF: Plaza y Valdés Editores.

Taylor, Diana
1996 "Making a spectacle: Mothers of the Plaza de Mayo," pp. 182–196 in Alexis Jetter, Annelise Orleck, and Diana Taylor (eds.), The Politics of Motherhood: Activist Voices from Left to Right. Hanover, NH: University Press of New England.

Townsend, Janet Gabriel et al.

1999 *Women and Power: Fighting Patriarchy and Poverty*. London: Zed Books.

Vargas, Virginia

1992 "The feminist movement in Latin America: Between hope and disenchantment." *Development and Change* 232(3): 195–214.

1995 "Women's movements in Peru: Rebellion into action," pp. 73–100 in Saskia Wieringa (ed.), *Subversive Women: Women's Movements in Africa, Asia, Latin America and the Caribbean*. London: Zed Books.

Vázquez, Norma

1996 "Revolution, war and women in El Salvador." *Lola Press*, no. 5 (May–October): 32, 34.

Waylen, Georgina

1993 "Women's movements and democratization in Latin America." *Third World Quarterly* 14(3): 583–587.

1994 "Women and democratization: Conceptualizing gender relations in transition politics." *World Politics* 46 (April): 327–354.

2000 "Gender and democratic politics: A comparative analysis of consolidation in Argentina and Chile." *Journal of Latin American Studies* 32: 765–793.

West, Guida and Rhoda Lois Blumberg

1990 "Reconstructing social protest from a feminist perspective," pp. 3–35 in Guida West and Rhoda Lois Blumberg (eds.), *Women and Social Protest*. New York: Oxford University Press.

Westwood, Sallie and Sarah A. Radcliffe

1993 "Gender, racism, and the politics of identities in Latin America," pp. 1–29 in Sarah A. Radcliffe and Sallie Westwood (eds.), *"Viva": Women and Popular Protest in Latin America*. London: Routledge.

Wieringa, Saskia

1995 "Introduction: Subversive women and their movements," pp. 1–22 in Saskia Wieringa (ed.), *Subversive Women: Women's Movements in Africa, Asia, Latin America, and the Caribbean*. London: Zed Books.

8

Chilean Women's Organizations and Their Potential for Change

Rosa M. Cañadell

Translated by John F. Uggen

During its 16 years in power, the military government of General Augusto A. Pinochet created an economic situation in Chile characterized by increasing misery for the poorest sectors of the population and increasing wealth for the upper-class elite (20 percent of the Chilean population receives 60 percent of the wealth and income, while 40 percent of the population receives only 11 percent), a re-concentration of private property, a reduction in social welfare spending, and a huge foreign debt. Of all the sectors in Chilean society, the lower class has been the hardest hit, with women being the most severely affected. In this article I will examine the consequences for women of the political and economic measures implemented by the hegemonic sectors of Chilean society. My purpose is to point out how, in these adverse circumstances, women have organized and developed strategies for opposing these hegemonic sectors that, at the same time, have helped them to increase their level of awareness and public participation, thus enabling them to play a primary role in the struggle against the dictatorship. In considering the various women's groups that have emerged in Chile since the coup d'état of 1973, I will focus on the factors that have made it possible for a large number of women to organize, the composition of the various groups, their impact on the development and self-awareness of the women themselves, their effect on the popular movement, alliances and contradictions among the different groups, the changes that have occurred as a result of the re-democratization process, and, finally, the prospects for the women's movement under the elected government.

This chapter first appeared in *Latin American Perspectives* 79, 20:4 (Fall 1977), pp. 43–60.

157

This work is a contribution to the study of recent popular struggles in Latin America and the Caribbean and women's participation in these struggles. The triumph of the Sandinista revolution in Nicaragua and the spread of other popular struggles in Latin America have resulted in criticism of the classical Marxist analysis of revolution, and intellectuals have begun to theorize about the new social actors that have emerged. In addition, the increasing participation of women in social movements and the advance of feminism have inspired research that concentrates specifically on discrimination against women. This has given rise to women's studies programs in almost all of the countries of the Southern Cone, a wide informal network dedicated to the dissemination of information about the situation of Latin American women (e.g., Isis International, Fem-Press), and feminist encounters that since 1981 have brought together women's organizations from throughout Latin America and the Caribbean.

In analyzing the conditions of the popular classes or of ethnic groups during moments of crisis, one must not overlook the different effects of the crisis on men and women in these sectors, its ramifications in the "private world" of relationships, and its reformulation of male and female power spaces within the overall social framework. At the same time, in analyzing the struggle for women's emancipation, one must not forget that women participate in different social strata with different socioeconomic conditions and have, therefore, different needs and interests that call for social changes that may be different or even contradictory. A popular revolution may bring changes in socioeconomic structures, emancipate the popular classes, improve living conditions, and increase access to political power while preserving intact women's subordinate condition, relegating them once again to their traditional societal roles. A formal democracy may incorporate relative progress in reducing discrimination against women and even integrate some feminist elements into the political hierarchy, but if it leaves the dominant economic relations and the unequal distribution of wealth and power intact it will maintain the great majority of women in the same state of oppression and double exploitation as any authoritarian regime.

Along with other oppressed groups women have always been instrumentalized by the official powers, both right and left, and their history silenced—thereby converting their participation in the social and political struggle into a conjunctural fact that disappears when the situation changes or the particular crisis is resolved. The traditional leftist parties have normally subordinated women's struggle to the class struggle and relegated women to their traditional roles. Reviewing history, we see that under the Popular Unity government women were glorified as "the mothers, daughters, and comrades" of the workers. During the popular government of Salvador Allende, if in fact women's participation increased at all it was only from within the unions and political parties and never with any real awareness of the specific problems facing women. Consequently, their role in the Popular Unity government was reduced to that of assuming and defending their traditional roles. Thus the bourgeois family and the proletarian family displayed a marked degree of subordination and hierarchy between the sexes—the same old relation between women and politics, with men once again in the dominant position. According to Julieta Kirkwood (1986, my translation):

> The most combative propositions of the leftist-progressive discourse are based on the dispute with the right over the condition of leader in the defense of the family—read proletarian family—defined as "the basic revolutionary nucleus" but leaving untouched the hierarchical and disciplinary internal networks that historically have made up the family without changing the reproduction of its order through the socialization of children. With this the left disputes, without actually wanting to, the reinforcement of traditional conservative values.

The women's groups that have emerged during the past 15 years in Chile are fundamentally different in that for the first time the majority of these groups have linked social and political to gender demands.

MECHANISMS OF HEGEMONIC POWER IN CHILE, 1973–1989

The current Chilean regime has been maintained in power by three sectors of society united by their mutual economic and political interests: (1) North American imperialism and multinational capital, with their loans, investments, and appropriation of mineral, agricultural, fishing, and other natural resources; (2) the local upper-class bourgeoisie, principally the sectors linked to agro-exports, with their financial and industrial capital; and (3) the military, linked to the upper sphere of high finance. (It should be pointed out that Chile has dedicated a very large percentage of its military budget to personnel.) Two types of mechanisms have kept these sectors in power: economic measures and the overwhelming deployment of state-sponsored terrorism and repression.

The system's main base of support is the implementation of neoliberal economic policies that have permitted a model of capital accumulation acceptable to the dominant sectors. This arrangement has produced a number of economic success stories (the so-called Chilean miracle) focusing on an increasing rate of growth in the GNP (which in 1987 was 5.5 percent) and a strict commitment to servicing the foreign debt. But in spite of these statistics, reality is very far from the so-called Chilean miracle, which has in fact left the country mortgaged to the hilt. Among the measures adopted, we can point to the following:

- Privatization of the principal publicly owned enterprises, such as energy, communications, mining, and the steel industry, which have been handed over to multinational interests from the United States, Japan, Germany, and Australia in association with local capitalists.
- Reconcentration of private landholdings with the return of land and businesses expropriated by the Popular Unity government and the subsequent conversion of the countryside to agrarian capitalism, leaving small proprietors without land or employment and a large number of peasants landless.
- Expansion of agricultural production for export and a corresponding drop in traditional agricultural production and the percentage dedicated to national consumption (daily consumption of food per inhabitant in 1975 was below the norm established by the Food and Agriculture Organization).
- Concentration of capital and de-industrialization, beginning with a massive influx of imported goods that ruined the manufacturing and small business sectors (from 1967 to 1983, 2,000 businesses disappeared) and increased unemployment and underemployment.
- Excessive foreign indebtedness arising from external financing dedicated primarily to the importation of luxury consumer items for the upper classes and a rescheduling of the foreign debt that has had no appreciable impact on production.
- A decline in social spending that has blocked the access of a high percentage of the population to education, health, and housing opportunities.

At the same time, state-sponsored terrorism has served as an instrument for the consolidation of the regime. The repression has been both physical—deaths, disappearances, detentions, exiles, torture, etc., aimed at workers' organizations and the popular sectors—and political/ideological—the dismantling of organizations, leftist political parties, and unions; permanent militarization, with the institutionalization of the secret police and systematic torture; the suppression of all kinds of democratic liberties; unrestricted access for partisans of the regime to job opportunities in the universities and the concomitant massive dismissal of educators suspected of not agreeing with the regime; and massive propaganda for a military-authoritarian ideology using women, especially from the upper class and wives of military officers, organized by the regime in a vast volunteer network directed by the dictator's wife.

WOMEN ORGANIZE

The political and economic aggression to which the population has been subjected has been met by intense opposition, with various popular movements fighting on different fronts to overcome the disastrous conditions they have faced. One of the most distinctive characteristics of these movements has been the incorporation of a large number of women into the social and political scene and the proliferation of groups organized by women. This female leadership is not in the least homogeneous. On the one hand, a great many women's groups—feminists, women from the popular classes, politicians, peasants—have arisen in opposition to the military regime. On the other hand, women from the upper classes and those linked to the military have been organized by the regime itself to support the dictator unconditionally and to fight feminism.

In spite of the efforts of the dictatorship to win the support and confidence of women, a large percentage of the female population has organized to fight it on various fronts and taken visible positions in the opposition movement. The brutality of the institutional repression, the serious deterioration in living conditions for the great majority of the population, and the regime's often authoritarian and violent discourse have been the most important factors in eliciting women's organized response. Although this response was at first only defensive, with the passage of time and the raising of consciousness it has tended to crystallize into a clearly anti-dictatorial and anti-patriarchal stance.

The mere appearance of conflict or of the necessary level of consciousness does not, of course, automatically result in the coalescence of a movement. Rather, a well-organized movement is the product of the evolution and interaction of many different factors. Four circumstances have converged to make it possible for women to assume active roles in the struggle and attain a high level of consciousness and organization: (1) a change in family roles: many women having become heads of households because of the absence (as a result of death, exile, disappearance, or abandonment) of their husbands or their unemployment; (2) the patriarchal ideology itself, which dignifies women as both mothers and wives while, through the repression, it takes their sons or husbands; (3) the absence of traditional political structures (parties and labor unions having been eliminated by the repression), leaving a vacuum that women can fill; and (4) the experience of political participation that many women had enjoyed, albeit in a subordinate position, under the Popular Unity government. In order to clarify this evolution, I will analyze the three main types of women's organizations that have emerged during the past 15 years: the popular women's organizations, women for human rights, and the feminists.

POPULAR WOMEN'S ORGANIZATIONS

Severely limited economically, the popular women's organizations have elaborated a large number of alternative strategies primarily having to do with subsistence and survival. According to studies carried out in 1986, it is estimated that in the metropolitan region alone there were 1,383 popular organizations in full operation, with a total of 46,759 active members, an overwhelming number of whom were women (Centro de Estudios de la Mujer, 1988). Community soup kitchens first appeared in 1982 when neighbors faced with the emergency agreed to prepare and cook their meals in common. From the beginning these women assumed the management of resources and the distribution of work assignments. Community purchasing activities allowed groups of women to pool their meager resources and thereby lower the cost of food and basic necessities. Productive workshops, many of them under the supervision of Catholic parishes, aimed at generating income to augment insufficient family budgets and to promote women's creativity on the basis of their own experiences and skills. The difficulty for the general population with scant resources of gaining access to health care has encouraged women to create popular health centers, and these women, supported and trained by middle-class women from the health professions or the church, have organized a network of first-aid stations, health workshops, primary care, health courses, children's hygiene, and a reassessment of traditional health-care practices and medicine (based on natural products, herbs, etc.).

The impossibility of obtaining adequate housing, along with popular experience during earlier periods of occupying land, has led to massive land invasions in which the participation of women has been of primordial importance. As one of the squatters told us, "The men are either not here or afraid; there are always many more women." Once the lands have been invaded, defense committees are set up: "We defend ourselves against the Pacos with sticks and clubs, but we also make clear that no one is going to kick us out of here," said a young mother of three. During this initial stage of occupation, women's actions belong to the domestic sphere, which is at once private and public, individual and collective—individual in that the objective does not transcend one's own household but collective because under the circumstances collective organization is indispensable. Once the necessary "space" has been won, the provision of services becomes the next common objective, and here again women play the primary role. As one camp resident put it, "Thanks to our organization we have grown. We have a great school, because we took over an excellent piece of property on which to build it."

Since the formation of the communal workshops and activities in the barrios, women are no longer isolated and therefore can begin to share their concerns and experiences. These women are well aware that their participation in these subsistence organizations represents but slight improvement in their material conditions, but they defend their own space and time outside of the family circle nonetheless. In this respect it is worth pointing out the significant increase in the number of women's organizations devoted primarily to self-examination and personal growth (from 38 in 1983 to 220 in 1986). Finally, these groups often come into contact with other groups of women—generally from the middle class and more committed to the feminist struggle per se—through their experience with women's centers that provide support services, legal, labor, and sexual counseling, and opportunities for training and reflection. These activities may be expected to raise their consciousness and self-esteem.

Popular organizations have meant not only personal advancement and self-examination but also an opportunity for women to increase their capacity for intervening in and even changing their personal and family lives. They have also meant a new interpretation of social realities and an increase in class consciousness that has fostered greater commitment to and participation in the process of change in which other sectors of the country are involved. Through the tasks that they have undertaken collectively and the discovery of common problems, women have been experiencing an awakening; they are beginning to realize that the situation that afflicts them is not personal or exceptional but social and therefore can be changed.

The experience of organizing and the problems of bureaucracy and repression that they encounter force women to reflect on the causes of these evils, and this in turn leads them to a much broader comprehension of the social problems that they suffer. The participation of women with experience in leftist politics and consequently a certain degree of political consciousness has helped to raise the level of political discussion and dialog within these groups. The tasks to be performed are many and urgent, however, and this has made in-depth political analysis of the situation difficult. Although the dictatorship has correctly been identified by each of these groups as the main enemy, there is seldom any detailed analysis of economic and power relationships.

Finally, these organizations, on the basis of their everyday experiences, can develop strategies that are in themselves counter-hegemonic and, though they may not be generalizable, can help form small nuclei of countervailing power. The communal activities carried out in the barrios have created relationships based on cooperation and solidarity rather than competition and individualism, and these values are considered appropriate and positive. Productive strategies also imply alternative values: cooperatives instead of private enterprises, cooperative commercialization of goods and services instead of mutual competition, etc. Artisanal workshops are helping Mapuche and

Aymará women to recover their cultures and to rediscover and recognize their ethnic heritage and identity. Land invasions and squatter encampments call for organization, thereby creating alternative sources of power and political action based on mass participation in public meetings and assemblies and the elimination of hierarchical forms.

WOMEN FOR HUMAN RIGHTS

Threatened with physical violence and the death and disappearance of their sons and husbands, women—often starting from the roles assigned to them of mothers and wives and taking advantage of their image as weak and non-threatening—are the first to take to the streets and denounce these abuses. Beginning on the emotional-affective level, their protests end up questioning the regime and being converted into political struggle. In the beginning this was a matter of relatives coordinating their activities so as to be able to visit prisoners in the detention centers. Later it was those looking for detainees and the disappeared, and from them emerged groups, consisting principally of women, that began to work against the government. Immediately following the military coup it was the Assembly of Relatives of Detained and Missing Persons and the Relatives of Political Prisoners that were the first organizations publicly to oppose the regime. Later it would also be women who would organize the relatives of political prisoners who had been executed, the Committee for the Return of Exiles, and many other organizations such as Democratic Women, the Committee for the Defense of Women's Rights, Women of Chile, and Women for Life.

Whereas the women's organizations mentioned earlier emerged out of the struggle for survival and the government's failure to fulfill its responsibilities, these organizations emerged out of the inability of traditional groups to force the government to comply with minimum demands for human rights. Thus, mothers and wives of the disappeared emerged when neither the political parties nor the Commission on Human Rights nor the national and international organizations had any impact whatsoever on the atrocities committed by the dictatorship. This type of organization brings together women of different economic and social strata not so much in opposition to the government or even necessarily as women per se as in their capacity as mothers and wives—making public what was formerly private (family, children, husband) and making political what was once personal. This active participation of women in the struggle against the dictatorship has been an important element of pressure on the regime and has achieved the recognition of women as social actors by the other actors in the social and political spheres.

FEMINIST WOMEN

A third type of women's organization has emerged to articulate gender demands, emphasizing theoretical reflection, active engagement aimed at the raising of consciousness, and the emancipation of women. These feminist groups consist of women, mainly middle-class and including university graduates and intellectuals, who belong to nongovernmental organizations financed by foreign capital or by elements within the Catholic church. Some of these groups (La Morada, Domus, Centro de Estudios de la Mujer, Fem-Press) form a network with a clear gender perspective. Others, such as the Movement for the Emancipation of Chilean Women or Women for Socialism, are more directly linked to parties, and still others, such as the Woman Settlers' Movement and the Feminist Liberation Front, are actively involved with the popular sectors. Their activities are various, including research on peasants, Mapuche women, and slum dwellers, organizational support for slum dwellers (soup kitchens, production workshops, commercialization of artisanal production), workshops for psychological support and workshops on health, sexuality, and personal development, and the dissemination of feminist perspectives.

Their relationships among themselves and with other political groups are, in general, sporadic and informal. "Very jealous of any outside intervention that might interfere with the management of their own organizations and worried about maintaining their identity and autonomy, these organizations operate, in general, in a very isolated and restricted environment" (Arteaga, 1988, my translation). The relations they maintain with certain popular sectors are more stable; these ties are important for what they can contribute to the development of self-awareness in and support for weaker and less-favored women, but they run the risk of creating asymmetric relations of power and dependence very much in contradiction with their theoretical discourse and their own principles of horizontal relationships. The assessments of this group by the poor women involved are diverse; some acknowledge the help they have received from contact with these groups, but others complain, in the words of one Mapuche woman, "They come, they observe us, they study us, they write a book, they make money from it, while we don't receive anything in return."

Nevertheless, these groups have played an important role in giving the private world political content and posing new topics—sexuality, violence, marginalization, etc.—for political debate. They have broadened the range of such traditional public issues as domination, politics, and peace by bringing to them the woman's perspective. The politicization of the private sphere has unveiled the power relations encapsulated within this sphere and their relationship with public power. This has led to the inclusion of specific women's demands within the general ones.

THE TRANSITION AND THE REALIGNMENT
OF TRADITIONAL POLITICAL FORCES

The events beginning with the "political opening" of 1983 and culminating in the plebiscite of 1988 and the elections the following December have introduced important changes in all social movements and particularly in women's organizations. From the outset of the political transition, political parties began to reassert themselves as the only channels of expression and representation in society, displacing many grass-roots and women's organizations by reclaiming their leadership roles and imposing their traditional orientation, priorities, and forms on all levels of political activity. The budding autonomy, self-government, and direct democracy of these organizations and their new ways of thinking about and conducting politics have already begun to show clear signs of disintegration as the reconstitution of the traditional political parties advances.

The different strategies employed against the dictatorship have also created divisions within and among the different women's organizations, fracturing them both vertically and horizontally. Furthermore, the class contradictions within the women's movement (between middle-class women and slum dwellers, intellectuals and workers, etc.) have split the various groups along political lines corresponding to different social class demands and interests. This split has created two large women's groups, Women's Reconciliation, aligned with the parties of the BPD, and the Coordinator of Social Organizations, whose point of reference is the most leftist parties. The feminist/politics dichotomy is consolidated in a third movement independent of the political parties, the Autonomous Feminist Tendency.

Friction has also developed within these groups as women who belong to different parties attempt to co-opt the group in terms of their particular needs. There would also seem to be a hierarchy based on degree of militancy, position within the party, etc. A young woman fighter explained, "For 15 years I struggled hard and was valued and appreciated as a woman, but lately my 'merits' have gone unnoticed; now that I am no longer a militant within a party, I begin to be ignored and relegated to a lesser role" (interview, January 1989, my translation). Another group of slum dwellers complained, "Ever since the parties have begun to organize again, they have all started fighting to see which one will take over our organization."

REVERSALS FOR THE WOMEN'S MOVEMENT

It is important to keep in mind that women's groups are subordinated not primarily because they are composed of women but because they are part of a so-

cial movement and therefore of an official political dynamic that gives priority to political parties and relegates all other groups to secondary status. This
phenomenon is nothing more than the dichotomy between direct and representative forms of political participation.

A social movement often represents a great variety of social classes. (The
women's movement is clearly a case in point.) This characteristic, as James
Petras (1987, my translation) notes, "constitutes not only its initial
strength but also its principal strategic weakness. Although the cumulative
impact of the combined action of diverse social classes places additional
pressure on the military regime, it also offers that regime a variety of possible negotiators and political alternatives when the time comes to abandon
the government." These alternatives will be the first to attack the unity of
the multi-class social movements.

Apart from these contradictions, the disintegration of the women's organizations vis-à-vis the political parties is a product of the particular character of
the transition. What is in fact taking place is a negotiated transition in which
neither the armed forces nor the hegemonic powers are prepared to cede an
iota of their political power. This type of agreement can be implemented only
with bourgeois political parties that, because of their very nature, objectives,
and relationships with the people, are capable of guaranteeing moderation in
socioeconomic change and limited innovation in the political and legal
spheres. Therefore the political parties directing the transition are those that
are willing to concentrate their efforts on governmental institutions, leaving
state power structures intact, and this can be achieved only if the problems
can be transferred from the street to the negotiating table—for which it is
necessary for social movements to disappear. Social movements represent a
profound alteration of the nature and structure of social and political participation. Controlled from below, they demand much more radical change and
are much less susceptible to being co-opted, making it necessary to neutralize
or eliminate them altogether.

This does not mean that the social and women's movements are weak or
have a tendency to collapse; rather, powerful institutional forces originating in
the economic, political, and military alliance of the hegemonic elites and their
political and class alliances (bourgeoisie/big capital/armed forces) are able to
override the aspirations of the great majority of the Chilean people.

The decline of the social movements, however, is not irreversible but conjunctural. As we have seen in the recent democratic transitions in Peru and
Argentina, neoliberal policies have not succeeded in resolving the economic
crisis, and once it is obvious that the new regime cannot bring about significant
change, popular mobilization resurfaces. "The trajectory of the movements
may not be lineal, but there is considerable continuity in their experiences,

particularly those of the informal leaders and the collective consciousness, to reconstitute the base of action of the movement in spite of political deviations" (Petras, 1989, my translation). Thus the women's organizations, and in particular those that belong to the popular sectors, that now find themselves subordinated to the political parties have ample opportunity to reorganize and take power in the not-too-distant future.

DIVISIONS WITHIN THE WOMEN'S MOVEMENT

To analyze the political divisions within the women's movement it is important to pose the following question: Is there an alternative program that can be supported by the majority of the women's organizations? The social world of women is neither unique nor homogeneous, and therefore the alternative must be not for women in general but for women who share a political or social agenda. Although women of course share a specific type of oppression simply by being women, they also share other defining characteristics—age, profession, race, and social class—and are subjected to other kinds of oppression depending directly on their particular social status. The dispersion of the women's movement at a time when opposition forces are fighting with every available means to force the dictatorship from power is inevitable. In these circumstances each group is seeking its own position vis-à-vis the various alternatives in accordance with its political ideology or social class. In this sense, what is important is not the divisions but whether the movement will be able to survive them.

My hypothesis is that the achievements of the past 15 years are not going to be reversible. The organization of women has meant a recognition by women and by a large proportion of the population of their oppression and subordination and the inclusion of their specific demands within the political and social demands. These are two fundamental advances that women will be unwilling to relinquish. This discourse from a woman's point of view will inevitably take various forms depending on political options and particular social realities, but this does not necessarily mean that it will disappear. The possibility of applying pressure from different angles and working together on common goals and strategies will continue to exist. This has been amply demonstrated by the mass protest demonstration in the Santa Laura stadium that brought together more than 2,000 women from all sectors and political tendencies, by the demands of Women for Democracy, subscribed to by more than 20 groups, and by the creation of a special group within the Human Rights Commission dedicated to protesting any act of violence against women.

Ultimately, what is at issue is not creating an alternative program that will include all women but articulating tactics and strategies that will make the inclusion of women's demands acceptable to every political and social sector and guarantee that this new dimension will not be lost no matter what Chile's political future may hold. It is important to keep in mind that this transition is only the beginning of a long struggle to make Chile once again a truly free and livable country, a country in which the majority of the Chilean people, both men and women, will be able to live in dignity. The progress that the women's organizations have achieved politically may serve as a point of departure for this struggle.

THE DIMINUTION OF WOMEN'S POLITICAL ROLE

In the absence of political parties, women's groups occupied a political space that allowed them to increase their participation in the various struggles against the dictatorship. Now that the political parties have reappeared, this leadership role is threatened. This is not simply a matter of the subordination of women's groups to partisan political conventions; as traditional institutions reemerge, a leadership is reasserting itself that is predominantly male. Not only at the public level but also within the human rights organizations and the popular groups, the traditional political leadership has once again given male politicians the dominant role. Women who have played important, active roles in their own organizations are being pushed aside and relegated to minor or secondary roles at the very moment at which their militancy in the party had begun to be important.

Past experience has not, however, been in vain. Many women who had played active roles during the dictatorship have been actively incorporated into the new political situation. In Women's Reconciliation, for example, a special committee has been created to develop strategies for increasing the participation of women in the new political scene. Socialist women have been able to place a significant number of women in positions of responsibility in their political party. Within the popular movement, strategies tend to be directed toward positions of authority for women at the local level (neighborhood boards, municipal councils)—in fact the same positions they have held, albeit unofficially, all along.

In other ways it will now be much more difficult for women to fulfill their political agendas. Basically, they will have to abandon many of their organizational practices, such as their preference for nonhierarchical structures. Women of the popular movement and feminists are more likely to be able to persist in these practices and thus to continue advancing not only in theory but also in practice in the direction of a new way of conducting politics.

CONCLUSION

During the past 15 years women's organizations in Chile have made the following important contributions to the struggle against the dictatorship: On the individual level, organization has fostered progress in women's self-esteem and self-evaluation and in the process of liberation as well as raising the general level of political and feminist consciousness. On the social level, the incorporation of women into the struggle for change is not only a quantitative contribution (in the sense that there are now more people involved) but also a qualitative one in that women have contributed to the development of new types of organizations (more participatory and less hierarchical) and new forms of struggle (integrating the private with the public sphere, for example) that presuppose a new way of understanding power.

Greater access for women to public roles, the fulfillment of their potential, the socialization of their experiences, and the rising level of consciousness achieved through experience in organization and participation in the women's struggle against the dictatorship have been internalized by women and can be considered irreversible gains. Awareness of their situation has given them a commitment to public service and participation that will not easily be surrendered.

Women's popular organizations, to the degree that they have begun to develop strategies combining their struggle against dictatorship and economic oppression with their own personal struggle for liberation, may become nuclei of resistance and generate not only new social movements but also new models of change that will succeed both in breaking with the current hegemonic powers and in resolving conflicts that arise from gender oppression. It is in this sense that one can speak of the potential for change that the women's movement represents by challenging conventional political concepts and schemes and thus broadening the scope of the system's contradictions and resisting a domination that penetrates the very web of social and family life. This potential calls for a redefinition of the concept of democracy and a new model of society based on equality and antiauthoritarianism in all its varied aspects.

NOTE

This article was written in November 1989, before the consolidation of the transition in Chile.

REFERENCES

Arteaga, Ana Maria
   1988 "Politización de lo privado y subversión de lo cotidiano," in Centro de Estudios de la Mujer (ed.), *Mundo de mujer.* Santiago: CEM.
Centro de Estudios de la Mujer (ed.)
   1988 *Mundo de mujer.* Santiago: CEM.
Kirkwood, Julieta
   1986 *Ser política en Chile.* Santiago: Facultad Latinoamericana de Ciencias Sociales.
Petras, James
   1987 *Estado y régimen en América Latina.* Madrid: Revolución.
   1989 "Movimientos sociales y clase política en América Latina." *América la Patria Grande* (Mexico City) 4.

9

El Comité de Amas de Casa de Siglo XX: An Organizational Experience of Bolivian Women

Moema Viezzer
Translated by James Dietz and Paula Tuchman

Si *permiten hablar* . . . is the title of the oral testimony of Domitila Barrios de Chungara, a woman from the Bolivian mines, whose story I collected and elaborated after meeting with her at the Tribunal of the U.N. International Women's Year Meeting in Mexico City in 1975. First published in Spanish in 1977 by *Siglo Veintiuno* in Mexico, the book has now been translated and published in nine languages and has recently appeared in English as *Let Me Speak* (1979).

"This life history is the book of one person, but it is also a book about a country and a class," said Eduardo Galeano commenting on the book. I would argue that it is also the first effort to present the organizing experiences of the group of mining women in the *Comité de Amas de Casa de Siglo XX* (Committee of Housewives of *Siglo XX*).

Comité de Amas de Casa de Siglo XX appeared in this context and linked with these struggles as an organization that brought together the majority of the women in the families of the mine workers.

Domitila, the protagonist in *Let Me Speak*, has been politically active in the Housewives Committee since 1963 and has held various positions, in particular that of secretary general. The lived experience of the Bolivian mining women when related by one of their representatives is unimpeachable when describing the oppression of Bolivian women in the environment in which they live and the manner in which they have persisted in the struggle to change their situation.

This article focuses on those aspects of Domitila's testimony specifically connected with the housewives' organization: How did the committee begin?

This chapter first appeared in *Latin American Perspectives* 22, 6:3 (Summer 1979), pp. 80–86.

What were the forms of action and struggle? What difficulties were encoun-tered by the women due to the fact that they had organized as women? What are the possibilities of the generalization of this experience? What theoretical contributions can be derived from this experience to further the women's problematic?

HOW THE COMMITTEE BEGAN

In 1961 all the union leaders of *Siglo XX* and the surrounding area were seized along with various workers who were then taken as prisoners to La Paz. The wives of the prisoners individually asked for the release of their compañeros, but in vain. Some sixty women decided to go together to make their claims. Arriving in La Paz, they declared a hunger strike and published a manifesto in which they asked for the freedom of the union leaders and the other com-pañeros, the back pay owed by the mining company to the workers for three months, and the stocking of the general store (the property of the mine) which had been empty while the people suffered from hunger.

The strike lasted ten days. Even though it had been spontaneous, it was successful, particularly because of the support offered the women by the unions of other mining centers, industrial unions, university students, and so on. Upon returning to *Siglo XX*, these women decided to organize themselves so that they could continue to be a part of the struggle in alliance with the workers. Today the committee still exists, having its recognized place in the different working class organizations.

FORMS OF ACTION AND STRUGGLE

The Housewives Committee has developed two forms of action:

First, in their alliance with the miners' struggle, the committee has partici-pated in such events of the working class as assemblies and union congresses of the federation of miners and of the *Central Obrera Boliviana* (Bolivian Work-ers Union) to which all union organizations in the country belong. The com-mittee has played an important role in activities related to the social well-being of workers' families, demands for improvement of hospital services and schools, for better living conditions, and so on. The committee has partici-pated, as well, in activities of a more political nature: strikes and demonstra-tions against government measures that have endangered the national econ-omy and political freedom. As a result, the women have been led to take part in many confrontations of the working class against the repressive state organs.

Second, with respect to the problems that more directly affect women, the activities of the committee can be summarized as follows: looking for sources of work for women; attempting to join together with women from other sectors, particularly from rural areas; attempting to organize housewives' committees on a national level (which failed as a result of government repression).

REPERCUSSIONS RESULTING FROM THE FORMATION OF THE COMMITTEE

The women of Siglo XX encountered many problems arising from various sources. These difficulties can be grouped as those arising from: (1) the men, (2) the women, (3) the government, (4) the family, and (5) the leadership. We will now turn to these in order.

The men of Bolivian mining centers—like the great majority of Latin American men—are educated (through the mechanisms of the capitalist system) to believe themselves superior to women, to accept as normal the harsh treatment of women, to believe the responsibility of childcare to be a woman's task, and so on. In a word, they are taught to be "macho."

Even the men conscious of their exploitation as workers do not have the perspective that permits them to understand the role performed by household labor in the productive process. In fact, as is realized by the women at the mine centers, household labor functions as a means of reproducing the labor power of their husbands, permitting, as a result, the mine owners to obtain labor at a lower wage.

Lack of consciousness leads the mine workers often to accept as "normal" the confinement of the women to the house, the prohibition of their social and political participation, and to bear an attitude of rejection or sarcasm in relation to the women who decide to participate in the struggle. Many men have changed now, but this attitude was prevalent among the miners when the women began to organize themselves.

Often, union leaders themselves did not support the committee by not understanding women's legitimate right of struggle in alliance with the workers for regaining what is "theirs" in production and by not understanding the power that women can express through their participation in the struggle. Other leaders, even though desiring to collaborate with the women forming the committee, did not have adequate preparation for a joint effort with them based on their situation as housewives, which is quite different from the situation of the workers.

In short, the difficulties created by the men often stemmed from the fear of losing their job or of being persecuted as a result of the participation by their wives—a situation that has occurred on various occasions.

The women have not always responded in a positive way to the committee. Unaware of the mechanisms of exploitation, which the maintenance of household labor represents as a means of reproduction of labor power, the majority of the women also were accustomed to considering the duty of household labor as exclusively their own and to accept as natural women's condition as wife and mother.

The committee also encountered difficulties in its work from organizations of other women serving interests different from those of the working class, like, for example, the women organized by the traditional Church and women's groups directed by the government.

The Bolivian government has reacted in different ways when it has seen itself affected by women's participation: at times by directly repressing them, ignoring the work of the committee, and by arresting and torturing some of the women. At other times, they have repressed the mine workers for the participation of their wives, getting them fired from their jobs, putting their names on the "black list," including sending workers into exile, and thereby hurting not only the worker but his family as well, which is left behind with little hope of income since there are few jobs for women in the mining centers.

Within the family many problems arose, the result of difficulties just noted, but not just because of a husband persecuted or fired on account of his wife, but also because of problems arising from the children that suffer the consequences of their father's unemployment.

Holding the position of director of the committee has placed some women in a dilemma that is not at all easy for them to resolve in the face of repression and torture: to choose between the life and well-being of her family or the cause of her people.

POSSIBILITIES OF GENERALIZING FROM THIS EXPERIENCE

The Committee of Housewives of *Siglo XX* has had a very valuable experience, but it is one that is limited and privileged in many ways. In the first place it has been a very localized experience that depends on exceptional conditions in relation to other productive centers. The committee deals with a mining camp where five thousand families live in a concentrated area and where not only the mine but all the social services belong to the company. As a result of this, the women can feel with much more force the relation with the owner for whom their husband works as well as how the economy functions in a dependent capitalist country. Besides, the *Siglo XX* mining center relies on the presence of an already politicized union. All these factors are unlikely to coincide in other workplaces, in the countryside, or in urban neighborhoods.

What elements of generalization can be derived from this experience? In relation to the situation of Latin American women, Siglo XX, in spite of presenting particular aspects, resembles the condition of the great majority of the women in Latin America who fulfill a similar function through the work they do in the home, thus permitting the reproduction of labor power.

As a women's organizing experience, that of Siglo XX invites a comparison with several similar experiences so as to discover how consciousness and commitment developed among these women. Perhaps the road to be followed by proletarian women can or must be distinct from other social groups. It is important to note also that in the same countries where the feminist movement already has a certain history, particularly in the United States and Europe, they have only included an insignificant minority of working class women (working women or housewives married to workers). A woman's organization like that of Siglo XX cannot be imposed from outside; it must take into account the socioeconomic, cultural, and political conditions in which it has developed.

CONTRIBUTIONS TO THE THEORY OF WOMEN'S PARTICIPATION IN STRUGGLE

In the Bolivian mining center, those who are directly connected to production are men. The women not only cannot enter the mine but have difficulty finding any source of work. The mine workers have in their union the mechanism for defending their rights. The women, since they are not directly involved in the productive work, organized themselves starting from their condition as wives who work to help maintain and reproduce labor in the home.

The Comité de Amas de Casa de Siglo XX is an organization of women who live from permanent domestic labor and who believe that they can win their liberation through indirect struggle connected with production. Their struggle is not isolated, but is in alliance with an organization that has a direct role in the struggle—the mine union. Nevertheless, the committee is more than a support committee to the union. For the housewife, it is the instrument of struggle that corresponds to her form of participation in the production process. The way in which the women of the mine lives her oppression determines the type of liberation that she demands.

The mining woman is directly connected with the exploitation that her compañero suffers in the mine and to which they are also subjected because of the effects of the capitalist system. These manifest themselves in distinct forms: (1) There are no sources of work for the women in the mines with the exception, for some, of gathering loose rocks or of finding work in some of the few services such as in the hospital, the schools, and the company store. (2) The woman is relegated to the "invisible" work of the home, which is considered economically and socially without value. (3) The pay of the workers (inside the mine it is on average U.S.$1.50 per day) is not enough for the maintenance of the family. Thus, besides domestic chores, the women do additional work for outside income: weaving, washing, selling, and so on. Some, for example, spend five to seven hours of the day preparing *empenadas* (meat pies) and selling them on the street with the help of their children. The rest of the day is dedicated to housework, thus resulting in almost a double shift. (4) Domestic work becomes, therefore, a form of indirect participation in production. Through the work that is realized in the home and other outside sources, the woman facilitates reproduction of the labor power of her *compañero*, which would not have been possible if the sole source of income was the salary that the worker receives. In this way, the woman is the object of the exploitation to which the worker is subjected, since it is her work that permits the mine owners to obtain more surplus value by paying less to the mine worker. (5) And still there is more: the situation of the women is such that after her husband retires from the company, often she must take charge not only of her prior responsibilities but also assume support of her children and her husband, whose working life was ended by the mine disease, silicosis.

The struggle for liberation of the mine women has to be thought about and organized starting from the previously mentioned elements of exploitation and oppression. In the first place, it is a struggle of classes. The mining women cannot imagine a women's movement separate from the popular movement and the struggle of the organized working class; she also cannot conceive of a movement that encompasses all women solely beginning from their "condition" as females. There is not equality among women solely because of the fact of being women. The interests of bourgeois women are antagonistic to those of proletarian women. And petty-bourgeois women who want to become part of the liberation struggle must guide their participation in the direction of the interests of the working class rather than starting from their own class interests.

Because of its class nature, the struggle of the mining women is distinct from the bourgeois feminist struggle which places the emphasis on the oppression of women as a result of the position of men and thus sees women's liberation starting from the relations between the sexes. What the mining woman pursues, as fundamental to every other change, is a change in the existing relations of production in the capitalist system. In fact, capitalism offers no alternative for men and women of the exploited and oppressed classes, while socialism creates the material conditions that can be favorable to the struggle of women, as women. Certainly socialism does not automatically bring women's liberation. The countries in transition to socialism illustrate this well in that they have not yet resolved many of the problems that affect women.

All of this leads us to the following. In our dependent countries of Latin America, we cannot become part of, predominantly, a struggle of "class against class." If women want to create the conditions that will permit them to benefit themselves—as women—from the process of liberation of our people, it is essential that we simultaneously approach the problem of "class and sex" from within a dialectical analysis of Latin American reality.

NOTE

This paper was originally presented at a workshop organized by the Institute of Development Studies in Sussex, England, September 19–23, 1978.

The Mother of the Nicaraguans: Doña Violeta and the UNO's Gender Agenda

Karen Kampwirth

[Doña Violeta] is not a political woman, better yet she's the symbol of the woman that the country needs. . . . She's the figure of a frail woman but at the same time [one] with the decision to maintain the unity of her family in spite of multiple problems and who even wants to maintain the unity of her people. . . . They say she is the Mom of all Nicaraguans.

—Ninoska Robles de Jarquín,
Nicaraguan Institute for Research on Women

Clothed in unsoiled white, arms outstretched to embrace her family, the Nicaraguan family, Violeta Barrios de Chamorro campaigned for president. She projected an image of herself as the mother of her country. Though a presidential candidate and a public figure, she was presented as symbolic of the private woman, the traditional mother. Doña Violeta promised that, just as she had reconciled her own politically torn family, she would reconcile the Nicaraguan people, torn by more than a decade of war.

Violeta Chamorro won the presidential election of 1990 with 54.7 percent of the vote (*Barricada Internacional*, 1990: 6). The symbolism of that campaign foreshadowed antifeminist[1] policies that have been put into place in a number of areas including education, day care, and macroeconomic policy. Yet despite her political successes, Doña Violeta's vision of proper family relations has not come to dominate Nicaraguan life. Gender in Nicaragua remains contested, though that, in and of itself, is a rather uninteresting observation. After all, where is it that gender relations are *not* contested? What is interesting in Nicaragua is the how and why of the contest. In Nicaragua, debates over gender take place with reference to the

This chapter first appeared in *Latin American Perspectives* 88, 23:1 (Winter 1996), pp. 67–86.

revolutionary mobilization[2] of the 1980s: rejecting it, embracing it, or, most often, in ambivalent relation to it.

Although the revolutionary project lost at the polls in 1990, it won within certain facets of civil society. By the end of 1992, women's organizations were at an all-time-high level of mobilization. The antifeminism of electoral symbols and state policies has been met by the feminism of the women's movement and by the laissez-faire conservatism of some representatives to the National Assembly from the *Unión Nacional Opositora* (UNO), the coalition that Doña Violeta represents.

This essay will explore debates over Nicaraguan gender relations from the 1990 election through the end of 1992. In focusing on the gendered content of political debates I am not suggesting that class issues are unimportant. These debates have a clear class content; indeed, economic policy is often at the forefront. Yet even policies such as structural adjustment that, on the surface, may seem to be exclusively about class have clear implications for gender relations (e.g., Benería and Feldman, 1992; Brenes et al., 1991: 208–232). In the case of other policies, such as those regulating education or sexuality, gender relations are clearly a prime concern, and the class issues, while still present, are more subtle (Lancaster, 1992; Leiner, 1994; Stromquist, 1992). In short, class and gender both matter in contemporary Nicaraguan politics. Unexpected political alliances sometimes form around common interests regarding gender, despite profound disagreements regarding class. After considering Chamorro and the gender agenda of the executive branch, I will analyze these alliances in the Nicaraguan case, building on the work of Rebecca Klatch (1987) and Sonia Alvarez (1990).

MOTHER ON THE CAMPAIGN TRAIL

Ever since President Chamorro[3] was candidate Chamorro, the image of the traditional mother, untainted by political experience, has been clear. The symbol of traditional womanhood is a multifaceted one. Principally, the facets involved here were (1) loyal wife and widow, (2) reconciling mother, and (3) Virgin Mary.

Doña Violeta's widowhood—specifically, her being the widow of one of the most important political figures in recent Nicaraguan history—made her an ideal candidate. Pedro Joaquín Chamorro was an outspoken opponent of the Somoza dynasty for decades in his capacity as editor of the daily newspaper *La Prensa* and in various political intrigues. His assassination in January 1978 set off general strikes that, in turn, set off several periods of popular insurrection. Riding the insurrectionary wave, the *Frente Sandinista de Liberación Nacional* (Sandinista National Liberation Front—FSLN) took control of the country on July 19 of the following year. Doña Violeta became a member of the original ruling junta, in her capacity as the widow of the martyred Pedro Joaquín, but she resigned within a year as it became clear that the revolutionary agenda went far beyond the overthrow of Somoza. Subsequent years were spent attacking the Sandinistas from the offices of La Prensa. Then, in the fall of 1989, she was once again asked to enter politics as the representative of Pedro Joaquín.

Doña Violeta did not miss an opportunity while campaigning to remind the public that she was the widow of this heroic figure. For instance, in a rally in Granada, the traditional center of the Conservative party and hometown of Pedro Joaquín, she told the crowd: "I love this city because it was the city of Pedro Joaquín and of his parents. From Pedro Joaquín I learned to know his values, and I never thought that I would return to Granada as a candidate, carrying Pedro Joaquín's bloodied flag" (La Prensa, 1990b).

During the campaign, emphasis was placed not only on the fact that she was the widow of Pedro Joaquín but also on the type of wife she had been. As Doña Violeta made clear, she was a good traditional wife. In an interview early in the campaign, she told a reporter, " 'I am not a feminist nor do I wish to be one. I am a woman dedicated to my home, as Pedro taught me.' Later she would claim 'to be marked with the branding iron of the Chamorros'" (Cuadra, 1990).

Doña Violeta presented herself not only as an exemplary wife and widow but also as an exemplary mother who had managed to keep her children united against the odds. Admittedly, those odds were considerable. Violeta has four children, two of them opposed to the revolution as she is and the other two fervent Sandinistas. All four have been actively involved in politics (see Christian, 1986; Edmisten, 1990; Heyck, 1990; Marquis, 1990; Larmer, 1990). Given their difference in political perspectives and their activism, it would not be surprising if they did not speak to each other, but that is not the case. The family's good relations are well known, and La Prensa made an effort to inform any who might be unaware of Doña Violeta's reconciliatory skills. For example, the caption of a page 1 photograph (January 4, 1990) points out that Doña Violeta was accompanied on a plane trip by her children Pedro Joaquín and Cristiana and seen off by her son Carlos Fernando.

Maternal love had triumphed over political divisions, and if it could work for Doña Violeta's immediate family, why not for the whole Nicaraguan family? Both messages—the reunification of individual families and the reunification of the national family—were present in the campaign not just at the level of symbols but also at the level of explicit policy. In a "New Year's Message" Doña Violeta said, "[In 1990] the Nicaraguan family will return to reunite with joy. In 1990 the people are going to choose our moral option, and there will not be any more war or misery or hate because we will all be brothers" (La Prensa, 1990a).

Consistent with the first two facets of the Doña Violeta symbol, those of loyal wife/widow and reconciling mother, was a third facet: that of the Virgin Mary. Throughout Doña Violeta's presidential campaign she was photographed in white. White is a symbol of purity, in this case of her freedom from the taint of politics. Many have suggested (e.g., *Envío*, 1991: 30; Mirna Cunningham, interview, April 9, 1991; Hazel Fonseca, interview, June 10, 1991) that she was trying to portray herself as the Virgin Mary. As National Assembly Representative Mirna Cunningham put it, "She was used in the elections, making herself ridiculous, dressing up like the Virgin Mary."

The Virgin Mary symbol is a powerful one in a predominantly Catholic country like Nicaragua. As Maurice Hamington has noted, "the phenomenon of the devotion to Mary in Catholicism rivals the attention focused on Jesus or even God" (1991: 1). Doña Violeta played on the Virgin Mary symbol in a number of ways beyond her choice of white clothing. Like the Virgin, who suffered the murder of her son, she had suffered the murder of her husband. Whereas the Virgin was the mother of a martyred savior, Doña Violeta was the widow of such a savior. Hamington identifies three other aspects of the Virgin Mary that Doña Violeta, to a degree, appropriated in her campaign. The Virgin Mary is compliant, impotent, and asexual (1991: 10–13). Like the Virgin, who always complied with the will of God and Jesus, Doña Violeta portrayed herself as compliant to her husband's will. Secondly, like the Virgin, who could only plead the case of humans before God the Father, Doña Violeta was unable to act without male direction. As she explained, Pedro Joaquín had even taught her how to be a "woman of the house." And though—unlike the Virgin Mary—Doña Violeta did not claim to have immaculately conceived her four children, part of the loyal-widow image is an assumption that she has been celibate since Pedro Joaquín's death.

Probably the most important element of the Virgin Mary image is that it provides an alternative to the most radical Sandinista image of womanhood, that of the woman guerrilla. Doña Violeta made it clear that she was not a guerrilla or even knowledgeable about politics and precisely *because* of that distance from politics she would be able to end the contra war. What normally would be a liability for a politician—lack of political experience—was presented as an asset. But this may have been more than just an electoral tactic. Long after she took office, Doña Violeta continued to be presented in such apolitical terms by the Chamorro family's own newspaper. In honor of the anniversary of her first year in office, *La Prensa* (1991) proclaimed on page 1 that Doña Violeta was "neither a guerrilla, nor aggressive, [but] a woman of the house."

The appeal to traditional womanhood resonated for many women, especially older women with draft-age children, who identified with the Nicaraguan stereotype of traditional womanhood: "an ideal of elevated motherhood . . .

[which] elevates planning over risk, self-abnegation over self-promotion, domesticity over worldliness" (Lancaster, 1992: 93). There were no exit polls, but polls conducted before the election suggest that older people, especially older women, were disproportionately represented in the 54.7 percent of the electorate that voted for Doña Violeta.[4] For example, a *Univisión* poll conducted in October 1989 showed that older voters (over 35 years old) favored Chamorro over Ortega 41 percent to 33 percent, while younger voters favored Ortega over Chamorro 44 percent to 37 percent (1989: 2). In a poll conducted in January 1990, Greenberg-Lake found that 61 percent of young men (between 16 and 24 years old) and 63 percent of young women thought that Daniel Ortega deserved reelection; only 42 percent of older men (over age 40) and 41 percent of older women agreed. These findings suggest that the division was not simply between men and women but between those who supported the old hierarchical model of family relations (generally older people) and those who benefited under the new, more democratic model (young people and especially young women).[5] With the election of Doña Violeta, traditional family values won this battle in the war between alternative models of family politics.

MOTHER BECOMES PRESIDENT

I have described Doña Violeta alternatively as a symbol of wife, widow, mother, and Virgin. All the facets of the symbol are characterized by subservience to males—a subservience that, in theory at least, is rewarded with respect and security. The symbol implies that women are basically incompetent, except within their traditional roles.

Although symbolism can hardly be divorced from politics, the import of Doña Violeta's gender agenda is not merely symbolic. The gender agenda suggested by the symbolism of the electoral campaign now manifests itself as policy (I am not arguing that the symbolism of the campaign caused the policies that followed, but the two are consistent). In particular, three policies that have emerged from the executive branch—education, day care, and "economic conversion"—have already had important effects upon gender relations. Many women, especially poor women, are seeing the gender gains of the past decade eroded away.[6]

One of the first tasks of Doña Violeta's administration was to reshape education. New textbooks, in a series called "Morals and Civics," were published soon after the UNO took office, financed with US$15 million from the United States Agency for International Development (USAID). In order to reinculcate proper family values at every grade level, these texts present images and discussions of correct gender and generational relations. Happy mothers are pictured cooking or scrubbing in their middle-class kitchens; happy fathers are pictured sitting in overstuffed chairs or engaged in paid employment. The texts emphasize the value of legal marriage, the only form of marriage recognized by the UNO (though the 1987 constitution recognizes both common-law and legal marriage), as well as the evils of abortion (which remains illegal in Nicaragua).

These gendered messages were not accidental. Rather, they were a conscious effort to reinstate traditional gender relations. As Elida Solórzano, adviser to the minister of education, explained, "Education [under the Sandinistas] was devoid of a lot of traditional family values that Nicaragua had known under the Somozas . . . Christian values were lost" (interview, January 31, 1991). The author of the new texts explained to me that their purpose was to recapture the family values of Somoza's time (César Escobar, interview, April 17, 1991). The sixth-grade text illustrates these traditional values through a nine-page-long discussion of the Ten Commandments, in apparent violation of the laws of the secular Republic of Nicaragua. Ministry of Education officials deny that such discussions can be seen as an attempt to substitute Catholic education for lay education. They acknowledge that such a substitution would be a violation of the constitution but insist that instead their goals are for the "educational system to be open to values of Christian inspiration" (Ministerio de Educación, 1990: 13).

A second area of gendered policy is social services. In contrast to Ministry of Education functionaries, who proudly proclaimed their desire to eliminate all vestiges of Sandinismo in education, most officials from the Instituto Nicaragüense de Seguridad Social y Bienestar (Nicaraguan Institute of Social Security and Welfare—INSSBI) refused to give me any information on cuts in services. For instance, the director of the Centros de Desarrollo Infantil (Child Development Centers—CDIs) for Region 3 (mainly Managua) denied that any of the ten CDIs in the region had been closed and claimed that the information on the other regions that she had was incomplete and therefore could not be shared with me (Livia Chévez, interview, June 27, 1991). Despite denials, it is widely believed that INSSBI has cut services.

A third manifestation of the changes brought about by the revolution that disturbs many UNO supporters is female employment. The massive entrance of women into the paid workforce is a trend with roots that go well beyond state policy but one that the previous administration did encourage. To the extent that it can, the current administration acts to curtail this trend. After all, the UNO ran on a platform of motherhood, and good mothers, like Doña Violeta, should be dedicated to their homes. Still, straightforward elimination of jobs would be unpopular, so the UNO softened the blow through a "plan for economic conversion." The plan was designed to encourage members of the state bureaucracy to quit their jobs in exchange for a cash payment of up

Women mobilizing to protest reversal of Sandinista land reforms, Managua, Nicaragua, 1991. *Photo courtesy of Cynthia Chavez Metoyer*

to US$2,000. Theoretically, these former state workers would then invest their cash payments in small businesses of their own. Given a disastrous economy, in which approximately 60 percent of the economically active population is unemployed (*Noticiero Univisión*, May 12, 1993), few believed that many of those businesses could survive, but the plan served other purposes besides improving the living standards of state workers.

Implemented with the encouragement of the U.S. government[7] and international lending agencies, the plan has one stated purpose and two important unstated consequences. The stated purpose is to reduce the size of the state bureaucracy. The two consequences may have been planned, but I will give the designers the benefit of the doubt and assume that they were unforeseen. Both are, however, consistent with the traditionally gendered symbolism of Doña Violeta's electoral campaign. In other words, from the perspective of the executive branch, these consequences can be seen as unintended benefits. One of these is a reduction in the number of Sandinistas in the bureaucracy, and the other is the return of women to their traditional roles as housewives. As Fatima Reyes, national director of the agency in charge of the plan, explained, "Of course [the plan] is going to impact quite a bit on family life. Before, women had to leave their children to work." Her figures showed that women took advantage of the plan in disproportionate numbers. This allows them to "return to their homes and take care of their children" (interview, July 18, 1991).

WILL ANTIFEMINISM TRIUMPH?

The state policies I have described, emerging out of the executive branch, are all tinted with antifeminism. But this does not mean that they will succeed unconditionally or that all sectors of the state controlled by the UNO coalition are antifeminist.

Although it is beyond the scope of this article, it is important to recognize that for every antifeminist act of the executive, the women's movement grows increasingly feminist and diverse.[8] Through participating in public debates and offering services (many of which used to be offered by the state when it was controlled by the FSLN), the movement actively challenges the model of gender relations represented by Doña Violeta. The women's movement is one of the most important legacies of the revolutionary period and an important check on the executive branch.

Within the state[9] itself there are tensions. That the state is divided is not surprising; elsewhere in the region the state has often been divided over gender policy. In her analysis of the Brazilian state in the transition to democracy, Sonia Alvarez (1990) points to distinct gender policies within parts of the same state. She concludes that while the state can generally be counted upon to uphold male power and privilege, there are "weak points" in the state (seen from the perspective of patriarchy) or what she calls "opportunity spaces" (seen from the perspective of feminism). Divisions within the UNO, I will argue, present a potential opportunity space for feminists. A comparison of the policies made by one particular space within the legislative branch, the National Assembly's Commission on Women,[10] with the executive-branch policies that I have just discussed illustrates these tensions within the Nicaraguan state.

First, however, it may be useful to recognize another cleavage in the UNO that roughly coincides with the division between these two branches of the state, one between what Rebecca Klatch (1987) calls social conservatives and laissez-faire conservatives. Klatch's arguments about political divisions in the United States can help illuminate Nicaraguan politics. As she argues, while both political positions are right-wing, they have different implications for gender and class politics.

Adherents of the social conservative model such as Doña Violeta, who originated in Nicaragua's Catholic landed aristocracy, tend to promote ascribed roles for women (and men). The images of traditional womanhood projected in her electoral campaign illustrate these gender roles. As Klatch argues, "social conservatives envision gender as a divinely oriented ordering in which men have natural authority over women. Women's roles are essentially defined in terms of support for men and a general orientation toward others" (1987: 9). In contrast, Klatch writes, notions of men's natural authority over women "are antithetical to the laissez faire conservative world view. Like many femi-nists, laissez-faire conservative women believe there are few natural differences between the sexes" (1987: 9). In terms of gender policies, then, these women tend to be to the left of the social conservatives. The same profound individ-ualism that pushes them to the left of the social conservatives on gender poli-cies, however, pushes them to the right of the social conservatives in terms of class. Unlike the social conservatives in the executive branch, who have cho-sen to ally themselves with moderate Sandinistas around economic policies, the laissez-faire conservatives seek to overturn all vestiges of Sandinista-era economic policies. Policies that were legitimated in terms of group rights (such as the rights of all peasants to land or the rights of all poor people to health care) run counter to the laissez-faire ideology that grants rights only to indi-viduals. Many female UNO representatives in the National Assembly sub-scribe to these laissez-faire views.

The division within the UNO between social conservatives and laissez-faire conservatives creates the potential for alliances between laissez-faire conser-vatives in the National Assembly and left-wing activists from the women's movement. One example of such an alliance was around legislation intro-duced on June 5, 1991, to enforce paternal child support. When the legisla-tion was initially proposed, many UNO representatives to the National As-sembly waxed eloquent about the need for it after a decade of what they regarded as attacks on the family by the Sandinistas. This was ironic in that the child-support bill had originally been introduced by the Sandinista ad-ministration.[11] Its passage was delayed for many months, reportedly because of pressures from the religious hierarchy which is allied with the social con-servatives in the executive branch (Cuadra, 1991: 13). There were, however, countervailing pressures from laissez-faire conservatives within the National Assembly, in alliance with the Sandinistas. For example, UNO Representative Adilia Sirias expressed her frustration that, six months after its introduction, the bill had not been sent to the commission but had been "misplaced." Sirias explained that "she [was] willing to defend, together with her Sandinista col-leagues, 'the rights of the women that voted for us'" (Cuadra, 1991: 13). The bill was finally approved and became law on June 11, 1992. The successful al-liance of women despite partisan affiliation would seem to confirm the words of UNO Representative Luisa del Carmen Larrios: "Independent of partisan stripe, our problems [as women] are the same, the cultural patterns are the same" (interview, October 5, 1992). Yet this alliance is fragile.

Another recent law points to the potential limits of the Commission on Women in addressing issues of gender relations and sexuality. In the spring of 1992 the commission proposed a revision of sex-crime legislation. It consid-ered this necessary because the 1974 penal code, which was still in effect with only minor changes, was itself very similar to the 1879 criminal code. The 19th-century logic that still defined rape in Nicaragua "reflect[ed] neither modern reform movements nor the changes brought to Nicaragua by the revolution" (Stephens, 1990: 75). Rape was defined very narrowly: only women could be raped, and vaginal penetration was required.

The first step in the process of revising the penal code was a draft bill signed by 12 Sandinista representatives, both women and men, and 5 female representatives from the UNO. This draft, the only one that was considered, called for broadening the definition of rape and strengthening its penalties. The two provisions of the draft that were to become controversial were proposals to eliminate the antisodomy provision of the 1974 code and to depenalize abortion in the case of rape (leaving abortion illegal in all other cases [*Proyecto de Ley de Reformas al Codigo Penal*, unpublished, Managua, 1992:4]).

Originally, the proposal to eliminate the antigay language was not controversial. Sandinista Representative Doris Tijerino explained that "effectively it [sodomy] was not the subject of consultation either in the discussions or in the [formal] consultations. In this law the people paid more attention to sexual crimes. I was very surprised [when the antisodomy provisions appeared in the final version]" (interview, October 27, 1992). The final version of the sex-crime law included Article 204, which read: "The crime of sodomy is committed by anyone who induces, promotes, propagandizes, or practices copulation with people of the same sex in a scandalous form. It will be penalized with one to three years' imprisonment."

In other words, the proposal to eliminate the antisodomy provision of the penal code was acceptable to most who were consulted, but in the final version of the law the National Assembly[12] did just the opposite: instead of eliminating the antisodomy language it strengthened it. The 1974 version penalized only sexual conduct; the 1990 version penalized both conduct and speech that might be construed as promoting such conduct.

The final version of the law, which was voted upon by the National Assembly on June 5, 1992, contained two controversial provisions: Article 204 and Article 208, which denied raped women the right to an abortion but did give them the right to collect child support from the rapists. Both were rejected unanimously by the FSLN and supported nearly unanimously by the UNO. Both articles passed. The most common explanation for this offered by members of the Commission on Women was that women were a small minority in the Assembly (holding 15 out of 92 seats), but in fact the lines that divided the final vote were not those of gender or sexual orientation but those of party.

It is not entirely clear why the coalition built around gender interests (laissez-faire conservatives in alliance with Sandinista feminists) held together to pass the child-support law but crumbled in the face of antigay Article 204. In part, it is probably a matter of simple vote counting: while the child-support law, if implemented, would benefit the majority of Nicaraguans, Article 204 would hurt only a small minority. This is also a case in which the influence of grass-roots organizing is evident. Women's groups have organized in favor of some sort of child-support law for years, while Article 204 caught many of the newly formed gay and lesbian rights groups by surprise. Ironically, the passage of Article 204 has had the unintended effect (from the perspective of the social conservatives who supported it) of mobilizing gays and lesbians and placing gay and lesbian rights on the agenda of many women's groups[13] (see Lancaster, 1992: 235–278; Randall, 1994: 265–285).

In addition to the partisan considerations that may have motivated UNO representatives there was a religious motivation. Leading up to the vote there was strong pressure from the Catholic church, especially Archbishop Miguel Obando y Bravo. There is reason to believe that the church strongly influenced Doña Violeta. After the National Assembly approved the sex-crime law, the president had 30 days either to veto the articles or to sign them. During this time, a public debate took place in the press. One contributor to the debate was Antonio Lacayo, minister to the president. When he came out against Article 204, many thought that Doña Violeta would be sure to veto it, since he typically enjoys tremendous influence with the president. Lacayo stated, "In any society, even in Italy, where the Vatican is located, homosexuals enjoy certain rights, and we do not see why we are to persecute them" (La Prensa, 1992). But his lukewarm defense of gay rights was not to sway the president. A few days later, during Sunday mass, Archbishop Obando y Bravo announced that homosexual practices were "immoral" and that "every sensible and responsible Christian should be in agreement with Article 205"[14] (Barricada, 1992). This was just one element of his campaign in favor of 204, a campaign that most likely was carried out in private as well as in public: Obando y Bravo is very close to the president and often at her side during public events. Once Obando had spoken, Doña Violeta had little choice. As one of the activists in the struggle against 204 and 208 noted, "The presidency could not veto when there was a great campaign from the cardinal. The cardinal appeared on television and practically told the president, 'Either approve this law or break with the church'" (Silvia Carrazco, interview, October 3, 1992).

The sex-crime bill was signed into law by Doña Violeta on July 8, 1992. It was published on October 31 but backdated to early September, which reduced the time available to submit a legal challenge from 60 to 9 days. Nonetheless, the women's movement, in coalition with a number of other groups, managed to submit a 20-page challenge (arguing that Article 204 violates more than 20 articles of the 1987 constitution). A year later, the Supreme Court ruled that Article 204 is constitutional.

The passage of Articles 204 and 208 indicates that the Commission on Women is only a limited "opportunity space." However, it remains important within the wider frame of feminist politics in Nicaragua. Once again, Sonia Alvarez's work can illuminate. She argues that, in Brazil, the limited attention given by political parties to radical gender appeals stems, in large part, from their lack of electoral appeal. For feminist action to be effective, she suggests, activists must pursue a multifaceted strategy, not just focusing on political parties and the state but simultaneously promoting progressive gender consciousness and mobilizing grass-roots constituencies (1990: 269).

Since about 1988, the women's movement in Nicaragua has been in a process of diversifying, expanding, and becoming more radical. Part of that new radicalism (in the case of some branches of the movement) includes vocal support for gay rights. Perhaps the inclusion of gay rights on the women's movement's agenda influenced the FSLN's unanimous vote against 204.[15] No doubt that vote was also (perhaps mainly) because they believed that 204 is unconstitutional.

Other contested gender issues illustrate Alvarez's argument regarding the importance of organized pressure from civil society. For example, Representative Mirna Cunningham argued that until the grass-roots organizes around abortion, there is no chance for its legalization. In 1991 she argued that other feminist demands, such as stricter legislation prohibiting domestic violence, had a better chance of being passed by the National Assembly than the legalization of abortion because of greater grass-roots support and mobilization (interview, April 9, 1991). In 1992, such legislation passed.[16]

To an important degree, the Commission on Women in the National Assembly is a feminist access point under an antifeminist government. Not only do feminists lack access to the Chamorro administration, but Doña Violeta's symbolism and policies place powerful constraints on the women's movement. The administration just might succeed in dismantling many of the feminist gains of the Sandinista period. But the words of Sonia Alvarez and Mirna Cunningham point to different possible outcomes. There is a potential for feminist gains by the Commission on Women if it allies itself with grass-roots organizations, especially the women's movement. Although the constraints imposed by the administration are powerful, they are not all-powerful. The existence of coalitions between UNO and Sandinista feminists in the National Assembly and the growth of the women's movement in the 1990s suggest that gender relations in Nicaragua, notwithstanding the influence of Doña Violeta, remain contested.

NOTES

1. By "antifeminism" I mean organizing that rhetorically responds to and practically attacks feminism. This concept builds upon the work of Sonia Alvarez, who argues that there are two basic ways in which gender becomes politicized—feminine organizing and feminist organizing. Feminine organizing "grows out of and accepts prevailing female roles and asserts rights on the basis of those roles," whereas feminist organizing "seeks to transform the roles society assigns to women, challenges existing gender power arrangements, and claims women's rights to personal autonomy and equality" (1990: 24). In the case of Nicaragua, Alvarez's concepts are most useful when complemented by a third, antifeminism. Antifeminism is not the same as feminine organizing, though both accept power differences between men and women as natural. The difference is that while feminine policies simply reinforce the status quo, antifeminist strategies are employed after a threat to the status quo (in this case, the decade of the Sandinista revolution). The difference is that while feminine policies simply reinforce the status quo, antifeminist strategies are employed after a threat to the status quo (in this case, the decade of the Sandinista revolution).

2. The ways in which women were mobilized under the Sandinistas varied by issue (certain issues, such as sexuality, were touchier than others, such as employment) and over time (early Sandinista policies tended to be more feminist than later ones). There is an extensive literature detailing the Sandinista record regarding women (see Brenes et al., 1991; Chinchilla, 1990; Collinson, 1990; Kampwirth, 1993; Lancaster, 1992; Molyneux, 1986, 1988; Murguialday, 1990; Pérez Alemán, 1990; Pérez Alemán et al., 1989; Randall, 1994, 1992, 1981; Rodríguez, 1990; Ruchwarger, 1989; Stephens, 1988, 1990; Wessel, 1991).

3. I will refer to her as Violeta Chamorro or Doña Violeta, because that is what she calls herself, though, according to the rules of naming in Latin culture, her name is Violeta Barrios de Chamorro, or Violeta Barrios for short. The "mistake" is quite intentional. Since her whole identity as a woman and legitimacy as a president are dependent upon her husband's memory, Doña Violeta prefers to defy the rules of grammar lest anyone forget that she is the widow of Pedro Joaquín Chamorro Cardenal.

4. I say "stated opinions" because the predictions of all the major polls of an FSLN victory were wrong. The polls seem to me to have some value nevertheless, since the generational differences hold between polls. Additionally, a month before the election, older people were more likely than young people to say that they were undecided. Only 9 percent of young men but 24 percent of older women claimed to be undecided. Some of those women might have been unwilling to admit their plans to vote against the revolution within earshot of their Sandinista children (for polling was conducted within the usually crowded homes of informants).

5. In contrasting the old hierarchical model of family relations with the new more democratic model, I am referring to ideal types of family relations, which exist at the level of public imagery of how families should be. These images are powerful precisely because they are linked to all citizens' lived experiences of power dynamics within their own households. Although family relations are often characterized by love and reciprocity, they are also characterized by power struggles and different degrees of inequality or democracy. Theorists writing about a wide range of countries have discussed how struggles to increase or limit the autonomy of women and youth within households have been linked to national political imagery (see Alvarez, 1990; Cohen, 1976; Fox-Genovese, 1991; Hunt, 1984, 1992; Kampwirth, 1993; Mattelart, 1980; Pateman, 1989; Stacey, 1983).

6. Although there is evidence that many of the UNO's policies have directly contributed to this deterioration in status, it is worth noting that, in some sense, this deterioration merely represents a continuation of the trend of the later Sandinista years. It is possible that, had the Sandinistas been reelected, poor women's status would have continued to deteriorate anyway. There is no reason to think that the economy would have improved significantly had the Sandinistas stayed in power (and it might have worsened, since the Sandinistas would not have enjoyed the minimal support from the U.S. government that the UNO has enjoyed). Moreover, as I have noted, the Sandinistas' gender policy tended to get progressively less feminist as their decade in power wore on. This was, I think, a response to fear of any additional divisiveness during the war, concern that feminist demands might cost money, and perhaps a general trend in post-revolutionary or postcolonial regimes toward increasing conservatism after the initial euphoric radicalism produced by the overthrow of the old regime (on this last point, see Fagen, 1986).

7. This "encouragement" might be better called economic coercion. Release of economic aid to the Chamorro administration was tied to many different conditions, one of which was layoffs of public employees. The Central American Historical Institute cites a report from the General Accounting Office permitting the release of US$5 million of this aid only "upon receipt of evidence that a total of 5,000 civilian employees had left the public sector and that total public sector civilian employment had declined by a corresponding number" (CAHI, 1991: 2).

8. This is not to say that the antifeminism of the Chamorro administration will result in a larger or more feminist movement than would have developed if the Sandinistas had won the 1990 elections. First, the increasing feminism and pluralism of the movement dates back to the late Sandinista period; it is not simply a response to the Chamorro administration. Secondly, while a clear opponent may be beneficial for mobilizing a movement, that opponent also may be a real threat. Nicaraguan feminists have far less access to state resources than they did in the 1980s, and many groups have had to disband or cut services. For more on the Nicaraguan women's movement see Kampwirth (1993), Randall (1994, 1992), Weiss (1992), and Furguson (1992).

9. Following Nora Hamilton, I understand the state to be "constituted by the civil and military bureaucracy, or state apparatus, on the one hand, and those having formal control of this apparatus, the government . . . on the other" (Hamilton, 1982: 7). A critical tool for gaining control of this apparatus is legitimacy or legitimation, which "involves not only a justification of the state's own authority but also of the existing social order" (1982: 7). It is here that Doña Violeta's electoral symbolism plays a (not always successful) role in the transformation of the Nicaraguan state.

10. The full name of this commission is the Permanent Commission on Women, Children, Youth, and the Family. Four of its seven seats, including that of the president of the commission, are held by members of the UNO coalition. The other three seats are held by Sandinistas. The members are Azucena Ferrey, Luisa del Carmen Larrios, Magdalena U. de Rodríguez, Leticia Herrera, Fidelina Rojas de Cerda, Doris Tijerino H., and Mirna Cunningham.

11. The law proposed by the Sandinistas was controversial and never approved because it would have required not only paternal economic responsibility but social responsibility as well. It required all members of Nicaraguan families, men as well as women, to carry an equal share of household chores. It was a much more radical proposal than the recent version, which addresses only economic responsibility.

12. I say that the "National Assembly" added it rather than attributing this to an individual representative because no one I interviewed knows who was responsible; the new language was simply inserted without attribution.

13. It is not that gay and lesbian rights had exactly been absent from the agenda of some of the more explicitly feminist groups prior to the fight over Article 204 but rather that the fight pushed the issues to the fore. In the case of some of the more middle-of-the-road women's groups, however, it seems to me that the fight over 204 forced them to take a stand that they had been avoiding. The Asociación de Mujeres Nicaragüenses Luisa Amanda Espinosa (Luisa Amanda Espinosa Association of Nicaraguan Women—AMNLAE), the women's organization that is most closely linked to the Sandinista party, traditionally had an ambivalent attitude toward lesbians—sometimes simply ignoring lesbian rights issues, at other times angrily denying that there might be lesbians within the ranks of AMNLAE. After 204 was passed, I was present at an AMNLAE meeting when the need to defend the rights of gays and lesbians was brought up—something that would have been unlikely to occur earlier. A key factor in this change may have been the activism of AMNLAE's former national director, Doris Tijerino, in the attempt to defeat the article within the Assembly.

14. Article 205 became 204 after an earlier article was dropped.

15. The vote was a surprise to many, as the FSLN has not always been a great defender of gay rights. Roger Lancaster summarized a discussion of the mixed Sandinista record regarding gays (1992: 252–265) by stating that "to say the Sandinistas' record was either exemplary or abhorrent would be to exaggerate the terms of their real engagement with the matter . . . In fairness, one should add that the Sandinista revolution was the first social revolution of the twentieth century not to persecute or scapegoat a sexual minority defined as deviant in its society" (1992: 263; gay rights observers Amy Bank [interview, October 27, 1992], Brick Blandón [interview, October 23, 1992], and Hazel Fonseca [interview, June 10, 1991] all gave me similar accounts of Sandinista ambivalence toward gays).

16. A number of the articles of Law 150 (the law which included the antigay provision) penalize sex crimes within families more harshly than those that occur outside of families. For instance, Article 195 penalizes rape especially harshly if the victim is married to or otherwise related to the rapist. All the sex crimes regulated in Law 150 (with the exception of the "crime" of sodomy) were made public crimes through this legislation. In other words, the state is now required to continue prosecution even if the victim withdraws his or her case (Asamblea Nacional, 1992). This legal reform, making sex crimes within families a public and not a "merely private" offense, is a nice example of a gain by Sandinista feminists in coalition with laissez-faire conservatives, even though the coalition broke apart around other articles within the same bill (representatives are permitted to vote differently on separate articles of the same bill).

REFERENCES

Alvarez, Sonia A.
    1990 Engendering Democracy in Brazil: Women's Movements in Transition Politics. Princeton: Princeton University Press.
Asamblea Nacional
    1992 "Ley no. 150: Ley de reformas al código penal." July 8.

Barricada
1992 "Cardenal apoya Artículo 205: Dice que prácticas homosexuales son inmorales."
June 22.
Barricada Internacional
1990 "Results of the Feb. 25, 1990, elections." March 10.
Benería, Lourdes and Shelley Feldman (eds.)
1992 *Unequal Burden: Economic Crises, Persistent Poverty, and Women's Work.* Boulder,
CO: Westview Press.
Brenes, Ada Julia et al.
1991 *La mujer nicaragüense en los años* 80. Managua: Ediciones Nicarao.
CAHI (Central American Historical Institute)
1991 "U.S. aid to Nicaragua: The first year." May 31.
Chinchilla, Norma Stoltz
1990 "Revolutionary popular feminism in Nicaragua: Articulating class, gender, and
national sovereignty." *Gender and Society* 4(3).
Christian, Shirley
1986 *Nicaragua: Revolution in the Family.* New York: Vintage Books.
Cohen, Abner
1976 *Two Dimensional Man: An Essay on the Anthropology of Power and Symbolism in
Complex Society.* Berkeley: University of California Press.
Collinson, Helen (ed.)
1990 *Women and Revolution in Nicaragua.* London: Zed Books.
Cuadra, Scarlet
1990 "Electorado feminino por la revolución." *Barricada,* January 13.
1991 "No support for child support." *Barricada Internacional,* December.
Edmisten, Patricia Taylor
1990 *Nicaragua Divided: La Prensa and the Chamorro Legacy.* Pensacola: University of
West Florida Press.
Envío
1991 "Women in Nicaragua: The revolution on hold." 10 (June): 30–41.
Fagen, Richard R.
1986 "The politics of transition, " in Richard R. Fagen et al. (eds.), *Transition and De-
velopment: Problems of Third World Socialism.* New York: Monthly Review Press.
Fox-Genovese, Elizabeth
1991 *Feminism without Illusions: A Critique of Individualism.* Chapel Hill: University of
North Carolina Press.
Furguson, Ann
1992 "A new woman, a new power." *Sojourner: A Women's Forum* (September).
Greenberg-Lake
1990 "Results of a poll conducted for Hemisphere Initiative." January.
Hamilton, Nora
1982 *The Limits of State Autonomy: Post-Revolutionary Mexico.* Princeton: Princeton
University Press.
Hamington, Maurice
1991 "The cult of Mary and feminist social agenda: Dual parenting and sexual ac-
ceptance." Paper presented at the conference "Boundaries in Question: Dialogues on
Theories and Practices," University of California, Berkeley, October 4–6.

Heyck, Denis Lynn Daly
1990 *Life Stories of the Nicaraguan Revolution*. New York: Routledge.
Hunt, Lynn
1984 *Politics, Culture, and Class in the French Revolution*. Berkeley: University of California Press.
1992 *The Family Romance of the French Revolution*. Berkeley: University of California Press.
Kampwirth, Karen
1993 "Democratizing the Nicaraguan family: Struggles over the state, households, and civil society." Ph.D. dissertation, University of California, Berkeley.
Klatch, Rebecca E.
1987 *Women of the New Right*. Philadelphia: Temple University Press.
La Prensa
1990a "Mensaje de Año Nuevo de doña Violeta." January 5.
1990b "Violeta: Mis muletas son símbolo de Nicaragua." January 22.
1991 "Doña Violeta, Presidenta: 'La mujer nicaragüense no se doblega.'" April 25.
1992 "Lacayo: Reformas serán revisadas." June 16.
Lancaster, Roger N.
1992 *Life Is Hard: Machismo, Danger, and the Intimacy of Power in Nicaragua*. Berkeley: University of California Press.
Larmer, Brook
1990 "Struggle to rule Nicaragua begins: Hints of dynasty." *Christian Science Monitor*, March 1.
Leiner, Marvin
1994 *Sexual Politics in Cuba: Machismo, Homosexuality, and AIDS*. Boulder, CO: Westview Press.
Marquis, Christopher
1990 "Preocupa a EU 'nepotismo' en Nicaragua: Afirma el nuevo *Herald.*" *Barricada*, December 20.
Mattelart, Michele
1980 "Chile: The feminine version of the coup d'état," in June Nash and Helen Icken Safa (eds.), *Sex and Class in Latin America: Women s Perspectives on Politics, Economics, and the Family in the Third World*. South Hadley, MA: J.F. Bergin.
Ministerio de Educación
1990 "Lineamientos del Ministerio de Educación en el nuevo gobierno de salvación nacional." Managua, July.
Molyneux, Maxine
1986 "Mobilization without emancipation? Women's interests, state, and revolution," in Richard R. Fagen et al. (eds.), *Transition and Development: Problems of Third World Socialism*. New York: Monthly Review Press.
1988 "The politics of abortion in Nicaragua: Revolutionary pragmatism—or feminism in the realm of necessity?" *Feminist Review* 29 (May).
Murguialday, Clara
1990 *Nicaragua, revolución y feminismo (1977–89)*. Madrid: Editorial Revolución.
Pateman, Carole
1989 *The Disorder of Women: Democracy, Feminism, and Political Theory*. Stanford: Stanford University Press.

Pérez Alemán, Paola
1990 Organización, identidad y cambio: Las campesinas en Nicaragua. Managua: Editorial Vanguardia.
Pérez Alemán, Paola et al.
1989 Industria, genero y mujer en Nicaragua. Managua: INIM.
Randall, Margaret
1981 Sandino's Daughters: Testimonies of Nicaraguan Women in Struggle. Toronto: New Star Books.
1992 Gathering Rage: The Failure of 20th-Century Revolutions to Develop a Feminist Agenda. New York: Monthly Review Press.
1994 Sandino's Daughters Revisited: Feminism in Nicaragua. New Brunswick, NJ: Rutgers University Press.
Rodríguez, Ileana
1990 Registradas en la historia: 10 años del quehacer feminista en Nicaragua. Managua: Companic.
Ruchwarger, Gary
1989 Struggling for Survival: Workers, Women, and Class on a Nicaraguan State Farm. Boulder, CO: Westview Press.
Saint-Germain, Michelle A.
1991 "Women in power in Nicaragua: Myth and reality." Paper presented to the convention of the American Political Science Association, August 29–September 1.
Stacey, Judith
1983 Patriarchy and Socialist Revolution in China. Berkeley: University of California Press.
Stephens, Beth
1988 "Changes in the laws governing the parent-child relationship in post-revolutionary Nicaragua." Hastings International and Comparative Law Review 12 (Fall).
1990 " A developing legal system grapples with an ancient problem: Rape in Nicaragua." Women s Rights Law Reporter: A Rutgers Law School Publication 12 (Summer).
Stromquist, Nelly P. (ed.)
1992 Women and Education in Latin America: Knowledge, Power, Change. Boulder, CO: Lynne Rienner.
Univisión
1989 "News release." November 14.
Weiss, Jean
1992 "Celebrating Nicaraguan women's resistance." Sojourner: The Women's Forum (September).
Wessel, Lois
1991 "Reproductive rights in Nicaragua: From the Sandinistas to the government of Violeta Chamorro." Feminist Studies 17 (Fall).

11

Constructing and Negotiating Gender in Women's Police Stations in Brazil

Sara Nelson

In 1985, in a gesture motivated both by progressive politics and political opportunism, the state government of São Paulo, Brazil, inaugurated the country's—indeed, the world's—first of many all-female police stations charged with investigating and prosecuting cases of violence against women. "The ground-breaking recognition of this gender-specific aspect of crime by the state was unprecedented in Brazil and indeed the women's precinct structure is unparalleled anywhere in the world" (Alvarez, 1989: 237). The idea behind its creation was that the traditional institutional response to grievances of violence against women was inadequate and even discriminatory. Police, almost always men, routinely ignored and rarely prosecuted cases of physical and sexual abuse of women and often blamed and harassed the victims. These female police stations or *delegacias de defesa da mulher* (hereafter referred to as DDMs) began in São Paulo as an experimental institutional response to the deficiencies of the regular police stations.

The DDMs represent a great achievement on the part of the Brazilian women's movement, but their location within the civil police engenders many political contradictions. The very existence of a feminist-inspired institution within the coercive arm of the state seems paradoxical, especially considering Brazil's history of military rule and police repression of resistance movements. However, it could also be seen as a *necessary* component of Brazil's transition to a multiparty democratic system. The DDMs are one of many civil initiatives to be implemented since the end of military rule, representing a systematic effort to legitimate the new regime and the position of the leading party

This chapter first appeared in *Latin American Perspectives* 88, 23:1 (Winter 1996), pp. 131–148.

or parties therein. Thus the role of the DDMs in Brazilian society is politically rather ambiguous.

This article is the product of two stints of fieldwork—the first conducted over a ten-week period during the summer of 1992 and the second from September 1994 to September 1995. The data are both quantitative (statistics on type and number of crimes against women and the corresponding rates of police investigation) and qualitative (interviews with police officers, government officials, crime victims, and feminist activists). After briefly describing São Paulo's first and main DDM, I will outline the factors that led to its establishment in 1985. Next I will discuss the status of the DDM system today and the complex political issues embedded in it. I will conclude by presenting what I consider to be the most provocative theoretical implications arising from my analysis. I must emphasize that my investigation into the DDMs' evolution and their present status is not intended as an evaluation of their performance. Rather, it is an attempt to understand the dynamics of converging forces—the liberalizing state and the women's movement in post-authoritarian Brazil—as they are negotiated in an institutional, bureaucratic setting. More specifically, my study will reveal the contradictions that emerge when gender issues are negotiated within the coercive arm of the state.

PORTRAIT OF A DDM

At the time of my first visit in 1992, São Paulo's first DDM was situated in the center of the city adjacent to a regular police station with which it shared police cars and holding cells.[1] The walls were decorated with posters of nature scenes and Catholic icons, and the "lobby" was sparsely furnished with benches and a desk behind which one of the staff sat to greet people and answer the phone. She took the names of women and told them to wait until they could see one of the female police officers (*delegadas*). In the privacy of her office, the officer would hear the victim's account of the incident that had brought her to the station. These details, along with the victim's vital statistics, such as age, occupation, color, level of education, address, and marital status, would be recorded by another employee who was also in attendance.

As I sat waiting for my interview with the head officer (*delegada titular*), Dr. Izilda Aparecida Carvalho Ferreira, I stole glances at the other women in the lobby, some accompanied by small children, relatives, or friends, and tried to imagine their stories. None of them seemed to be in visible physical distress; rather, they looked bored, restless, or weary. Then, just as I was called into Dr. Ferreira's office, a woman staggered up the stairs, leaning on two others, obviously in great pain. I soon found out that she had just been violently raped on the street by a stranger. In order to initiate an investigation, she, like all victims,[2] had to be examined by a doctor at the medical-legal institute, where official injury reports are compiled. This report would serve as the most important piece of evidence in the future trial. Only four such facilities exist in São Paulo, a city of 15 million; the closest one to that DDM was quite far away, and the DDM did not have enough police cars to drive victims there. This woman did not have any bus money, so Ferreira reached into her pocket and gave it to her.

The ambiance of the DDM was otherwise rather cheerful, with much chatting and joking among the staff members. Ferreira informed me that her DDM was the only one in the city open 24 hours a day, seven days a week. All the others observed regular business hours and were closed on weekends. This seemed odd to me, as I would expect most violence to occur late at night on weekends. She told me that most women wait to report crimes of domestic violence until Monday morning when their husbands or lovers are at work and their children are in school or in the care of a friend or relative. During this delay much of the medical evidence of a rape or a beating will have disappeared. Ferreira said that it would be difficult to estimate the number of women who were attended to each week because violence fluctuated widely in accordance with paydays and the various holidays throughout the year. The only reason that this particular DDM had extended hours and a seemingly full staff was that it was the first one and the staff and hours had been expanded to accommodate the public's needs before other DDMs had been created. My first encounter with this enigmatic institution raised more questions for me than it answered, and it is precisely this complexity that renders Brazil's DDMs such a compelling site for anthropological research.

MURDER TRIALS AND SOS-MULHER: THE FIRST STEPS

The establishment of the first DDM in São Paulo in 1985 was the result of a long struggle on the part of various sectors of the women's movement to implement some sort of institutional response to the increasingly visible problem of violence against women. Male-to-female violence and its inadequate redress became a nationally visible, if not sensationalized, issue following two cases of murder that captured public attention between 1979 and 1984. The first case, in 1979, involved Raúl Doca Street, who murdered his lover when she decided to break off their relationship. The court accepted the defense's argument that the crime was motivated by "violent emotion" (*emoção violenta*) due to the unjust provocation by the victim and sentenced Street to a mere 2 years in jail. The decision was appealed in 1980—partly because of the

thousands of protesting women gathered outside the courthouse—and Street
was sentenced to 15 years in prison. The second murder, which occurred in
1981, involved a famous Brazilian singer, Lindomar Castilho, who shot his
wife, Elaine, and her cousin, who Lindomar believed to be her lover. Elaine
died, but her cousin survived. During the pretrial phase, the judge accepted
"violent emotion" as a mitigating factor, but women's rights activists protested
this ruling. When the case was finally brought to trial, the jury rejected the
"violent emotion" defense, and Lindomar was sentenced to 12 years in prison.
These two cases, in addition to similar ones heard in other states, contributed
to galvanizing a national women's movement to protest domestic violence and
the inadequate, often discriminatory response of the Brazilian police and ju-
diciary (Americas Watch, 1991: 9).

The movement emerged against the background of Brazil's military dictatorship and in the context of gradual political liberalization. This process of
opening (abertura) began in the mid-1970s and culminated in the indirect election of a civilian president in 1985 and the creation of the New Brazilian Republic. Reports of sexual abuse, torture, and murder of political prisoners during the dictatorship led to a national debate about violence and the creation
of human rights organizations within the opposition movement, in which
women were very active. At the same time, women were beginning to organize and advance their specific gender interests. It is not possible here to trace
the development of the autonomous women's movement or the pro-
democracy movement. Suffice it to say that the interplay of the two movements enlarged the debate on violence to include many forms of its exercise beyond those employed by the authoritarian state (Pitanguy, 1991: 2). The many
women's groups that emerged during this time began to focus on gender-specific issues such as rape and domestic violence, elevating them from "private,
personal" matters to major public policy concerns (Americas Watch, 1991: 9).

The most active and visible organization was SOS-Mulher, devoted exclusively to combating violence against women. Chapters of SOS-Mulher were
established first in the state of São Paulo in 1980 and soon sprang up in other
states. SOS-Mulher recognized that crimes against women were grossly un-
der-punished and that a woman's access to legal redress was severely limited.
The members of SOS-Mulher were primarily middle-class women educated in
law, social work, or medicine. Their main objective was to provide female victims of violence with emotional support, legal counsel, and assistance in registering these incidents with the police (Gregori, 1992).

The above discussion of the two famous murder trials touches on the discrimination inherent in Brazil's judicial system. In addition to the defense
based on "violent emotion," many defendants in cases of domestic abuse or
homicide were permitted to use the related "defense of honor" (defesa de

honra) which sanctions violence in circumstances of alleged unfaithfulness. Although the honor defense was declared illegitimate by Brazil's highest court in 1991, it continues to be employed in trials that escape media coverage and public oversight. But Brazil's criminal law is only part of the problem. The police officers responsible for registering and investigating the incidents frequently treated the victims with hostility and indifference and failed to instruct the women of their responsibilities for initiating investigation procedures. They neglected, for example, to inform women that they had to *return* to the station to provide formal testimony and the medical examiner's report of their injuries (moreover, many women lacked the time or money to return repeatedly to the station). The SOS-Mulher activists attributed this breach of protocol to the *machista* nature of the police system and society in general. In response to this "culture of impunity" these women volunteered their time in obtaining the necessary services or, if possible, providing the services themselves.

THE WOMEN'S MOVEMENT AND THE BIRTH OF THE WOMEN'S POLICE STATION

In 1983 SOS-Mulher in São Paulo dissolved as a result of internal conflicts and a shortage of material resources (Gregori, 1992), but many of its members continued to fight against gender-specific violence in various other organizational capacities. Meanwhile, the diverse and increasingly influential women's movement acquired leverage during the political ferment associated with the first direct elections for state governments in 1982. Some leaders of the movement—women closely allied with the winning opposition party—gained entry into the new, democratizing state apparatus in the form of an advisory council called the *Conselho Estadual da Condição Feminina* (State Council on the Status of Women—CECF), established in 1983. The CECF consisted of representatives (*conselheiras*) from women's organizations and ten state-level executive departments (education, health, etc.). In principle, its president was nominated by the representatives and approved by the governor. The CECF was, in essence, the movement's reward for its endorsement of the triumphant opposition party, the *Partido Movimento Democrático Brasileira* (Party of the Brazilian Democratic Movement—PMDB). The new state administration, headed by Governor André Franco Montoro, demonstrated its indebtedness to and support of the women's movement by appointing as the CECF's first president Dr. Eva Blay, well known for her feminist politics and scholarly work on gender issues. The CECF was designed to give the women's movement a voice within the state government, but it held no executive power.

Many sectors of the women's movement were, in fact, *against* the creation of the CECF, which they felt compromised the autonomy of the movement and facilitated its co-optation. Many feminists backed more left-wing parties such as the *Partido dos Trabalhadores* (Workers' Party—PT). Others preferred not to be associated with any party at all. Those who supported the PMDB generally viewed traditional arenas of political power (that is, political parties and government ministries) as the most appropriate and expedient means for advancing the movement's interests. These partisan divisions within the movement ultimately fractured its unity. The CECF did indeed become vulnerable to the increasingly conservative political agenda of the subsequent administrations, ultimately compromising the effectiveness with which it could champion women's interests and undermining the militancy of the movement as a whole. This illustrates the extent to which the institutional women's movement (that which is represented by the CECF) is linked to Brazil's political party dynamics, which are rife with opportunism and clientelism.

The first CECF administration prioritized the problem of violence against women and its inadequate institutional response and set up a subcommittee to propose ways of addressing it. In the eyes of the activists, the most viable solution appeared to be installing in a police station in central São Paulo a team of women who would be trained to receive and investigate reports of violence and provide the social services needed by the victims to reconstruct their lives.

The secretary of public security, Michel Terner, however, had an even more ambitious idea: the establishment of a separate police precinct, staffed exclusively by women, that would process incidents of violence against women. I should note here that the civil police in Brazil is administered by the individual states and is distinct from the federal police. Although its structure differs slightly from state to state, the civil police is generally divided into separate departments—narcotics, homicide, etc.—that preside over specific offenses. The specialized structure of the civil police thus facilitated the establishment of yet another division, the DDMs. Like officers of the regular precincts, female officers would be empowered to carry guns and make arrests. The first DDM was to be a pilot project and if successful would be replicated throughout the city and the rest of the state.[3]

The women on the committee were wary of the implications of this proposal and articulated their concerns during the initial planning meetings. Instead of "movement" women's interacting with female victims, the responsibility would fall upon police women. This was potentially problematic because female officers were trained at the same academies as male officers and therefore likely to subscribe to the same gender stereotypes that manifested themselves in the sexist practices and attitudes of the ordinary stations. Likewise, female police officers might refuse to give priority to the needs of women so as not to jeopardize their hard-won position within the police by appearing "soft" or "overly sensitive" in the eyes of their male colleagues.

Consequently, one of the conditions of the proposal stipulated that DDM personnel receive additional special training on issues of gender-specific violence. To this end, an intensive two-day seminar was conducted with the first chief officer, Rosmary Correa, and her team before the opening of the first DDM. According to the coordinator of the CECF's commission on violence, this meeting between members of the women's movement and police personnel dispelled the initial tension and helped establish a positive relationship between the two, as well as opening a channel for future input from the activists. As a result of these formal and informal encounters, Correa, who had had no previous contact with the women's movement or feminist politics, assumed her position adequately informed of the philosophy and goals of the DDM. "When I was chosen to head the first DDM I had been in the police for fifteen years. I was never a feminist, never worked with women's groups, never worked specifically with discrimination or violence against women. I accepted the position because as a professional I had to carry out this mission and carry it out well." After the first discussion sessions with members of the CECF, Correa became "aware of the specific problems women suffer." Now she announces with pride that "if being a feminist means fighting for women's rights, I am this country's biggest feminist."

The first DDM opened in downtown São Paulo on August 8, 1985, drawing attention from around the state and outside the country. Correa became a popular public figure, conveying in media and public appearances profound pride and conviction in her work. She was also in charge of the orientation of new officers and thus reinforced the original goals of the DDMs and the feminist vision and politics upon which they were founded. Their perspective that violence against women derives from women's structurally subordinate position in society departed from the conventional view of the criminal justice system and the public at large that gender-specific violence is simply another form of random (male) aggression.

In September 1989 a special organ called the *Assessoria Especial das DDMs* was created within the civil police to facilitate the administration of the rapidly multiplying DDMs. This was headed initially by Correa, but when she was elected to the state assembly in 1990 the leadership was transferred to Dr. Carlinda de Alemeida, a high-ranking woman officer appointed by the new secretary of public security. In essence, the administration of the DDMs was transferred from the officers and activists involved in the creation of the first DDMs and the informal training of their personnel to a bureaucracy headed by individuals who had never worked in a

DDM or had any ties to the grass-roots movement combating violence against women. The widening gap between the movement and the DDM bureaucracy resulted in the fact that the officers chosen by the police hierarchy to work in the DDMs assumed their positions without any introduction to issues relevant to gender-specific violence beyond the required curriculum in the police academy.[4] In addition, as material resources decreased due to the faltering economy and increasingly conservative state and municipal political agendas, very few subsequent DDMs were equipped with a social worker or psychologist as originally intended,[5] and many were grossly understaffed and lacked police cars, guns, and office supplies.

Nevertheless, the DDM system entered a period of accelerated expansion throughout São Paulo and was even replicated in other states, partly because of the extraordinary degree to which the DDMs had captured the public imagination. Launched with a media blitz and caricatured in a popular evening television series, the first DDM was touted as a triumph for all abused women. Voters began to clamor for DDMs in their neighborhoods. As of February 1995, 126 DDMs are operating in São Paulo state and over 200 throughout the country.

PRESENT STATUS OF THE DDM SYSTEM

Despite the proliferation of the DDMs and the impressive number of women served by them, evaluations of their performance by Brazilian and foreign researchers (Americas Watch, 1991; Pitanguy, 1991; Alvarez, 1990; Hautzinger, 1991) have not been altogether favorable. Indeed, the DDMs are accused of many of the same negligent practices considered commonplace in the male-run stations. One female union activist (who agreed to be interviewed on the condition that her identity be kept confidential) recounted her impressions of a DDM to which she had accompanied a fellow factory worker who wanted to report her involuntary sterilization following a miscarriage:

> She [the officer] didn't seem to care about my friend's suffering at all. At first she refused to take down the report because she said there was nothing the police station could do. When I insisted, she finally listened but made us wait a long time. She kept repeating her questions as though she didn't believe the answers my friend was giving her. She was very cold and business-like. It was as though she'd rather not be bothered.

This indifference is reflected in the very low rate of punishment of violent crimes against women. In the first semester of 1994, of a total of 54,472 registered incidents statewide, only 16,219 (roughly one-third) of these cases resulted in a police investigation and far fewer still in prosecution or conviction. The large majority of reported cases are simply archived and forgotten. In spite of these dismal figures, the academics I interviewed who are familiar with the DDMs[6] warn that judging the performance of the DDMs on the basis of prosecution rates alone is misleading and obscures the more subtle and complex factors that impinge upon their effectiveness. Moreover, this simplistic evaluation unfairly casts them as ineffectual and denies the very real, albeit flawed or truncated, services they provide to thousands of women annually.

It could be argued that the DDMs have been impressively successful in rendering highly visible a social problem that has historically been played down in the media and public discourse. The numbers of women who use the DDMs and the vast increase in reports of violence against women is evidence that the DDMs are effective in sensitizing the population to this issue. One would like to think that this heightened awareness would deter men from resorting to violence, but the low prosecution rate takes the bite out of this threat of punishment. Is this low prosecution rate the result of weaknesses inherent in the criminal justice system itself, such as bureaucratic red tape and overflowing courtrooms? Or is it a manifestation on the part of the women officers of the indifference perceived in males? Or, yet again, does it underscore the conviction of many of the officers that the women victims simply sabotage their own pursuit of justice by refusing, for whatever reason, to comply with the proper procedures?

Jacqueline Pitanguy, a Brazilian scholar and women's rights activist, presents some further difficulties that undercut the potential effectiveness of the DDMs (1991):

> The prestige of [DDMs] inside police structures varies, but, in general they're not given the importance of traditional specialized police stations like Homicides or Drugs. In many cases, police women working at a DDM complain of having difficulties with their professional careers . . . One other problem of [DDMs] has to do with its personnel. Police women also have to learn how to perceive crime in certain violent behaviors. Many of them have relationships with violent men and bring this contradiction to their professional lives. They are also brought up in a society where culture ascribes to men the role of aggressor/protector.

This last point underscores the need for special training courses within the police academy to sensitize both male and female officers to the issues involved in gender-specific violence. The line between acceptable and unacceptable treatment of women remains fuzzy in the minds of police officers. For example, one woman officer, when asked about the punishment of marital rape, replied that the only form of marital rape that is recognized as criminal is rape aggravated by a weapon and visible physical abuse (cuts, bruises, broken limbs). "After all," she continued, "a woman has an obligation to sleep with her husband; if she doesn't want to, her recourse is divorce. If no signs of violence were left, rape by a husband or companion would not be provable."

The DDMs' lack of prestige within the police structure has several ramifications. My interviews revealed that many of the officers had not chosen to work in a DDM, fearing that it would compromise their long-term career goals. Others expressed resentment about the seeming futility of their work: battling a social problem that showed no signs of diminishing and working with female victims who took no personal responsibility for getting out of abusive relationships. Such low morale is bound to be reflected in poor or negligent job performance.

The preceding discussion reinforces my point that the complexity of factors influencing the DDMs' performance precludes simplistic evaluations of their effectiveness. Moreover, I refrain from speculating whether the DDMs currently represent a victorious or a co-opted form of feminist resistance, because such dichotomous characterizations are reductionist and misleading. I am interested instead in tracing the redefinition of this institution throughout the process of its bureaucratization and analyzing how gender identity and feminist politics are negotiated within a governmental arena. Such inquiries address the problematics of identity politics (Fuss, 1989; Escobar and Alvarez, 1992). Can the primarily white, university-educated, middle-class women of the movement that gave rise to the DDMs legitimately claim to represent the majority of Brazilian women? More to the point, are the women police officers—also primarily white and middle-class—equipped to deal with the abuse suffered by (predominantly) poor women of color?

PARADOXES AND CONTRADICTIONS

The capacity of the DDMs to fulfill many of their original objectives is *necessarily* limited by their problematic position within the police bureaucracy—problematic because the DDMs were created in resistance to the very male-dominated criminal justice system in which they themselves are located. In order to exist and proliferate, they must succeed at the basic police duties with which they are charged. Yet they must also, in a sense, fail, or otherwise pose a threat to the legitimacy of the police bureaucracy. That is, they must perform their bureaucratic function while concealing the feminist premises upon which they were founded. Their presence within the police structure must be stripped of its political or ideological (that is, feminist) rationale. The fundamental raison d'être of the DDMs is to compensate for the sexist practices of the male-dominated criminal justice system in which they are located. However, the absence of special training programs to educate officers about issues relevant to gender-specific violence coupled with a lack of social work professionals seriously compromises crucial components of the DDMs' function. Consequently, the sole rationale for the DDMs' existence seems to rest on the essentialist notion that providing a private "women's space" in which to report an incident of violence will facilitate justice.

Feminist critiques of essentialism (Fuss, 1989; Riley, 1988; Butler, 1990; Mohanty, 1991) have questioned the validity of assumed female solidarity based on gender alone in light of the diversity of women's life experiences, mediated by other factors such as race, class, sexuality, age, etc. Indeed, the deconstruction of the unified, undifferentiated category "woman" as a unit of theoretical analysis problematizes feminism's political agenda by questioning the presumed "natural" solidarity among women deriving from their supposedly shared subjugation to patriarchal domination. Chandra Mohanty echoes many feminist theorists when she states: "Sisterhood cannot be assumed on the basis of gender; it must be forged in concrete historical and political practice and analysis" (1991: 58). Likewise, sisterhood cannot be inserted into the Brazilian police system in a sweeping gesture of enlightened public policy. The same critiques levied against feminist representational politics that purport to articulate a stable, unitary subject (Butler, 1990: 5) also apply to the DDMs, which operate according to a logic based on essentialist notions of womanhood.

Reporting a rape or beating to a woman officer in a private office will not ensure that a female victim will receive better treatment at a women's police station than she would at an all-male one. What is crucial is that victims are attended to by officers who are trained to be sensitive to the gender politics inherent in violence against women. In the absence of such training, the DDMs' performance will predictably be unsatisfactory. Indeed, my interviews with DDM personnel suggest that women are no more "naturally" compassionate and responsive to their sisters' needs than men.

Although most of the women activists acknowledged the DDMs' disappointing performance, they stopped short of recognizing how seriously the above factors undermined their foundation. Instead they stressed the important and necessary role still played by the DDMs in Brazilian society in order to lend continued support and legitimacy to the fruit of their struggle. These women blamed the deteriorated relationship between the movement and the administration of the DDM system—caused by an unwillingness on the part of the police hierarchy to interact with movement members—for most of the DDMs' shortcomings.

In sharp contrast, DDM personnel blamed the "perceived" weaknesses of the DDMs on the unrealistic expectations of the feminists who created them.

Illustrative of this position are the opinions of the DDMs' former chief administrator, Dr. Carlinda de Alemeida,[7] who openly expressed her animosity toward the CECF and the women's movement in general.

Alemeida questioned the very legitimacy of the DDM system, contending that it violated the judicial system's anti-discrimination laws by catering only to women. She also resented the burdening of the DDMs with extra, social-service-type responsibilities, which she regarded as superfluous to the police duties with which they were charged. In her view it was the responsibility of the feminists (i.e., the CECF) to educate the women victims instead of insisting on enlightening the police through seminars or additional courses in the police academy. According to Alemeida, the feminists should be educating the women of poor neighborhoods about their rights and how to raise their children properly; it was the mother's failure to educate her children that was at the root of the problem. "If a man is *macho*, who educates the man?" Alemeida's strong views should not be dismissed as merely idiosyncratic. They represented the politics of the police and the greater governmental hierarchy that appointed her. At the same time, they motivated her administrative decisions and the explicit and implicit messages conveyed to her subordinates and thus influenced the character of the DDM system itself.

To rephrase, the feminists acknowledge that the DDMs have been stripped of much of their original power and intent, but they deny that this transformation renders them completely invalid. Concomitantly, the officers and other police personnel deny that the original rationale of the DDMs was to correct the negligent and sexist practices of the traditional criminal justice system in order to preserve the legitimacy of the bureaucracy in which they work. Meanwhile, politicians continue to vie for public support by championing the important role of the DDMs in combating violence against women and ordering their replication.

CONCLUSION

The DDMs are a fertile field for anthropological investigation because they are sites where notions of gender, class, and race are constructed and contested. When Alemeida asserts that "those Northeastern [read poor, black] women deserve to be beaten if they don't leave their husbands because they're too lazy to work," she is not merely reinforcing the classist, racist, and sexist stereotypes endemic to the Brazilian criminal justice system but reformulating these hegemonic state values under the institutional guise of feminist resistance. The DDMs are social spaces that, following Bourdieu (1985), embody a

field of forces, a set of power relations that impose themselves on all who enter it. They have become sites in which a gendered hierarchy is produced that
reconfirms rather than redresses traditional power relations. This is yet another
example reinforcing the views of Laclau and Mouffe (1985), Hall (1985), and
others who reject the determinism of orthodox revolutionary theory. "The in-
determinate, unexpected, unfixed aspect of subjectivity and the politics of
identity is deeply rooted in the post-Marxist understanding of movements"
(Slater, 1994: 17). Just as there are no privileged political subjects (the working class) poised for the unleashing of a socialist political practice, there are
no given feminist subjectivities ready for deployment in the struggle against
gender oppression. The articulations of DDM personnel undermine traditional gender ideology that presupposes officers' "feminine," compassionate,
sensitive subjectivity. As the former head of the Assessoria, Dr. Izilda Ferreira,
wisely said, to be an effective officer, "being a woman is not enough." The politics of political agents—be they feminist activists or police officers—cannot
be assumed on the basis of personal characteristics such as gender, ethnicity,
class, or professional responsibilities.

In terms of praxis, the implications of identity politics can appear either
paralyzing or empowering depending on the contextual specificities. Although
I have sought to avoid judging the effectiveness of the DDMs or their value
as public policy, it is clear from my analysis that after ten years in operation
their role within Brazil's criminal justice system—indeed, their very political
nature—has been transformed through the system's institutionalization and
expansion. This makes them a fascinating case study that underscores the
contradictions that arise when feminist policy agendas are incorporated into
the state apparatus. Feminist theorists and women's rights activists must
weigh the benefits of integrating women's issues into institutional politics in
light of the possibility that such inclusion could result in movement compla-
cency and/or ineffectual public policy. Cross-cultural evidence (Hanmer, Radford, and Stanko, 1989) demonstrates that the police (male *or* female) cannot
effectively treat violence against women as a serious crime without undermining the institutionalized basis for specifically male authority. Thus gender-
based, racially based, and class-based political struggles led by grass-roots
movements can and must take place both within and outside the political apparatus of the state (Alvarez, 1990: 31). And social scientists must strive for
a more nuanced understanding of state and civil relations and the complex
politics of representation entangled therein.

Examining the evolution and present status of the DDM system therefore sheds light on the processes by which notions of gender, race, class, and
sexuality are constructed and negotiated in public policy and discourse.
This comes at a crucial moment in which the analysis and redefinition of

the nature of citizenship—encompassing the political and social rights won during the transition and their legal ramifications—are critical components of the consolidation of Brazil's New Republic.

NOTES

This article is based on research funded by grants from the National Science Foundation, the Wenner-Gren Foundation for Anthropological Research, and the North-South Center of the University of Miami and with the institutional support of the Gender and Social Relations Studies Unit of the University of São Paulo. An earlier version was presented at the 18th International Congress of the Latin American Studies Association in Atlanta, GA, March 10–12, 1994.

1. Two weeks later the facility relocated to a much larger building closer to downtown. Staff and material resources were also expanded.

2. I recognize the political implications of the word "victim," but I use it for the sake of simplicity and brevity.

3. The fact that the idea for and the structure of the DDMs came from the police and not the activists is very significant. It might be argued—and I have no evidence to support such a conspiratorial hypothesis—that the police hierarchy proposed such a structure with the intention of subverting the movement's radical demands by creating an institution that would occupy a marginalized position within the greater police system and would be easily manipulated—financially, for example—and under the direct surveillance and administration of the state.

4. Suggestions by the CECF that a course on gender-specific violence be included in the police academy curriculum were repeatedly rejected by officials within the Secretariat of Public Security.

5. Only ten DDMs in the state of São Paulo have social workers, and only one, the first, has a psychologist. The last governor of São Paulo approved a proposal to put a psychologist in every DDM, but it remains to be seen whether this will be implemented by the new administration.

6. Most of them have also published on the DDMs, among them the current First Lady and anthropologist Ruth Cardoso (1992 taped interview), Danielle Ardaillon (1989), Heleieth Saffioti (1994: 179), Miriam Grossi (1994), and Barbara Soares (1994)

7. These interviews were conducted in 1992. In April 1994, as the result of personnel changes within the civil police hierarchy, Alemeida was transferred, and the current head of the first DDM, Dr. Izilda Ferreira was promoted to the position. Her involvement with the system since its very inception endowed her with a strong loyalty and motivation to invigorate the morale of its personnel and recuperate its public image, and in the first months of her term she initiated sweeping reforms to this end. Sadly, with the change of administration, she was dismissed from her position in February 1995, and her successor, a close friend of Alemeida, has taken command of the Assessoria. It is probable that the reforms commenced or proposed during Ferreira's short term will be disregarded. During her brief tenure, she also reopened channels of communication with members of the CECF (which Alemeida had deliberately shut), facilitating cooperation in the improvement of the system by making possible greater participation by the women activists.

REFERENCES

Alvarez, Sonia
1989 "Politicizing gender and engendering democracy," in Alfred Stepan (ed.). *Democratizing Brazil.* Oxford: Oxford University Press.
1990 *Engendering Democracy in Brazil: Women s Movements in Transition Politics.* Princeton: Princeton University Press.
Americas Watch
1991 *Criminal Injustice: Violence against Women in Brazil.* New York.
Ardaillon, Danielle
1989 "Estado e mulher: Conselhos dos direitos da mulher e delegacias de defesa da mulher." Final report, Fundação Carlos Chargas, São Paulo.
Bourdieu, Pierre
1985 "The social space and the genesis of groups." *Theory and Society* 14: 723–744.
Butler, Judith
1990 *Gender Trouble: Feminism and the Subversion of Identity.* New York: Routledge.
Escobar, Arturo and Sonia Alvarez (eds.)
1992 *The Making of Social Movements in Latin America: Identity, Strategy, and Democracy.* Boulder, CO: Westview Press.
Fuss, Diana
1989 *Essentially Speaking: Feminism, Nature, and Difference.* New York: Routledge.
Gregori, Maria Filomena
1992 *Cenas e queixas: Um estudo sobre mulhers, relações violentas e a prática feminista.* São Paulo: Paz e Terra.
Grossi, Miriam Pillar
1994 "Lutas feministas, violência congugal e novas violências contra as mulheres no Brasil." Paper prepared for the 4th World Conference on the Woman, São Paulo.
Hall, Stuart
1985 "Signification, representation, ideology: Althusser and the post-structuralist debates." *Critical Studies in Mass Communication* 2(2): 91–114.
Hanmer, Jalna, Jill Radford, and Elizabeth Stanko (eds.)
1989 *Women, Policing, and Male Violence: International Perspectives.* New York: Routledge.
Hautzinger, Sarah
1991 "Policing violence against women in Salvador da Bahia, Brazil." Manuscript.
Laclau, Ernesto and Chantal Mouffe
1985 *Hegemony and Socialist Strategy.* London: Verso.
Mohanty, Chandra
1991 "Under Western eyes: Feminist scholarship and colonial discourses," in Chandra Talpade Mohanty et al. (eds.), *Third World Women and the Politics of Feminism.* Bloomington: Indiana University Press.
Pitanguy, Jacqueline
1991 *Violence against Women: Addressing a Global Problem.* Report for the Ford Foundation, New York.
Riley, Denise
1988 *"Am I That Name?" Feminism and the Category of "Women" in History.* Minneapolis: University of Minnesota Press.

Saffioti, Heleieth I. B.
   1994 "Violência de gênero no Brasil contemporâneo," in Heleieth I. B. Saffioti and Monica Munoz-Vargas (eds.), *Mulher brasileira assim*. Rio de Janeiro: Rosa dos Tempos.
Slater, David
   1994 "Power and social movements in the other Occident: Latin America in an international context." *Latin American Perspectives* 21(2):11–37.
Soares, Barbara Musumeci
   1994 "Delegacia de atendimento á mulher: Questão de gênero, número e grau." Paper prepared for the 18th Annual Meeting of ANPOCS.

Reading between the Lines: Women, the State, and Rectification in Cuba

Sheryl L. Lutjens

Because we are not a rich country Cuba will always have a frugal socialism, even as we continue to develop. In the immediate years ahead, as Fidel has correctly said, our women may have to wear the same clothes for five years.

—Carlos Rafael Rodríguez "Cuba's Predicament" (1991)

SOCIALIST WOMEN, SOCIALIST STATE

The Cuban state is at the heart of a reconsideration of women and a socialist strategy for their emancipation, in both theoretical and practical terms. The centralization of power and policy characteristic of the modern socialist state has been identified by many as the source of intractable economic and political problems. For feminists working from a variety of positions, specific indictments include official policies that have little to do with women's interests or potential emancipation and the imposition of policies from on high. Haug, for example, writes that despite a weighty presence in public employment, "nowhere did women achieve decision-making positions in numbers that could sway masculinist cultures; socialisms too, besides being authoritarian administrative structures, were above all patriarchies" (1991: 40–41). Einhorn refers to paternalism and rights "given" by the socialist state "as opposed to won," arguing that the "fundamental contradiction inherent in the paradigm adopted by state-socialist countries lay in a definition of women as workers *and* mothers

---

This chapter first appeared in *Latin American Perspectives* 85, 22:2 (Spring 1995), pp. 100–124.

without any parallel conceptualization of men's role" (1991: 25, 19). Key in such critiques of the socialist state is the perception that women's organizations lack autonomy.[1] As Molyneux (1990: 26) explains:

> Within these authoritarian political systems founded upon centralism and the imposition of orthodoxy, no autonomous women's movement, and no feminist critique of socialist theory and policy, were allowed. Official women's organizations mobilized women in the service of the economic and political goals of the state, in accordance with a narrowly defined set of "questions of everyday life." They did not challenge state policy, or tackle the gender inequalities which survived the substantial social transformations.

The *Federación de Mujeres Cubanas* (Federation of Cuban Women—FMC) and the official positions voiced by its president, Vilma Espín, thus reveal important aspects of the relationship of Cuban women to the socialist state.

Created to bring women into the revolutionary process, the FMC has functioned within the centralization characteristic of the first decade and the institutionalization that followed. The main report of the Second FMC Congress in 1974 explained that the organization's goals were still those of the revolution (FMC, 1975: 141). The party program adopted in 1975 identified the "struggle for the creation of the objective and subjective conditions that permit the full exercise of the equality of women" and authorized the FMC to "organize the great female masses and reflect their interests and worries" (PCC, 1978: 119). Supported by the constitution's definition of mass organizations as representing "specific interests" while fulfilling state functions, the basis was laid in the 1970s for the FMC's increasingly self-conscious efforts to mobilize and represent women. Autonomy was not claimed for or by the FMC, however; centrally defined goals have disciplined its work in the areas of health, education, resource conservation, defense, and women's voluntary and paid labor. The objectives and activities of the FMC in the current period still reflect the overall priorities of the socialist state, while its agenda shows where change has occurred since reforms began in the mid-1980s.

In accepting central goals, the FMC has had certain advantages in its work. It has the backing of the state and state resources, for example; its status as the sole organization of women permits comprehensive planning that is reinforced by the orientation of all mass organizations to national goals. Although structured hierarchically like other mass organizations and presided over since its founding by Vilma Espín, the wife of Raúl Castro, the FMC is far from being a simple or authoritarian "transmission belt."[2] It has not coerced total participation; although it had nearly 3.4 million members in 1989, approximately 17 percent of women chose not to join, and women participate in other organizations (though men do not join the FMC). Some activities that have been vital among the FMC's aims and accomplishments show grassroots initiative, such as the Movement of Militant Mothers for Education, with more than 1.4 million participants in 1990 (Berges, 1990). And according to Evensen's 1986 assessment, the relationship of the FMC to centralized decision making changed after 1975: "the content of Party policy today is derived in large measure from information and proposals made by the FMC" (1986: 304).

The FMC continues to organize women in pursuit of goals determined by the socialist ideology and material conditions of the rectification period. It has shared the official view of equality and the causes and consequences of ongoing inequalities and discrimination, actively rejecting "bourgeois" feminism and the idea of a separate struggle of women. Adequate laws and material supports have been considered essential for achieving equality, while women themselves have been included among those "subjective" factors seen to sustain both public and private discrimination. As Espín explained in a 1985 interview, "Fulana," the average working mother, limits her own possibilities on the job when she sees no solution for the burdens of home and children (1990c: 55). Men and their consciousness are also recognized as part of the subjective constraints on equality; Fulana has a husband, noted Espín, one who has the same number of children as she (1990c: 55). The formal antifeminism of the FMC has been modified with time, however.[3] In 1989 Espín used words that reflect some of the central issues in feminist debates: "Personally, yes, I believe in feminist groups that link the solution of the oppression of women, of the liberation of women, with the liberation of all those who are exploited, oppressed, discriminated against, which means approaching present-day problems, economic as well as social, political, and ideological, through a prism of analysis of classes, sex, and race" (1990c: 215, my translation). The positions of the FMC and Espín still coincide with official priorities. Despite the provocative themes raised in the preparations for the Fifth FMC Congress in March 1990, the congress turned on solidarity with the goals of rectification and the impending fight for survival in the special period that began later that year.

The special period is the backdrop for seeing how official policies and the content of FMC work have together become more feminist. Rectification sustained criticism of the double load of working women created by the caretaking assigned to wives and mothers, for instance, emphasizing men's acceptance of the benefits and burdens of shared obligations in the home and the family. Men have long been asked to participate more in the home, and several studies reported in the documents of the Fifth Congress explain the ongoing concern with domestic inequalities at the end of the 1980s. According to the National Study of the Budgeting of Time, stubborn imbalances in domestic work meant that working women still contributed a much greater share (more than 22 hours each week, compared with nearly 5 hours of work by men [FMC, 1990: 24]). A 1988 study by the FMC found that more than 90 percent of those surveyed believed that men did participate more in household chores, though more than 80 percent saw women as "naturally" better at caring for small children (FMC, 1990: 24–25). The redistribution of domestic responsibilities is not a matter of asking men for help, as Espín explained in 1985 (1990b: 65–66, my translation):

> This is very important: not using "help," because a woman wasn't born with a little card that said: "all the domestic tasks and all the child care are yours." Nature made her different inasmuch as she is the carrier of the child that will be born, nature's workshop where life is forged—as Fidel poetically said. This is her biological function, and breastfeeding joins these functions. But in the rest the father and the mother have a fundamental participation—not only to lighten the double burden of the woman but because the child also needs its father.

According to Espín's speech to the February 1989 meeting of women leaders from socialist countries, achieving equality in the home requires improvement in parent-child relations, the division of labor, and the "attitude of people about the social role that each family member should play, on the basis of equal rights, duties, and opportunities of each and every one of them" (Espín, 1990d: 242, my translation). The needed lightening of women's load is explained in terms of parents and children as well as women and men. It is also explained in terms of women's mental well-being (Espín, 1990e: 253).

A concern with the family is thus evident in the policies of rectification. The official view still offers an ideal of the nuclear family as fundamental to socialism, grounded in the 1975 Family Code and a belief that the family is the site of an "intense fight between old criteria and the sweeping and new revolutionary reality" (FMC, 1990: 34). While an anticipated review of the Family Code by the National Assembly has not yet occurred (see Gómez Treto, 1988), a National Family Group has been created, and the sixteenth national congress of Cuban unions in 1990 gave formal attention to the families of workers for "the first time ever." And by 1992, 40 casas de la mujer (women's houses) had been created throughout the island as new centers for cultural and educational activities, problem solving, and support for women and families (Mujeres 31 [January–March 1992]: 11).

Private life is in other ways important within the rectification process. A concern with the reproductive health of women continues, for example, apparent in the FMC's educational campaign aimed at reducing the number of abortions and in the attention to problems of teen pregnancy and single mothers needing social assistance.[4] The call for improved sexual education in the schools is found among the educational reforms of rectification, while the so-

Casa de la Mujer, Cienfuegos, Cuba, February 1998. *Photo courtesy of Mary Ann E. Steger*

cial and health issues of sexuality inside and outside families have been raised in the press and in policy.[5] Criticism of a sexual morality that permits men what is denied women continues; "our socialist society cannot allow double standards," asserted Espín in her 1986 article on women and equality in Cuba, "in this important aspect of daily life, equal rights and equal obligations should prevail" (n.d.: 41–43). Both traditional preferences and post-revolutionary transformations are apparent in the public agenda, noticeable in the rigorous measures adopted to control HIV and such concerns as parents' role in sexual education in the home. The Federation further demonstrates where adjustments within Cuba's strategy for women reflect the larger aims of rectification. The FMC and other mass organizations were asked to improve their organizational practices and performance, and the especially harsh criticisms of the Federation produced speculation about its demise (see Espín's 1985 justification of its existence, 1990b: 79). Although such problems as the quality of grassroots meetings are not new, the self-criticism emblematic of rectification assumes a new phase in the work of the FMC. Espín's scrutiny of successes and shortcomings on the 30th anniversary of the Federation identified several areas needing attention, including work with young members, with women in bigger cities, and with rural women. As Espín explained, geographical and occupational differences among women had been taken seriously beginning with the Third FMC Congress in 1980; housewives are not the only or the predominant concern, and the FMC must meet the needs of working women in such a way that their participation is "useful" to them. Espín also referred to the overloading of the Federation and its cadres with work and meetings "that have nothing to do with our tasks and programs" (and duplication of efforts among mass organizations) and to the use of voluntary labor to compensate for what are really administrative failings—a problem shared by all mass organizations (Espín, 1990f). As one FMC official explained, the talk of eliminating the Federation prompted serious discussion of what they had done wrong. With all the work of the FMC, why wasn't it noticed by women (Agramonte, 1992)?

The FMC's organizational response included visits by the national leadership to different provinces and extensive base-level meetings and discussion of local FMC activities. More than 1,000 meetings were held in Ciudad de La Habana, for example, and over 4,000 women participated in discussions in Santiago de Cuba (*Mujeres* 30 [February–March 1991]: 2–4 and [June–July 1991]: 2–4). Accounts published in the FMC magazine *Mujeres* noted accomplishments, cited the problems seen by leaders and members, and assessed the process itself in terms of new organizational standards. In Las Tunas province, for instance, more than 47,000 members had participated in agricultural mobilizations, and 96,000 homes had the *parcelas de autoconsumo familiar* (plots for family food production) encouraged in the special period; their problems included the poor articulation of health brigades with local delegations and a lack of knowledge of the leading role the province had taken in resolving the problem of paternal child support (*Mujeres* 30 [October–November 1991]: 2–5). Among the issues raised in Ciudad de La Habana were "cold" and boring meetings, problems in food distribution, delinquents, and early pregnancy and other problems of youth. Commentary on the process stressed that the old, top-down practices were inappropriate; "the key to success in these meetings was that they weren't for giving orientations from above but for an interchange of opinions and views on how to ensure that in each locale the problems affecting local women are treated" (*Mujeres* 30 [February–March 1991]: 2–4, my translation).

An awareness of differences among Cuban women is a formal part of the current efforts of the FMC. In organizational terms, the identification of who the members are and what they do, need, and want is considered mandatory for altering the FMC's style of work. This new process of differentiation, called *caracterización* (characterization), joins the call for open discussion and meetings that facilitate the creative consideration of the problems of women, families, and the community as a whole (*Mujeres* 30 [February–March 1991]: 2–4, [August–September 1991]: 8–10).

While conclusions about the desired grassroots revitalization of the FMC are premature, other modifications associated with the organization and its work confirm that policy and the Federation are both more feminist. Most noticeable, the official study of women has been established in institutions of higher education in a number of provinces, and women's studies was instituted at the University of Havana in 1991. The *casas de la mujer* also offer an intriguing demonstration of official attention to women in the special period. The *casa* in Habana Vieja, for example, was to be a center for women and the family with multiple objectives. According to the announcement in *Granma*, it would be a place for "reflection and debate," though not only about women's issues, also serving as a site for non-formal education with classes in yoga, aerobics, and haircutting; future plans included legal consultations, advice about herbal medicine (a problem-solving measure to cope with shortages), a video room, and classes in modeling and massage (*Granma*, March 5, 1992).

Despite the FMC's lack of organizational autonomy, its official positions and those of Vilma Espín reflect some of the essential concerns of contemporary feminist theory, including a critique of biologism. Charged with both representing the specific interests of women and pursuing the goals of the revolution, it demonstrates some of the less noticed dynamics of a reform process that has defiantly resisted predictions of its failure from both the Right and the Left. If one feminist criticism of the socialist state is that it is not "woman-friendly" (Dölling, 1991), the continued attention of the Cuban state may be a necessary condition for maintaining the achievements of women in a decidedly unfriendly international order. Given the state's concern with the family and personal life and the constraints imposed by intensifying material scarcity, the private sphere holds important clues about the meaning of socialism for women. Indeed, in Cuba there is an official recognition that the special period affects women in distinctive ways. As a recent article in *Bohemia* magazine explains, the special period is changing women's lives, and their attitudes are crucial (Rodríguez Calderón, 1992: 38–40).

REREADING INTERESTS

Instead of drawing predetermined conclusions about the socialist state, centralization, and a missing autonomy, it is possible to view the FMC as an organization that mediates women's relationship to the state. The idea of mediation recognizes a more complex relationship between the organizational arrangements of the public sphere and the realities of home and private life. Gotkowitz and Turits have identified such a relationship with regard to state policies on the family and the private sphere in the previous period of institutionalization: "During . . . the 1970s, there is an essentially equivocal articulation of the domains of private and public in which the two realms are to be equilibrated via the mediation of social workers, official discourse, and the mass organizations" (1988: 14). The notion of mediation requires an understanding of women's interests, however. Important here is Molyneux's differentiation of "women's interests" and "gender interests"—"those that women (or men, for that matter) may develop by virtue of their social positioning through gender attributes" (1986: 283–284). Judgments about what women's *gendered interests* are and about what is or is not in women's interest thus requires a careful reading of cultural context and current conditions.[6]

How women are officially seen in the policies and practices of the state and how they see themselves are two sides of enacting *women* as a social/gender category rather than an economic or biological category stuffed full of preassigned interests. An official recognition that women have different interests is thus at odds with suspicions that the state imposes a single policy for women. That such a recognition is apparent in the formal efforts of the FMC supports an interpretation of its mediating role or function. Yet the circumstances of rectification reveal where conclusions about the socialist state and women confront the dilemmas of *imputing* interests rather than uncovering interests that are reflected and created by women's wide-ranging participation in public life.

The formal awareness of differences among women seen in the official perspective of the FMC is also found in the policies and public discussions characteristic of rectification and the special period. Cuban research, almost always associated with policymaking and problem solving, shows that differences still exist among Cuban women. For instance, rural and urban women differ in terms of a number of indicators, according to a study of 3,302 women in three municipalities in the first part of the 1980s (conducted by the ILO Global Research Project with the aid of the FMC [Catasús et al., 1988]). The study focused on fertility, and findings included differences in employment, the rate of consensual unions, education, and the type of family problems perceived by women. Rates of participation in mass organizations (reported as the assuming of "concrete responsibilities") varied, ranging from 43.8 percent of the urban sample to 31.2 percent of the rural and 47.1 percent of the midrange community, with the largest differences those between the youngest and the oldest women. If the amenities of urban life have been extended deep into rural Cuba, shifting the definition of "urban" and narrowing gaps, distinctions in standard of living or opportunities occasioned by terrain and tradition have not been entirely eliminated. The specificities of women's experiences can also be traced in a recent book surveying 17 years of research on the Cuban family (Reca Moreira et al., 1990).

Lingering and newer differences are associated with the more and less prominent policies of rectification. The decline in the number of women working in Cuba's agricultural cooperatives has prompted a focus on retaining or reincorporating women in line with the emphasis on agricultural production and what is called the food program. The troubling performance of the service sector that exacerbates the distributional difficulties of the special period is recognized, as is the fact that women make up over 60 percent of service workers. In postrevolutionary Cuba, problems are often discussed with reference to cultural level, using the standards of consciousness to replace both color and class in explaining the progress and problems that Cubans see. Yet there are occasionally telling allusions to problems of consciousness particular to socialism and, more recently, to issues of race discrimination. For example, an article about the results of new regulations permitting fathers to accompany children during hospital stays—an FMC victory often cited as an example of its organizational strength—explains that "no father is exonerated from attention to his child, neither the simple worker nor the busiest functionary" (*Granma*, August 18, 1990, my translation), and a 1992 Valentine's Day article in *Bohemia* surveys the "contradictions" of interracial relationships ("Talking about Love," 1992).

Current Cuban policy explicitly and implicitly grants a multiplicity of potential interests of women—as wives, mothers, daughters, workers, students, farmers, consumers, scientists, and sometimes single women, among others. Indeed, multiple and conflicting "identities" of women thrive in the context of rectification, available in a kaleidoscopic array of images that range from women in military uniforms to the dancers in the Tropicana extravaganzas, from the fashions in *Mujeres* to newspaper vignettes celebrating women engaged in traditionally male occupations, from the occasional reference to women whose work in the homes of others remains invisible to the fame of such female athletes as Ana Fidelia Quiroz, and from the newspaper picture of a breastfeeding mother to Castro's comment in his December 1991 speech to the National Assembly that with regard to improving the quality of elected representatives, "it seems that the future belongs to the women, since here during the first speeches there were almost ten straight given by women" (1992a: 3).

Which identities—and interests—are given priority by Cuba's strategy for women? Cuban women still adhere to traditional standards of beauty that have been abetted, not thwarted, by state policy providing hairdressers, manicurists, and fashion shows. At the same time, Medin's (1990: 107) study of ideology in Cuba finds that in Cuban detective fiction women are "presented neither as sex symbols nor characterized by traditional 'feminine' traits of innate fragility or weakness; they appear on equal footing with men, sometimes as an observant neighbor, sometimes as president of a CDR, sometimes as the victim, sometimes as the murderer." Rectification's call for "opening up" the mass media, moreover, invited the advice of the FMC with regard to the representation of women and the family. The television series *La Delegada*, for example, showed a family life "so perfect" that, according to one FMC official, few if any could identify with the *delegada plástica* (plastic delegate): "She had time to attend to her functions as delegate, time to attend to her children, time to attend to her work, to attend to her family, to go out, for everything; it was absolutely perfect" (Berges, 1990). Among the themes in Cuban film, the quandary of the revolutionary woman torn between children, work, politics, and the unfaithful or unsupportive husband is intriguingly repeated even though women are underrepresented as writers and directors. And in the 1989 editorial on the banning of two Soviet publications popular in Cuba, one of the reasons offered was that writers advocated "domestic servitude for women" (*Granma Weekly Review,* August 13, 1989).

There are authentic dilemmas involved in sorting out interests and images, however, some of which are posed in an article on Cuban views of beauty and bodies published in *Allure* (Hanly, 1991). Here, the need to invent cosmetics and the lasting search for fashion amidst the accelerating scarcity of the special period are explained by a woman official in Cuba's world of design: "All through our history we've invented. Otherwise the island would simply fall into the sea. This is a culture of extravagant imagination" (1991: 44). And "What law says a coquette can't be an effective militant?" she asks (1991: 50). Another woman official recognizes what others might see, acknowledging that "our sexuality can seem at odds with our revolutionary ideals." Referring to the women in the Tropicana shows, she is "more concerned about whether a divorced man continues child support than any number of feathers rising from a woman's head. We've all grown up some" (1991: 50). Similar dilemmas were raised by a March 1991 *Playboy* story on Cuba's women; the FMC was "outraged" and considered the incident the result of a "bureaucrat's 'gross misjudgment'" (Murphy et. al., 1991).

The dilemmas of assigning interests are also posed by the proliferation of the underground market in dollars, domestic products diverted from official distribution, and female bodies. Prostitution and other "antisocial" behavior fomented by the tourism strategy for hard currency earnings have been officially—and quite publicly—viewed as choices, not necessities. According to the director of *Juventud Rebelde*, "A lack of things inevitably produces economic crimes and corruption. . . . It's interesting what hookers charge: hard currency, the latest clothes, various electrical appliances. We find almost no cases of people living off of what they make" (quoted in McKerrow, 1991: 24). Castro reiterated the official judgment that prostitution is voluntary rather than a necessity in his April 1992 speech at the Congress of the Union of Young Communists (1992b). The FMC has not ignored the fact of prostitution, though it has shared in the official view that it is neither "alarming" nor a widespread problem (Agramonte, 1992). A noticeable lack of repression of the activities of women whose trade is their bodies suggests more pressing priorities in the state's policing of the public behaviors of both women and men, as well as the challenge of interpreting—or repressing—the interests and needs behind a burgeoning underground that may be only partially defined by the expressly illegal pursuit of profits.

The FMC continues to organize women in a context in which *paternalismo* (paternalism) is a word often used in rectification's criticisms of the poor results of past practices. The problems of Cuba's socialist state and Cuban women are not, however, reducible to a Western feminist critique of the Cuban strategy for the emancipation of women or to the centralization of socialist organizations. The FMC hopes to assert itself as a more responsive link between women and the state and has increased its attention to the obstacles to women's full participation, including the need to recognize the "differential character of ideological work" (Espín, 1990f). Together with the commitment to democratizing the family—replacing "anachronistic patriarchal authoritarianism" with "shared responsibilities" (Espín, 1990d: 244)—women with diverse interests have officially recognized places in Cuba's process of reform. Seeing only orthodoxy and presuming only problems ignores the substantial gains made by Cuban women and the range of gender interests actually present in official policies. The problems of the special period, of course, cannot be ignored in assessing the meaning for women of what is traditional or new in the strategies of Cuba's socialist state.

CONCLUSIONS ABOUT CUBAN WOMEN

The meaning of women's participation in the public sphere needs to be better explained in order to understand the fate of Cuban women as part of the future of Cuban socialism. Quantitative measures are useful in charting the configuration of formal roles and legal rights, but interpreting the significance of postrevolutionary change in women's lives requires more. The tendency to judge whole systems on the basis of assumptions about formal institutional arrangements that naturalize the standard of autonomy is unlikely to provide an explanation of women's relationship to the Cuban state or the social relations and dynamics of any socialist society. Similarly inadequate is a view of participation that imputes theoretically derived interests to organizational forms, replacing the study of real women with ahistorical categories and/or a predetermined and perhaps "essential" woman whose interests can be discovered everywhere. If feminist perspectives provide the foundation for reconsidering women's experiences in socialism, moving us beyond mainstream categories and conclusions, their contribution to an understanding of the Cuban case will be limited if they provide only another set of fixed meanings.

The startling changes in the socialist world are the framework within which conclusions about the past progress of Cuban women and their place in the current process of rectification encounter this problem of meanings. The matrix of unprecedented constraints on Cuban choices, attributable in good part to the dissolution of the socialist bloc and U.S. policy that has provoked hardship through decades of intentional isolation of the island economy, is also an ideational one. The reconstruction of the world economic order is enforced by a global discourse about the proper organization of economic and political life; its arguments for markets, political pluralism, or even an autonomous feminist movement do not go unnoticed in Cuba. Given this altered global context and the sweeping predictions it promotes, it is necessary to restate the argument for using gender and everyday life to read between the lines.

The severity of the special period affects Cuban women—and the socialist project—in ways that are predictable only with an understanding of the gendered dynamics that join public and private life in Cuba. Where food, household necessities, and everything else are stringently rationed or simply unavailable, shopping, cooking, and otherwise maintaining the home and family are ever more difficult and time-consuming. From the scarcity of soap and cooking oil to the promotion of bicycles for transportation, adapting to shortages has specific consequences for Cuban women who are still inequitably burdened by the duties of family life. The survival of the revolution may indeed be charted by macroeconomic indicators of the adjustment and outcomes of economic strategy, including the "socialist" opening of the economy to foreign investment that is now an accepted necessity. Yet the economic struggle is also one of maintaining homes and families. Cuban women can be expected, quite predictably, to defend their families. Others have done so in different times and places with sometimes powerful expressions of their gendered interests as mothers—or wives, sisters, daughters.

The feminism of Cuban policy becomes more obvious in the light of women's pivotal position in the resistance required in the special period, a position symbolized by lines or queues and the increasingly time-consuming "participation" needed to secure food and other essentials of homes and families (see Tax, 1988: 459–460). Asserting men's responsibilities in the home implies a needed sharing of the myriad practical difficulties of everyday life, while problem-solving efforts show the state's awareness of the problems of the private sphere, including more than one modification of the arrangements for working women's (and men's) access to the distribution system—such innovations as local delivery and permission for job-switching that brings work closer to home. Yet the Cuban strategy for women in the 1990s recognizes and responds to women's other interests even while unexpected modifications are made to past policies. In the summer of 1991, for instance, the age of entry into the system of day care was raised from 45 days to six months, requiring a quick revision in state policy on maternity leave (women receive 60 percent of their salary for six months). Both actual and still only potential shifts in all areas of state policy bear directly on the pursuit of gender equality, the past successes that the revolution can quite rightly claim, and the diverse interests reflected in women's responses to the day-to-day and longer-term exigencies of survival.

The island, in the words of one Cuban, is "still afloat" despite the dreadful uncertainties that the current crisis has imposed on it. Among the encouraging signs are a growth in tourism, foreign investment, and the constitutional reforms adopted by the National Assembly in July 1992. With regard to the last, the new constitution reflects some of the adjustments in Cuba's strategy for women, including an elevation of the standing of the family in relation to the state and modification of Article 43's association of "physical makeup" with women's right to work (Cuba, 1992). The National Assembly rejected language identifying work "compatible with their functions as mothers," instead approving a restatement of maternity leave and the addition of "temporary options for work compatible with her maternal function" (*Cuba en el mes,* 1992: 27). Arguments over the nuances of constitutional definition—and redefinition—of women are not tangential to the Assembly's approval of alterations in the legal foundations of the economy and the socialist state. Economic recovery and the directions of political change—including the opening up of the electoral system and the legalization of dollars and private enterprise in 1993—are intimately related to women's place within an ongoing process of reform.

Cuban women and Cuban men provide the most reliable testimony about what the future holds. Dissent exists in Cuba; women have participated in opposition groups, and some are found among the internationally recognized critics of the state and its leadership—Maria Elena Díaz Varela is probably the most prominent case.[7] In the troubling times of the special period, there are clear signs of frustration, anger, and sadness (bus stops are acknowledged sites of debate and criticism), as well as formal defections and more dangerous unofficial departures by sea. Repression is not, however, the determining factor in the resilience of Cuba's socialist state.[8] Indeed, one scholar's 1992 projection of alternative scenarios for Cuba perceived the regime as having both support and legitimacy, "although this cannot be substantiated with confidence" (Ritter, 1992: 251). The search for substantiation best proceeds with less confidence about the imported measures of support and legitimacy and a closer look at the continuing participation of Cuban women—and Cuban men. If the experiences of women are overlooked or misread, valuable insight into the societal dynamics of the process of rectification is lost. Gendered conclusions, moreover, can actually point the way to more careful reading of other categories of experience, including race, youth, men, labor or class.

Cuban history, the actual conditions of women's lives, and the squeeze of the international political economy must all be considered in interpreting the meaning of socialism and the years of rectification for Cuban women. Extensive and dramatic gains have been made by women since 1959, while the official strategy for women has assumed a more feminist tone. Yet new certainties lament the lack of an autonomous women's organization, and even friendly observers suppose that "more could be achieved in the sphere of personal and family life if Cuban women, while remaining committed to the revolution, could name their own problems and seek their own solutions" (Quant, 1990: 110). Autonomy, however, may be an inadequate standard for interpreting the commitment(s) that sustain Cuban socialism or for knowing which problems remain unnamed and why. The devotion of women to the revolution can be as principled as men's, supported by a combination of nationalist and socialist aspirations. Women's specific gains can also be the source of particular, gendered commitments that balance the state's intentions against the limits of policies made in an imperfect world in which economic constraints threaten even the most feminist policies. As the reforms of rectification and the compelling necessities of the special period continue to open up the organized discussion of the problems that different women see, and with the situation of postsocialist women in mind, it is easier to believe in the prospects for Cuba's survival and a future decided on Cuban terms.

NOTES

1. Discussing the epistemological and ontological "phallocentrism" of socialist theory, Campioni and Grosz (1990: 367) explain that "a radically *women-centered* version of 'socialism'" is needed, one "conceptualizing a space which allows women to be considered autonomous spheres and creators of meaning." The issues of autonomy considered here are simpler.

2. Einhorn (1991: 24) calls women's organizations in socialism a "bureaucratic arm of the state"; Molyneux (1990: 29) notes that some were "moribund" or "corrupt" and points to personal connections between female and male leaders (here including Espín).

3. Molyneux (1990: 32–33) identifies "Cuba's hostility to feminism" in Espín's "regular denunciation of its 'bourgeois' and 'imperialist' character"; she explains change in terms of the increasing acceptance of feminism by socialists everywhere and the FMC's engagement in international feminist events and dialogue.

4. Without a formal population policy, the official position is that women should have the right to choose an abortion, that safe conditions should be available, and that abortion should not be viewed as a method of family planning (FMC, 1990: 48–49). See Espín's response to "What is the FMC's position on family planning?" (1990a: 57–58) and the ILO fertility study by Catasús et. al. (1988). In 1975 there were 1,178 births to girls under 15 and more than 48,000 in the 15–19-year age group; in 1987 the figures were 1,372 and 44,775, respectively (FMC 1990: 15). In 1988 there were 36.9 abortions per 1,000 women under 18 (*Granma International*, May 19, 1991) while 30 percent of those having abortions in 1989 were adolescents (FMC, 1990: 49).

5. For example, "Caballo grande, ande o no ande . . . ?" *Juventud Rebelde*, January 7, 1990; "Does frigidity exist?" *Granma Weekly Review*, September 30, 1990; "Sexuality: Neither a dilemma nor a sport," *Granma Weekly Review*, January 37, 1991.

6. Also relevant is Molyneux's further distinction between "strategic" and "practical" gender interests, a widely used pairing that will not be addressed here.

7. Few are the memoirs of women among the anti-Castro exile testimonials, and women seem to receive little attention in men's stories. See the essay by La Silenciada (1984) in Morgan's feminist anthology and reference to the Mothers for Dignity in Pérez-Castellón (n.d.). *Foreign Report* (January 9, 1992) noted a Christmas 1991 march of some 200 women to deliver a letter requesting Castro's resignation (with two reported arrested), though one FMC official had no knowledge of it; she explained that an event of that size would surely be known in Havana even if it was not reported in the Cuban press, though it was quite possible that a few women had participated in such an activity (Agramonte, 1992).

8. A number of factors might help account for the absence of widespread opposition, including nationalism, the PCC's development within the revolution, and a low level of corruption among the leadership. See Rodríguez's discussion of the problems of "weak socialism" in Eastern Europe (1991:11).

REFERENCES

Agramonte, Elsa
    1992 Interview, Federation of Cuban Women, Havana, August 6.
Berges, Célia
    1990 Interview, Federation of Cuban Women, Havana, June 8.
Campioni, Mia and Elizabeth Grosz
    1990 "Love's labours lost: Marxism and feminism," pp. 366–397 in Sneja Gunew (ed.), *A Reader in Feminist Knowledge*. London: Routledge.
Castro, Fidel
    1975 "Discurso del Comandante en Jefe Fidel Castro en el acto de clausura," pp. 279–305 in *Memoria: Il Congreso Nacional de La Federación de Mujeres Cubanas*. Havana: Editorial Orbe.

1992a "Speech . . . at the closing of the 10th regular session, 3rd Legislature of the National Assembly of People's Power . . . December 27,1991 . . . " *Granma International*, January 12, 1992, pp. 2–6

1992b "Discurso pronumciado . . . en la clausura del VI Congreso de la UJC . . . 4 de abril . . . " *Granma*, April 7, suppl. 2-11.

Catasús, S. et. al.
1988 *Cuban Women: Changing Roles and Population Trends*. Geneva: International Labour Office.

Cuba
1981 *Constitution of the Republic of Cuba*. Havana: Editora Política.
1992 *Constitución de la República de Cuba*. Havana: Editora Política.

Cuba en el mes
1992 "Proyecto de modificaciones a la Constitución de la República." Havana: Centro de Estudios sobre América.

Dölling, Irene
1991 "Between hope and helplessness: Women in the GDR after the 'turning point.'" *Feminist Review* special issue, no. 39 (Winter): 3–15.

Einhorn, Barbara
1991 "Where have all the women gone? Women and the women's movement in East Central Europe." *Feminist Review*, special issue, no. 39 (Winter): 16–36.

Espín, Vilma
n.d. *The Struggle for the Full Exercise of Women's Equality*. Havana: Federation of Cuban Women.
1990a "Conclusiones en la sección 'A Debate' sobre la plena igualdad de la mujer, en el periódico *Juventud Rebelde*, Agosto 1984," pp. 47–68 in Vilma Espín Guillois, *La mujer en Cuba, familia y sociedad: Discursos, entrevistas, documentos*. Havana: Imprenta Central de las FAR.
1990b "Entrevista concedida a Mirta Rodríguez Calderón, del periódico *Granma*, agosto de 1985," pp. 37–81 in Vilma Espín, *La mujer en Cuba, familia y sociedad: Discursos entrevistas, documentos*. Havana: Editora Política.
1990c "Entrevista concedida a la periodista griega Elizabeta Popogay, febrero 1989," pp. 211–221 in Vilma Espín Guillois, *La mujer en Cuba, familia y sociedad: Discursos entrevistas, documentos*. Havana: Imprenta Central de las FAR.
1990d "La familia en el socialismo: Intervención en la reunión de dirigentes femeninas de paises socialistas, Ciudad de La Habana, febrero 1989," pp. 223–245 in Vilma Espín Guillois, *La mujer en Cuba, familia y sociedad: Discursos entrevistas, documentos*. Havana: Imprenta Central de las FAR.
1990e "¡¿Cosas de mujeres?! Entrevista concedida a la periodista Mirta Rodríguez Calderón revista *Bohemia*, marzo 1989," pp. 247–266 in Vilma Espín Guillois, *La mujer en Cuba, familia y sociedad: Discursos entrevistas, documentos*. Havana: Imprenta Central de las FAR.
1990f "Vilma Espín habla para *Granma*." *Granma*, August 23.

Evensen, Debra
1986 "Women's equality in Cuba: What difference does a revolution make?" *Law and Inequality: A Journal of Theory and Practice* 4 (July): 295–326

FMC (Federación de Mujeres Cubanas)
1975 "Informe central," pp. 93–114 in *Memoria: II Congreso Nacional de la Federación de Mujeres Cubanos*. Havana: Editorial Orbe.

[1989] *Draft thesis, V Congreso FMC, 5 al 8 de marzo de 1990.* Havana

[1990] *Proyecto de informe central, V Congreso FMC, 5 al 8 de marzo de 1990.* Havana

1990 *Mujer y sociedad en cifras 1975–1988.* Havana: Editorial de la Mujer.

Gómez Treto, Raúl
1988 "¿Hacia un nuevo Código de Familia?" *Revista Cubano de Derecho* 17 (July–September): 32–35.

Gotkowitz, Laura and Richard Turits
1988 "Socialist morality: Sexual preference, family, and state intervention in Cuba." *Socialism and Democracy* 6 (Spring/Summer): 7–29.

Hanly, Elizabeth
1991 "Allure in Cuba." *Allure* (July): 44–51.

Haug, Frigga
1991 "The end of socialism in Europe: A new challenge for socialist feminism?" *Feminist Review*, special issue, no. 39 (Winter): 37–49.

McKerrow, Richard
1991 "Cuba Libre!" *Details* (August): 20–26.

Medin, Tzvi
1990 *Cuba: The Shaping of Revolutionary Consciousness.* Translated by Martha Grenzback. Boulder, CO: Lynne Rienner.

Molyneux, Maxine
1986 "Mobilization without emancipation? Women's interests, state and revolution," pp. 280–302 in Richard Fagen, Carmen Diane Deere, and José Luis Coraggio (eds.), *Transition and Development: Problems of Third World Socialism.* New York: Monthly Review Press.

1990 "The 'woman question' in the age of perestroika." *New Left Review*, no. 183 (September/October): 23–49.

Murphy, Julien S., Ofelia Schutte, Jan Slagter, and Linda López McAlister
1991 "Feminism in Cuba: Report from the Third Conference of North America and Cuban Philosophers." *Hypatia* 6, 3 (Fall): 227–232.

PCC (Partido Comunista de Cuba)
1978 *Plataforma programática del Partido Comunista de Cuba: Tésis y resolución.* Havana: Editorial de Ciencias Sociales.

Pérez-Castillón, Ninoska
n.d. "Coping in Cuba: The internal opposition," pp. 21–27 in *Cuba in Crisis: Proceedings from a Conference Sponsored by the Cuban American National Foundation, Washington D.C., Tuesday October 26, 1993* n.p.

Quant, Midge
1990 "Women's liberation in Cuba." *Z Magazine* (October): 108–110.

Reca Moreira, Inés, Mayda Alvarez Suárez, María del Carmen Caño Secade, Gilda Castilla Garcia, Maritza García Alonso, Orlando García Pino, Consuelo Martín Fernández, Alicia Puñales Sosa, and Maysu Ystokazu Morales.
1990 *Análisis de las investigaciones sobre la familia cubano 1970–1987.* Havana: Editorial de Ciencias Sociales.

Ritter, Archibald R. M.
1992 "Prospects for economic and political change in Cuba in the 1990s," pp. 235–252 in Archibald R. M. Ritter, Maxwell A Cameron, and Donald Pollock (eds.), *Latin America to the Year 2000: Reactivating Growth, Improving Equity, Sustaining Democracy.* New York: Praeger.

Rodríguez, Carlos Rafael
  1991 "Cuba's predicament: A fate worse than imperialism? [Interview with Abraham Lowenthal and Nathan Gardels, Havana, November 1990]." *New Perspectives Quarterly* 8 (Winter): 10–14.
Rodríguez Calderón, Mirta
  1992 "Sin tiempo para el desaliento." *Bohemia* 84 (March 6): 38–42.
La Silenciada
  1984 "Cuba: Paradise gained, paradise lost—the price of 'integration,'" pp. 169–177 in Robin Morgan (ed.), *Sisterhood Is Global: The International Women's Movement Anthology*. New York: Anchor Books, Doubleday.
"Talking about Love, Whites and Blacks: Obstacles?" (my translation)
  1992 *Bohemia* (February 14): 4–7.
Tax, Meredith
  1988 "The sound of one hand clapping: Women's liberation on the left." *Dissent* 35 (Fall): 457–462.

13

Seeking Our Own Food: Indigenous Women's Power and Autonomy in San Pedro, Chenalhó, Chiapas (1980–1998)

Christine E. Eber

This article explores indigenous women's pursuit of power and autonomy in San Pedro, Chenalhó, a highland Chiapas township. Specifically, it describes women's grassroots initiatives since the early 1980s in the context of two social movements—the weaving cooperative movement and the Zapatista democracy movement. Within these two movements I focus on two cooperatives— *Mujeres Marginadas* (Marginalized Women), which is a bakery cooperative of approximately 20 women, and *Tsobol Antzetik* (Women United), which is a weaving cooperative composed of about 18 women and several of their children. Women in the bakery cooperative live in one hamlet of Chenalhó and belong to a Zapatista *base de apoyo* (support base). Women in the weaving cooperative live in a three-hamlet area and sympathize with the Zapatistas but for the most part do not belong to Zapatista support bases. The four hamlets lie along the mountainous side of a valley about 45 kilometers from San Cristóbal de Las Casas, the urban center of highland Chiapas. The hamlet populations average 550; the township population is 30,680 (Viqueria, 1995: 25). The majority of women in Chenalhó and in the two cooperatives are monolingual in *Tzotzil*, a Mayan language.

I draw data for this article from two sources—my own and others' ethnographic research in Chiapas and the experiences and views of one woman, Antonia, current president of the bakery cooperative and past president of the weaving cooperative.[1] Although the value of ethnographic research may be apparent, in this article I address recent critiques of ethnographic studies of resistance movements stating that these often scant the cultural richness,

This chapter first appeared in *Latin American Perspectives* 106, 26:3 (May 1999), pp. 6–36.

spiritual aspects, internal politics, and long-term consequences of these movements (e.g., Ortner, 1995). In response to these criticisms, I discuss how culture, spirituality, and political factionalism influence individual women's actions and participation in collective projects.

My decision to situate my discussion of women's seeking of power and autonomy within a narrative of Antonia's adult life responds to another criticism
of ethnographers—that they fail to represent the subjectivities of the people
whose experiences they study (Nash, 1997; Ortner, 1995). For the purposes of
this article, I draw one woman out of the complex whole in which she is embedded to shed light on the complexity of individuals' actions and the multi-
dimensional nature of their identities. Through exploring Antonia's different
identities—weaver, Zapatista supporter, co-op representative, mother, and
wife—I show how each of these may help define her without telling her whole
story. Antonia calls on different identities to embrace, negotiate, and change
the organizations in which she is involved. Her choices illustrate the agency
of individual women whose daily lives require them to shift their positions in
complicated and changing social structures. They also suggest that her importance as a subject lies as much in the projects in which she is involved as
in who she is. Antonia's actions combined with those of the other women in
the two cooperatives create the dynamic mix that leads to social change.
Through their collective acts, the women create and transform both their personal identities and the social universe to which they belong (Ortner, 1995:
187; Rus, 1997).

My discussion of women's collective and personal experiences in a few
hamlets of Chenalhó focuses attention on the diversity and complexity of responses to the Zapatista rebellion within communities and townships. Scholars' analyses of indigenous people's efforts to renegotiate their place in Mexican society reveal quite different histories, points of view, and social
configurations within and between townships (Hernández et al., 1999). Diverse responses to the rebellion, contextualized within their specific histories,
remind us that although the Zapatistas articulated a platform for indigenous
autonomy and women's rights, it has been and continues to be small groups of
women and men in their local communities who are doing the hard work of
creating a viable framework in which to realize these ideals.

Focusing on local responses also involves attending to how women and
men have been responding differently to the rebellion. My discussion of the
two cooperatives shows that indigenous women are working apart from men
but in complementarity with them to respond to new ideas about democracy
and women's rights. They also provide much needed economic support that
their kinsmen have not been able to provide in ways that are meaningful to
them as men, for example, as semi-subsistence farmers. Through my discus-

sion of the two cooperatives, I argue that women's collective initiatives demonstrate how working from group identities in small grassroots projects is relevant to building social movements and how cultural traditions can serve as foundations on which to create movements that expand rights for women.

Last, exploring women's grassroots initiatives since well before the Zapatistas came on the scene makes it clear that women have been continually seeking and finding ways to support themselves and their families and to create a more just world for future generations. Through their participation in various organizations from cooperatives to religious groups, women have worked hard to prepare the soil in which the democracy movement has taken root.

The article is divided into three parts: ethnographic background about women in Chiapas, women's grassroots initiatives in Chenalhó, and a commentary integrating the women's experiences into conceptual frameworks developed by social scientists. Antonia's story weaves through the three parts.

ETHNOGRAPHIC BACKGROUND

Drawing on indigenous women's diverse experiences and perspectives, I aim here at a more nuanced point of view somewhere between the stereotypes of "total oppression" and "harmonic complementation" (Heidi Moksnes) that writings by and about indigenous women of Chiapas sometimes reproduce.

The total-oppression stereotype is common in the responses of young indigenous women soldiers in the *Ejército Zapatista de Liberación Nacional* (Zapatista Army of National Liberation—EZLN) when asked to comment on women's rights. Most women rebels came of age in training camps where gender roles and relations differed radically from those of their home communities (*El Tiempo*, 1994; K'inal Antzetik, 1995; *La Jornada*, 1994; Rojas, 1994; Rovira, 1997). Women combatants rarely mention anything positive about indigenous women's lives and stress the unfairness of girls not being able to pursue formal education. They report that education is the first activity in which they become involved when they enter a base camp (Commander Ramona, quoted in *La Jornada*, 1994). First, they learn to read and write if they do not already know how. After that, they read about Mexico's history and the liberation struggles of people in other countries. Rebel camps provide a respectful environment for young women to pursue their education and to explore the challenges they face in charting new territory as women in their communities.[2]

In Chenalhó, girls and boys rarely go beyond sixth grade. One reason for this is the lack of a junior high school in their vicinity, but another is parents' concern that attending school past the sixth grade will increase the chances

that their children will get involved in relationships with members of the opposite sex or enter a path on which they may abandon their connection to the
land, their families, and their traditions. Parents have also refused to let their
daughters go farther in school out of a legitimate fear that teachers will treat
them with disrespect or physically molest them. To most parents, indigenous
teachers represent agents of modernization and purveyors of mestizo gender
ideology (Eber and Rosenbaum, n.d.).[3] Girls who go past the sixth grade or
work in nontraditional jobs must leave their communities. In the township
head towns or cities where they go, girls usually work as servants in mestizo
households to pay for their room, board, and education. In these settings, girls
are often abused and say that they feel vulnerable and lonely.

When Antonia graduated from sixth grade she begged her parents to let
her go to junior high school, but they would not let her leave home. When
she was newly married, she defied her parents and took a brief teachers' training course and then taught in a primary school for a few months in a neighboring township. But with a new baby, the loneliness of being away from her
family, and a husband who felt threatened by his wife's being away from home
a lot, she gave up her teacher training. Since then, she has sought knowledge
about the world outside her township in the weaving cooperative she helped
form and in the relationships she has established with Catholic clergy, foreigners assisting the weaving cooperative, and several researchers who have
studied in her township. But as the children began to come, her workload increased, and she did not have time to pursue her interests. The Zapatistas
have awakened in Antonia a desire to study the history of Mesoamerica and
of women in other countries. In March 1997, Antonia wrote her first song and
poem and performed them with her 13-year-old son at an International
Women's Day celebration organized by the EZLN in Oventic.

Young women rebels are justified in pointing out the ways in which traditional gender systems constrain women. Women do marry early instead of
continuing their education; they have many children and spend their lives
taking care of their families. Yet, women rebels' views on marriage and education give the impression that indigenous women have no value to their people except as workhorses and baby machines. To a young woman embarking
on the rest of her life and engrossed in a radical movement to restructure her
society, this conception may be the one she needs to justify her divergent
path. However, it obscures the ways in which beliefs and practices in communities such as Chenalhó foster a variety of socially meaningful roles for women
while keeping their kinsmen in check.

The total-oppression stereotype also characterizes many non-indigenous
people's views of indigenous women. An often-heard comment laments the injustice of men's walking ahead down trails in shoes while their kinswomen walk

behind them barefoot. This detail of their lives does not hold nearly the same interest for many indigenous women. When I mentioned to Antonia what people say, she replied: "It doesn't matter to me if my husband walks in front of me on the trail wearing shoes. He needs boots to work in the milpa, while I work at home. What matters to me is that my husband works hard and respects me."

Ideally, people concretize respect and complementarity in their traditional division of labor. While roles are flexible and constantly changing, men traditionally work in the fields, planting corn and beans to feed their families and other crops to sell for cash, while women work in and around the house compound, caring for children and animals, weaving for household use and sale, and performing myriad other chores aimed at maintaining the household unit. Men and women pass on their traditional division of labor in their ideas about marriage and in the rituals that encode them (Nash, 1973). Traditional marriages begin with a bride petition initiated by a young man. Girls learn early that no man has the right to speak to them, much less touch them, unless he first shows respect to their parents by approaching them with a formal petition. Despite these proscriptions, boys and girls often find ways to talk to each other. Sometimes they even have sex. But more often, if they desire each other, they will go off together for a few hours or perhaps a day and then return to ask their parents' blessing.

When Domingo petitioned her parents to marry her, Antonia was 18 years old. Antonia and Domingo lived almost four years with her parents while Domingo fulfilled his bride service working in her father's fields.

Marriages such as Antonia and Domingo's function to bind young couples in networks of rights and obligations that extend existing kin bonds rather than starting new, separate families. Many women who have married this way in Chenalhó say that the extended arrangements strengthen them throughout their lives because many people are there to help them and to keep their husbands in line if they fail to respect them or to treat them with kindness. Traditional marriages also give men the same support if their wives do not live up to their responsibilities.

Women in highland Chiapas are also involved in meaningful roles that bring them self esteem and social power outside of their households as midwives, shamans, weavers of festival garments, and leaders of fiestas and cooperatives (Eber, 1995; K'inal Antzetik, 1995; Komes Peres, 1990; Rosenbaum, 1993; 1996). Women call these roles *cargos*, service that they provide to their communities without pay and that they are often called to perform in a dream. In *Tzotzil*, *cargo* is glossed as *nichimal abtel* (flowery or sacred work). The concept evokes the responsibility that people carry to assist powerful spiritual beings in keeping the world in flower and in balance (Eber, 1995: 187). Observing and interviewing female shamans and fiesta leaders in the late

1980s, I learned that they saw their service to their people as an occasion of power, beauty, and suffering, a time during which they shared with their husbands the burden of mediating between the gods and ordinary people (Eber, 1995; Rosenbaum, 1993).

From their positions in both their communities and households, indigenous women continually adapt traditional ideas of respect, service, and complementarity to meet their own and their society's changing needs and ideals. For example, in response to her own and her people's problems with alcohol, María substituted sodas for rum in rituals she conducted during the fiesta. Over the past decade, many women have been substituting sodas for rum in their *cargos* as fiesta leaders and as shamans. By doing so, they convey the message that while rum may be a symbol of respect and an offering to the gods, people so often abuse it that it is more respectful to God and each other to use sodas instead (Eber, 1995: 101–106). In a prohibition movement during the late 1980s, women used alcohol as a rallying point to confront patriarchal domination, challenging men's prerogative of getting drunk and powerful men's right to dominate less powerful people through alcohol sales (1995: 231–234). Many men heeded the women's words because women pointed out that men who abused alcohol could no longer fulfill the requirements of a good person (i.e., to be respectful, to complement one's spouse, and to serve one's family and community). Today in Chenalhó, it is accepted and common to find male *cargo* holders using sodas and only bringing rum to their lips as a sign of respect.

Despite continued belief in the rightness of a way of life based on *milpa* production, gender complementarity, and community service, the reality of life in Chiapas often collides with these ideals, sometimes dramatically. Many Pedranos have been rejecting *cargos* as a result of converting to Protestant religions or becoming involved in the Catholic Church's preferential option for the poor (Chojnacki, n.d; Kovic, 1998; Sullivan, 1997). Before Protestant missionaries and Catholic missionaries committed to the option for the poor began to work in highland Chiapas, in mid century, indigenous people did not separate spiritual concerns from other concerns. Today, while this tendency still exists among most Pedranos, they now divide themselves into three religious groups: Traditionalists who follow the folk Catholicism that has evolved out of almost five centuries of contact with the Catholic Church; Protestants of diverse denominations, who reject many aspects of Traditional beliefs and practices as idol worship; and followers of *La Palabra de Dios* (The Word of God), the Catholic Church's option for the poor (known elsewhere as liberation theology).

An additional dimension of social life contributing to resistance to assuming *cargos* has been the lack of land, especially productive land, which has forced young people to seek alternative ways of making a living as wage laborers or in commerce. In neighboring Zinacantán, the advances that young men have made in economic independence through wage labor have reduced their interest in fulfilling bride service and accepting *cargos* (Cancian, 1992; Collier, 1994: 114–116). In most highland townships, young men and women are caught between the world of their parents, rooted in service and the *milpa*, and the urban world of mestizos, with wage labor, educational opportunities, religious diversity, and nontraditional gender roles and relations. Today, the increasing frequency of elopement and women's choosing not to marry or to be single mothers reflect young people's rejection of elders' and men's control over their lives as well as the monetization of the economy (Flood, 1994; Garza Caligaris and Ruiz Ortiz, 1992; Siverts, 1993).

Statistics on maternal death and domestic violence vividly reveal the collision between ideal and real gender relations. Freyermuth Enciso and Pinto's (1996) research on women between the ages of 10 and 49 who died in Chenalhó reveals that maternal death (the death of a woman during the course of pregnancy, childbirth, or within 42 days after giving birth) ranked second to death caused by diarrhea and intestinal infections. Their study also indicates that domestic violence was a factor in some of the women's deaths.

Anthropologists have recorded many testimonies of domestic violence over the past decade (e.g., Eber, 1995; Freyermuth Enciso, 1996; Freyermuth Enciso et al., 1997; Rosenbaum, 1993). The Zapatista uprising and the work of women's organizations have brought to light many more (Rovira, 1997; K'inal Antzetik, 1995; Hernández Castillo, 1998). These narratives show a shift from those collected before the rebellion, in which women tended to contextualize their stories within the suffering that their kinsmen endured in the normal course of their lives (Eber, 1995). Until recently, women may have said that they suffered differently from men, but they rarely argued that women suffered more than men. Even today when describing abuses, women tend to focus on those related to poverty and racism that affect their whole communities, for example, the lack of health clinics in their communities or social assistance in times of need (Freyermuth Enciso, 1996; Rovira, 1997: 216–220). Overall, however, women seem to be developing a more critical perspective on the abuses that they suffer as women.

Political violence in recent years has brought additional suffering to women. Women symbolize change in Chiapas, especially the thrust of the democracy movement, through their growing quest for personal and communal autonomy, their greater participation in political affairs, and their fierce defense of their children's right to a better future. The threat women pose to those who resist change became painfully clear on December 22, 1997, when a paramilitary group of 75 men known as Red Mask massacred 18 adult women, 5 of them pregnant, in Acteal, Chenalhó. The 45 people massacred in Acteal, including 15 children, were members of Las Abejas, a sector of the democracy movement in Chenalhó. Along with their neighbors who support the Zapatistas, these people oppose the communitarian power structure and the hegemony of the *Partido Revolucionaria Institucional* (Institutional Revolutionary Party-PRI), the official Party in Mexico (see Garza et al., 1998, for women-centered accounts of the massacre).

Survivor of December 1997 massacre in Acteal, Chiapas, Mexico, May 1998. *Photo courtesy of Richard Stahler-Sholk*

Even before the escalation of violence in Chenalhó in 1997, women had been suffering the effects of the low-intensity war that began with the February 1995 invasion by the Mexican army of strongholds of Zapatista support. The presence of army and paramilitary troops in their midst creates fear, discord, and exploitation. Prostitution, uncommon in indigenous communities before the rebellion, has led to increased family violence and increased confinement of women by fearful kin (*La Jornada*, 1997). In villages divided into pro- and anti-Zapatista factions, human rights observers have reported suicides, also rare in indigenous communities. One young woman committed suicide as a result of her family's reaction to her having a boyfriend on "the other side" (Heather Sinclair, personal communication, Jan. 17, 1997). Many indigenous women have also been victims of rape (Eber, 1997; Hernández Castillo, 1998: 138).

Women who join cooperatives or political groups risk being targets of vicious rumors, physical assault, or murder. Petrona de la Cruz Cruz, co-founder with Isabel Juárez Espinosa of *Fortaleza de la Mujer Maya* (Strength of the Mayan Woman-LA FOMMA), an organization that involves indigenous women in playwriting and acting, had to stand up to her family's accusations that she was a prostitute when she first began acting. Ironically, she said, "It is more acceptable for me to be a servant than an actress" (Laughlin, 1991: 89). In Amatenango in the 1980s, two women were murdered for leading a craft cooperative—one of them for challenging the male-dominant civil-religious hierarchy by running for township president (Nash, 1993: 127–129). Rosa Gómez, an indigenous woman from Jitotol, was killed with a machete by her husband, who resented her frequent trips to meetings to discuss women's issues, even though she participated with her husband in a peasant organization (Hernández Castillo, 1998: 138).

Experiences that women have had with violence and reprisals for political participation have compelled them to seek support from other women and to create formal women's organizations. *Grupo de Mujeres* (the Women's Group) began in 1989 in San Cristóbal de Las Casas through a collaboration between indigenous and non-indigenous women formalized in the *Colectivo de Encuentro entre Mujeres* (COLEM). Since its inception, the group has focused on educating women about their legal rights, responding to the needs of women migrants from rural areas to San Cristóbal de Las Casas, and investigating women's health and welfare issues such as reproductive health and domestic and political violence (Freyermuth Enciso and Fernández Guerrero, 1995). Since the rebellion, the Women's Group has documented 50 cases of violence against women in Chiapas linked to political reprisals.

The dissemination in 1994 of the Zapatistas' agenda for women's rights, spelled out in "The Revolutionary Women's Law" (*Doble Jornada*, 1994), provided the Women's Group a context in which to join with other organized women in Chiapas to intensify their participation in political spaces. The Zapatista agenda addresses many of the basic gender issues that concern indigenous women, for example, women's having the right to pursue an education, to choose whether to marry, and to be free of physical or emotional abuse, but it goes beyond these basic rights of individuals to include the rights of communities, ethnic groups, and interest groups to make claims based on their distinct identities and needs. In this conception of citizenship, indigenous women can be at once individuals, women, indigenous, and Mexican. The Zapatista agenda raised hopes that this time a democratic movement would result in full emancipation for women. But the failure of the EZLN to protest the continued abuse of women both within their communities and by the Mexican military, police, and paramilitary groups diminished many feminists' faith in its commitment to confronting gender inequality on a par with other issues (Hernández Castillo, 1998).

Spurred on by the contradiction between rhetoric and practice, women in Chiapas are pushing the boundaries of the Zapatista agenda for women (Hernández Castillo, 1998; Palencia, 1998; Rojas, 1994; Rovira, 1997). In their organizations, they are developing a new framework within which indigenous women can incorporate gender into their analyses of oppression. The demands women are making (e.g., those made at the 1994 State Convention of Chiapanecan Women) include demands directed toward the state as well as toward their communities. They question the traditional-versus-modern dichotomy that the official indigenous state policies promote and insist on the right to hold to distinct cultural traditions while at the same time changing aspects of those traditions that oppress or exclude them. In their conventions and workshops at the state and national level, indigenous women have challenged the patriarchal premises of "traditional" culture intrinsic to men's demands for autonomy (cf. Nash, 1997). Specifically, they are extending the concept of autonomy, central to the Zapatistas' demands for control over territories and resources, to cover their rights as women, among them political autonomy, physical autonomy, economic autonomy, and social and cultural autonomy (Hernández Castillo, 1998).

Women's diverse experiences of the democracy movement in Chiapas argue strongly for serious study of the strengths of social embeddedness, cultural traditions, and collective identity. At the same time, as women take on more individualistic ideas or behavior for particular purposes, they often frame these behaviors in culturally significant ways. For example, Antonia has referred to her leadership role in the weaving cooperative as her *cargo*—her service to others in her community. *Cargo* work requires that individuals subordinate their personal egos and needs to the group. Since the rebellion, Antonia has extended the sacred qualities of *cargo* work to her work in the Zapatista base and the bakery cooperative. She calls this work *la santa lucha* (the holy struggle). With this phrase she refers to the complex whole of spiritual, political, and economic meanings that this work has traditionally embodied for women and men in her community.

COMMENTARY: TOWARD NEW CONCEPTUAL FRAMEWORKS

Women's collective work in Chenalhó and the localized nature of responses to the Zapatista democracy movement throughout Chiapas illustrate the kind of data that has influenced researchers of social movements to shift their theoretical focus from modernization forces or dependency structures to individual agency, subjectivities, and cultural meanings (Escobar and Alvarez, 1992). This shift has shed light on participants' social embeddedness, specifically the importance of their social networks based on race, ethnicity, gender, class, and religion (Mueller, 1992).

Ethnographic research examining the specificity of women's collective experiences in Latin America has been particularly helpful in shaping this new framework for understanding social movements (see Jelin, 1990; Lind, 1992; Rivera Cusicanqui, 1990; Safa, 1990; Stephen, 1996; 1997). Findings from studies of women' s roles in popular social movements reveal their central importance and the need to bring gender to the core of analyses of these movements. Research on women's collective action argues convincingly that women' s internalization of specific class and gender identities is a primary motivation to participate in social movements (Stephen, 1996; 1997). Antonia's experiences and those of other cooperative members in Chenalhó reveal that it is their inability to fulfill valued and expected roles as mothers, wives, craftswomen, and household managers that compels these women to become involved in social movements.

NOTES

Research in Chenalhó in 1997 was funded by a minigrant from New Mexico State University (NMSU) and a grant from the NMSU Mexico Small Grants Program. The author thanks the women in the two cooperatives and others who have helped with the ideas she presents in this article. She especially thanks Antonia (not her real name), Robert Dentan, and Elizabeth Kennedy for their guidance and support during her initial research in Chenalhó. She also thanks Diane Rus for encouraging her to try to present the complexity of individual women's lives. Others whose assistance she wishes to acknowledge include Lisa Bond-Maupin, María Victoria Quiroz-Becerra, Elaine Chamberlain, Jennifer Abbassi,

Graciela Freyermuth Enciso, Judith Gleason, Sheryl Lutjens, Carol Jean McGreevy, Heidi Moksnes, June Nash, Robin O'Brian, Beth O'Leary, Milagros Peña, Susan Rippberger, Brenda Rosenbaum, Jan Rus, Heather Sinclair, Cookie Stephan, and Isabel Zambrano. This article is dedicated to the 34 women and girls who died on December 22, 1997, in the massacre at Acteal, San Pedro Chenalhó, Chiapas.

1. At points in this article I use a third source of data—my applied work on behalf of the weavers and bakers. This work is based on a key assumption of feminist scholarship that research unfolds within ongoing dialogues aimed at decentering the researcher from positions of privilege in order to ameliorate the worst effects of inequality between ourselves and the people we study as well as within the communities we study (Nash, 1997; Wolf, 1996). My support work has produced understandings that I otherwise would not have had about how women are reconfiguring their communities and linking them to the region and beyond in ways that are meaningful to them as women (Eber, n.d.).

2. Unfortunately, no bilingual/bicultural schools exist in civilian contexts to do the same for young civilian women. However, indigenous people are currently constructing a junior high school in Oventic under the direction of the *Ejército Zapatista de Liberación Nacional* (Zapatista Army of National Liberation-EZLN) and with assistance from Mexican and U.S. volunteers. With assistance from non-indigenous advisers, indigenous people are creating a curriculum to provide bicultural, bilingual education for about 400 indigenous boys and girls from the highlands.

3. While gender relations in indigenous communities are rapidly changing, elders continue to distinguish their gender ideology from that of mestizos by emphasizing men's responsibility for nurturing children and both spouses being virginal and chaste. In contrast, *machismo* and *marianismo*, the poles of mestizo gender ideology, give men license to have extramarital affairs and often excuse them from responsibility for their children while holding women accountable for sustaining families and upholding society's morals.

REFERENCES

Cancian, Frank
  1992 *The Decline of Community in Zinacantám: Economy, Public Life, and Social Stratification, 1960–1987*. Stanford, CA: Stanford University Press.
Chojnacki, Ruth
  n.d. "Indigenous apostles: Notes on Maya catechists working the word and working the land in highland Chiapas." Manuscript.
Collier, George A. with Elizabeth Lowery Quaratiello
  1994 *Basta! Land and the Zapatista Rebellion in Chiapas*. Oakland, CA: Institute for Food and Development Policy.
Doble Jornada
  1994 "Ley Revolucionaria de Mujeres." February 7 .
Eber, Christine E.
  1995 *Women and Alcohol in a Highland Maya Town: Water of Hope, Water of Sorrow.* Austin: University of Texas Press.
  1997 "Communique on violence toward women in Chiapas." *Latin American Perspectives* 23: 6–8.

n.d. "'That they be in the middle, Lord': Women, weaving, and cultural survival in Highland Chiapas." Manuscript.

Eber, Christine E. and Brenda P. Rosenbaum
n.d. "Making souls arrive: Enculturation and identity in two highland Chiapas towns." Manuscript.

El Tiempo
1994 "Mujeres Zapatistas: La lucha dentro de la lucha." March 17–18.

Escobar, Arturo and Sonia Alvarez (eds.)
1992 *The Making of Social Movements in Latin America: Identity, Strategy, and Democracy.* Boulder, CO: Westview Press.

Flood, Marielle
1994 "Changing patterns of interdependence: the effects of increasing monetization on gender relations in Zinacantán, Mexico." *Research in Economic Anthropology* 15: 145–173.

Freyermuth Enciso, Graciela
1996 *Morir en Todos Santos: En catorce estampas de mujeres mexicanas.* Mexico City: Menciones DEMAC.

Freyermuth Enciso, Graciela and Mariana Fernández Guerrero
1995 "Migration, organization and identity: The Women's Group case in San Cristóbal de Las Casas." *SIGNS: Journal of Women in Culture and Society* 20: 970–995.

Freyermuth Enciso, Graciela, Anna Maria Garza, and Gabriel Torres
1997 *Campaña en contra de la muerte materna: Porque damos la vida tenemos derecho a ella.* San Cristóbal de Las Casas, Chiapas: COLEM Grupo de Mujeres de San Cristóbal de Las Casas.

Freyermuth Enciso, Graciela and Delmi Marcela Pinto
1996 *Carpeta informativa: Muerte materna en el municipio de San Pedro Chenalhó.* San Cristóbal de las Casas, Chiapas: Centro de Investigaciones y Estudios Superiores en Antropología Social del Sureste.

Garza Caligaris, Anna María and Juana Maria Ruiz Ortiz
1992 "Madres solteras indígenas." *Mesoamerica* 23: 67–77.

Garza, Anna María, Juana María Ruiz, R. Aída Hernández, Martha Figueroa, and Mercedes Olivera
1998 "Antes y después de Acteal: Voces, memorias y experiencias desde las mujeres de San Pedro Chenalhó," pp. 15–36 in R. Hernández Castillo (ed.), *La otra palabra: Mujer y violencia en Chiapas, antes y después de Acteal.* Mexico City: CIESAS/COLEM/CIAM.

Hernández Castillo, Aída
1998 "Construyendo la utopía: Esperanzas y desafios de las mujeres chiapanecas de frente al siglo XXI," pp. 125–142 in R. Aída Hernández Castillo (ed.), *La otra palabra: Mujer y violencia en Chiapas, antes y despues de Acteal.* Mexico City: CIESAS/COLEM/CIAM.

Hernández, Aída, Jan Rus, and Shannan Mattiace
1999 *Taking the Future into Our Own Hands: The Impact of the Zapatista Uprising Four Years After.* Manuscript.

Jelin, Elizabeth
1990 *Women and Social Change in Latin America.* London: Zed Books.

K'inal Antzetik
1995 *Mujeres indígenas de Chiapas: Nuestros derechos, costumbres y tradiciones.* San Cristóbal de Las Casas, Chiapas.

Komes Peres, Maria, with Diana Rus and Salvador Guzman
    1990 *Bordando milpas* (in *Tzotzil* and Spanish). San Cristóbal de Las Casas, Chiapas: Instituto de Asesoria Antropológica para la Región Maya.
Kovic, Christine
    1998 "Walking with one heart: Human relations and the Catholic church among the Maya of highland Chiapas." Ph.D. dissertation, City University of New York.
La Jornada
    1994 "Don't Abandon Us!" in *La Jornada's* special supplement for International Women's Day. March 7.
    1997 "Prolifera la prostitución en zonas militares de Chiapas." January 27.
Laughlin, Miriam
    1991 "The drama of Mayan women." Manuscript.
Lind, Amy Conger
    1992 "Power, gender, and development: Popular women's organizations and the politics of needs in Ecuador," pp. 134–149 in Arturo Escobar and Sonia E. Alvarez (eds.), *The Making of Social Movements in Latin America: Identity, Strategy, and Democracy.* Boulder, CO: Westview Press.
Mueller, Carol McClurg
    1992 "Building social movement theory," pp. 3–25 in Aldon Morris and Carol McClurg Mueller (eds.), *Frontiers in Social Movement Theory.* New Haven: Yale University Press.
Nash, June
    1973 "The betrothal: A study of ideology and behavior in a Maya Indian community," pp. 89–120 in Henning Siverts (ed.), *Drinking Patterns in Highland Chiapas.* Bergen: Norwegian Research Council for Science and the Humanities.
    1993 "Maya household production and the world market: The potters of Amatenango del Valle, Chiapas, Mexico," pp.127–154 in June Nash (ed.), *Crafts in Global Markets: Changes in Artisan Production in Middle America.* Albany: State University of New York Press.
    1997 "The fiesta of the Word: The Zapatista uprising and radical democracy in Mexico." *American Anthropologist* 99: 261–274.
Ortner, Sherry
    1995 "Resistance and the problem of ethnographic refusal." *Journal for the Comparative Study of Society and History* 37: 173–193.
Palencia, Diana Damían
    1998 "A manera de epílogo testimonial de mujeres: Temores y retos de la experiencia urbana," pp. 143–153 in R. Aída Hernández Castillo (ed.), *La otra palabra: Mujer y violencia en Chiapas, antes y después de Acteal.* Mexico City: CIESAS/COLEM/CIAM.
Rivera Cusicanqui, Silvia
    1990 "Indigenous women and community resistance: History and memory," pp. 151–183 in Elizabeth Jelin (ed.), *Women and Social Change in Latin America.* London: Zed Books.
Rojas, Rosa (ed.)
    1994 *Chiapas: ¿Y las mujeres qué?* Mexico City: Ediciones La Correa Feminista.
Rosenbaum, Brenda
    1993 *With Our Heads Bowed: The Dynamics of Gender in a Maya Community.* Albany: Institute for Mesoamerican Studies, State University of New York.

1996 "Women and gender in Mesoamerica," pp. 321–352 in Robert Carrnack, Janine Gasco, and Gary Gossen (eds.), *The Legacy of Mesoamerica: History and Culture of a Native American Civilization.* Albany: Institute for Mesoamerican Studies, State University of New York.

Rovira, Guiomar
1997 *Mujeres de maíz: La voz de las indígenas de Chiapas y la rebelión Zapatista.* Barcelona: Ediciones La Lletra.

Rus, Diane
1997 *Mujeres de tierra fría: Conversaciones con las coletas.* Tuxtla Guitierrez, Chiapas: Universidad de Ciencias y Artes de Chiapas.

Safa, Helen
1990 "Women's social movements in Latin America." *Gender and Society* 4: 354–369.

Siverts, Kari
1993 "'I did not marry properly': The meaning of marriage payments in Southern Mexico," pp. 225–236 in Vigdis Broch-Due, Ingrid Rudie, and Tone Bleie (eds.), *Carved Flesh/Cast Selves: Gendered Symbols and Social Practices.* Providence: Berg.

Stephen, Lynn
1996 "Democracy for whom? Women's grassroots political activism in the 1990s, Mexico City and Chiapas," pp. 167–186 in Gerardo Otero (ed.) *Neoliberalism Revisited: Economic Restructuring and Mexico's Political Future.* Boulder, CO: Westview Press.
1997 *Women in Social Movements in Latin America: Power from Below.* Austin: University of Texas Press.

Sullivan, Kathleen
1997 "Religious change and the re-creation of community in an urban setting among the Tzotzil Maya of highland Chiapas, Mexico." Ph.D. dissertation, City University of New York.

Viqueria, Juan Pedro
1995 "Chiapas y sus regiones," pp. 19–40 in Juan Humberto Viqueria and Mario Humberto Ruz (eds.), *Chiapas: Rumbos de otra historia.* Mexico City: Universidad Nacional Autónoma de Mexico, Ciudad Universitaria.

Wolf, Diane
1996 "Situating feminist dilemmas in fieldwork," pp. 1–55 in D. Wolf (ed.), *Feminist Dilemmas in Fieldwork.* Boulder, CO: Westview Press.

III

CULTURE, HISTORY, AND FEMINISMS

14

Introduction to Part III

The scholarship on women in Latin America and the Caribbean has helped write them back into the national and regional past and present, and it has gendered political economy by finding women's agency as economic and political actors. A new interest in culture has raised more and different questions about women, gender, and political economy, however. Feminists have joined other scholars who, in Mallon's words, may still aspire to an "emancipatory bottom-up analysis," but "can no longer simply ride one of our various Marxist or Marxian horses into the sunset" (1994: 1491). The problems of traditional left politics, and various "post" critiques of Marxist, liberal, and indeed any modernist projects, have created fertile grounds for the cultural trends in critical theory. These trends head in sometimes different directions to redefine culture and how it is studied, departing from multiple disciplinary locations and creating new academic spaces—ranging from literary studies, anthropology, sociology, and political theory, to the innovations of cultural studies, subaltern studies, and postcolonial theory, among others. Culture is no longer understood only as the "high" or elite culture of literature and the visual arts; nor is culture conceived as "static—embedded in a set of canonical texts, beliefs, and artifacts" (Alvarez, Dagnino, and Escobar, 1998: 3). Boyle defines culture in her study of women in Chile, revealing the focus on people, the everyday, and a new materialism.

> Culture is how people express their daily lives and how people express themselves in their daily lives. Cultural expression is the material expression of the interaction between an internal self and experience with an external reality. Culture cannot be seen as an immutable solid apart from or pinned on to society, for it is integral to society, it grows from it and feeds it, it elucidates its day to day workings, and provides ways of talking about ourselves within our different contexts. Without cultural expression a society is void of forms and means of reference. (1993: 165)

Cultural power and politics are matters of much debate. As Yúdice explained at the start of the 1990s, with the waning of the "revolutionary" in Latin America and "the transformation of politics into struggles for interpretive power, the cultural sphere has opened up to all kinds of challenges" (1992: 11).

Contemporary globalization frames the challenges in Latin America and the Caribbean in the material and theoretical terms of what has been called a new global cultural economy (Appadurai, 1994; Hopenhayn, 2000). Culture, explain Arizpe and Alonso, "provides the images—and the underlying values—with which people construct their view of the world" (1999: 37), and they discern three types of cultural issues in the global cultural economy. Trade in cultural commodities creates one set of issues; it refers to export and import of printed matter and literature, music, visual arts, cinema and photograph, radio and television, and sporting goods. World trade in these cultural commodities rose dramatically from $67 billion in 1980 to $200 billion in 1991 (Arizpe and Alonso, 1999: 41). A second set of issues includes the cultural consequences of global information technologies and flows. In 1997, for example, there were 107 telephones per 1,000 persons in Latin America and the Caribbean, compared to 61 in 1990; there were also 31 personal computers and forty-nine Internet hosts per 1,000 persons, while there were 274 computers and 3,411 hosts in North America (United Nations, 2000: 95). A third set of issues concerns cultural heritage and rights, as well as identity politics. Theorizing in and about Latin America has engaged these and related issues in the study of cultural politics and power (Beverley, Oviedo, and Aronna, 1995; Mallon, 1994; Sánchez and Pita, 1999; Jones and Munck, 2000).

Feminists have participated in the theoretical reformulations at the heart of new cultural approaches to power and politics, although cultural studies are not always feminist. These approaches reflect postmodern social theories' concern with the conceptual decentering of power—freeing it from grand ideological projects, from economic determinism, and from the unitary subjects of modernist theory and epistemology. Culture and its practices then become the means for finding power as it operates at the everyday—or micro—level, through language, symbols, and even bodies. Distinguishing two tendencies in the efforts to rethink the relationships of culture and politics helps order the controversies in this area of theory and research. On one hand, and as Alvarez, Dagnino, and Escobar articulate, a textual tendency embraces the semiotic and linguistic currents within critical cultural studies, and though treating "grounded practices and representations as central to culture," it emphasizes "textual and artistic forms" (1998: 3). On the other hand, the political culture tendency prioritizes cultural agency, the materiality of cultural forces, and collective action, wary of "disembodied struggles over meanings and representations" (Alvarez, Dagnino, and Escobar, 1998: 5; Munck, 2000). Cultural studies still focus on traditional cultural production—literature, music, art. Yet power and politics are tracked through architecture, public ceremonies, humor, clothing, and other innumerable places and ways that they find local, or cultural, expression. Feminists have studied the cultural practices that produce and reproduce gender, explored the changing topography of politics, and debated and defended the materialist foundations of a "red feminism" (Ebert, 1995).

The transformations in feminist perspectives of Latin American women are part of the flowering of transnational feminism. As feminists join ranks to uncover the historical and geographical specificities of gender ideologies and practices, inspecting the intersections of gender with class, race, ethnicity, and sexuality to find what is shared—or universal—and what is not, they cross boundaries of time and space. Such traveling is not entirely new, however. The history of Latin American and Caribbean women and their feminisms reveals that the search for representation and self-representation as cultural actors began long ago. That history is charted by changing access to knowledge and the production of knowledge, as well as border-crossing movements of women, ideas, and practices that shed valuable light on the constructed cultural realities of gender. In Chile, for example, access to formal education expanded in the nineteenth century; the first woman graduated from medical school in 1887, distinguishing Chile as one of three countries worldwide with female doctors (the others were the United States and England) (Lavrín, 1995). Education may foment consciousness and new claims by women, promoting both striking and more quotidian cultural reinterpretations. It also discloses the state's regulation of gender and its practices, as Mary Kay Vaughan shows in the following excerpt, recounting public education policies promoted in the Mexican revolution. The study of women and gender in cultural perspective carries us beyond the schools to other less familiar places for thinking about power and politics.

<hr />

THE STATE, WOMEN, AND THE FAMILY (1915–1928)

Mary K. Vaughan

Selection from "Women, class, and education in Mexico, 1880–1928," *Latin American Perspectives* 4:1/2 (Winter/Spring 1977), pp. 135–152.

Although the Mexican revolutionary state did not begin to take shape until 1917, a general approach to education was earlier laid out by petty-bourgeois revolutionaries for whom a vast extension of public schooling was to serve as an instrument of social control and integration and as a means of training an increasingly differentiated and hierarchically structured labor force for advancing industry. Unlike their *Porfirian* counterparts, revolutionary educators focused on poor women in their response to the general social upheaval of the day. In 1915, Felix F. Palavicini, acting official in charge of education under Venustiano Carranza (head of the Constitutional Army), was especially fearful of the socialization unschooled mothers would give to their children:

> Children abandoned to the immortality of the gutter, the filth of the factories, and the temptation of vice will be the men who form our society of tomorrow, citizens and a people sovereign by law. . . .
> From the pallid lips of wives and mothers will come the first phrases of children emerging in a seething oration of hate. They will grow with incongruent impulses, without discipline or orientation. . . . While the disciples of Max Stirner and Nietzsche await the triumph of a superman, a stronger force can emerge from the union of proletarians who organize, form unions, and join hands as a single strong body sustaining the torch which illuminates consciences and the hatchet which breaks their chains. If this force surprises us as enemies rather than as allies, we will be the losers. (Palavicini, 1910: 12–15)

In his concern, Palavicini was assisted by a core of educated women who had emerged from or worked within *Porfirian* women's schools. In 1915, they reached out to open technical education to poor women as a means of upgrading their skill, curbing prostitution, and reforming family structure. Such education was to "Aid [*la mujer pobre*] by theoretical-practical training to save her from the dangers into which she stumbles and habilitate her to duly fulfill her social duties as well as her duties as a woman of the home" (*Secretaría de Instrucción Pública y Bellas Artes*, 1914: 126). Many *gente decente* women participated in the *Universidad Popular*, Mexico's first university extension program created in 1912 to pacify and incorporate the capital's workers, then in a state of growing consciousness and agitation. Wrote Laura Mendez de Cuenca, a leading educator and participant in the *Universidad Popular*:

> If we ignore woman leaving her in . . . ignorance we would establish in the Mexican home a regrettable disequilibrium tending to multiply marital disasters so unfortunately abundant in our society. If someone is in need of education it is the woman. Her mission is to raise and care for the family; she is the exquisite engraver of society. The man sustains the home materially—he represents the physical force of the home . . . but the woman, wife and mother, nourishes the soul of her children and strengthens that of her husband with wise teachings and prudent advice. (*Universidad Popular Mexicana*, 1916: 188–189)

The instruction of women in household duties and efficiency, hygiene, and childcare, had its counterpart in general lectures to men and women on the importance of averting strikes, practicing savings, and respecting law and work. The disciplined working-class home could presumably sustain itself on a minimum income. The purpose of the *Universidad Popular* was to divert the public life of the working class from streets, taverns, and politics, and to orient it in defined directions, i.e., lectures on cultural and social organization, the formation of choirs and sports teams. Part of this scheme involved an effort to refocus working-class life on the family as the primary unit of association and emotional attachment. This thrust deepened in the 1920s with the *Secretaría de Educación Pública's* organization of workers' cultural centers and night schools.

In the 1920s a larger number of schools opened to women for training in clerical work, home economics, and domestic-related industries such as sewing, soap and artificial flower-making, cooking, toy and shoe-making. These, as well as night centers for working women, were designed more explicitly to remove women from factory production—preparing them for household work while providing them with a trade they could practice independently at home such as sewing, embroidery, or candy-making (Secretaría de Educación Pública, 1922: 238; 1923: 81, 109–112; 1923–24: 111–117, 133–36, 300–02; 1927c: 69–62). This morally motivated trend suggested an attempt to strengthen woman's primary role in the home as a replacer of labor power while marginalizing her participation in the labor force. It in fact suggested a return to domestic piecework, one of the most exploitative forms of work in which women had been engaged. The trend was further strengthened by limiting skilled training for increasingly capital-intensive industry to men.

Women's vocational training reflected and reinforced a class-stratified society and woman's pervasive subordination within it. Different curricula were offered to middle-income women in homemaking and clerical work, to domestic servants in household industries, and to working-class women in household work and home industries for market sale. The product models and consumer values promoted by the schools reflected those of the bourgeoisie with the consequences that less affluent women would be encouraged to desire and to subordinate themselves to such models and values. Annual exhibits at women's schools included richly furnished homes replete with crystal flower bowls, tiffany lamps, and fine linen, and fashions which the press called "chic" (*Secretaría de Educación Pública*, 1923–24: 134, 296–312; 1925b: 136–137). Further, the industries open to women whether in fashions, cooking or beauty parlors were almost entirely designed to please men and so tended to perpetuate the subordinate role of women in society. The type of work was often individual or confined to the small shop such as the beauty parlor or clothing store, and thus was not propitious to the development of political consciousness. Even if women worked in production, because the school emphasized their primary role in the home and defined for them an apolitical and submissive role, their potential for politicization through work might be limited.

More than simply returning women to the home, educators saw the need to restructure working-class family life. Women educators were concerned with increasing the economic efficiency of the workers' home to perform the double function of sustaining labor on a minimum income and internalizing values such as subordination, discipline, and efficiency of time and space, which the worker needed in factory production. In lectures in schools and over the government radio station, home economics professors discussed the function of the housewife:

> The head of the household has to be active; if she is lazy or indolent, there will never be enough time and her tasks will always be behind, the meal will not be served when it should, the clothes will not be ready, and she will look dirty and disheveled. Nearly always these things arise from laziness and disorder. . . . In the home the lack of order is failure since without order, it is impossible to develop faculties and to form good habits; if the child is made to wash his face one day and stops doing it for three or four, to ask him again on the fifth day—and if he does not do it again for eight days—means he will not acquire the habit of washing himself. (*Secretaría de Educación Pública*, 1926: 162)

The educators portrayed the wife as a worker who had to efficiently balance the factors of time, work, and money to facilitate a regular performance of tasks with appropriate rest periods to avoid exhaustion. Such budgeting was not only essential to the economical organization of the home, but to the inculcation of proper values among family members.

As the state attempted to define a specific role for the family, it simultaneously sought to absorb family functions such as socialization, health, protection, and other social services in such a way as to suggest an attempt to subordinate and limit the family as a source of authority, ideas, and independent thought and action. Thus in the extension of schools in the 1920s, the *Secretaría de Educación Pública* sought to organize parents to support the school but without giving them any say in what took place in the school (*Secretaría de Educación Pública*, 1925a: 24; 1928b: 292).

While in this period of Mexican history such a move has stemmed specifically from the state's fear of the growing opposition of the Church to the revolution, this created disjuncture is typical of the expansion of public school systems. Further, the teacher was to instruct parents on the proper moral and economical home life for children (*Secretaría de Educación Pública*, 1925a: 25, 75; 1927a: 79, 81; 1927c: 282–283; 1928a: 12, 152, 168, 202–203, 219, 260). In 1927, an effort was made to organize mothers' clubs by identifying their socializing role with patriotism. To be truly patriotic, however, the mother had to reform herself or "Your children will lack this moral formation which will make them useful and vigorous citizens" (*Secretaría de Educación Pública*, 1927b: 180–181). The content of this reform involved instruction in childcare and household organization and narrowed political and social participation to the formulation of choirs, drama clubs, saving associations, and cooperative sewing machine centers.

This effort to subordinate the family to the authority of the state and by implication to inflict or reinforce a sense of inferiority was apparent also in the extension of other social services. The beneficial school health service intruded upon the home to upgrade its hygiene. In 1925, a Protective Council for Children requested patria potestad over the "integral development" of childhood (*Secretaría de Educación Pública*, 1925a: 140). Seeking control over delinquent and unattended children and the right to place them in day-care centers and special homes, it bid also for the right to intervene in labor contracts negotiated between families and employers to see that the minor had a school certificate, a state medical certificate, and a safe job. The council proposed to introduce to the home the social worker, who equipped with a knowledge of hygiene, childcare, home economics, psychology, history, and civics, would provide "moral" education to the family.

This intervention was by implication an ideological act at once suggesting the inferiority of the working-class home and the authority of the state and its bourgeois representatives. While at the same time transmitting direct information tending to legitimize a specific social order (instruction in history and civics), to individualize the worker in his performance of a specific task within a sanctified socio-economic hierarchy, and to focus upon the family as an extension of the atomized worker at the expense of the collective experience of work and community, the social worker was to teach forms of recreation which could be enjoyed at home. In short, the extension of social services by the state was not a neutral undertaking: it was ideologically loaded to mirror an existing class structure and to legitimize the subordination of labor to capital, specifying at the same time an important but circumscribed role for the family in the reproduction of the social relations of production.

REFERENCES

Palavicini, Felix F.
    1910 *Problemas de la educación.* Valencia: F. Sempere y Compañia, Editores.
Secretaría de Educación Pública
    1922 *Boletín*, I, 3 (January).
    1923 *Boletín*, I, 4.
    1923–24 *Boletín*, 1, 5 and 6.
    1925a *Boletín*, IV, 8 (November 1925).
    1925b *Boletín*, IV, 9 and 10 (November–December).
    1926 *Boletín*, V, 6 (June).
    1927a *Boletín*, VI, 3 (March).
    1927b *Boletín*, VI, 4 (April).
    1927c *Boletín*, VI, 6 (June).
    1928a *Boletín*, VII, 1 (January).
    1928b *Boletín*, VII, 4 (April).
Secretaría de Instrucción Pública y Bellas Artes
    1914 *Boletín de Educación*, I, 1 (September).

Universidad Popular Mexicana
1916 Boletín de la Universidad Popular Mexicana, vol. II. Mexico: Universidad Popular Mexicana.

❦

DIFFERENCES IN CULTURAL PERSPECTIVE

The current engagement with cultural studies underscores difference as a crucial concern for thinking about women and about Latin America. Despite shared imperial roots, the patriarchal construction of masculine and feminine intersected with race and class hierarchies of pre- and postconquest practices to produce the often quite specific national and local expressions of gender relations. The concept of identity, meaning the deep psychological "sense of self" and/or "self-ascription" to a group's values and practices, has been important in the exploration of difference (Young, 1997; Minh-Ha, 1989). The exploration of the mobility of gender as racialized, classed, and more recently "sexualized" identities has focused on the cultural construction of marriage and family, heterosexuality, public and private spheres, and the nation. If struggles over interpretation inhere in the construction of people and their lives, as critical cultural perspectives suggest, key questions include the fixity and fixing of individual, group, and national identities.

The recovery of race and ethnic differences has contributed to the study of women in Latin America and the Caribbean. Pérez Sarduy and Stubbs (1994) chart distinctive subregional variations in population patterns and relations: a Euro-Latin America in the southern cone; a mestizo America in Mexico, Guatemala, the Andes, and the Amazon areas; and an Afro-Latin America slave plantation-based subregion in Northeast Brazil and the Caribbean (Pérez Sarduy and Stubbs, 1994: 3). The indigenous population in Latin American is some 50 million, with great variation among countries—from more than 70 percent in Bolivia and 66 percent in Guatemala, to 1 percent in Argentina, 2 percent in Colombia, and 14 percent in Mexico. The transatlantic slave trade carried between 10 million and 50 million Africans to Latin America and the Caribbean. European immigration in the late nineteenth century shaped population patterns in Argentina, Chile, and Uruguay, and Chinese, Japanese, Turkish and Syro-Lebanese, and Jewish immigration in the twentieth century has also contributed to regional patterns of cultural diversity (Mörner, 1970; Elkin, 1998).

State practices have contributed to an official invisibility that belies the realities of exclusion and inclusion of race and ethnic identities. The Minority

Rights Group notes that there is a lack of research and evidence about Afro-Latin Americans, since most states fail to collect statistical data and those that exist are imprecise (Minority Rights Group, 1995: viii). The group cites estimates by the Organization of American States (OAS) of some 130 million to 170 million African-ancestry persons in Spanish- and Portuguese-speaking Latin America, a third of the population. Estimates for countries vary greatly, from 34 percent to 62 percent of the Cuban population, for example, and from 9 percent to 70 percent in Venezuela and 33 percent to 75 percent in Brazil. The 1990 census in Brazil recorded 55.3 percent of the population as white, 39.3 percent as brown, 4.9 percent as black, and 0.5 percent as Asian; a study conducted to improve the classifications found 134 terms popularly used to describe color (Brazilian Institute of Geography and Statistics, 1999). In addition to official misrecognition, the construction and regulation of racial and ethnic identities has included state policies of extermination and geographical exclusion. In Argentina for example, the indigenous population dropped from 5 percent in 1869 to .07 percent in 1895, and blacks from 25 percent of Buenos Aires population in 1838 to 2 percent by 1887. In part a result of immigration from Europe, racist policies prevailed in the 1880–1930 period, buttressed with positivism, social Darwinism, and eugenics, according to Helg (1990: 38).

Gender is shaped by and shapes the historical construction of racialized and ethnic identities. The complexities of race and ethnicity included *mestizaje*, or mixing, and Spanish-Indian, Spanish-Black, and Indian-Black relations found names and cultural roots that superceded phenotypes. Language, social customs and organization, and consciousness all contribute to the practices that mark race and ethnicity with power. *Mestizaje* always involves women, and as Townsend explores in the chapter "Story without Words: Women and the Creation of the *Mestizo* People in Guayaquil, 1820–1835," her historical research on day-laboring *mestizas* in Guayaquil, Ecuador, meaning and consciousness is created in living an identity. The study of race and ethnic identities and their cultural practices has expanded rapidly in recent years, including work on Cuba where state policies since 1959 have pursued the elimination of structural racism. Gender relations may offer special insight into the difficulties of change, a possibility examined in Fernandez's study (1996) of interracial romances in Cuba in the early 1990s.

In the context of the modern state, race and ethnic consciousness may be at odds with the generic identity of citizen. Protections of threatened peoples have been created at the international level, and are also found in constitutions in Brazil, Colombia, and Nicaragua. Identity-based demands and the movements that organize them have surfaced in Latin America and the Caribbean (see the country studies in Minority Rights Group, 1995; Gordon, 1998; the essay by Gomes da Cunha and others in Alvarez, Dagnino, and Escobar, 1998; Torres and Whitten Jr., 1998). The Pan-Mayan movement, for instance, has become increasingly visible, both inside and outside the region. In 1950, a first Congress of Brazilian Blacks was held; in 1978, the Movimento Negro Unificado emerged in São Paulo, including women; subsequent associational activities include the Geledés Black Women's Institute, a nongovernmental organization (NGO) created in São Paulo in 1988, and the Center for Mobilization of Marginalized Populations founded in Rio de Janeiro. An Afro-Brazilian working class woman, Benedita da Silva, has became a city councilor in Rio, the first Afro-Brazilian member of congress in 1987 and senator in 1997. In Colombia, Zulia Mena, an Afro-Colombian, has also run for office.

Benedita da Silva, 1998. *Photo courtesy of Kit Miller*

Regulated in the state's control of marriage and family law, and the social enforcement of proper gender behaviors, sexualities present other understudied realities of everyday life in Latin America and the Caribbean. Lavrín argued that:

> Marriage was neither the only outcome of courtship nor the only channel for the expression of sexuality in colonial Latin America. Premarital sexual relations, consensuality, homosexuality, bigamy and polygamy, out-of-wedlock births, and clandestine affairs between religious and lay persons have been a common daily occurrence since the sixteenth century. (1989:2)

The needed historical research on the private and social practices of sexuality had only just begun, she noted, and it has expanded (Stern, 1995; Caulfield, 2000). Contemporary discourses of sexuality reflect the state's regulation through law, the Catholic Church's concerns with conserving traditional family structures, and tensions, conflicts, and struggles over representations. Kunzle, for example, in the chapter "Róger Sánchez's 'Humor Erótico' and the *Semana Cómica*: A Sexual Revolution in Sandinista Nicaragua?" explores what he calls the sexual economy of revolutionary Nicaragua, tracing the dangerous appeal of humorizing the private world of sex. A growing scholarship includes research on the lived experiences of male homosexuality in Cuba, Mexico City, and Nicaragua (Gutmann, 1996; Lumsden, 1996; Lancaster, 1992), and sometimes of lesbians (Randall, 1995; Babb, 1998). Even motherhood is no longer an obvious category of being, as Scheper-Hughes confirms in an ethnographic study of poverty-stricken Brazilian mothers' disturbingly distant relationship with babies they expect to die (1992).

Homosexual—and bisexual—identities have also organized in public ways in recent decades. The AIDS crisis in Brazil prompted open discussion and activism beginning in the mid-1980s; by 1994 there were more than fifty NGOs working on AIDS in Brazil (Klein, 1998: 27). In Chile, the first public gay march took place in 1972, raising "third sex" demands in the context of the socialist administration of Allende though without an organizational foundation or support from left political groupings (Robles, 1998). Military rule repressed such alternative sexualities and their demands, though redemocratization has allowed a more organized presence of gays and lesbians in the public sphere in Chile—and elsewhere (for example, Bonfil and Brito, 1998). The first regional *encuentro* (meeting) of lesbians was held in 1987 in Mexico City.

Questions have also been raised about regional and national identifications in Latin America (Beverley, Oviedo, and Aronna, 1995; Mignolo, 2000). Feminist scholars have focused attention on nationalism and how it constrains and conduces the formation of identities, obscuring some differences and creating others. From representations of history to the territorial state's sovereignty and its enemies, both gendering and racialization are vital in re-producing a "national" identity. Masculinities and femininities can be used to map the national space—a gendered geography—including the construction of "mothers" who reproduce the nation, of racialized ideals of beauty, the family, and heroes, and of the deeply gendered bodies that symbolize and defend the nation (Radcliffe and Westwood, 1996; Alarcón, Kaplan, and Moallen, 1999; Ranchod-Nilsson and Tétrault, 2000). Benhabib (1999) wonders if the violent conflicts and new insecurities of the world order might invite fresh claims for the stability of fixed and universal identities in practice and in theory, shifting the focus from difference, the unfixing of identities, and what she calls the "hermeneutics of suspicion."

INTERPRETING TEXTS

The cultural turn takes critique and recasting beyond the more visible exclusions to explore representation, self-representation, and interpretative struggles. Scholars have examined literary texts for their representations of race, ethnicity, sexuality, and gender, locating them within the regulatory practices of culture in Latin America and the Caribbean and the new global cultural economy. Searching for women's voices, feminist theorizing has traveled this path with its (re)reading of writing by and about women, including such authors as poet–journalist Alfonsina Storni of Argentina or Chilena Gabriela Mistral, Latin America's first female Nobel Prize-winner (1945). Genres of literature are many, however, and the texts that are read and interpreted are not always written.

Travel writing offers an intriguing example of the issues of representation and self-representation. As Hahner (1998) explains in introducing a collection of nineteenth-century accounts of Latin American women written by women, travel literature is now a literary genre as well as a resource for social historians. Such writing from the past may be viewed as colonial discourse—narratives of the subordinated colonial society that serve as a tool of imperialism, and in actuality provide an exposé of the author's own culture (Hahner, 1998: xx–xxi). While the motives for their travel varied, nineteenth-century women writing about women often said more about the "models of femininity" in their own societies; their interpretations of Latin American women's duties, desires, and differences reflected their own locations. There are thus dangers in writing women out of and into history, including rendering them as "exotic" or victimized "others." In the following excerpt, Margaret Randall's explanation of the turn to oral histories by

women journalists working in Latin America suggests how writers and readers are implicated in the problems of traveling, representation, and interpretation.

✦

TESTIMONIAL JOURNALISM

Margaret Randall

Selection from "Reclaiming voices: Notes on a new female practice in journalism,"
Latin American Perspectives 70, 18:3 (Summer 1987), pp. 103–113.

I'd been in El Salvador two weeks and I was walking home one day when I heard shots.
There were tanks all along the block, and some fifty soldiers and police. They had mor-
tars, machine guns, and they were attacking one house in particular. It was incredible,
because they had all this trained on just one house, and the only thing you could hear
coming from inside the house were the shots of a small caliber pistol. Then the shots
from inside were heard no more. Everything grew quiet. The smoke cleared and the
first group of policemen and journalists entered the house. There was a young man
dead in the bathroom. And there was a woman, maybe forty or forty-five, wearing an
apron and with a kerchief around her head. She was lying in a pool of blood. . . . I was
the only woman in the group, and the only journalist from the U.S. who had stayed in
El Salvador for more than a couple of days that month. And I just couldn't believe what
happened next: the Chief of Police went into another room and got a machine gun. He
knelt beside the older woman and placed it in her hand. "This was the weapon, this
was the machine gun she used against us," he said. He got a box of bullets, unused
bullets still wrapped in paper, and he threw them on the floor on top of her blood.
"Those were her bullets," he said. And the international press took photos and they
said, "Right, right," and they took notes: ". . . she had a machine gun, she was shoot-
ing at the Government Forces, terrorist, guerrilla" and so on. (Ann Nelson, quoted in
Randall, 1985: 56)

There was something wrong with "free journalism."

In the late 1960s and early 1970s two important forces came to bear on
the work of a number of women who lived in and wrote out of Latin America. The first was a disparate but growing awareness of the relationship between U.S. government foreign policy and the reality of life for most Third
World peoples. It wasn't difficult for us to understand why real news about
these people did not, for the most part, find its way into the mainstream U.S.
press.

The second important force was feminism. It exploded across our collective consciousness, catching each of us wherever in our own lives we happened to be standing. As women reevaluating our present we began to realize we had a past, a history hidden or distorted, a memory we needed—for

our own health and well-being—to retrieve. As writers, as journalists, we gradually came to feel it was no longer satisfying to try to "write like the men." We were no longer sure we accepted male criteria for what good writing, or accurate journalism, was. We began to listen to our own voices, play by our own rules.

The change was sometimes uneven, an ascending spiral rather than an immediate shift. Some of us wrote essays about our discoveries. Others were less analytical, more intuitive. We learned to trust our—and each other's—analyses and intuitive powers. Our work changed.

We began to understand that our collective as well as our individual memories have been invaded, raped, erased. Recreating these memories has been an ongoing concern, taking place in many ways and in a number of disciplines. Listening—to ourselves as well as to our grandmothers, mothers, sisters, and to women of different histories, ethnicities, social classes, and cultures—has been important in the context of this changed vision.

A new practice of listening and telling is sometimes called oral history. Sometimes it's called testimony, or testimonial journalism. Some people refer to it more simply as in-depth interviewing. Whatever the label, it has created a body of voice and image, a new resource literature—much of it from the so-called Third World and much of it from and about women. This new literature provides a whole other way of listening to and looking at life in places like Latin America.

REFERENCES

Randall, Margaret
    1985 *Women Brave in the Face of Danger.* Tromansburg, NY: Crossing Press.

The reading of women's literature has in other ways considered the implications of writing, cultural power, and the politics of interpretation (Ippolito, 2000). Jean Franco's work on Mexico offers insight into the location and nature of women's writing. Franco is concerned with the gendering of peripheral subjects, and though Mexico might seem "ex-centric, off center as far as the normative power of metropolitan nations is concerned," she is keen to reveal "struggles for interpretive power, struggles waged not on the high plane of theory but very often at the margins of canonical genres—in letters and life stories" (Franco, 1989: xi). Franco explores mysticism and nuns, the national allegory, and family, arguing that taking struggles for interpretation seriously moves feminist theorizing forward with the "politics and poetics of transgression." It is "the contradictory claims between life practices and textuality, political power and the virtues of marginality, that mark this present and as yet uncrystallized stage in feminist theory" (Franco, 1989: xxii). Many literary scholars are pursuing feminist textual interpretation (for example, Guerra, 1994). Erotic writing by women is another instance of claims for a different cultural power (Fernández Olmos and Paravisini-Gebert, 1993; Alvarez, 1992), as is the burgeoning of published writing by and about lesbians (Martínez, 1996; Fiol, 1995).

Women's narratives have thus become a rich resource for studying the politics of cultural interpretation. Testimonials, a new genre related to oral histories that is examined by Sternbach in the chapter "Remembering the Dead: Latin American Women's 'Testimonial' Discourse," is another revealing example of the often deeply contested terrain of representation. Aided by editors, translators, journalists, or oral historians, some notable testimonials are now classics in this literature, including those of Domitila Barrios de Chungara (Bolivia) (1978) and Rigoberta Menchú Tum (1984) (also see Randall, 1979, 1981). Menchú's story recounts her life as a Quiché-Maya woman, born in 1959 in the highlands of Guatemala and politicized by the genocidal military attack against her people. Exiled in Chiapas for twelve years, Menchú was acclaimed for bringing the actualities of Guatemala to the international eye; she won a Nobel Peace Prize in 1992 and has since written a second story of her life (Menchú, 1998). Franco calls Rigoberta and the Mothers of the Plaza de Mayo in Argentina the "organic intellectuals" of feminism (Franco, 1989: xxii). Menchú's testimonial offers insights into matters of agency, strategy, and interpretive struggles inside and outside Latin America (see Sánchez and Pita, 1999; Bueno, 2000). Anthropologist David Stoll decided to investigate the truthfulness of Menchú's narrative account of atrocities against the Mayan people and the logic of the violence in Guatemala. She mystified conditions, claims Stoll, though many defend Menchú against the media-intensive attacks that followed publication of Stoll's research as a book (*Latin American Perspectives*, 1999; Matthews, 2000). As Jan Rus suggests in the following excerpt that introduced an issue of *Latin American Perspectives* devoted to the Stoll-centered controversy, facts are not the only issue in the debate. Indeed, Stoll waged an aggressive offensive against an indigenous woman's voice, a rare self-representation that may be especially vulnerable to a white male, academic call for individualism and objectivity.

IF TRUTH BE TOLD

Jan Rus

Selection from "If truth be told," *Latin American Perspectives* 109, 26:6
(November 1999), pp. 5–14.

Within just a few months of its publication in late 1998, David Stoll's book *Rigoberta Menchú and the Story of All Poor Guatemalans* had been reviewed or at least noted in the better part of the mainstream press in the United States. Indeed, some newspapers had treated it as front-page news—one, the *New York Times*, going so far as to seek out some of the rural Guatemalans who had talked to Stoll in order to reinterview them. This was quite an unusual reception for an "academic" book that set out to sift through the details of events in the remote mountains of western Guatemala almost 20 years ago.

The reason for this extraordinary attention, of course, is that Stoll's book is not just another monograph about rural Guatemala but a critical reassessment of *I, Rigoberta Menchú* (Burgos, 1984), the oral autobiography of a young K'iche' woman who was an eyewitness to the genocide of her people in the early 1980s. Published during the worst years of the Maya holocaust, the book helped rally the universal condemnation of the Guatemalan state that eventually forced it to begin negotiating for peace. Almost a decade after its appearance, in 1992, its author, by then perhaps the best-known indigenous person in the Americas, was awarded the Nobel Peace Prize in recognition of her tireless work on behalf of reconciliation and social justice.

Why would anyone want to reexamine the life of such a revered figure? According to Stoll, the idea first occurred to him in the late 1980s while he was doing anthropological fieldwork in the general region of Rigoberta's village. As he talked to residents about the civil war in the beginning of the decade, he repeatedly encountered discrepancies between Rigoberta's testimony and descriptions of the same events by others who had lived through them. Eventually, he began to perceive enough of a pattern to the discrepancies that he decided to try to reconstruct both Rigoberta's own history and the course of the violence in the area where she had lived. In the revised version of Rigoberta's story that resulted, Stoll concludes, among other things, that contrary to what Rigoberta had claimed, her father had not been a traditional villager who had lost his fields to predatory *ladino* landlords but a progressive and fairly well-off man whose land fights had mostly been with his in-laws; that her immediate family had not been forced by poverty to become migrant workers on Guatemala's coastal plantation, where one of her brothers died of malnutrition, but had sufficient land to make a living without ever leaving the highlands; that she herself had not been monolingual in K'iche' and unlettered until she joined the revolutionary movement but had received secondary education at catholic boarding schools; and finally, that when she and her family joined the revolutionary movement at the beginning of the 1980s, it appears to have been not so much because that was the logical next step from having been leaders of local struggles for peasant rights as because they had been swept up in a factional fight within their village to which the army had overreacted. In short, Rigoberta's testimony of deprivation, racial discrimination, and repression, eventually leading to redemption through the act of taking up arms against her people's oppressors, appeared to have been at least partly fictionalized. The most renowned modern document of Native Americans' resistance to conquest and disappearance seemed not to be true.

Presented with the discrepancies Stoll had discovered, many of the mainstream reviewers turned on Rigoberta. In the "gotcha" atmosphere of the U.S. press in 1998 and 1999, such contradictions were simply too tempting a target. Both in press conferences and interviews, Rigoberta tried to defend herself. Some of the details of her story had been changed, she explained, to protect teachers and religious workers who had helped her but who in 1982 were still within the reach of the death squads in Guatemala; others had been made more generic in order to make her story typical of a larger number of people. Most of all, though, she appeared pained that the doubt cast on her own story might strengthen those who wished to minimize what had happened in Guatemala or even deny that the killing had taken place. To be sure, numerous writers came to her defense, trying to remind the world—as if it were necessary—of the urgency of the situation in Guatemala in the early 1980s, of Rigoberta's untiring work on behalf of human rights and peace, and of the fact that not even Stoll claims that the discrepancies he found in her book suggested that the genocide was not as she described it. Unfortunately, such explanations and qualifications were relegated to back pages and small-circulation journals.

At stake in the argument between Menchú and Stoll is much more than the literal truth of Rigoberta's story. Indeed, both in the introduction to his book and in later statements to the media, Stoll himself has been at pains to try to direct attention onward from the specific contradictions of *I, Rigoberta Menchú* to the construction of the testimony as a whole and its relationship to the history and politics of 1980s Guatemala.

Although there are numerous points of contention between Stoll and his critics, the most important ones can be grouped in two sets. The first concerns the participation of indigenous people in the guerrilla movement of the 1970s and 1980s. The second set of issues concerns the text of *I, Rigoberta Menchú* itself: just what kind of document is it? In recent months, both Rigoberta Menchú and her collaborators . . . have reminded us that it was never meant to be a simple autobiography.

Some of the issues between Stoll and his critics may eventually be resolved empirically. Clearly, though, much of it cannot. Even more than the facts and argument of her *testimonio*, what Rigoberta Menchú—and Elizabeth Burgos—brought to the discussion of events in Guatemala was a face and a voice—a human presence. Before *I, Rigoberta Menchú*, Guatemala's horrors were discussed in terms of statistics and anonymous descriptions of abuses. After it, there were human beings with families, lives, and hopes for the future—real people whose suffering one could identify with. In one sense, by taking Rigoberta's testimony seriously as a document, by interrogating it and attempting to discover its hidden and collateral purposes, Stoll is completing the process of taking indigenous voices seriously as interlocutors. He is subjecting *I, Rigoberta Menchú* to the same skeptical treatment with which one would hope scholars would receive statements by David Stoll. What many of the critics objects to, however, is that despite his avowal that he is not doing any more than scholars do to each other every day, his treatment of Rigoberta Menchú is actually much rougher because the indigenous voices in our public conversation are not really conditioned to that conversation. Not only are they vastly fewer and in that measure alone more delicate but—as was noted above—they are generated according to different rules about time, person, and literal accuracy of detail. If we were to begin disqualifying them on the basis of such cultural differences, we would put ourselves back in the condition of knowing rural, non-Western places only from statistics, impersonal case studies, and our own voices. Is there a balance that can be struck between respectful and critical listening?

REFERENCES

Burgos-Debray, Elisabeth (ed.)
    1984 *I, Rigoberta Menchú: An Indian Woman in Guatemala*. London: Verso.

Rigoberta Menchú's story is not simply about her life, multiple identities, or cultural rights, as many have concluded. Nor is it just about women. And writings about and by women are not the only texts that invite interpretation. Boyle calls the famed weavings (*arpilleras*) of Chilean women under Pinochet's dictatorship "testimonial tapestries" (1993: 167), for instance, and women's distinctive artistic practices have been studied elsewhere (La Duke, 1985). McAllister (1996) studied the annual Mayan Queen "beauty" contests and how the "authenticity" of indigenous culture is used and consumed, and Hendrickson (1995) the weaving of dress and "self" in Guatemala. Music, the media, and movies, too, produce and reproduce the gendered cultural scripts and routines of national and daily life. Savigliano, for example, reads Argentina's First Lady Evita into and through the cinematographic production of "Evita."

From *telenovelas* to food, studies of popular culture invoke bodies, customs, and visualities as places for creative rethinkings of women and others (Beezly and Curcio-Nagy, 2000, Bueno and Caesar, 1998; Melhus and Stølen, 1996).

TRANS/NATIONAL FEMINISMS
FROM A LATIN AMERICAN PERSPECTIVE

Interpretive struggles seem to flourish as electronic transmissions and the movement of people facilitate unprecedented movement in what Appadurai (1994) calls the "ideascape"—one of several "scapes" that conform the global cultural economy. In their feminisms, Latin American women offer a useful vantage on the interplay of the global and local in cultural politics. Many approaches to globalization, postperspectives included, tend to ignore feminisms' contributions, however (Kaplan and Grewal, 1999). The forging of collective political identities is of keen concern in thinking about the decentered cultural dynamics of power. Wieringa writes, "Feminism is a discursive process, a process of producing meaning, of subverting representations of gender and of re-creating new representations of gender, of womanhood, of identity and the collective self" (1995: 5). Much as a careful look at Latin American debates about postmodernism reveals that regional intellectuals are not simply recipients of others' theories, the experiences of women-as-feminists include their contributions to global discourses and practices.

The historical experiences with feminist organizing—and theory—vary from country to country and regionally. Miller (1991) provides an overview that periodizes shifting contexts and goals as general trends: 1890–1938 is a period called social motherhood where women's claims for change emphasized traditional gender virtues; the 1938–1958 period is explained as democracy and the search for social justice, including the quest for suffrage; and the 1959–1973 period is one of revolution and counterrevolution (Miller, 1991). Women and feminisms are thus set against the backdrop of social change, including industrialization and urbanization, immigration and the influx of ideas, and national political struggles. Organizing is traced through claims for education and cultural production in journalism and other writing. Researchers are discovering more about movements of women and their variations. The early travels by Latin American women have garnered new attention, for example (Boschetto-Sandoval, 2000); intriguing details have been uncovered regarding Latin American women's participation in the transnational organizing of Pan-Americanism (Ehrick, 1999), as well as the distinctive rooting of liberal and other feminist claims in the region.

The particularities of national feminisms are thus explored and sometimes extolled, ranging from Cuba to Colombia to Peru (Stoner, 1991; Gargallo,

Wayúu Woman, Riohacha, La Guajira, Colombia, July 2000. *Photo courtesy of Isa Ponce*

1990; Vargas, 1995). Lavrín's (1995) historical study of the emergence of Southern Cone feminisms in the 1880–1940 period documents a subregional pattern. She finds that liberal feminism developed in a shared, transborder fashion in Argentina, Chile, and Uruguay in this period, promoted by women in the urban capital cities who successfully crossed class lines to link liberal so-cial reformers, the political left, and feminists. These liberal feminists organized around the rights of working women and mothers, at different points including such sexual issues such as the double standard and notions of honor, abortion and reproductive rights, and sex education. This feminism, argues Lavrín, was not simply of the middle class, though its focus on nationalism discounted con-sideration of "diverse ethnic groups" in the nation; "feminist writing, even in the earliest periods, focused on the integration and improvement of the nation" (Lavrín, 1995: 356). In contrast to the Southern Cone but sharing a subordi-nation within national goals, feminism in postrevolutionary Mexico is seen to have faced race and class cleavages, as well as the power of the Catholic church (Ehrick, 1999). The two women's congresses organized by the socialist government in Yucatán in 1916 included hundreds of women in discussion of the public education they needed to better serve the nation as mothers and wives, an example of "feminism-in-nationalism," according to Pérez (1999). The possibilities of a shared regional feminist identity can be explored in other ways. Wieringa concludes that Third World feminism has a distinctive bent, one reflected in the "insistence on the materiality of power relations, not only in cultural practices, but in all aspects of daily life" (1995: 19). Structural inequalities and the aggravation of poverty under the neoliberal economic strategies of past decades, might support such an interpretation of Latin American and Caribbean feminisms in terms of the class materialities of power. The 1975 United Nations Women's Year meetings held in Mexico City are often cited in this regard. The meetings included 133 delegates from around the world—half of them men—who gathered to inaugurate the international discussion of women's equality, as well as a second organization of interested participants, including NGOs, called the Tribune. As Franco (1989: 184–185), Miller (1991: 198–201), and others point out, Domitila, the Bolivian miner's wife, and other "gendered subalterns" raised the class- and race-stakes of the discussion of women's equality, introducing issues of exploitation and repression and arguing for joining with men in the larger struggle of the left. The left positioning was important in the period of "revolution and counterrevolution," though military rule and violence raised the stakes for such women "at the very moment," writes Franco, "when they had begun to emerge as a force in the public sphere" (1989: 186). Indeed, Miller claims that "socialist feminism became the predominant strain of feminist thought in Latin America in the twentieth century" (1991: 14).

Franco considers the decade of the 1980s as an "extraordinary one for women." Some women passed through painful periods of exile during military rule, encountering and engaging European feminist ideas and organizing, as de Brito's explains in the chapter "Brazilian Women in Exile: The Quest for an Identity." The "extraordinariness" of the 1980s was not imported, however. Franco (1989) cites the international recognition of research centers and activist organizations in the region, including the *Centro Flora Tristán* in Lima, the *Casa de la Mujer La Morada* in Santiago, and the *Fundaçao Carlos Chaga* in São Paulo. Feminist journals emerged in various countries, including *Nos Mulheros*—the first, founded in São Paulo in 1976—and *fem, Debate Feminista, Ventanas, Géneros, Estudos Feministas, Feminaria*, as well as networks and information services. Women's studies programs were created during the 1980s and 1990s. In 1991, *Casa de La Mujer La Morada* created *Radio Tierra* (Radio Earth), the first feminist radio station in the world (Boyle, 1993: 171). The recovery of the contributions of women to history and the arts moved ahead, as did feminist theorizing (Franco, 1998; Miller, 1991). Regional gathering called *encuentros* also began in the 1980s, the first held in Bogotá in 1981 with some 200 women. Participation grew rapidly (2,500 to 3,000 women attended the V *Encuentro* in 1990) and Lavrín considers the debates and discussions in the first seven *encuentros* the "distinguishing features" of Latin American feminisms of the 1990s (1999: 179). From the debates about women's relationship to the left in the first *encuentro* to indigenous women and armed conflicts in Central America, reproductive rights, the weakening or fragmentation of feminism as a transformational project, and arguments about the co-optation of feminists by governments and NGOs, the *encuentros* recorded changing practices and theory-building debates (see Sternbach, 1992; Franco, 1998; and S. Alvarez, 1998).

Yet whose practices matter? And whose theories? The transnationalization of feminism is a live question for many women inside and outside Latin America. In the early 1990s, Olea denied that the debate about postmodernity had

> concerned Latin American feminist discourse in a central way. Our own ambiguous integration as women in cultural processes deriving from Eurocentrism always/already prevents us from positioning ourselves in relation to our own complex reality. . . . feminism comes from "no-where" to spaces where its discursivity does not yet have a history. (1995: 197)

Lavrín offers a complementary view, naming Latin American women's concrete contributions to international debates, among them the extending of the struggle for democracy to the home and the debate about empowerment from maternalist—or other nonfeminist—positionings in extraordinary national and everyday situations (Lavrín, 1999: 189). The complexities of the global "ideascape" raise further questions about theorizing and the organizational linkages that transport, enact, or resist cultural power. Sonia Alvarez (1998), for example, calls attention to the problems and the potential of new international connections, expressed locally through the mediating work of NGOs and globally through the U.N. conferencing that rather effortlessly orients national programs and associational activities, as well as the representations of an "international sisterhood."

The positionings of feminist movements with and to each other, "women," and theorizing itself invite more reflection. As Sinha, Guy, and Woollacott explain in the introduction to *Feminisms and Internationalism*,

> The real challenge for feminisms and internationalism today lies in a historical critique both of a *false* universalism that would subsume the diversity of feminisms within an elite or "provincial" understanding of feminism and of a relativism that would abandon any universalist claim for feminism in obeisance to reified and absolute conceptions of difference. (1999: 2)

Stabile suggests the depth of the challenge in warning that center feminist debates may create and celebrate discursive conflicts, freed from "economic or historical contexts" (1997: 401). At issue in the new cultural trends, still though not for all, is the understanding of gender and the materialities of power.

SUGGESTED READINGS

Sonia E. Alvarez, Evelina Dagnino, and Arturo Escobar (eds.), *Cultures of Politics, Politics of Cultures: Re-Visioning Latin American Social Movements*. Boulder, CO: Westview Press, 1998.

John Beverley, José Oviedo, and Michael Aronna (eds.), *The Postmodernism Debate in Latin America*. Durham, NC: Duke University Press, 1995.

Elisabeth Burgos-Debray (ed.), *I, Rigoberta Menchú: An Indian Woman in Guatemala*. London: Verso, 1984.

Ingrid E. Fey and Karen Racine (eds.), *Strange Pilgrimages: Exile, Travel, and National Identity in Latin America, 1800–1990s*. Wilmington, DE: SR Books, 2000.

Jean Franco, *Plotting Women: Gender and Representation in Mexico*. New York: Columbia University Press, 1989.

Roger N. Lancaster, *Life Is Hard: Machismo, Danger, and the Intimacy of Power in Nicaragua*. Berkeley: University of California Press, 1992.

Sarah A. Radcliffe and Sallie Westwood, *Remaking the Nation: Place, Identity, and Politics in Latin America*. London: Routledge, 1996.

Susan Migdal Socolow, *The Women of Colonial Latin America*. Cambridge: Cambridge University Press, 2000.

REFERENCES

Alarcón, Norma, Caren Kaplan, and Minoo Moallen (eds.)
    1999 *Between Woman and Nation: Transnationalism, Transnational Feminisms, and the State*. Durham, NC: Duke University Press.

Alvarez, Cecilia et al.
    1992 *Mujeres de mucha monta, cuentos*, 3rd ed. Montevideo: Arca Editorial.

Alavarez, Sonia E.
    1998 "Latin American feminisms 'go global': Trends of the 1990s and challenges for the new millennium," pp. 293–324 in Sonia E. Alvarez, Evelina Dagnino, and Arturo Escobar (eds.), *Cultures of Politics, Politics of Cultures: Re-Visioning Latin American Social Movements*. Boulder, CO: Westview Press.

Alvarez, Sonia E., Evelina Dagnino, and Arturo Escobar
    1998 "Introduction: The cultural and the political in Latin American social movements," pp. 1–39 in Sonia E. Alvarez, Evelina Dagnino, and Arturo Escobar (eds.), *Cultures of Politics, Politics of Cultures: Re-Visioning Latin American Social Movements*. Boulder, CO: Westview Press.

Appadurai, Arjun
    1994 "Disjuncture and difference in the global cultural economy," pp. 324–339 in Patrick Williams and Laura Chrisman (eds.), *Colonial Discourse and Post-Colonial Theory: A Reader*. New York: Columbia University Press.

Arizpe, Lourdes and Guiomar Alonso
    1999 "Culture, globalization and international trade," pp. 37–56 in *Globalization with a Human Face; Background Papers, vol. 1, Human Development Report 1999*. New York: Human Development Report Office, U.N. Development Programme.

Babb, Florence E.
    1998 "Gender and Sexuality in LAP." *Latin American Perspectives* 103, 25:6 (November): 28–29.

Barrios de Chungara, Domitila with Moema Viezzer
   1978 *Let Me Speak! Testimony of Domitila, a Woman of the Bolivian Mines.* New York: Monthly Review Press.
Beezley, William H. and Linda A. Curcio-Nagy (eds.)
   2000 *Latin American Popular Culture: An Introduction.* Wilmington, DE: SR Books.
Benhabib, Seyla
   1999 "Sexual difference and collective identities: The new global constellation." *Signs* 24 (Winter): 335–361.
Beverley, John, José Oviedo, and Michael Aronna (eds.)
   1995 *The Postmodernism Debate in Latin America.* Durham, NC: Duke University Press.
Bonfil, Carlos and Alejandro Brito
   1998 "Asamblea de diversidades." *Debate feminista* 18 (October): 334–344.
Boschetto-Sandoval, Sandra M.
   2000 "Engendering cultural formations: The crossings of Amanda Labarca between Chile and the United States," pp. 113–128 in Ingrid E. Fey and Karen Racine (eds.), *Strange Pilgrimages: Exile, Travel, and National Identity in Latin America, 1800–1990s.* Wilmington, DE: SR Books.
Boyle, Catherine M.
   1993 "Touching the air: The cultural force of women in Chile," pp. 156–172 in Sarah A. Radcliffe and Sallie Westwood (eds.), *"Viva": Women and Popular Protest in Latin America.* London: Routledge.
Brazilian Institute of Geography and Statistics
   1999 "What color are you?" pp. 386–390 in Robert M. Levine and John J. Crocetti (eds.), *The Brazil Reader: History, Culture, Politics.* Durham, NC: Duke University Press.
Brito Peña, Alejandra et al.
   1995 *Voces femeninas y construcción de identidad.* Buenos Aires: Consejo Latinoamericano de Ciencias Sociales.
Bueno, Eva Paulino
   2000 "Race, gender, and the politics of reception of Latin America *testimonios*," pp. 115–147 in Amal Amireh and Lisa Suhair Majaj (eds.), *Going Global: The Transnational Reception of Third World Women Writers.* New York: Garland.
Bueno, Eva P. and Terry Caesar (eds.)
   1998 *Imagination beyond Nation: Latin American Popular Culture.* Pittsburgh, PA: University of Pittsburgh Press.
Caulfield, Sueann
   2000 *In Defense of Honor: Sexual Morality, Modernity, and Nation in Early Twentieth-Century Brazil.* Durham, NC: Duke University Press.
Ebert, Teresa L.
   1995 "(Untimely) critiques for a red feminism," pp. 113–149 in Mas'ud Zavarzadeh, Teresa L. Ebert, and Donald Morton (eds.), *Post-ality: Marxism and Postmodernism.* Washington, DC: Marxist Boundary Work in Theory, Economics, Politics and Culture, vol. 1, Maisonneuve Press.
Ehrick, Christine
   1999 "*Madrinas* and missionaries: Uruguay and the Pan-American women's movement," pp. 62–80 in Mrinalini Sinha, Donna Guy, and Angela Woollacott (eds.), *Feminisms and Internationalism.* Oxford: Blackwell.

Elkin, Judith Laikin
1998 *The Jews of Latin America*, rev. ed. New York: Holmes and Meier.
Fernandez, Nadine T.
1996 "The color of love: Young interracial couples in Cuba." *Latin American Perspectives* 88, 23:1 (Winter): 99–117.
Fernández Olmos, Margarite and Lizabeth Paravisini-Gebert (eds.)
1993 *Pleasure in the Word: Erotic Writing by Latin American Women*. New York: Penguin Books.
Fiol, Matta
1995 "The 'schoolteacher of America': Gender, sexuality, and nation in Gabriela Mistral," pp. 201–229 in Emilie L. Bergmann and Paul Julian Smith (eds.), *¿Entiendes? Queer Readings, Hispanic Writings*. Durham, NC: Duke University Press.
Foster, David William (ed.)
1999 *Chicano/Latino Homoerotic Identities*. New York: Garland.
Franco, Jean
1989 *Plotting Women: Gender and Representation in Mexico*. New York: Columbia University Press.
1998 "The long march of feminism." *NACLA: Report on the Americas* 31 (January-February): 10–15.
Gargallo, Francesca
1990 "El feminismo en América Latina: ¿Cómo construir un movimiento político intransigente?" *fem* 14 (November): 4–7.
Gomes da Cunha, Olivia Maria
1998 "Black movements and the 'politics of identity' in Brazil," pp. 220–251 in Sonia E. Alvarez, Evelina Dagnino, and Arturo Escobar (eds.), *Cultures of Politics, Politics of Cultures: Re-Visioning Latin American Social Movements*. Boulder, CO: Westview Press.
Gordon, Edmund T.
1998 *Disparate Diasporas: Identity and Politics in an African Nicaraguan Community*. Austin: University of Texas Press.
Guerra, Lucía
1994 *La mujer fragmentada: Historias de un signo*. Havana: Casa de las Américas.
Gutmann, Mathew C.
1996 *The Meanings of Macho: Being a Man in Mexico City*. Berkeley: University of California Press.
Hahner, June E.
1998 "Introduction," pp. xi-xxvi in June E. Hahner (ed.), *Women through Women's Eyes: Latin American Women in Nineteenth-Century Travel Accounts*. Wilmington, DE: SR Books.
Helg, Aline
1990 "Race in Argentina and Cuba, 1880–1930: Theory, policies, and popular reaction," pp. 37–69 in Richard Graham (ed.), *The Idea of Race in Latin America, 1870–1940*. Austin: University of Texas Press.
Hendrickson, Carol
1995 *Weaving Identities: Construction of Dress and Self in a Highland Guatemala Town*. Austin: University of Texas Press

Hennessy, Rosemary and Chrys Ingraham
1997 "Introduction: Reclaiming anticapitalist feminism," pp. 1–14 in Rosemary Hennessy and Chrys Ingraham (eds.) *Materialist Feminism: A Reader in Class, Difference, and Women's Lives*. New York: Routledge.

Hopenhayn, Martin
2000 "Globalization and culture: Five approaches to a single text," pp. 142–157 in Anny Brooksbank Jones and Ronaldo Munck (eds.), *Cultural Politics in Latin America*. New York: St. Martin's Press.

Ippolito, Emilia
2000 *Caribbean Women Writers: Identity and Gender*. Rochester, NY: Camden House.

Jones, Anny Brooksbank and Ronaldo Munck (eds.)
2000 *Cultural Politics in Latin America*. New York: St. Martin's Press.

Kaplan, Caren and Inderpal Grewal
1999 "Transnational feminist cultural studies: Beyond the marxism/poststructuralism/feminism divide," pp. 349–363 in Caren Kaplan, Norma Alarcón, and Minoo Moallen (eds.), *Between Woman and Nation: Nationalisms, Transnational Feminisms, and the State*. Durham, NC: Duke University Press.

Klein, Charles
1998 "Gender, sexuality and AIDS prevention in Brazil." *NACLA: Report on the Americas* 31 (January–February): 27–32.

La Duke, Betty
1985 *Compañeras: Women, Art, and Social Change in Latin America*. San Francisco: City Light Books.

Lancaster, Roger
1992 *Life Is Hard: Machismo, Danger, and the Intimacy of Power in Nicaragua*. Berkeley: University of California Press.

Latin American Perspectives
1999 "If truth be told: A forum on David Stoll's *Rigoberta Menchú and the Story of All Poor Guatemalans*." 109, 26:6 (November).

Lavrín, Asunción
1989 "Introduction: The scenario, the actors, and the issues," pp. 1–43 in Asunción Lavrín (ed.), *Sexuality and Marriage in Colonial Latin America*. Lincoln: University of Nebraska Press.
1995 *Women, Feminism, and Social Change in Argentina, Chile, and Uruguay, 1890–1940*. Lincoln: University of Nebraska Press.
1999 "International feminism: Latin American alternatives," pp. 175–190 in Mrinalini Sinha, Donna Guy, and Angela Woollacott (eds.), *Feminisms and Internationalism*. Oxford: Blackwell.

Lumsden, Ian
1996 *Machos, Maricones, and Gays: Cuba and Homosexuality*. Philadelphia, PA: Temple University Press.

Mallon, Florencia E.
1994 "The promise and dilemma of subaltern studies: Perspectives from Latin American history." *American Historical Review* 99 (December): 1491–1515.

Martínez, Elena M.
1996 *Lesbian Voices from Latin America: Breaking Ground*. New York: Garland.

Matthews, Irene
2000 "Translating/transgressing/torture . . . ," pp. 85–112 in Marguerite R. Waller and Jennifer Rycenga (eds.), *Frontline Feminisms: Women, War, and Resistance*. New York: Garland.
McAllister, Carlota
1996 "Authenticity and Guatemala's Maya Queen," pp. 105–124 in Colleen Ballerino Cohen, Richard Wilk, and Beverly Stolltje (eds.), *Beauty Queens on the Global Stage*. New York: Routledge.
Melhus, Marit and Kristi Anne Stølen (eds.)
1996 *Machos, Mistresses, Madonnas*. London: Routledge.
Menchú, Rigoberta
1984 *I, Rigoberta Menchú*, ed. Elisabeth Burgos-Debray. London: Verso.
1998 *Crossing Borders*, translated and edited by Ann Wright. London: Verso.
Mignolo, Walter D.
2000 *Local Histories/Global Designs: Coloniality, Subaltern Knowledges, and Border Thinking*. Princeton, NJ: Princeton University Press.
Miller, Francesca
1991 *Latin American Women and the Search for Social Justice*. Hanover, NH: University Press of New England.
Minh Ha, Trinh
1989 *Woman, Native, Other*. Bloomington: Indiana University Press.
Minority Rights Group (ed.)
1995 *No Longer Invisible: Afro-Latin Americans Today*. London: Minority Rights Publications.
Mörner, Magnus
1970 "Historical research on race relations in Latin America during the national period," pp. 199–230 in Magnus Mörner (eds.), *Race and Class in Latin America*. New York: Columbia University Press.
Munck, Ronaldo
2000 "Afterword: Postmodernism, politics, and culture in Latin America," pp. 185–205 in Anny Brooksbank Jones and Ronald Munck (eds.), *Cultural Politics in Latin America*. New York: St. Martin's Press.
Olea, Raquel
1995 "Feminism: Modern or postmodern?" pp. 192–200 in John Beverley, José Oviedo, and Michael Aronna (eds.), *The Postmodernism Debate in Latin America*. Durham, NC: Duke University Press.
Pérez, Emma
1999 "Feminism-in-nationalism: The gendered subaltern at the Yucatán Feminist Congresses of 1916," in Caren Kaplan, Norma Alarcón, and Minoo Moallen (eds.), *Between Woman and Nation: Nationalisms, Transnational Feminisms, and the State*. Durham, NC: Duke University Press.
Pérez Sarduy, Pedro and Jean Stubbs (eds.)
1994 *AfroCuba: An Anthology of Cuban Writing on Race, Politics and Culture*. Melbourne: Ocean Press.
Radcliffe, Sarah A. and Sallie Westwood
1996 *Remaking the Nation: Place, Identity, and Politics in Latin America*. London: Routledge.
Ranchod-Nilsson, Sita and Mary Ann Tétrault
2000 "Gender and nationalism: Moving beyond the fragmented conversations," in

Sita Ranchod-Nilsson and Mary Ann Tétrault (eds.), *Women, States, and Nationalism: At Home in the Nation?* London: Routledge

Randall, Margaret
1979 *El pueblo no solo es testigo: La historia de Dominga de la Cruz.* Rio Piedras, Puerto Rico: Huracán.
1981 *Sandino's Daughters.* Vancouver: New Star Books.
1995 "To change our own reality and the world: A conversation with lesbians in Nicaragua," pp. 127–151 in Margaret Randall (ed.), *Our Voices, Our Lives: Stories of Women from Central America and the Caribbean.* Monroe, ME: Common Courage Press.

Robles, Victor Hugo
1998 "History in the making: The homosexual liberation movement in Chile." *NACLA: Report on the Americas* 31 (January-February): 36–43.

Sánchez, Rosaura and Beatrice Pita
1999 "Mapping cultural/political debates in Latin American Studies." *Cultural Studies* 13 (April): 290–318.

Sarduy Pérez, Pedro and Jean Stubbs
1995 "Introduction," pp. 1–17 in Minority Rights Group (ed.), *No Longer Invisible: Afro-Latin Americans Today.* London: Minority Rights Publications.

Scheper-Hughes, Nancy
1992 *Death without Weeping: The Violence of Everyday Life in Brazil.* Berkeley: University of California Press.

Sinha, Mrinalini, Donna J. Guy, and Angela Woollacott
1999 "Introduction: Why feminisms and internationalism?" pp. 1–13 in Mrninalini Sinha, Donna J. Guy, and Angela Woollacott (eds.), *Feminisms and Internationalism.* Oxford: Blackwell.

Stabile, Carol A.
1997 "Feminism and the ends of postmodernism," pp. 395–408 in Rosemary Hennessy and Chrys Ingraham (eds.), *Materialist Feminism: A Reader in Class, Difference, and Women's Lives.* New York: Routledge.

Stern, Steve J.
1995 *The Secret History of Gender: Women, Men, and Power in Late Colonial Mexico.* Chapel Hill: University of North Carolina Press.

Sternbach, Nancy Saporta et al.
1992 "Feminisms in Latin America: From Bogotá to San Bernardo." *Signs* 17 (Winter): 393–434.

Stienstra, Deborah
2000 "Dancing resistance from Rio to Beijing: Transnational women's organizing and United Nations conferences, 1992–6," pp. 208–223 in Marianne H. Marchand and Anne Sisson Runyan (eds.), *Gender and Global Restructuring: Sightings, Sites and Resistances.* London: Routledge.

Stoner, K. Lynn
1991 *From the House to the Streets: The Cuban Woman's Movement for Legal Reform, 1898–1940.* Durham, NC: Duke University Press.

Torres, Arlene and Norman E. Whitten Jr. (eds.)
1998 *Blackness in Latin America and the Caribbean: Social Dynamics and Cultural Transformation.* Vol. II: *Eastern South America and the Caribbean.* Bloomington: Indiana University Press.

United Nations
    2000 The World's Women 2000: Trends and Statistics. New York: Social Statistics and Indicators, Series K, no. 16, United Nations.
Vargas, Virginia
    1992 "The feminist movement in Latin America: Between hope and disenchantment." Development and Change 232(3): 195–214.
    1995 "Women's movements in Peru: Rebellion into action," pp. 73–100 in Saskia Wieringa (ed.), Subversive Women: Women's Movements in Africa, Asia, Latin America and the Caribbean. London: Zed Books.
Wieringa, Saskia
    1995 "Introduction: Subversive women and their movements," pp. 1–22 in Saskia Wieringa (ed.), Subversive Women: Women's Movements in Africa, Asia, Latin America and the Caribbean. London: Zed Books.
Young, Iris Marion
    1997 Intersecting Voices: Dilemmas of Gender, Political Philosophy, and Policy. Princeton, NJ: Princeton University Press.
Yúdice, George
    1992 "Postmodernity and transnational capitalism in Latin America," pp. 1–28 in George Yúdice, Jean Franco, and Juan Flores (eds.), On Edge: The Crisis of Contemporary Latin American Culture. Minneapolis: University of Minnesota Press.

Story without Words: Women and the Creation of a *Mestizo* People in Guayaquil, 1820–1835

Camilla Townsend

A woman sat silently on her raft in the river; the water made only the faintest lapping sound. She looked out at the city of Guayaquil and listened to the music and laughter, the yells and scuffling. During the chaos of the recent wars for independence, a small floating city had come to be anchored next to this big port town. A network of creeks and streams ran into the River Guayas, and then the river ran its course down to the Pacific. People came and went along these watery highways, depending on where the current war trouble was. Some built up little houses on their rafts; a few operated temporary taverns. They were proud of the fact that the foundations of their structures, unlike those of the city folk, never rotted away in the rainy season. Whenever the police chased them away, they came back a few weeks or months later (Terry, 1834: 81; Stanley, 1850: 70).

The woman certainly spoke sometimes to people on neighboring crafts. She might have told them where she had come from or where she was going. But neither she nor they ever wrote down anything she said—or, if they did, they destroyed the paper not long after. And yet this ordinary woman, with little or no property to her name, was regularly scrutinized, judged, and criticized by people who wrote long and often. Elite city officials mentioned her in their newspapers, their court cases, their church records, and their letters to each other. Thus, although we do not know much of what she said, we do know much of what she did. Her actions are themselves testimony to her life. In studying them, we can come to terms with at least part of her life's significance—with the impact that she and her contemporaries had on their society

This chapter first appeared in *Latin American Perspectives* 95, 24:4 (July 1997), pp. 50–68.

and its future. Without their words, we can still try to tell their story and articulate its relevance to others.

The extent of the record keepers' commentary on these women is a measure of their fear and concern about them. The *jornaleras*, or women day laborers of Indian and African descent, were the least powerful members of society, and yet they of all groups, except perhaps for the unpaid military troops, apparently provoked the most unease among the elites. They were more active in certain ways than many members of the elite wished them to be. Their ability to remain so even in the face of their extreme powerlessness was probably the basis for the elites' concerns. Although the record keepers complained about the women's lifestyles and their insistence on talking or refusing to talk in the wrong situations, the elites may have been unaware of the more serious long-term consequences of their actions: Despite being buffeted by economic change and by the deployment of cultural power all around them, the late-colonial and early-republican women day laborers managed to negotiate their own path, choosing their own relationships and raising their children to create a people with a new identity. Albeit unconsciously, they created a people whose members could later move consciously toward a definition of themselves as *guayaquileños* and as workers.[1]

The concept of *mestizaje* is at issue here. *Mestizaje* is often accepted uncritically as a key process in the unfolding history of the region, but in fact its occurrence was hardly a foregone conclusion. Three races existed together, but it did not necessarily follow that women would choose to disown their communities' traditions and establish relationships with partners from outside their own groups. And even if we were to take random sex for granted it would not necessarily follow that the mixed children would think of themselves as something different rather than simply as children of their mothers' group. People of a range of colors might have continued to think of themselves more decidedly than they in fact did as "Spanish" or "black" or "indigenous." The women day laborers transformed not only the population but also the population's self-understanding. The importance of this phenomenon is underscored by the fact that it did *not* occur everywhere that different groups of people lived in close proximity.

It is more than time to look at this well-known phenomenon very concretely in a specific time and place. In the long run, comparative studies will be necessary for the full elucidation of its causes and implications, but for now I have chosen my moment: in the late-colonial and early-republican era, the common women of indigenous, African, and Spanish descent forged a *mestizo* people on the coast of the former Kingdom of Quito. They came to be the majority of the residents in the city of Guayaquil and in other towns, and there they met and interacted daily with people different from themselves. Out of an array of possibilities, they chose how to conduct their relationships and raise their children. The Spanish words categorizing whites, blacks, Indians, and various combinations thereof came to have less and less meaning or, at least, different and hazier meanings. The word *guayaquileño*, which had referred only to elites, began to take on new meaning when it became difficult or impossible to describe someone effectively in a legal document as *indígena* or *Negro, natural de la costa*. I contend that we can best explore the reasons for this change by studying working women's lives in depth.

The project of historicizing the identities of subaltern women in Latin America is necessarily fraught with problems. Perhaps first and foremost is the obvious one already presented—that we have few or no words of their own. More worrisome, however, is the possibility that in debating these issues of individuals' internal consciousness of themselves we may lose sight of broader patterns in the deployment of power. That is, our new knowledge of the ways in which these women conceived of themselves and why they made the decisions that they did will become self-referential and of limited interest if we do not also explore the social and political *impact* of their self-conceptions and decisions. These women in fact altered the array of possible futures for their grandchildren by changing the population's self-understanding. One scholar has gone so far as to call *mestizaje* "the ultimate Achilles' heel of colonialism" (Dunbar Ortiz, 1993).

It was with the latter concerns in mind that I originally turned to a study of women and *mestizaje* in the province of Guayas. Despite the growing number of studies of *mestizaje* on the part of anthropologists and literary critics, there are few works that consider women's agency in the process. Claudio Esteva Febregat (1995) includes women as a category in his comprehensive work but does not consider that they may have had perspectives of their own, and Manuel Espinoso Apolo (1995) does not address gender in his otherwise pathbreaking study of the Ecuadorian case. Indian and black women have generally been assumed to be pawns at worst or enactors at best of discourses concerning identity. But when we think about it, it seems clear that such women have been making their own decisions for generations. We should listen to what they tell us, for what might we learn about *mestizaje*? Florencia Mallon recently posed this question eloquently when she asked, "If th[ese women] are supposed to be the *tabula rasa*, the ground onto which men inscribe ethnicity or national identity in their struggles for power, what happens when the ground moves and speaks?" (Mallon, 1996: 176). I decided to try to listen to what such women had to say, through their deeds if not through their words. A few Andeanists had gone before me in exploring the territory of the early colonial period. An early book emphasizing the importance of these issues was Magnus Mörner's *Race*

Mixture in the History of Latin America (1967). In the days before there was a feminist historiography to consult, Mörner touched on the central role of women in the processes of conquest and miscegenation. In the late 1970s, Elinor Burkett, referring to Mörner's ideas, wrote about dislocated Indian women in the aftermath of the conquest and their importance in the formation of an early mestizo society in the Andean region (Burkett, 1978).

Most scholars agree that between the period Burkett describes and the late colonial there were no cataclysmic disruptions to established social patterns and hierarchies in the area, but the late-18th-century Bourbon reforms and then the independence wars brought a new period of flux to women and their families. This was a period of relatively dramatic migration in the region. People moved toward the city of Guayaquil from four directions. It was at least as much the push from the countryside as the pull from the city that brought the people to town. Over the course of the previous two generations, many native people had come down from their Andean villages because of the declining production of their traditional textiles in the face of British competition and rumors of jobs on coastal plantations growing cacao for export and lowered Indian tribute payments in the lowlands, dominated by political liberals. Yet, having apparently come in search of agricultural work, these newcomers, along with some of the local indigenous people and freed slaves, often chose to move to the city. What these three groups had in common was their landlessness. Former slaves of course had been given nothing but freedom, and as cacao production became more profitable some of the coastal Indians began to lose their land. The wealthy expanded their plantations along the riverine network through clever legal maneuvers; by 1830 in the province of Machala, for example, most indigenous residents were landless. And there simply were not enough jobs on the large cacao plantations to provide for an army of day laborers composed of immigrant highlanders, uprooted lowlanders, and some descendants of slaves (Hamerly, 1973; Contreras, 1990).[2] Worst of all were the times when the troops of one side or another in the independence wars came through, taking food and farm animals wherever they found them and sometimes raping women and drafting men as well (*El Patriota de Guayaquil*, June 2 and 30, 1821; *Biblioteca Municipal de Guayaquil* [henceforth BMG], vol. 67, March 7, 1827).

In rural areas where mass dislocation was not an issue, the indigenous people most resented the centuries-old *contribución* or tribute in cash and labor time that they were still expected to pay. In colonial times women had been excluded; some enthusiastic early-republican collectors included them until 1827, when an order came to spare them, given that they were theoretically dependents (Van Aken, 1981; *Archivo Nacional de História, Fondo Gobierno*, vol. 75, January 29, 1827). But even then, when a woman's husband or father was taken to a labor site for weeks or even months at a time she sometimes had no choice but to head toward a populous center in search of some kind of paid work. When the collectors approached, many and sometimes most of the tribute-paying men disappeared for a while, and according to the frustrated officials, the women simply did not seem to know what had happened to them (BMG, vol. 92, October 26, 1830, and vol. 118, March 28, 1831). Many indigenous people who came to the city and passed as mestizos no longer had to pay the tribute: the rising numbers of "white mestizos" (Hamerly, 1973) indicate that many natives acted on their knowledge of that fact.

A small proportion of the migrants were runaway slaves. Plantation owners wrote irate letters to the city's chief of police demanding that he do his job and find someone who had escaped from them and was assumed to be in the city. Three such women, María Enrique and Paula and María Rivera, were caught in February 1834 and returned to their angry masters (El Colombiano, February II, 1834). We do not know what happened to them afterwards.

The attraction of the city lay in the possibility of anonymity and work. The pull was stronger for women than for men. The limited jobs that did exist on the plantations were primarily jobs for males. Men could also become fishermen, cut timber, herd cattle, work in the salt mines, or dive for pearls or for the caracolillo shells used to make purple dyes. Women were not hired for such work. If they lived in the city, however, they could labor as cooks, maids, peddlers, bakers, laundresses, seamstresses, dancers, barkeepers, and prostitutes. The statistics bear out this commonsense interpretation. A church census taken in a central parish in 1832 demonstrated that in every age-group except those of children under 14 and men and women over 60, the number of women exceeded the number of men. On average, there were half again as many women as men. In the rural areas, in contrast, there were often more men than women (Hamerly, 1973: 93–97). We can assume that slaves were distributed by their owners in town and country houses in order to maximize their usefulness; not surprisingly, in the same central parish of the city, there were only 86 percent as many enslaved men as enslaved women.

This count does not take into consideration the poorest people living at the edge of the city on the savannah or in the floating city of rafts. The church census covered only the clearly demarcated city blocks, but government correspondence leaves no doubt that there were many people living beyond their boundaries. A large number of women apparently not only lived there but also headed households. The chief of police commented, "There are many married women [that is, with children] who live separately from their husbands and maintain themselves" (BMG, vol. 68, February 6, 1827). He is unlikely to have been speaking of the central parish, for in the census there appear only about 100 women heads of household, and even combined with similar numbers from two other central parishes such a total in a city of approximately 20,000 would hardly have been enough to arouse comment.

Marriage records prove that some of these women were choosing interracial relationships. For example, "Alejo de Silva, a free *zambo* from Paita, resident in this city . . . and Martina Flores, a mestiza from Puertovieja . . . [are] free to marry without any Impediment which may prevent them" (*Archivo Histórico del Guayas* [henceforth AHG], document 500, 1827). Even a complete count of the many such cases would fail, however, to yield an accurate calculation of the proportion of mixed relationships, for many and possibly most of the city's poor did not legally marry. They even went so far as to complain about the cost of the service, which some said prevented them from going through with it (*9 de Octubre*, July 6, 1833). Sometimes city residents who had been taken for Indians by the authorities and had had the tribute demanded of them went to court; although they could not produce marriage certificates belonging to their mothers or grandmothers, they were able to produce witnesses testifying that they were indeed of mixed descent (AHG, documents 585, 1818; 898, 1830; 6240, 1830).

There is other evidence, however, concerning the scope of the phenomenon of interracial relationships. When the Spanish colonized the area, a thin stratum of white "pure bloods" ruled over a population of coastal indigenous and imported African slaves. There were words referring to "mixed bloods": *mulatto* (white and black), *mestizo* (white and Indian), and *zambo* (black and Indian). The category *zambo*, once a relatively rare designation, eventually included anyone who had any percentage of black and Indian ancestry, such as the child of a mulatto and a mestizo, for example. By the 1820s and 1830s, court records indicate that it was this word that came to dominate people's descriptions of themselves before judges and people's designations of each other in recounted conversations: the word *zambo* appears more often in the notarial documents than any other racial designation.

It is important to remember that we are talking about more than sexual ties between people. Emotional bonds were being forged in what should be seen as cross-cultural relationships. Unless coercion is involved, as in the case of slavery, miscegenation depends upon women's interest and willingness, which generally depends on their forming affective ties. To understand why and how these ties were formed, we must look at the situation in which the women found themselves. It is not enough to say that they lived in close proximity to many kinds of men: if that were all that were needed, all cities would rapidly undergo the process of *mestizaje*. In fact there was more to the story. The women were often newcomers or the immediate descendants of newcomers and thus people who had broken their traditional community ties and needed to forge new ones. They were also poor, with limited options and often with children to support. Relationships with men—even temporary ones—could be a significant help.[3] There may not have been enough men of a woman's own particular group to go around, but men could of course be shared. Thus there had to be other, more significant reasons for women's not limiting them-selves to men of their own group; some women, especially the fugitives, were consciously seeking to discard old identities, and those who were not soon learned that they were no longer bound by the traditional practices of an In-dian village or a slave plantation.

THE QUESTION OF SURVIVAL

If, however, the women day laborers experienced in common with others a high degree of cultural interplay and were familiar with many of the same sights and sounds, they still experienced a degree of poverty as unfamiliar to wealthy residents as to most modern readers. Whatever the pleasures of life in the Ciudad Nueva, most working women did not live there. To get to the Ciu-dad Vieja, where most of them would end up living, they had to cross a bridge that traversed a small estuary running into the river. Looking up over the war-ren of houses, a pedestrian could just see at the top of the hill the Iglesia Santo Domingo, built of heavy stone two centuries earlier. Smoke from the cooking fires hovered in the houses; filth ran down the narrow alleys and stone steps, and disease spread rapidly (Estrada, 1973: 85; Hamerly, 1973: 16–17).

Often a woman's way lay not along these winding streets but rather away from the hills and the central area toward the savannah. Between May and December it was hot and dry there until the sun went down; from January to April it was steamy hot and often raining. Then many of the streets ran with mud, making it impossible to use a carriage or a cart. There was a decent road to the cemetery on the edge of town, but if a person's way lay toward the slaughterhouse or the tannery instead it would be a difficult walk (BMG, vol. 133, December 21, 1832). Recently, more and more people had been building bamboo houses on stilts as the indigenous peoples of the coast had been used to doing for generations. In the sheltered area under the house the women cooked and kept any animals they had, and when they were ready to go inside they climbed a ladder into the house. Those who were better off partitioned their one room into two; usually the only furniture consisted of a hammock (Stevenson, 1825: 201).

Here the people shared many of the problems of the inhabitants of the Ciu-dad Vieja. Water had to be carried for a long distance or up a steep incline or bought at a high price. The entire city swarmed with mosquitoes, but only in these parts was mosquito netting scarce. It was difficult to keep the unfloored living quarters free of snakes, scorpions, and the *niguas* that laid their eggs in bare feet (Terry, 1834: 83–84). When it rained, muddy rivulets formed on the dirt floor. And when an army of ants carried off the bread it was often impossible to find the money to buy more. Sometimes 15 people lived in one room; even with so many helping, it usually required all their resources to obtain food from day to day.

A day could begin like any other day and end in an inferno if sparks flew from a kitchen fire or even from a frigate anchored in the port (*Et Patriota de Guayaquit*, May 23, 1827; BMG, vol. 92, June 4, 1830). Sometimes whole city blocks exploded in flames. People came to stare and then to hurry away, for the troops called in to fight the disaster hurled insults and abuse as they worked (*El Colombiano del Guayas*, November 12, 1829; BMG, vol. 109, January 11, 1831). Afterwards, the wreckage smoldered.

Every person on every street was subject to the epidemic diseases that struck with deadly effect, but some neighborhoods were more dangerous than others. In early colonial days, the Guayas River had been considered healing water, but in recent times, as more and more migrants poured down from the Andes, the river's reputation had deteriorated. These migrants were used to cooler, drier air and had never been exposed to these tropical maladies before, so they succumbed easily and painfully (Pineo, 1990: 612–618). By 1813, the dockyards area adjacent to the savannah and the Cerro Santa Ana was already notoriously unhealthy, to the point that some doctors would not even go in (Hamerly, 1973: 182). Yellow fever, cholera, and smallpox were perhaps the greatest enemies. There was nothing to be done about the first two except to check incoming ships for signs of disease, but people could fight against smallpox. The local government tried to stop its coming, ordering vials of the "best-quality" vaccinating serum from Bogotá, where it had been sent from London. These men were not afraid of the miracles of modern science. They hung a flag to advertise the vaccine from the windows of the *Casa Consistorial* and wrote articles for the newspaper to try to bring people in. Few came. The authorities stormed against "the indolence of parents" who did not look out for their children, but still few came. They seemed to be more afraid of the vaccine than they were of the disease. Perhaps they thought they would be forced to pay a great deal of money for it, and perhaps they were right (BMG, vol. 61, December 15, 1826; *Archivo de la Secretaría Municipal* [hereafter ASM], *Particulares*, April 23, 1832).

After all, the government was short of money, especially for hospitals, and poor women bore the brunt of the shortages. Those who were better-off brought nurses and doctors into their own homes, but the women day laborers needed to be able to go somewhere for help. In some years there were hospitals or hospices for them to visit, but the doors of these opened and closed depending on the availability of resources. They never seemed to be considered very important by the people who made the decisions about them. There had been a women's hospital, for example, but it had been transformed into a military hospital despite protests in 1826. Even that hospital was always short of sheets (BMG, vol. 61, January 6,1826, and vol. 84, September 21, 1829; ASM, *Documentos Varios*, February 26, 1828). There was a charity hospital, rebuilt each time it burned down, but one could not be admitted to it without legal proof of poverty. Slaves could not receive attention there at all, as their masters or mistresses were supposed to care for them. Women slaves frequently suffered from venereal disease that their masters may have communicated to them (BMG, *Actas del Cabildo*, January 22, 1827, December 24, 1827, and January 4, 1828).[4]

In these circumstances, women raised their children, only sometimes with the help of men. In multiple ways, their lives were marked by new and unfamiliar forms of devastation, and in defense of their children and themselves they learned to meet it. Those who were trying to extricate themselves from slavery were committed to saving money each week toward buying themselves or members of their families (Townsend, 1993). Even those who did not face that predicament had to come up with enough resources every day to buy food for several persons, itself no easy task. A handful became midwives or seamstresses, but most did not have such an opportunity. There were really only three categories of legitimate work open to women: they could be peddlers, domestic workers, or barkeepers. Those who hawked food often worked in partnership with husbands and brothers from rural areas, who brought them canoes full of foodstuffs to sell in the city. A few gathered enough capital to become vendors of bread or of used clothing. Most domestic workers had less freedom than the peddlers in that they generally lived in the households of their employers. They carried water and messages, cooked and cleaned, laundered and ironed. Many were also subject to the sexual advances of the men in the house. In the larger houses the responsibilities were divided, but in a house with one servant a lone woman was expected to do everything. Some women elected to live on their own and take in laundry, although then they often faced more seriously straitened circumstances.

Many *guayaquileñas* subsisted on what they made working permanently as *chinganeras*, or bartenders. Foreign ship captains complained that their sailors always came back from the city thoroughly inebriated: it was true that the bars in Guayaquil were numerous and entertaining (*Archivo del Banco Central de Quito, Fondo Jijon y Camaaño*, vol. 52, p. 141, 1826). There, a man could drink, enjoy the music and the dancing, play cards, hire a prostitute. Judging by the frequency of references, more than half of the establishments were owned and operated by women. Sometimes a *chingara* sprang up informally and disappeared quickly: a group of young black women rented a room and offended the neighbors with their late-night dances and bawdy behavior. But in other cases the bars were well-known establishments: another black woman had two floors, a hired girl, and an investment in jewels (BMG, vol. 104, 1831; AHG, document 549, 1823).

The barkeepers were willing to take risks to increase their profits. They often allowed gambling with cards, even though such activities were illegal, and took precautions to make sure that they were caught as seldom as possible. Acting on a tip, the police chief burst into a billiard hall one night, where he found "no disorder at all" (BMG, vol. 73, March 8, 1827). Apparently, the hall's grapevine had worked with at least a minute to spare. The bars were frequently fined several pesos for staying open after hours (they were supposed to close at 10 or 11) and sometimes for leaving their doors open. Since the owners continued to make the same decisions despite the fines, we can only suppose that they were calculating a certain investment in fines, increasing their profits by more than they lost.

This was the only business in which common women could end up doing exceedingly well. Most female entertainers remained poor and lived with more violence and vulnerability than other women, but a few came to own their own bars, and in 1832 six were so successful as to have to join the elites in making a financial contribution toward the public debt. One Beatríz López made money in the 1820s but then lost her investment. At this point she decided to take the risk of sponsoring illegal gambling to attract more customers. Having been fined once, she continued to allow the profitable but reprehensible activity and was reported again by angry losers—and one of their wives—when her gamesters cheated once too often. In court she spoke in her own defense, attempting to portray herself as pathetic: "The debts that plague me are huge, for I have to pay 50 pesos a month for the rooms I use and 32 pesos within four months for the taxes levied against me. . . . The solution I chose was motivated by the fact that I am a pitiable woman who cannot bargain for herself" (*El Patriota de Guayaquil*, August 17, 1822; AHG, document 415, 1822). The judge rejected these excuses and forced her to sell the tavern (to a man) as punishment.

Still, the majority of the *chinganeras* had far less control over their lives than Beatríz López. Ana Yagual lived on the outskirts of the city with her aunt, an indigenous woman who had migrated from the coast, and together they operated an informal bar. Someone played the guitar outside to attract customers, and they sold rum and probably sexual services. Once when Ana's uncle was visiting them, he saw Ana protest that a departing guest still owed her money for unspecified services. The client was a Spanish soldier; when Ana went after him, he laughed, insulted her and her uncle, and left. Ana and her uncle apparently had their own ways of making a public statement, however; the soldier was found dead later that night, and the murderer was never discovered (AHG, document 536, 1823).

Many women were reduced to supporting themselves through some form of crime. Court records indicate that they often acted as receivers and processers working in partnership with men. The meat sold in the warren of narrow streets in the Ciudad Vieja rather than in the market had often been stolen. Men could take a cow from a nearby hacienda's herd, tie it in the savannah, slaughter it by candlelight when most people were asleep, and then bring it to sell in the early morning. When such cases were uncovered, they revealed a complex network of thieves and receivers, including people of all colors and both sexes, slave and free. The contraband trade also provided an illegal living. Most of the work available was for men, but families living in the Ciudad Vieja were paid to store goods, and in one case they secretly processed smuggled tobacco right in the house (AHG, document 754, 1823; BMG, vol. 130, February 26, 1832).

WOMEN'S DECISIONS

Given their extensive interactions and their limited material options, many—and probably most—women depended on relationships, at least from time to time, both to make ends meet and to survive psychologically. These relationships certainly were not always sexual and not always with men. Sometimes women looked to employers for help, but they had to be prepared to defend anything they gained at their hands. Vidala Plazarte, for example, had been a slave in a wealthy woman's house. Her dying mistress had freed Vidala and Vidala's daughters in her will and left her worldly wealth to a fund established to help found a school for elite girls, with special instructions that enough be set aside to buy Vidala and her family a small house. But the executor refused to spend the money. Vidala went to court, and the executor, the wealthy María Urbina, was enraged: "The maid has had no other motive than to plot against me." Besides, she argued, the school needed the money. Vidala answered that they were talking about a house, not "the school, which has nothing to do with us" (AHG, document 457, 1823).

More often women depended on personal relationships with men—some of whom were also their masters or employers. The arrangement was most useful (but perhaps also most dangerous and confining) when the men were of higher social status. A woman might move in with a printer, a lieutenant, or a baker. She would serve as both his mistress and his maid, but her standard of living and that of her children were the same as his as long as the relationship lasted. Usually other people—neighbors or the man's employers—ascribed her the status of a wife in their dealings with her (AHG, documents 2607, 1828; 888, 1829; BMG, vol. 80, January 26 and March 7, 1828). There were two exceptions. First, women who entered into relationships with the city's clergy, who were quite wealthy, were obviously not treated as wives. (In at least one case such a woman, who had met a monk while working in a bar, was clearly viewed as a prostitute.) And the women who formed attachments to foreign sailors, mostly from Britain and the United States, while not considered prostitutes, were understood to be living under purely temporary conditions. Despite this, priests and sailors could be quite useful in that they had some material resources; they could also help a woman transcend some of the frustrations of her straitened existence in that they had traveled and had stories to tell (AHG, document 1418, 1823).

In establishing relationships with men from outside their traditional communities—men who generally had more money and power than they—women ran certain risks. There were a few recorded cases of violent assault each year, and the end of a relationship could spell economic disaster. But many of the women fought for what they viewed as their rights. If they felt there was any hope of success, they frequently made legal demands on former partners for financial help in raising their children; in one case a woman demanded years of back pay for all the domestic work she had done for a lover who had now abandoned her—and the judge found in her favor (AHG, document 3561, 1825). During Carnaval the women often informally meted out their own brand of retribution on men whom it was no use taking to court. A foreign observer (Terry, 1834: 80) wrote:

> I saw one unfortunate fellow who had fallen into the clutches of about a dozen women. They had pinioned his arms, and plastered him from head to foot with paint, flour, soot, and mud, and were driving him through the streets, shouting, beating him, and covering him with all sorts of abomination. It appeared he had been a very active tormenter of these gentle beings, who had formed a conspiracy to punish him.

However, the same women who fought back against such men would still side with them if they were under attack by the elite. One woman, for example, who lived with a shoemaker, once fought actively to defend herself in a "domestic dispute" and did not hesitate to express a negative opinion of him, but the very next day, when he was accused of plotting a rebellion, she gave the authorities no help in locating him. "What hat was he wearing when he left the house?" they asked her. "The same hat as always," she said. "Yes, but what kind of hat was that?" And she described almost all the hats in the city when she answered, "A white straw hat with a dark ribbon." "Was it old?" No. "Was it new?" No. The questioners soon gave up (AHG, document 1420, 1823).

This woman was surviving in the city both materially and psychologically by choosing this cross-cultural relationship. She felt some antagonism toward the shoemaker, but she also drew a line around the two of them and against certain others. In siding with him she was defining herself very differently than her rural foremothers had done. Were she and other similar women conscious that they were forming an urban mestizo identity? Probably not. And yet they did make indirect political statements about this issue. When the government demanded a new head tax in 1827, for example, they not only insisted that they did not have the money but also verbally insulted the chief of police to his face and made disparaging comments about "the tribute"—rather than calling it "the tax." Only Indians paid tribute. In using that language, they were underlining the fact that whatever their past, they rejected for themselves the status assigned to indigenous people. The police chief was forced to write to the government that he was being asked to carry "an immense hatred." He complained that the behavior of the women was far worse than that of the men, but the government could do little to help him (BMG, vol. 73, February 3, March 16, and March 21, 1827).

Many women day laborers also did their best to undermine coercive labor practices. About a third of the fines recorded by the police were issued to women—a high proportion, considering their supposedly lesser role in public activity. They were penalized, for example, for sheltering army deserters and fugitive slaves and for transporting travelers unknown to the authorities in their boats. Once the city police, acting on a tip, entered a woman's house and found her hiding a runaway slave. They marched him away in the mud. The next month's paper printed the woman's name and the fine she owed in order to shame her. We cannot know if this was the last time she ever committed such a crime or if she ever saw her runaway friend again. We do know, however, that she was not the last woman in Guayaquil to act as she did.[5]

What seemed to anger elite families was not only that such women continued, despite their pain and the poverty, to rebel against authority, but that they did it with flair. They certainly knew that for many of their problems there was no way out, and yet they still seemed glad to be living free in the city. Every Sunday they annoyed the best families by appearing in fine clothes. One traveler—whose opinions were probably influenced by his elite hosts—wrote: "On holidays, troops of women, displaying satin shoes, silk stockings, golden and pearl ornaments . . . issue from holes and corners fitter for the residence of the mole, earthworm and bat, than for a human being" (Terry, 1834, 70). Other observers' comments also indicate that the women spent a significant portion of their lives repairing and embroidering, salvaging cast-offs, and pawning and redeeming goods in their efforts to appear occasionally as ladies.

Much of the elites' nervousness concerning these women was centered on the women's ability to talk. They did not like it that the women hurled insults in the street and testified in court, and they were afraid of the power of the women's gossip. When a respected merchant who had been active in the patriot cause learned that his slave and lover was pregnant with his child, he tried to send her to Cuenca, far up in the mountains, in order to preserve his "honor"— a plan that she sarcastically rejected. When the police learned that some black citizens had been heard complaining about whites at a baptismal party organized by women, they panicked, launching a full-fledged investigation that turned up nothing (AHG, document 698, 1822; BMG, vol. 104, 1831).

The irony in these women's having such a fearsome reputation is that they in fact could have participated in a real rebellion but chose not to.[6] Beginning in early 1827, other women and men gathered on the mountain of Chilintomo, north of the city near the town of Babahoyo. They were Indians who had lost their land, runaway slaves, military deserters, and other "fugitives from justice" who had built their community on the mountain, and they made war on the government's troops for three years (Nuñez, 1978; BMG, vol. 77, October 15, 1828; vol. 84, November 29, 1829). The women in the city had chosen to avoid the trouble in the countryside. They behaved as though they wanted only to be left alone by city authorities; they negotiated the maze of urban life on their own, largely without recourse to institutions. They bore children by whomever they chose and raised them as they saw fit, neither indigenous nor black. If they gave up the safety of familiar and traditional social bonds, they were able to form new ones and willing to fight to defend themselves. Theirs was a quieter revolution than that of Chilintomo: almost certainly without intending to, they created a mixed people, who thought of themselves as *guayaquileños* before they thought of themselves as the children and grandchildren of Indians, slaves, or Spanish. At the time, although the activities of the women did give them some cause for concern, the elites did not seem to realize how momentous such a change might be. Such a phenomenon would have to occur if it were ever to be possible for the people of Guayaquil to make demands as a class of workers. Later in the 19th century and deep into the 20th, that story would unfold.

NOTES

1. This is of more than academic interest in the case of Guayaquil, given the great strike of 1922 (see Pineo, 1988). I would argue that such events need to be placed in the context not only of labor history but of women's history as well.

2. The combined story told by these two historians is also confirmed in the extensive provincial government correspondence housed in the archive of the *Biblioteca Municipal de*

Guayaquil (hereafter BMG) (see e.g., vol. 70, September 15, 1828; vol. 80, September 22, 1828; vol. 112, January, 1831; vol. 132, February 11, 1831).

3. This point is to some extent self-evident. It has also been statistically proven for women in other cities for which more detailed census records exist. During the same period in Mexico City, for example, poorer women were less likely to choose to head their own households permanently (that is, remain outside of relationships with men) than wealthy women (see Arrom, 1985). Lebsock (1985) has uncovered the same statistical phenomenon in a Virginia city among women both white and black, some of them of Caribbean descent.

4. There are literally scores of cases in the AHG in which a male purchaser of a female slave sued to return the woman and get his money back on grounds that she had come to him from her former master with a venereal disease.

5. Police reports were published in *El Colombiano del Guayas* between August 1829 and February 1830. Most fines were for more minor offenses, such as keeping a bar open after hours.

6. Eric Van Young (1988) has described a similar situation in the cities of war-torn Mexico. There, too, migrants from the countryside had had their traditional ties severed and were in the process of forging new ones rather than uniting to plot revolution. Van Young does not discuss an additional factor, the preponderance of women in the cities, but Arrom (1985) has demonstrated that, at least in Mexico City, their being in the majority was a demographic fact.

REFERENCES

Arrom, Sylvia
    1985 *The Women of Mexico City, 1790–1857.* Stanford: Stanford University Press.
Burkett, Elinor
    1978 "Indian women in white society: The case of sixteenth-century Peru," in Asunción Lavrín (ed.), *Latin American Women: Historical Perspectives.* Westport, CT: Greenwood Press.
Contreras, Carlos
    1990 *El sector exportador de una economía colonial: La costa del Ecuador, 1760–1830.* Quito: Abya-Yala.
Dunbar Ortiz, Roxanne
    1993 "Invasion of the Americas and the making of the Mestizocoyote nation: Heritage of the invasion." *Social Justice* 20: 52–55.
Espinoso Apolo, Manuel
    1995 *Los Mestizos Ecuatorianos y las Señas de Identitad Cultural.* Quito: Ediciones Centro de Estudios Felipe Guaman Poma de Ayala.
Esteva Fabregat, Claudio
    1995 *Mestizaje in Iberoamerica,* translated by John Wheat. Tucson: University of Arizona.
Estrada, Julio
    1973 *El puerto de Guayaquil.* Vol. 2. Guayaquil: Archivo Histórico del Guayas.
Hamerly, Michael
    1973 *Historia social y económica de la antigua provincia de Guayaquil, 1763–1842.* Guayaquil: Banco Central del Ecuador.

Lebsock, Suzanne
1985 *The Free Women of Petersburg: Status and Culture in a Southern Town, 1784–1860.*
New York: W. W. Norton.
Mallon, Florencia
1996 "Constructing *mestizaje* in Latin America: Authenticity, marginality, and gender
in the claiming of ethnic identities." *Journal of Latin American Anthropology* 2(1):
170–179.
Mörner, Magnus
1967 *Race Mixture in the History of Latin America.* Boston: Little, Brown.
Nuñez, Jorge
1978 "Las luchas campesinas en la costa en el siglo XIX," in *Segundo Encuentro de Historia y Realidad Económica y Social del Ecuador,* vol. 1. Cuenca: Instituto de Investigaciones Sociales.
Pineo, Ronn
1988 "Reinterpreting labor militancy: The collapse of the cacao economy and the
general strike of 1922 in Guayaquil, Ecuador." *Hispanic American Historical Review* 68:
707–736.
1990 "Misery and death in the Pearl of the Pacific: Health care in Guayaquil, Ecuador,
1870–1925." *Hispanic American Historical Review* 70: 609–638.
Stanley, Edward
1850 *Six Weeks in South America.* London: Privately printed.
Stevenson, William Bennet
1825 *Historical and Descriptive Narrative of Twenty Years' Residence in South America.*
London: Hurst Robinson.
Terry, Adrian
1834 *Travels in the Equatorial Regions of South America.* Hartford: Cooke.
Townsend, Camilla
1993 "En busca de la libertad: Los esfuerzos de los esclavos guayaquileños por garan-
tizar su independencia después de la Independencia." *Procesos: Revista Ecuatoriana de
Historia* 4: 73–85.
Van Aken, Mark
1981 "The lingering death of Indian tribute in Ecuador." *Hispanic American Historical
Review* 61: 429–459.
Van Young, Eric
1988 "Islands in the storm: Quiet cities and violent countrysides in the Mexican Independence era." *Past and Present* 118: 130–155.

16

Brazilian Women in Exile: The Quest for an Identity

Angela Xavier de Brito

Translated by Charlotte Stanley

Following the military coup of 1964 and especially after the hardening of the repressive regime that followed in 1968, a number of Brazilians—mostly political activists—were forced to leave their country and plunge into the "dark tunnel" of exile. The first exodus just after 1964 turned toward Latin American countries, especially Cuba and Uruguay. Several years later Chile, under the government of Salvador Allende, attracted a great number of exiles. The 1973 coup in Chile, however, pushed them further, toward Europe (France, Sweden, Switzerland, Belgium, and West Germany for the most part), because Latin American countries no longer accepted them on a permanent basis. These exiles simultaneously lost their sociocultural frame of reference and were plunged into a different environment in which they had to confront and adapt to new cultural forms—a process made all the more difficult by great geographic and cultural distance.

The story of exile has not been written. Although a few books are beginning to appear on this period, they are more in the nature of personal accounts and memoirs, and like most of the history of our era, they are written by men (Gabeira, 1980; Sirkis, 1981; Polari de Alverga, 1982). With the exception of a few novels that give a partial image of women in exile through the bias of fiction (Fischer, 1982), I know of no work that deals with this specific population.

Of course, efforts have been made to preserve a little of this story of exiled women. But the raw material thus collected by Costa et al. (1980) has not been developed except in the unpublished works of one of the coauthors,

This chapter first appeared in *Latin American Perspectives* 49, 13:2 (Spring 1986), 58–80.

Valentina da Rocha Lima (1980, 1982). No one else to my knowledge has given this oral testimony the significance it deserves.

The objective of this article is to attempt to analyze the process of a quest for identity on the part of these exiled women. My central hypothesis is that the period of exile has exercised a fundamental influence on building the identity of the Brazilian women who have lived this experience either out of necessity or some form of choice. I will strive above all to show the social significance of feminine and feminist organizations in the context of the Brazilian community in exile and the influence of the country of refuge on their development.

I have used two collections of primary material: a series of undirected and in-depth conversations with forty Brazilian women (Costa et al., 1980) and the content analysis of the documents published by the *Circulo de Mulheres Brasileiros* (Circle of Brazilian Women) in Paris between 1975 and 1979.

My personal experience is certainly not foreign to this analysis. However, I have tried to take the necessary precautions so that it does not disproportionately influence the construction of my argument.

THE FIRST JOURNEY

In societies in which patriarchal values take root and have considerable importance, the "natural" functions of women are the only ones on which their socially recognized identity is based. With the modernization of society, some Brazilian women—belonging mostly to the middle class—have broken with certain of these values such as virginity, traditional marriage and family structures. This rupture goes hand in hand with a process of more or less successful professionalization and, usually, with their inclusion in revolutionary organizations. Because this rupture is individual, it is very fragile.

The inherent limitations of an article do not allow us to introduce here an in-depth critique of the situation of women in the Brazilian, or even Latin American, Left. However, an illumination of the principal traits concerning the political inclusion of women in these groups, the ideology in force, the structures and the behavior of male or female activists, can help us understand their situation prior to leaving their native land.

Being unable to escape the ideologically charged reality of the society that these groups wanted to combat, but of which they were a part, most women activists were content to occupy a subordinate role and to participate in the secondary tasks assigned them.

The organizations that were most directed toward mass action[1] certainly had feminine sections intended to politicize the mass of women habitually kept apart from politics. This did not prevent this work from being perceived as less important for ideological reasons: "the problems of women were explained by the class struggle and derived from a secondary contradiction, the essential differences being class antagonism" (Vazquez, 1982c: 23). They would not be resolved before the revolution because there was a cause and effect relationship between the latter and the liberation of women. That is why the few leading women refused to assume this type of work. It also explains the hierarchy established between activist women and those who were not, which has long been an impeding factor in any solidarity between them.

In the militarist groups an egalitarian relationship predominated, however. The theoretical principle of equality among human beings postulates the equality of the sexes and implicitly refuses any discrimination with respect to women, without taking into account the objective conditions of their lives in a society steeped in "machismo": the woman is *a* combatant, *an* activist, and combatants, like angels, have no sex. Thus women were included at the expense of their specificity, striving to imitate the behavior, attitude, and language of their masculine comrades whose positive identity seemed to them "a model that was both ideal and unattainable" (Marc-Lipiansky, 1978: 67)— while striving to wipe the slate clean of their own limitations arising from a differentiated socialization.

For example, in principle military training was imparted with no sex discrimination, but the handicaps accumulated by the women in the course of their prior education made it unequal. This explains a certain "paternalism" of the male comrades in dangerous actions and also the fact that the men rose more rapidly to positions of responsibility and direction. The centralism of these organizations served to reinforce this aspect, because these positions were reserved "for the best," for those who had "proved themselves" in the heat of action. Women were especially excluded from theoretical formulation and the elaboration of the political line (strategic or tactical).

Their role is important but secondary. "In the reality of combat, the woman is a comrade who will bring the qualities innate in her sex." Such was the current thinking, inspired by the military writings of Che Guevara. And these qualities were the same ones valued by society that they were seeking to destroy: to feed, clothe, and nurture (the activists); to educate (politically, that is, to transmit to new recruits the political line developed elsewhere); to be attractive (that is, to serve as a liaison among the combatants and as a legal facade for the clandestine hiding place) (Araujo, 1980: 129ff).

The weakness of the theoretical instruments with respect to the situation of women available to these groups, as well as the absence of moments of reflection that would make possible the collective taking in charge of the women's struggles, resulted in the fact that the women who participated in these organizations never felt this oppression as such and, hence, never were able to begin to build a positive identity.

But the concept of identity can be treated on two levels that complement each other: the first on the level of the individual and intragroup relations; the second on the level of intergroup relations. If we define the concept identity as did Erikson (1972), that is as a system of feelings and representations of oneself starting which one can define oneself, know oneself, and make oneself known, we are more on the first level.

"Erikson defines identity as both consciousness and process. As consciousness, he refers to the feeling (sense of identity) that the individual has of his own specificity. As process, he suggests an unconscious effort tending to establish the continuity of the lived experience and, finally, the solidarity of the individual with the ideals of the group" (Marc-Lipiansky, 1978: 70). He stressed this last aspect—belonging to a group whose characteristics make possible an identification—in the process of development of a positive identity.

On the other hand, according to Noelle Bisseret (1974: 7), the term domination expresses a social relation between groups such that one, the group dominated, is subject by the other, the dominant group, to a system of real constraints in the realm of the economic, the political, the juridical, and the ideological. The social identity of any group is based on relations of domination whether it exercises power in fact or is subject to it (in this way the identity of classes and that of sex categories are formed in their historical relativity) in such a way that the relations between groups identified as dominant and dominated can be considered as forming a system. This is the second level of analysis.

According to the elements described above, Brazilian women corresponded in all points and at all levels to the characteristics of a dominated group before leaving their country. On the other hand, they lacked that "sense of identity" that is determined by a consciousness of specificity. Even the functions of wife and mother were diffuse. On the other hand, at the time there was no feminist movement in Brazil that could give them a positive identification with a social group.

EXILE IN LATIN AMERICA

Even if we agree with Candido (1984) that our country has always looked to Europe while turning its back on its neighbors, the cultural distance between each Latin American country is, in certain respects, less than between the latter and the United States or Europe.

Deeper ties were woven among the countries of the continent, especially after the great hope of the Cuban Revolution in 1959 and the concept of a revolution on a continental scale that began to circulate in 1966.

Thus the first wave of Brazilian exiles, just after 1964, was directed essentially to the Latin American countries: Cuba, Uruguay and, to a lesser extent, Chile and Mexico. This was especially true in the case of political, trade union, and student leaders. The proximity of Brazil allowed them to pursue political struggles that favored their entrance into the countries of refuge and the maintenance of their status.

For the majority of women, this first exile was more a personal than a purely political decision. Their roles in the trade union and the student organisms, for those who were politically active, did not justify their departure in the early years after the coup.

> In 1964, I left for Uruguay because I was married. I was an activist but I had no objective reason to flee, I was not a leader, I had my work in the *União Nacional des Estudantes* (National Union of Students, UNE), my trade union work and in the campaign against illiteracy—and I was gaining ground in that work. Suddenly I had to live in a house, relegated not only to the category of nonactivist but to that of housewife, of "a type of woman who dabbles in politics." Even though Uruguay was a sympathetic country, I was living in a frustrating situation not only because of what I had lost, but above all because of the impossibility of being active there. Conditions were such that *he* continued to be the political activist, go to meetings, speak, argue and as for me . . . I was his wife. He continued to be a political activist and I ceased being one. (conversation with Sandra; Costa et al., 1980: 270–272)

Thus, political activity continued to be a benchmark for certain women, from which they felt excluded by the restrictions of Latin American society. The nonactivist women did what they had always done in their function as wives and mothers. The conditions in the countries of refuge, the dispersion of the Brazilian women, and the short duration of this first period of exile did not even allow them to ask questions, let alone organize themselves in some way or another.

EXILE IN CHILE

The subsequent period of exile is characterized by the massive exodus toward Chile, especially after 1970. A socialist experiment was being constructed there under the Unidad Popular (UP), which made Chile the crossroads for all the Latin American nationalities in exile.

However, the choice of the majority of Brazilians in exile was the recreation of the national political organizations along the same lines as the originals. For men, this was the guarantee of continuity of experience, of their identity as activists.

> The great majority (of the women) were there because of their husbands. They were completely on the fringes of Chilean society, because they did not speak the language and in their own families, because the men pursued their political activities while they stayed at home. (conversation with Zuleika Alembert; Costa et al., 1980: 60–61)

As in the previous exile, the women stayed at home, at least at the beginning. Like the men, the activist women clung to the only activity that gave them a semblance of an identity as precarious as it might be: they re-created their old organizations.

> I had a problem of loss of identity. I had political activity in Brazil, a center of interest. Suddenly, we arrive in Chile and we are displaced, unlike the men. They quickly reestablished themselves because they came with reputations as revolutionaries with a political entree. The fact that they were coming into another "macho" culture made it all the easier for them to make contacts. As for us, we stayed in their shadow. (conversation with Angela B; Costa et al., 1980: 426)

The precarious and individual rupture experienced by some could not withstand the move to a foreign country.

> There was a time in Chile when I felt that I was like my mother and that drove me crazy. In the final analysis, I had made a break and once again I was dying of jealousy and insecurity; I was doing domestic work, that is, I was repeating on another level exactly the same behavior of my mother. (conversation with Glorinha; Costa et al., 1980: 416)

Another woman stated: "For me Chile represented a step backward, my consciousness regressed ten years. Once again I was setting up housekeeping with a man, in a house, with a dog . . . 24 hours of political action every day counted for little . . . " (Conversation with Regina; Costa et al., 1980: 416).

We must point out that the structure of the society and the vision that Chilean political organizations of the Left had of women hardly facilitated their integration under a new form. The Chilean Left, even during the period of intense social struggles under Allende (and perhaps even because of that) did not break free from the traditional conception of the Latin American Left on the problems of women, "did not dare (nor was it able) to conceive of a new feminine identity" (Vazquez, 1982c: 23).

At the time of the coup in 1973, foreigners constituted the scapegoats on whom the military government's propaganda concentrated. Those who were not imprisoned in the national stadium or killed sought refuge in embassies or refugee centers set up by religious groups. Most of them were able to leave Chile thanks to the action of international groups that organized their departure to European countries in the face of the refusal of other Latin American countries to accept them on a permanent basis.

EXILE IN EUROPE

It was in Europe and most notably in France that the process of a new consciousness on the part of Brazilian women began to take shape.

According to Daniel Bertaux (1980), in the analysis of life histories, statistical validity is replaced by the search for the saturation point, the phenomenon seen in the majority of the chosen and constructed data. "The researcher can only be sure of having reached saturation to the extent that he has consciously sought to diversify his sources to the maximum" (Bertaux, 1980: 207–208).

If it is true that my data is not diversified in terms of social class, this is essentially due to the characteristics of the Brazilian population in exile, which was made up mostly of middle-class people and a minute number of working-class ones. But my data is certainly diversified from the point of view of age, social function, and status of women in it.

At every step of the testimony, the fact is affirmed that the process of reflection on the conditions of oppression of women could only be done in exile and especially in societies whose social conditions favored its appearance. It never could have been done in societies such as Brazil or Chile, imbued in patriarchal values.

Whether they were members of an activist family, like Dedna, wives, like Maricota da Silva and so many others, students, like Beatriz, or activists like Zuleika, Regina, or Sandra, they were unanimous in recognizing the influence of French society in the development of their reflections on women: "through the debates going on in Europe from the time I arrived there, I began to realize that there was something that had been hidden from me until then" (conversation with Regina; Costa et al., 1980: 414), and "for most of us, feminist consciousness arose in France because of the social movement going on there which served as a point of reference. There is a whole process of exchanging experiences with other women" (conversation with Zuleika Alembert; Costa et al., 1980: 62).

For the majority of Brazilians, exile in Europe was a prolongation of exile in Chile, but it was treated as if it was a new exile. The same themes that characterize the first phase of all exiles were found there, which Vazquez (1982a: 85) describes as: withdrawal into a national ghetto, sensation of provisional life, the anguish of loss of identity, and difficulties of fitting into a new culture.

The economic situation in Europe at the time of their arrival already showed warning signs of the economic crisis that would follow in 1974 with the abrupt rise in oil prices. They had to settle into the new reality more rapidly before the crisis made the conditions of their social adjustment more difficult.

The Latin American activist arriving in exile profited from a good image, that of someone who had fought for the liberation of his country and democracy, universal values that enabled the activists to recognize one another and to be recognized in the country of refuge. No doubt the myth of the Latin American *guerrillero* helped to "make the Latin American exile be accepted and even valued by an important sector of the population in the particular case of France, so that, even dispossessed of power, he is looked on positively" (Vazquez, 1982a: 85). This image worked much more in favor of the men than the women. For the latter, the image of the past was too weak to be of use. In exile, women had the same roles as before—roles in which they were "invisible" and little valued.

A certain number of male political activists continued to be supported in exile by organizations with the same ideological affiliation. Thus it was easier for them to remain in a secure and prestigious post. Those who tried to find a professional niche profited from the help of like-minded groups, in which suitable employment was given them more easily than to women—not only because of their image but also because of their prior achievements, their greater ease of abstraction and articulation, and their status as "head of family."

Women were never asked what they did in their home country: "In exile no one ever asked me what I had done in Brazil because the point of reference was my husband. . . . The woman is a shadow, the shadow of her husband or her companion" (conversation with Maricota da Silva; Costa et al., 1980: 40). Nevertheless, it was often the woman who supported the family in Brazil:

> In my organization, the woman was in fact the man of the house. In matters of security, we were expected to support our companions. In my case, for example, I had a job while he read, studied and participated. He was a professional cadre. The women were assigned to support the men while the men devoted themselves to the grand revolutionary tasks. But we women also participated in political activities; we had responsibilities; we did everything. I felt like an inferior being who made it possible for superior beings to read all day long. (conversation with Vania; Costa et al., 1980: 111–112)

No doubt this situation sharpened the contradictions that had long been latent.

Direct or indirect contact with women who affirmed "their differences with respect to individual or collective identity and [who] in this role participate

in the creation of a culture [that] directly pursues the construction of tomor-
row's world" (Michaud, 1978: 20) upset Brazilian women's perception of the
world and themselves.

> All of the women with whom I had contacts—all, without exception—had a femi-
> nine consciousness, an awareness of the discrimination to which women are subject
> and the role of women in society. Contact with these women marked the beginning
> of my being interested, of reading and realizing the degree of truth contained in the
> problems that they brought up. (conversation with Beatriz; Costa et al., 1980: 132)

Nevertheless, the women's movement in French society frightened a number of these Brazilian women in exile. We must not forget that most of them
arrived in France in 1973, which saw the launching of the *Mouvement pour la
libération de l'avortement et la contraception* (Movement for the Freedom of
Abortion and Contraception, MLAC), and of family planning,[2] in which
neighborhood feminist groups thrived. Accustomed to male supremacy and
subject to the ideas current in Latin American revolutionary groups, for
whom the women's struggle was an element of disunion in the working class,
they fell back on the old familiar forms of organization and declared themselves hostile to feminist ideas in the beginning.

> I never considered myself feminist. I even had a certain hostility to the word, or
> rather, I was afraid for political or pseudo-political reasons. I was afraid that the
> women's movement might compromise the workers' movement by causing division
> or contradiction. (conversation with Nora; Costa et al., 1980: 324)

As a subject group, women submitted to this universal vision of the Brazilian
Left, a vision that later helped to make them feel guilty after they had become
feminist.

Thus, around 1973 we see the creation of various feminine groups within
Brazilian political organizations, as for example, the female unit of the Debate
group.[3] At the same period the *Circulo de Mulheres Brasileiras No Exterior* re-
constituted itself in Paris. Most of these groups began a discussion on the theoretical causes of the oppression of women in capitalist society, generally
based on Marxist authors, their favorite reading being Engels's *Origins of the
Family, Private Property and the State*. Concrete, everyday experiences and
questions coming from the interaction with French society were once again
excluded from the debate.

But the feminist tide was much too strong to be resisted. Gradually within
these very groups we see the first contradictions between those who upheld
the old vision of the problems of women and those who wanted an analysis
and a more active denunciation of the foundations of feminine oppression, a
deeper questioning of the power relations between the sexes and of everyday

life. "Often the confrontation between two cultures entails a questioning of taboos and rites, in such a way (that they) are led to contest the traditional values that they should be preserving" (Vazquez, 1982a: 82). Thus,

> to accept ourselves as feminists . . . took a long time full of ideological contradictions and discoveries. One could assume the women's struggle sociologically, on behalf of far away people, but to assume that we ourselves, living abroad, were also a part of that half of humanity which experiences woman's condition everyday was a more complicated proposition. (*Circulo*, 1978a)

THE *CIRCULO DE MULHERES BRASILEIRAS* IN PARIS

The collective aspect of the process of building an identity was, as we have seen, basic, and the group dimension played a very important part in it. In the Brazilian community in exile, one organization played this role in a striking way, not only because of its longevity but also its makeup. The *Circulo de Mulheres Brasileiras*, or *Circulo* as it was known familiarly by its adherents, was a feminist-type group that gathered together a great number of Brazilian women between October 1975, the date of its creation, and the end of 1979. In its title we find the chief elements that define this organization: feminist, autonomous, Brazilian. It was *feminist* because "from our point of view, feminism is the fight which we women are making against specific oppression, tied to the social movement for the creation of new collective relations which are opposed to the dominant ideology in every domain" (*Circulo*, 1976b). It was *autonomous* in the sense that "the oppressed person is the best situated to fight against her oppression. Only women themselves, organized autonomously, can be the avant-garde of this struggle in defense of the demand issuing from their specific problems" (*Circulo*, 1976c: 5). And finally, it was *Brazilian* because, "the problems of the Brazilian woman have their own cultural characteristics which are not conducive to being fit into a European mold" (*Circulo*, 1976b).

Its first actions were noticeably marked by manifestations of solidarity with the nascent Brazilian feminist movement: they attempted to create ties with feminist groups in Brazil through an exchange of letters, publications, the analysis of the contents of the Brazilian feminist press, discussions on the paths to follow, rescue campaigns for feminist journals in financial difficulties, etc.

Even if it demanded autonomy, we must not forget that most of its members were also affiliated with leftist political groups whose first goal was to influence the women's movement to orient itself in the direction indicated by their political line. But the most "radical" faction of the *Circulo*—the group that concentrated on sexuality, the practice of "self-help" and knowledge and control over the body, called the "birth control group"—was composed mostly of *Campanha*[4] activists.

The contradictions that riddled the *Circulo* at that time are well illustrated in its political charter (1975), which gives the principal guidelines for its activists:

- denunciations of the forms of oppression to which Brazilian women—especially those of the lower classes—are subject in all social arenas: domestic, professional, political and sexual;
- integration of the women's struggle into all of the struggles for social liberation, especially under an authoritarian regime;
- struggle for the building of new social relations between the sexes and the classes;
- demystification of the idea that only socialism will put an end to the oppression of women.

Even this contradictory definition was not formed in a direct way: situated in a community that rejected the idea of feminism in any form, the *Circulo* felt the need to justify itself for its feminist stands in almost all its documents.

> The idea of the independent organization of women should not be taken to mean separating, dividing or distinguishing our struggles from those that men and women carry on together for the destruction of all relations of domination in the capitalist society. (*Circulo*, March, 1976a)
> Starting with their specific demands, they [the women] are organized and integrated into a large movement of opposition to military dictatorship. (*Circulo*, 1977a)
> Our struggle should not be taken as a struggle against men but as a struggle against any ideology which creates and maintains this (phallocratic) behavior. (*Circulo*, 1976b)
> Women in each social class are affected by oppression in different ways . . . thus we do not believe there is a purely feminine question which could unify all women in a common struggle against a common oppression. (*Circulo*, 1976b)

The Brazilian community was long in recognizing them as a political force. Note that the first public presentation of the *Circulo*—which was defined by its national character—was done within the framework of the French feminist movement, on the occasion of a meeting entitled "A Word to the Women of Latin America," organized by the French feminist journal, *L'information des femmes* on March 4, 1976.

In the document presented by the *Circulo* on that occasion, they still emphasized the denunciation of working conditions, forced birth control, prostitution as a means of survival for women with no training, and the repression and torture suffered by political activists in the non-feminist women's groups that had always existed in the Brazilian community. The last part of the document, however, posed another issue in a timid way: that of daily life, the unequal division of domestic chores and repressed sexuality. They began to paint a picture of a woman doubly exploited, both socially and in her daily life, in contrast to the picture of the fighting Latin American woman who battled side-by-side with men in a process of social change. And they registered their reactions to the current ideas of the Brazilian Left concerning the women's struggle, in statements such as "in Latin America, the struggle against hunger is uppermost"; "feminism is a trick of the developed capitalist countries"; and they protested that "this anti-feminist propaganda has lulled us far too long, it is true. . . . It is time to change this state of affairs, and thus to get organized" (*Circulo*, 1976a).

But however closed it may be, a community in exile cannot remain impervious to the social influences surrounding it. Thus, the *Circulo*, a year after its founding, was finally invited to participate in a debate on "Women and Political Action" in the context of discussions that were organized regularly by all the political forces of the Brazilian community. This debate was a total failure from their point of view and ended with the *Circulo*'s chilly withdrawal into itself.

From that time on, a double movement took place that expressed very well the contradictions running through the *Circulo*: in the general assemblies and in their tracts, the members spoke especially about political themes such as solidarity with the Brazilian women's struggle whether feminist or not, and of course, with the struggles of women workers; the defense of women political prisoners; the struggle for amnesty and against the dictatorship.

In the subgroups, which met more frequently, discussion of private life and the everyday were thriving, which contributed to changing the participants' relationships and creating a solidarity among them.

> Ever since I started discussing with other women, the image that I had of myself has changed a lot: I am more sure of myself, of my value as a human being who thinks, feels, and acts in an autonomous way. From the beginning, I realized that 'my' problems and 'my' anxieties were not only mine but those of all women. (*Circulo*, 1977b)

Following the example of American blacks who declared, "I am because we are and because we are, I am," Brazilian women for the first time began to have the feeling of identifying with something of their own, of belonging to a specific group. This process culminated in the organization of the first "feminist weekend," an occasion when close to 80 women left their husbands and children in order to discuss their experiences as women freely among themselves. And it certainly was not purely by chance that shortly after this weekend, in June of 1977, they were invited to be formally presented to the whole Brazilian community as part of a day of solidarity with the Brazilian people.

Progressively the *Circulo* acquired legitimacy that political organizations could no longer deny: the scope of their activities would oblige the community to deal with them as equal partners, to recognize the specificity of the women's struggle, and to grant it status on a par with other forms of political struggle. As a result, the need to be recognized by the Brazilian community became less; they even allowed themselves the luxury of passing judgment on the content of the political campaigns of the community and of choosing whether or not to participate in them—a sign of their new self-regard and of the strength born of an awareness of their specificity.

But the influence of Brazilian political circumstances remained strong. The liberalization of the military regime announced in mid-1978 caused both male and female exiles to dream of returning home. The plans of the *Circulo* then began to center on "what to do as feminists in Brazil." They sought information and documentation in planning for self-help groups, feminist bookstores and publishing houses, battered-women's groups; they made contacts with French feminist groups and sought means of financing, all with the hope of transferring their plans to Brazil once the amnesty law was promulgated in August 1979.

Too few studies have been devoted to the clear influence that women who have lived in exile have exercised on the feminist groups that existed at the time of their arrival in Brazil. Goldberg (1982) gives us a short description of the way that some of these women intervened in the CMB in Rio de Janeiro, with their criticism of authoritarianism, the hierarchical structure, the existence of taboo subjects, the academic approach of the feminism there and above all, the absence of solidarity and affection among the participants. The same criticisms were raised by former *Circulo* activists who were members of feminist collectives in other Brazilian cities, and these criticisms helped bring about splits everywhere, starting in 1979, and, as a consequence, the appearance of feminist groups of a new type.

CONCLUSION

Thus, throughout this article we have seen that the society of refuge had a preponderant influence in the formation of a comprehensive, positive identity for the women in exile—in the context of that process of transculturation of which Ana Vazquez speaks (1982a and 1982b).

Certainly they had centers of identity in Brazil: for some it was their work; for others, membership in a political party or group, often both.[5] These centers of identity, which they valued, were denied in the Latin American countries of refuge without any alternative being proposed. The void created by this denial would only be filled in France. If we consider again the various dimensions of the concept of identity, we will see that it was in France that they first became a reality for these women in exile.

First of all, on the level of a "sense of identity," the existence of a strong and active feminist movement allowed them to become aware of their status as individuals entirely separate in their specificity. Exile in Chile certainly encouraged them to question themselves about the precariousness of their individual rupture with the values of the patriarchal society, their inferior position in the hierarchy of political groups, their segregation in the family, and their greater difficulty in adjusting to a foreign country. In their conversations, these women often complained of a "loss of identity," and of "a break with their past lives." But Chilean society had no means of responding.

It was only in France that the contact with and then the participation in the feminist movement made it possible for them to retrieve the history of women as their own and to identify with a whole social movement based on the specificity of women. By offering alternative models, this movement freed them from constant reference to the dominant groups as the only model of positive identity.

Secondly, it was in France that they first constituted an autonomous feminist exile group. This area, created by them and for them exclusively, allowed them to attribute to private space all of its political importance and to learn to recognize the subversive value of the social movement of women. The acceptance of feminism was not a linear process. All the contradictions between their *habitus* and the new values that French society revealed to them were there. In the course of this process, they had to confront not only themselves but also the antifeminist prejudices current in the Brazilian community, and, ever more, in political groups of which some of them were members.

Thirdly, the group that they formed gradually acquired political visibility. Their practices, timid and hesitant at the beginning, progressively stood out until their organization was recognized as an independent political speaker. The relations between oppressor and oppressed became less as the women became more conscious of the justice of their struggle and less dependent on masculine recognition.

I do not think that this process of the building of an identity was the exclusive province of Brazilian women. The direction taken by other Latin American women shows strong similarities, with a few temporal differences, however (see Vazquez, 1982b, concerning Chilean women). In the limited scope of this article, I have not tried to establish comparisons.

It is still necessary to inquire into the permanence of these new values upon contact with the society of origin—the same society that it was necessary to leave for the process of consciousness-raising to be nurtured. How has the process of the reentry of these women into the Brazilian reality taken place once exile was over? As I have emphasized, they belonged to the middle class of the population. On their return, they almost all inhabited large cities in which feminine and feminist organizations developed in their absence, in parallel fashion with their own modalities. The debate that began on several levels between those who "ate the bitter fruit of exile"[6] and those who, never having left the country, underwent the hardest years of the repression, took on forms of a rare intensity and usually ended in schisms and ruptures.

It is important to know what will become of this identity forged under socially favorable conditions when it is confronted with a very sticky political situation, like the Brazilian one. Can it hold up, and under what conditions? What forms will it take? Will there be differences depending on whether the returnees live in regions that are more or less developed? What will be the forms of organization adopted: autonomous women's movements, specific inclusion in political parties, contested elected post, action with working-class women in peripheral urban areas, inclusion in the university world, and if so, on what basis? These are some of the many questions that are yet to be studied and are especially important at a time when Latin American society appears to be entering a new political stage of democratization.

NOTES

1. The Brazilian Left at the time described in this article was divided *grosso modo*, into two groups; (1) organizations more oriented toward mass action instead of armed struggle; they were called "nonmilitarist" (*Partido Communista Brasileiro*—PCB; *Partido Communista do Brazil*, or PC doB; *Acão Popular*, or AP); and (2) the groups that preached urban or rural guerilla action, called the "militarists" (*Vanguarda Popular Revolucionaria*, or VPR; *Vanguarda Armada Revolucionaria Palmares*, or VAR-Palmares; *Movimento Revolucionario Oito de Octubro*, or MR-8) among others.

2. MLAC is an organization of mixed origin that has fought since 1973 for free legal abortion and for information about the various contraceptive methods available to men and women. This last objective is also that of family planning.

3. *Debate* was a Marxist political group in exile in Paris between 1970 and 1979. It published a mimeographed review of the same name, which published two special issues on women.

4. *Campanha* was a Trotskyist group begun in Chile in 1972 around the journal of the same name. It still exists in Brazil under the name *Movimento de Emancipacão do Proletariado* (MEP).

5. It is intentional that I do not mention the roles of mother and wife as elements of identity. At that time in Brazil, these roles were perceived as "natural" functions of women and, if they formed their socially recognized identity, as we have said, they did not constitute a conscious element of specificity around which women could organize

and make demands, in contrast to certain women's movements in other Latin American countries.

6. An expression used ironically by those remaining in Brazil with regards to the exiles. As bitter as it was, it was still compared to fruit.

REFERENCES

Araujo, Ana Maria
1980 *Tupamaras—Les femmes de l'Uruguay*. Paris: Des Femmes.
Bertaux, Daniel
1980 "L'approche biographique: Sa validité methodologique, ses potentialités." *Cahiers Internationaux de Sociologie* 69: 197–226.
Bisserct, Noelle
1974 *Les inéqaux ou la sélection universitaire*. Paris: PUF.
Candido, Antonio
1984 Conversation with Antonio Candido in *Le Monde* (January 13).
Circulo (*Circulo de Mulheres Brasileiras*)
Packet containing all the documents listed below was published by the *Circulo* in Paris in 1979
1975 Political Charter, October.
1976a "Parole aux femmes de l'Amérique Latine," section on Brazil, March.
1976b Manifesto of June.
1976d Document on the Campaign of Support for Political Prisoners.
1977a March.
1977b October.
1978a May.
1978b Document, Testimony of a Militant, October.
1978c Synthesis, Document of the General Assemblies.
Costa, Albertina Oliveira da, Maria Teresa Prociuncula de Moraes, Norma Marzola, and Valentina da Rocha Lima
1980 *Memorias—das mulheres—do exilio*. Rio de Janeiro: Paz e Terra, Projeto Memorias do Exilio (II).
Erikson, Erik H.
1972 *Adolescence et crise: La quête d'une identité*. Paris: Flammarion.
Fischer, Carmen
1982 *Travessia do sonho á realidade, uma brasileira no exilio*. Rio de Janeiro: Record.
Gabeira, Fernando
1980 *O crepusculo do macho*. Rio de Janeiro: Codecri.
Goldberg, Anette
1982 "Feminismo em regime autoritario: A experiência do movimento de mulheres no Rio de Janeiro." Presented to the Twelfth World Congress of the International Association of Political Science (IPSA), Rio de Janeiro, August 9–14.
Marc-Lipiansky, Edmond
1978 "Groupe et identité," pp. 59-88 in G. Michaud (ed.) *Identités collectives et relations inter-culturelles*. Paris: Editions Complexe, PUF.

Michaud, Guy
1978 "L'ethnotype comme systéme de signification," pp. 19–34 in G. Michaud (ed.) *Identités collectives et relations inter-culturelles*. Paris: Editions Complexe, PUF.

Polari de Alverga, Alexis
1982 *Em busca do tesouro*. Rio de Janeiro: Record.

Rocha Lima, Valentina da
1980 "Why did feminism become an issue for Brazilian women in exile?" Presented at Washington University, Department of History (unpublished).
1982 "Memoirs of a project: Memorias do Exilio. Steps of a methodological search." Ad-hoc group for the use of autobiographical accounts (life histories) in social research. Tenth World Congress of Sociology, Mexico, August.

Sirkis, Alfredo
1981 *Roleta chilena*. Rio de Janeiro: Record.

Vazquez, Ana
1982a "Das troubles d'identité chez les exilés," *Amérique Latine* 12 (October–December). Paris: CENTRAL.
1982b "Mujeres en el exilio. La percepción del exilio de las mujeres exiliadas en Francia." *Mensaje* 314 (November): 618–634.
1982c "Preface," pp. 15–31 in *Chilenas—Des Chiliennes*. Paris: Des Femmes.

17

Remembering the Dead: Latin American Women's "Testimonial" Discourse

Nancy Saporta Sternbach

La memoria guardará loque valga la pena. La memoria sabe de mí más que yo; y ella no pierde lo que merece ser guardado. (Galeano, 1983: 10)
To speak the name of the dead is to make him live again . . . [it restores] the breath of life of him who has vanished.

—Egyptian tomb inscription, cited in Noblecourt and Kenett 1963: 625

In the past decade we have witnessed an abundance of what has been called women's "testimonial" literature.[1,2] Although this phenomenon may be explained strictly within a literary context—the flourishing of women's literature both in Latin America and elsewhere—it is also necessary to situate it within its Latin American sociohistoric and political context. By this, I do not mean to suggest that we ignore or disregard the growing interest in women's literature brought about to some degree by the efforts of the women's movement and the advent of feminist criticism. However, examining Latin American women's recent testimonial literature as a direct offshoot of and response to the military repression of the 1970s must also inform our analysis of this discourse. Military repression and authoritarian rule are no newcomers to the Latin American political scene, but women's open and direct opposition to and participation in them is. Thus when we ask: why women's testimonial literature? and why now? our answers must be grounded in both literary and extraliterary conditions. May we affirm, as feminist historians have done, that times of "advance" for men are notoriously "backward" for women? or its converse: that times of repression for men generally tend to be more favorable for women's advance? Or shall we place women's testimonial discourse within the

This chapter first appeared in *Latin American Perspectives* 70, 18:3 (Summer 1991), pp. 91–102.

context of women and resistance in Latin America, an ingenious and creative grassroots activism that has literally sprung up across the continent, sparking a political consciousness of women's condition of marginality, that has contributed to this sudden flourishing of the testimonial genre? Then again: is this mushrooming of women's testimonial literature a product of the fluctuations and demands of an international market that revels in essentializing indigenous and revolutionary women as exotic others and whose "writing" is a profitable object of consumption?

At first glance, there hardly seems to be anything specific about women's testimonial literature that would differentiate it from men's. On the contrary, the naming of the genre itself— *testimonio*—appears to have much more to do with men than with women, as its etymology demonstrates. It has occurred to critics to refer to the Latin roots of *testimonio*, but one of its characteristics— viewing oneself, according to René Jara (1986: 1), as *"testigo"*—has not been studied etymologically. The fact that *testigo* (and therefore *testimonio*) derives from *testes* will not only obviously exclude women both legally and anatomically,[3] but would also tend to confirm the fact that if women and *testimonio* are binary opposites biologically speaking, the language of the genre itself manifests women's exclusion from it and from power. It is also interesting to note that the word *testigo* has no feminine form in Spanish. When women are witnesses, they must be referred to as *la testigo*.

The same condition of marginality of women and the oppressed in Latin America that gave so much impetus to the testimonial genre was also instrumental in feminist theory in retrieving, reconstructing, and recovering women's history. Even the characteristic traits of the two sound familiar: both include theory based on and grounded in the reality of a people who are breaking silences; both include theory for those who envision a future distinct from their past of oppression; both use discourse, which gives voice to many others in their same situation; and both influence and are influenced by people who, with their new consciousness as a political subject, make evident the relationship between the personal and the political in a historic moment when the subject sees herself/themselves as an integral part of the collective process. These categories have been elaborated exclusively by male theorists of testimonial literature, but it is striking that they elucidate women's particular situations so eloquently without ever noticing that they do so, or without alluding to women's discourse specifically (i.e., breaking silences, giving voice, envisioning a new future, equipped with a new consciousness, aware of the relationship of the personal and the political). Of the many traits shared by women's discourse and testimonial literature, in this essay, I am interested in focusing on three: (1) the vindication and use of oral history as a means by which to obtain a narrative, (2) the use of the paradigm of female sexual slavery as the cause of the *testimonio*, and (3) the understanding of the personal as the political. Oral history, female sexual slavery, and the personal as the political are all familiar to us as forming an integral part of feminist discourse and can thus be said to be women's domain.

ORAL HISTORY

In English the terms "oral historian" or "interviewer" have been used to denominate the person who mediates between the narrator-protagonist and the text, and in Latin American *testimonios*, that person is most frequently known as an *intermediario*,[4] or for our purposes *intermediaria*. In either case, their role is similar: to "document a vanishing way of life" (see Bloom, 1977: 1), "refusing to be rendered historically voiceless" (see Gluck, 1977: 3), and to counteract and denounce the official version of history.[5] Furthermore, as in the case of the two *testimonios* that I propose to examine here, those of Claribel Alegría and Darwin Flakoll (1983) and Hebe de Bonafini (1985), both serve as repositories of memory, thereby requiring survivors of the dead to recreate those lives posthumously. In so doing, history is enacted and politically evaluated in order to create a consciousness of what has been silenced, or what could be forgotten—the dead. Alegría's text, then, celebrates a revolutionary Salvadoran woman who refused to be taken alive; Bonafini's chronicles an Argentine mother, the survivor of her children who were taken alive and never returned, either dead or alive, and whose remains continue unfound.

Both texts were elaborated on the basis of interviews by skilled writers, same-sex "intermediaries" who are politically committed to the narrator-protagonists who recount the story. Nevertheless, unlike anthropological intermediaries whose ethnographical disciplinary rigor forms a pithy component of the introduction to their *testimonio*, writers Alegría, Flakoll, and Sánchez, provide only the barest explanations of their "methods" of interviewing, the hours of tapes, or the amount of time spent with the narrator-protagonist or her family.[6] In both texts, however, normal categories of literary definition and genre mesh, intertwine, become indistinguishable, and finally beg for new definitions, for a new dialectic articulation.[7] In both texts, the memory of the survivor is paramount to the testimonial enterprise; for these women's testimonies are either the texts of survivors, or a tribute to the memory of those who did not survive. This explains why Hebe de Bonafini, president of Madres de Plaza de Mayo, can bear to retell and reconstruct her tragic story in spite of having lost two of her children: why Claribel Alegría evokes an unfailing desire to live in spite of the fact that she labels herself a "cemetery." It is in her cemetery, the intimacy and privacy of her heart and mind, where memory resides (Alegría, 1987).[8]

Both Alegría and Bonafini claim that the purpose of their text is to conserve memory, to avoid a national or collective amnesia. *No me agarran viva* is dedicated to *la memoria* of the heroic revolutionary woman who is, in the words of the intermediaries, *un caso típico y no excepcional* of Salvadoran women who have dedicated their lives to the liberation of their country. In this sense, it is a memory of the dead, appropriate for a woman who has called herself a cemetery. Yet, in contrast to the usual morbid symbolism of the cemetery, here, Alegría subverts and transforms its meaning; for instead of death, this cemetery gives life. In dismantling the traditional metaphor, this inverse process *un*earths, rather than buries; has transformed death into life with the act of writing, with her memory. In the same manner, Hebe de Bonafini's testimony is also a tribute to memory. Denied the traditional mourning process, a ritual of grieving that includes burial, here there is an *un*burial, an unearthing of the truth that translates into an invasion of the space occupied by official history, necessary for future generations of children who need to know this buried, silenced, and forgotten chapter of Argentina's history.[9] Both texts are committed to the proposition of creating a foil to the official discourses of their countries who would silence them again with a *punto final* or whatever other tactic might be invented to discredit their voice. Both texts, then, serve as a model of inspiration and action to Latin American women whose word on the printed page insists on our not forgetting this story, till now untold. They resurrect their dead through language: they do not "make the word flesh," rather they "make the flesh word," and in so doing establish an entirely new reading of "writing the body." Likewise, they inform us that we can no longer rely solely on the oral histories that passed from woman to woman, from generation to generation, as Rigoberta Menchú's testimony so clearly demonstrates. This becomes especially clear as the stories become more complex, as Bonafini writes: "at first we knew all the stories by heart. Then we had to start writing down the information and names; there were too many stories and we could no longer trust memory alone."[10]

But such manners of transcribing oral history to a written text create concomitant problems with reference to the authorship of the testimonial text. When we, as readers, are amazed, astonished, and admiring of the heroism present in the *testimonio*, who is it we admire: the narrator- protagonist or the intermediary? The narrator-protagonist individually, or the collective group from which she emerged? Whose book is it: the intermediary's, the narrator-protagonist's or the collective group's? Or does it belong to the dead? What happens when the author or "ownership" of the text foreshadows the circumstances that propelled the individual or group into the public domain?

FEMALE SEXUAL SLAVERY[11]

Theorists of Latin American testimonial literature are very useful in creating categories of reference, characteristics of and maxims applicable to the testimonial genre, as well as establishing its academic validity; but, for the most part, they have rarely addressed the specificity of women's testimonial literature. Such omissions occur in spite of the fact that many of the testimonies that document their theory are, indeed, written (see Partnoy, 1986), or "co-produced" (McKracken, 1986)[12] by women[13] and tend to suggest that women's testimonial literature is no different from men's. However, in the same way that we have seen the shared components of testimony and women's discourse in regard to oral history, we may also evaluate other significant elements that testimony shares with women's literature: breaking silences, raising consciousness, envisioning a new future, and seeking collective action. Hence, in testimonial literature, it is not the women who are conforming to a male model; on the contrary, the dimensions of male testimonial literature tend to incorporate those characteristics we normally attribute to women's discourse, that is the circumstances of viewing oneself as a marginal subject who has taken history into her or his own hands for the first time.[14]

Nevertheless, when such circumstances do arise for the male narrator-protagonist, the above-mentioned reversal is possible because he also finds himself in an *estado límite*,[15] a crisis situation which bears remarkable resemblance to a women's state in patriarchy; his treatment by the military makes those connections especially evident. As Ximena Bunster-Burotto (1986: 310) has written, the military state, "the patriarchal state in distillation . . . uses the paradigm of female sexual enslavement, rape, in as many forms as it can image."[16] Thus this paradigm of female sexual enslavement that includes but is not limited to sexual torture, humiliation, voyeurism, cruelty and domination, among other tactics, is exercised on victims regardless of gender[17] as Bonafini (1985: 127) has expressed in regard to her son's tortured body:

> Why should we continue to outrage those bodies that have already been tortured so many times in every imaginable form? I can't talk about Jorge's body because I gave birth to it, I held him in my arms and he drank my milk until he became a man . . . To speak of the torture is like opening the wound . . . I close my eyes and I imagine that body full of blood and bruises and it makes me feel terribly ashamed. Because I see him with a different nakedness, and to describe it is to humiliate him; it's like repeating the torture and deepening the violation.[18]

It is clear from the above passage that Jorge was (mis)treated, abused, humiliated and tortured within what we can call this female paradigm: it is no coincidence that Hebe uses the double meaning of the word *violación* to express this horror. This is to say that his treatment echoed, paralleled and reproduced—to a greater or lesser degree—the abuse and oppression of women in patriarchy.

Recently, women's increasing participation as activists in Latin American politics has tended to blur those gender-specific theoretical categories that defined men as "warriors" (*guerrilleros*) and their *testimonios* as "epic" (Ché Guevara, Omar Cabezas) and in which women remained "marginal" with unnamed, uncategorized *testimonios*.[19] Moreover, in the past decade, those "epic" circumstances that caused the testimony-as-genre to be written in the first place have increasingly become women's domain as well. Women's participation in revolutionary struggles (see Randall, 1980)[20] witnessing murders of loved ones (Menchú, 1984; Partnoy, 1986),[21] suffering disappearances (Bonafini, 1985),[22] rapes, tortures, and perhaps most poignantly, women's specific resistance to military rule, all attest to their own *estado límite*, a condition that propels them to insure that their story is heard, written, and read. Furthermore, the traditional spaces occupied by women are no longer immune from attacks, break-ins and violations, as events in the past decade have shown (see Franco, 1985).[23] In ever-increasing proportions, women who enter the testimonial discourse tend to understand their roles both as women and as political subjects, with all of the consequences that this *doble militancia* implies. "Eugenia," in a letter to her *compañero*, which forms part of the text of *No me agarran viva* (Alegría and Flakoll, 1983: 131), writes: "I don't know how long all this will last, my love, but I'm prepared for everything, to sacrifice everything, though I find it very painful." And Bonafini (1985: 73) permits herself the following reflection in hindsight:

> What makes me angriest of all is that the boots, the slaps and the kicks were necessary before we good housewives would finally go out and participate and actually produce a shout of protest instead of listening to it on the radio. So I'm angry for not having left my knitting and pots and pans earlier to go out and complain about the tanks.[24]

It is in this trespassing on and usurping of patriarchal space, undermining the personal and the political, that we may begin to speak of women's specific testimonial discourse.

PERSONAL AND POLITICAL

One of the most predominant features of testimonial discourse, and therefore its most cited characteristic, is its function as the site of nexus between the much-used feminist category of the personal and the political. In this sense, "personal" refers to a private, domestic, or intimate sphere, and "political" may be viewed as the public, historic or collective one. The political aspect of the testimonial is often seen as the crossroads between official history and literature (see Chevigny, 1986: 181).[25] Nowhere has this term, "the personal is the political," been used so often in reference to protagonists other than women than in testimonial theory, which becomes obvious from examples. René Jara (1986: 3) writes that in the *testimonio*, "los límites entre lo público y lo privado desaparecen . . . la intimidad pertenece a todos."

For this reason Bonafini can challenge the public and official discourse, take and appropriate the Plaza de Mayo both physically and symbolically and, in so doing, transgress the previously delineated female space in the name of her disappeared children. Her actions vivify Manuel Jofre's affirmation that testimonial discourse is a convergence of "una voz personal y una voz colectiva" (1981: 155), for she is one mother among many, with the strength of a collective female force behind her.

In a woman's testimony, that line between personal and political is often expressed in terms of her family; it is not unlikely that her role as mother compels her as testimonial subject to enter the public arena. For example, in one of the interviews of *No me agarran viva* (Alegría and Flakoll, 1983: 97, 99), a woman states: "Having children is the most beautiful and most revolutionary experience there is . . . As a mother, I can't just watch out for one child, there are millions of children in the country . . . Maternity has a historical dimension and not just an individual one."[26]

Indeed, it is the condition of motherhood redefined within a new revolutionary context that often motivates today's Latin American woman, the new narrator-protagonist of testimonial literature, to enter this discourse. Such an understanding gives a new political dimension to the term and the experience of motherhood; it transcends the private sphere and invades the political one. Consequently, in women's *testimonios* we not only establish a new genre, but also a new speaking subject, that is, a new discursive articulation. In male *testimonios*, the bonding relationships of and with the *compañera* are certainly present (Cabezas, 1982), but the family tends to figure less significantly than in women's texts. For example, Jacobo Timerman's (1988) *estado límite* was so pronounced that any mention of tenderness reduced his resistance; and, in any case, it was not the cause for his having written the text. Miguel Barnet (1973), on the other hand, is fascinated either by Esteban Montejo's celibacy or his liaisons with women, but neither was responsible for the writing of the text itself. For Omar Cabezas, the loss of love is only bearable in the light of his love for Nicaragua. As for women's *testimonios*, the narrator-protagonist is clearly more concerned with her children or with her "woman-family" (Cervantes, 1981: 11) than solely with her *compañero*.

Thus, in women's testimonial discourse, it is either having lost her children, or imagining for them a social change and political transformation that motivates the act of writing. The text itself becomes the symbol for an act of love: not simply an abstract love of one's country, one's race, or one's revolution (although these characteristics are also present) but rather, love for the human being to whom they gave life. In this sense, these tests are "cathartic" for their authors, for in both cases the act of writing itself serves as a tribute to the memory of the dead: what has been silenced is spoken and written. It allows Alegría to wash away the wounds inflicted on a cemetery. For Bonafini its publication assures that it shall enter the historical process side by side with official history. In this manner, neither story can be lost again, either in the amnesia and political machinations of official memory and history, or by making it accessible to the new generations who did not live it. For this reason, in Alegría and Bonafini, the cemetery functions as a metaphor for not forgetting, a re-membering, *re-memorando*: putting together memories, enacting history, chronicling the loss, carrying pictures, and naming the dead. Ultimately, the act of re-membering is really an act of birthing and re-birthing; the offspring is the woman's *testimonio*.

NOTES

1. Throughout this article the author has translated the Spanish quotations from de Bonafini (1985) and Alegría and Flakoll (1983) into English.

2. In the period from 1969 to 1986, the best-known testimonials published were by Elena Poniatowska (1969), Domitila Barrios de Chungara with Moema Viezzer (1977), Rigoberta Menchú (1983), Claribel Alegría and Darwin Flakoll (1983), Hebe de Bonafini (1985), Doris Tijerino (1978), and Alicia Partnoy (1986), to mention only a few.

3. Corominas' (1983) *Diccionario crítico etimológico* says of *testigo* "derivado del antiguo *testiguar* (= *atestiguar*) que es descendiente semiculto del latín *testificare* (compuesto de *testis* 'testigo' y facere "hacr")." The *Oxford Latin Dictionary* tells us that "testiculus" (testicle) derives from "testis" + "culus." Mary Daly (1978: 435n) further elaborates: "*testiculus,* diminutive [sic] of *testis*: witness (the organ being evidence of virility). Since women do not have testicles, they cannot really be qualified to testify—give evidence."

4. See Prada Oropeza (1986: 15). Another form of "address" is *gestor* (gestator) or *editor*. See Elzbieta Sklodowska (1982: 380).

5. Elena Moya-Raggio writes that they are "urgent responses to immediate events that have been glossed over in official channels" (1987: 275).

6. Such a technique varies sharply with the models of Oscar Lewis (1965), Moema Viezzer (see Barrios, 1977), Miguel Barnet (1973), and Elisabeth Burgos-Debray (see Menchú, 1983, 1984), though it tends to be more in line with Elena Poniatowska's methodology. Although Poniatowska worked with Lewis on his project, she, too, is a professional writer rather than an anthropologist.

7. Eliana Rivero (1984–85: 219) has written that testimonial discourse "*rompe las fronteras intergenéricas.*"

8. In many of her poems, Alegría alludes to the image of the tomb or the cemetery. See Alegría (1982), especially "Sorrow" and *"Mis adioses."*

9. Although Bonafini does not refer to herself as a "cemetery," as does Alegría, it is interesting to contemplate the massive marches of the Madres, each one holding a larger-than-life size photograph of her lost children. Seen from afar, such posters, with their rows of faces and names, also evoke the sensation of a walking cemetery with rows of tombs. Such a reading is especially suggestive considering that one of the platforms the Madres have defended is "no a las exhumaciones." That is to say, that rather than unearth the actual physical bodies of their dead children, the Madres have reversed, uncovered, unearthed and unburied the truth. I am especially grateful to Alberto Sandoval for the conversations we had on this subject and his sensitive reading of an earlier draft of this article.

10. *Al principio sabíamos los relatos de memoria. Luego hubo que escribir la información, los nombres, las historias eran demasiadas y en la memoria no se podía confiar* (1986: 126).

11. I am indebted to Kathleen Barry (1979) for the title of this section.

12. For use of the term "co-produced." Such is the case of testimonies by Domitila Barrios de Chungara, Rigoberta Menchú, and Hebe de Bonafini. Elena Poniatowska, and Claribel Alegría are good examples of co-producers.

13. In her essay Doris Meyer (1983: 6) states, "the testimonial style is so often associated with the 'feminine.'" Although Meyer does not actually give examples of such an association, her essay refers to works of fiction and not what I call the testimonial genre. See also René Jara (1986); Willy O. Muñoz (1987); David William Foster (1984); Roberto González-Echeverría (1980); Mary Ellen Kiddle (1985); and Eliana Rivero (1984–85).

14. Such self-perceptions are not often the case with male narrators unless, of course, they were so marginal as to fall into the same category as women described above. Jacobo Timerman, for example, devotes a lengthy portion of his testimony detailing Argentina's situation in 1976. In such descriptions, he describes his political clout at clubs whose entrance was only available to the very highest elite of Argentine political and military power (1988).

15. I consider an *estado límite* to be one in which the narrator-protagonist takes action because s/he feels there is nothing else to lose. Obviously, I am borrowing this term from Alejo Carpentier's celebrated discussion of "lo real maravilloso" (1967: 11), which I do in spite of the fact that in the same essay, he also considers that "lo maravilloso" includes raping women.

16. Later in the same article, Bunster-Burotto writes (316), "the military state sadistically literalizes patterns of female sexual slavery."

17. Bunster-Burotto stresses the fact that light-skinned, bourgeois women received "better" treatment than their dark-skinned, working-class counterparts although the repression was spread across class lines.

18. *Para qué volver a vejar esos cuerpos que ya fueron humillados tantos veces de todos los modos imaginables? No puedo hablar del cuerpo de Jorge porque lo parí, lo tuve entre mis brazos . . . y tomó mi leche hasta transformarse en un hombre . . . Hablar de las torturas a ese cuerpo . . . es como revolver la tijera en la herida . . . cierro los ojos y me imagino ese cuerpo lleno de sangre y moretones y tengo una horrible vergüenza. Porque lo veo con otra desnudez y describirlo es humillarlo, es repetir la tortura y ahondar la violación.*

19. Such is the case in González-Echeverria's essay (1980: 257). He writes: "it is perhaps no coincidence that [these testimonies] tend to have female protagonists . . . by turning back to origins suggests a return to the womb."

20. A translated and abridged version of this *testimonio* exists in English as *Sandino's Daughters* (see Randall, 1980; and Doris Tijerino, 1978).

21. Rigoberta Menchú witnesses the murders of most of the members of her family; in her incarceration in the Little School, Alicia Partoy recounts the "transfers" (read murders) of her *compañeras/os*.

22. Bonafini's call to action came as a result of the disappearance of her son. Her own militancy, she feels, caused the military's continued reprisals, which resulted in the disappearance of her second son.

23. Franco (1985: 416) has written that the "sacred space and the immunity" traditionally occupied and enjoyed by women and the clergy have been destroyed with the "modernization" of Latin America's armies.

24. *Lo que más rabia me da es que hayan sido necesarias las botas, las cachetadas y puntapiés para que las buenas amas de casa saliéramos a participar, produjéramos un grito de protesta en lugar de escuchar el ajeno por la radio. Me da rabia, entonces, no haber dejado antes los tejidos y las cacerolas para salir a mirar y quejarme de los tanques.*

25. Chevigny (1986) calls it "the site of the encounter between writing and history."

26. *Tener hijos es la experiencia más linda que hay, la más revolucionaria . . . yo como madre no puedo velar sólo por un niño, hay millones de niños en el país. . . . la maternidad tiene dimensión histórica y no sólo individual.*

REFERENCES

Alegría, Claribel
  1982 *Flowers from the Volcano*, translated by Carolyn Forché. Pittsburgh, PA: University of Pittsburgh Press.
  1987 Interview on National Public Radio, October.
Alegría, Claribel and Darwin Flakoll
  1983 *No me agarran viva: La mujer salvadoreña en lucha.* Mexico City: Ediciones Era.
Barnet, Miguel
  1973 *The Autobiography of a Runaway Slave, Esteban Montejo.* New York: Vintage Books (originally published as *Biografía de un cimarrón*, 1968).
Barrios de Chungara, Domitila with Moema Viezzer
  1977 *"Si me permiten hablar . . . " Testimonio de Domitila, una mujer de las minas de Bolivia.* Mexico City: Siglo XXI.
Barry, Kathleen
  1979 *Female Sexual Slavery.* Englewood Cliffs, NJ: Prentice Hall.
Bloom, Lynn Z.
  1977 "Listen! Women speaking," *Frontiers* 2 (Summer): 1–2.
Bonafini, Hebe de
  1985 *Historias de vida: Hebe de Bonafini.* Edited with a prologue by Matilde Sánchez. Buenos Aires: Fraterna/Del Nuevo Extremo.
Bunster-Burotto, Ximena
  1986 "Surviving beyond fear: Women and torture in Latin America," pp. 297–325 in June Nash and Helen Safa (eds.), *Women and Change in Latin America.* South Hadley, MA: Bergin & Harvey.

Cabezas, Omar
1982 *La montaña es algo más que una inmensa estepa verde.* Havana: Casa de las Américas.
Carpentier, Alejo
1967 "Prólogo," pp. 7–17 in *El reino de estemundo.* Mexico City: Cía General de Ediciones.
Cervantes, Lorna Dee
1981 *Emplumada.* Pittsburgh, PA: University of Pittsburgh Press.
Chevigny, Bell Gale
1986 "Twice-told tales and the meaning of history: Testimonial novels by Miguel Barnet and Norman Mailer." *Centennial Review* 30 (Spring): 181–195.
Corominas, Joan
1983 *Diccionario crítico etimológico caste llano e hispano.* Madrid: Editorial Gredos.
Daly, Mary
1978 *Gyn/Ecology: The Metaethics of Radical Feminism.* Boston: Beacon Press.
Foster, David William
1984 "Latin American documentary narrative." *PMLA* 99 (January): 41–55.
Franco, Jean
1985 "Killing, priests, nuns, women, children," pp. 414–420 in Marshall Blonsky (ed.), *On Signs.* Baltimore: Johns Hopkins University Press.
Galeano, Eduardo
1983 *Días y noches de amor y de guerra.* Managua: Editorial Nueva Nicaragua.
Gluck, Sherna
1977 "What's so special about women? Women's oral history." *Frontiers* 2 (Summer): 3–11.
González-Echeverría, Roberto
1980 *"Biografía de un cimarrón:* And the novel of the Cuban revolution." *Novel: A Forum on Fiction* 13 (Spring): 249–263.
Jara, René
1986 "Prólogo: Testimonio y literatura," pp. 1-6, in René Jara and Hernán Vidal (eds.), *Testimonio y literatura.* Minneapolis, MN: Institute for the Study of Ideologies and Literature (3).
Jofre, Manuel
1981 "Literatura chilena de testimonio." *Casa de las Americas* 21 (November–December): 150–156.
Kiddle, Mary Ellen
1985 "The *Novela testimonial* in contemporary Mexican literature." *Confluencia* 1 (Fall): 82–89.
Lewis, Oscar
1965 *La vida.* New York: Random House.
McCracken, Ellen
1986 "Gender and revolution: Women's and men's testimonial discourse in Central America. " Paper read at the XIII International Congress of the Latin American Studies Association, Boston, Massachusetts, October.
Menchú, Rigoberta
1983 *Me llamo Rigoberta Menchú y así me nació la conciencia.* Elisabeth Burgos-Debray (ed.), Havana: Casa de las Americas.
1984 *I, Rigoberta Menchú.* Elisabeth Burgos-Debray (ed.). London: Verso.

Meyer, Doris
1983 "'Feminine' testimony in the works of Teresa de la Parra, María Luisa Bombal and Victoria Ocampo," pp. 3–15 in Doris Meyer and Margarite Femández-Olmos (eds.), *Contemporary Women Authors of Latin America: Introductory Essays*. Brooklyn, NY: Brooklyn College Press.

Moya-Raggio, Elena
1987 "Three testimonies from Latin America." *Michigan Quarterly Review* 26 (Winter): 272–277.

Muñoz, Willy O.
1987 "La consciencia de sí como arma política en *Si me permiten hablar . . . Testimonio de Domitila.*" *Confluencia: Revista Hispánica de Cultura y Literatura* 2 (2): 70–77.

Noblecourt, Christiane Desroches and F. L. Kenett
1963 "Tutankhamun's golden trove." *National Geographic* 124 (October): 624–646.

Oxford Latin Dictionary
1976 Oxford: Clarendon Press.

Partnoy, Alicia
1986 *The Little School: Tales of Disappearance and Survival in Argentina.* Pittsburgh, PA: Cleis Press.

Poniatowska, Elena
1969 *Hasta no verte, Jesús mío.* Mexico City: Era.

Prada Oropeza, Renato
1986 "De lo testimonial al testimonio: Notas para un deslinde del discurso testimonio," pp. 7–21 in René Jara and Hernán Vidal (eds.), *Testimonio y Literatura*. Minneapolis, MN: Institute for the Study of Ideologies and Literature.

Randall, Margaret
1980 *Todas estamos despiertas: Testimonios de la mujer nicaragüense hoy.* Mexico City: Siglo XXI. (A translated and abridged English version appeared in 1981 as *Sandino's Daughters.* Vancouver: New Star Books.)

Rivero, Eliana
1984–85 "Testimonios y conversaciones como discurso literario: Cuba y Nicaragua." *Literature and Contemporary Revolutionary Culture* 1: 218–228.

Sklodowska, Elzbieta
1982 "La forma testimonial y la novelística de Miguel Barnet." *Revista/Review Interamericana* 12 (Fall): 375–384.

Tijerino, Doris
1978 *Inside the Nicaraguan Revolution.* Told to Margaret Randall, translated by Elinor Randall. Vancouver: New Star Books.

Timerman, Jacobo
1988 *Prisoner without a Name, Cell without a Number,* translated by Toby Talbot. New York: Vintage Books.

Róger Sánchez's "Humor Erótico" and the *Semana Cómica:* A Sexual Revolution in Sandinista Nicaragua?

David Kunzle

How do you manage to combine two mortal enemies, humor and the left?

—Tim Patterson

My study of the sex humor of the cartoonist Róger Sánchez, like Nicaragua itself in recent years, has undergone many vicissitudes. I first wrote on this topic in 1988, optimistically, at the height of the contra war, against which Sandinista Nicaragua seemed to be standing firm. But something was missing, other work supervened, and I began to write on Nicaragua revolutionary murals instead (Kunzle, 1995). Since my first draft in 1988, there have been some (unfortunate) closures that have facilitated an evaluation of Roger's sex humor in toto rather than in progress, as I had intended: first, a literal (if temporary) closure by government order of his notorious satirical magazine and then, more significant, the electoral defeat of February 1990, coding 10 years of Sandinista rule, followed toward the end of that year by the death of the artist and, soon afterwards, the *Semana Cómica* itself.

If in 1988 I was too optimistic about the health of Sandinismo and the revolution, including the sexual liberation that, I still argue, Róger promoted in his and Nicaragua's own confused, contradictory, but always stimulating way, there is every reason to be pessimistic about the long-term effects of the Chamorro government's neoliberal market policies and a future dominated by the former Somocista Arnold Alemán. The most conspicuous contribution of the latter, elected mayor of Managua (in a process of very doubtful legitimacy) in 1996, to Nicaraguan culture has been to destroy many of the best Sandinista murals.

This chapter first appeared in *Latin American Perspectives* 101, 25:4 (July 1998), pp. 89–120.

The UNO government, headed but not controlled by President Violeta Chamorro, was party to a rollback of revolutionary achievements on all fronts, sexual or moral as well as political, social, and economic. If Róger contributed, as I argue, to female as well as male social and moral emancipation, his aims in this respect are undermined by ongoing campaigns against sex education, contraception, abortion, and women's and gay rights generally (see "Women in Nicaragua," 1991; Randall, 1992; "Censorship Unmasked," 1991; Aleman, 1993; "Anti-Condom Crusade;' 1994; Quant, 1990).

Those hostile-to-leftist revolutions and revolutionaries often stigmatize leftists as humorless and repressive of sexual as well as political freedom. To recognize that the enemy has a sense of humor is to humanize that enemy. Yet our own revolutionary spasm of the 1960s offers ample proof that efforts at political liberation bring about psychic liberations, of which humor and sex are both instruments and celebrations, means and ends. From the 1960s we inherit a vision of political and sexual liberations marching (often comically) hand in hand. There is all the more reason, then, for us to look curiously and sympathetically at a Nicaraguan effort to achieve, through humor, a kind of sexual emancipation within and as a critical part of the revolution, and even as "a reaffirmation of the value of human life and dignity in a country . . . wracked by war, struggle, and injustice" (Clark, 1990).

Róger Sánchez Flores was a name familiar to readers of the daily *Barricada* (and *Barricada Internacional*), the official organ of the Sandinista National Liberation Front (FSLN), the Sandinista party that from 1979 to 1990 ran the Nicaraguan government. He signed as "Róger" the daily political cartoons, later gathered into two albums under the title *Muñequitos del Pueblo* (Cartoons of the People) (1981; also published in West German and British editions),[1] which featured a working-class Sandinista cartoon character called *Polidecto* who demonstrated how wrong, futile, and ridiculous were the policies of the United States against Nicaragua. His political cartoons occasionally appeared in the U.S. alternative press. He was not so much the best as probably the only true political cartoonist in Nicaragua, which now has virtually none. His true popularity, in terms of a mass and enthusiastic regular readership, however, derives not so much from his political as from his sexual humor, which was not admissible in the Sandinista dailies. He may be a unique figure in the history of the cartoon in the extent to which he successfully combined such very different modes of humor.

There was and is another Róger whose existence one would scarcely suspect from the political cartoons: he was from 1985 to his premature death in 1990 the director of the humorous weekly *La Semana Cómica* and author of a regular feature in it called *Humor Erótico* that was, I dare say, unique in Latin America. If in his *Barricada* cartoons Róger registered the political heartbeat of the revolution, his *Humor Erótico* laid bare a sexual nerve that was another manifestation of the revolution and a peculiarly Nicaraguan one. It would be hard to find even in the "sexually liberated" advanced capitalist world, not to speak of Latin America, so flagrant and so massively distributed an outrage against traditional Christian sexual taboos—and this, moreover, in a country still largely beholden to Roman Catholic and machista Christianity. Róger made no attack on religion in its institutional form (as does, for instance, the Mexican cartoonist Ríus), and he had no interest in offending Catholic sensibilities as such, especially those of the country's many "revolutionary Christians." But his *Semana Cómica*, with its conspicuous sexual component, was nonetheless profoundly subversive of hallowed Christian attitudes, and in later years he repeatedly attacked the hypocrisies of individual reactionary clerics. By 1988 he could "expose" the reactionary priest Bismark Carvallo, who supported the contras even in their worst sadistic (sexual) atrocities, exposing his Reagan-headed penis to the readership in a full page front cover drawing in *Semana Cómica*, no. 392 (August 1988).[2] A cartoon showing a Catholic cleric kneeling by the bed occupied by a naked girl and praying "Give us this day our daily bread," first drawn in 1981, was published only many years later; by the late 1980s cartoon priests up to the highest ranks were shown lusting, leching, and copulating like the average Nicaraguan (only they seemed to prefer the "cross" position in bed).

MEGA-ACTION IN A MINI-BED

Róger's *Humor Erótico* offered to males (the primary audience) a platform for a kind of sexual emancipation in Nicaragua: sex was explicit, eclectic, recreational, tricky, promiscuous, adulterous, and decidedly extramarital ("I demand an explanation! What is your husband doing here [with you in bed]?" [1986:194]). Permissible variations included group sex, homosexuality, oral sex, masturbation, and, fancifully, bestiality.[3] Sex is existential: ". . . therefore I am!" cries the triumphant lover. Sex is situated between work and play, in power and deceit, rather than in sentiment ("This can't go on. I'm falling in love with you").

Many of Róger's *Humor Erótico* cartoons (my sample includes several hundred), as a comment on sexual relations in a bourgeois society, would be readily understood in our own and could appear in any relatively emancipated organ of the Western capitalist press, although they would be excluded from our mainstream mass media. Róger's sex war is in part a familiar bourgeois cartoon sex war: it expresses alienation, frustration, and failure. It is about status and competition. A revealing comparison could be drawn with

Playboy, the magazine that the *Semana Cómica* both plagiarized and mocked. Like *Playboy,* the *Semana Cómica* jokes are about sexual fear and hostility. The differences, however, are considerable. They are partly those between a culture of wealth and a culture of poverty; they are also those between the political agnostic or ignoramus and the political partisan. Another major level of difference is technological: quality of print and paper reproduction. Unlike *Playboy* and its many luxurious progeny, *Semana Cómica* lacked the means to eroticize sexual situations in a visually appealing way. Róger never in his cartoons emphasized the primary sexual parts and did not offer sexual encounters for titillation and vicarious consumption, that is, for their own sakes. Compared with the lush seductions of *Playboy* cartoons and center-folds, Róger's is an austere art. His latter-day use in the *Semana Cómica* of photographs, much degraded on the cheap newsprint available, from *Playboy* and the like virtually mocked the sexual fantasies of a culture unable to af-ford the "real" (i.e., colored, glossy) thing, which was of course supremely un-real and supremely deceptive as the *Semana Cómica* could never be. Had some millionaire decided to endow Róger with the necessary hi-tech equip-ment, it is doubtful that he would—or could—have used it, for Nicaraguan law under the Sandinistas forbade the exploitation of the female body in ad-vertising, which even the crude Nicaraguan billboard technology, under So-moza and now once more, makes truly alluring.

The ever-recurring stage set of *Humor Erótico* is the bedroom or, rather, the bed. The implications range well beyond it, but the bed sheet is the obligatory fig leaf for activities that cannot be completely revealed. The bed is also a module of graphic convenience and a concession to both orthodoxy and de-cency: "In a bed!" complains one, amorous female, "How orthodox!" (i.e., boring [1986: 57]). In compensation, a minority of cartoons takes copulation into nature, treetops, the sea, the open road, generating a new kind of high-way symbol: "Watch out for Recumbent Lovers" (1986: 15). This is a pansex-ual world, and paradise itself cannot be imagined without sex: "This is Par-adise, isn't it?" protests the couple bringing its bed up to the gate of heaven, against the ultimate denial of St. Peter (no. 251).

The bed is single, narrow, and far too short. It is in a way an emblem of the Nicaraguan economy, short on so many essentials. Urban living space in Nicaragua (as of course in any Third World country) is by our standards ex-tremely cramped. But the great sexual energy that can be generated from this bed is out of all proportion to its size, as the revolutionary energy generated from Nicaragua is out of all proportion to the size of the country. The bed is further cramped by an apparently superfluous but conventional headboard and footboard, obstacles smashed, on occasion, by flailing extremities (1986: 30, 34). The bed is apt to collapse and to need shock absorbers. Sex is shocking.

ATTACKS FROM THE LEFT:
SANDINIZED SEX OR REVOLUTIONARY PORNOGRAPHY?

Róger's audience included many who did not share the Sandinista ideals, who voted the Sandinistas out of office in 1990. It is true that Nicaragua voted massively for the FSLN in the 1984 elections: 67 percent of the vote cast went to the Sandinistas. But these votes were concentrated among the less educated masses, while the appeal of Róger and of the *Semana Cómica* as a sophisticated and intellectual magazine had to be disproportionately concentrated among an urban, educated male elite, including many in the apolitical (nonvoting) 25 percent of the population and non-Sandinista elements.[4] (This is not to say that all the readers were well educated: from a comic sexual personality test it emerged, to the editor's surprise, that many did not know the meaning of the word "phallic" [no. 320].)

For Róger, the non-Sandinistas among his readership were targets for political persuasion. The political cartoons in the *Semana Cómica* are as clearly Sandinista as those he did concurrently for *Barricada*. Róger wanted his readers to understand that the sexual humor, indeed, everything in the magazine, also shared that ideology—or at least shared in the debate that it aroused. By "Sandinista" Róger does not mean "partisan" in any narrow sense, much less "sectarian"; sectarianism was like sexual prejudice and an enemy of the total liberation for which Róger-style Sandinism, broadly conceived, was striving.

A revolution can turn repression into expression. The Nicaraguan Revolution opened up topics that had never before been debated and Róger's *Humor Erótico* was part of that debate, part of that release. In an often repeated editorial manifesto he defined his magazine, with comic tortuosity, as a

> sometimes unpublishable publication, which exercises its right to say whatever wishes to reserve to itself the right to hear what it doesn't want [to hear]. In principle we are against all evil, even our own. In this publication anyone can contribute anything as long as it doesn't injure the emotional interests of the Directorate. We confess we are Sandinista, but we don't need to go around saying so all the time. (no. 340)
>
> We are Marxist . . . not with a Marxism like any other, but still a Marxism . . . [down to] every headline, every caption, every photo, every joke, every buttock we draw. (no. 317)

Originally subtitled *Semanario de la Jodarría Nicaragüense* (Weekly of Nicaraguan Fun),[5] from June 1987 (no. 337) on the *Semana Cómica* substituted on the cover *Semanario de Humor, Marxismo, Sexo y Violencia*. This outspoken assertion of Sandinism and Marxism provided a political cover for avowedly violent sexual humor that many of the left as well as the right (of course) found offensive. The editorials quoted above respond to certain attacks from the left, primarily feminists, communists, and orthodox Sandinistas. To an accusation in the pro-FSLN *Nuevo Diario* of sexism and degradation of women (no. 301), Róger responded evasively to defend what went on "under the sheets of *Humor Erótico*: "it depends what goes on under the shaggy skin of each reader." Róger deemed the attack not a personal one but a "monkish" reaction based on an "antiquated moral system." Against this system, which condemned sex as such, Róger offered a drawing typical of a category of his cartoons celebrating sex as such, showing a fireman hosing down an excessively ardent and grateful pair (no. 301). The other accompanying cartoon was typical of another, more dubious category, the woman-blames-man-for-failure— here, failure to "commit [the] outrage on morality and decency" she desires. Was this sort of thing a degradation of women as the *Nuevo Diario* claimed? No, said Róger, for the true degradation was wife abuse, a tremendous problem in Nicaragua (since 1990 on the rise again) and a topic exploited (as Róger implied) for sensationalist purposes by the *Nuevo Diario* itself in its reportage on the subject. Róger's sex could be violent, but it was not a violence directed *against* women or against *women*.

THE COMMUNIST ATTACK

The polemic was sharpened, two issues later, by the Communist party organ *Avance*. The Communist Party of Nicaragua is a minuscule, "hard-line" party "with perhaps a few hundred members" (Rosset and Vandermeer, 1985: 64). In 1990 it joined the rightist UNO coalition against the Sandinistas. *Avance* was closed in 1980 for calling for strikes against a regime it regarded as petty-bourgeois reformist. The *Semana Cómica* was at this time riding high on a wave of increased circulation, warming to an "idyll," a "love affair" with weekly sales that, since the open declaration of Marxism, were approaching 60,000. "When we get there," added Róger in a typical dig, "our ego will be greater than that of all the poets in this country put together in a no. 108 bus." But for having arrived at Marxism without the advice of the Nicaraguan Communist party head Eli Altamirano, the *Semana Cómica*, with Róger's *Humor Erótico* as its standard-bearer, was excoriated in a ferocious polemic. According to Róger's account, printed on the front cover of the issue for St. Valentine's Day, 1987 (no. 319), specially dedicated to lovers and love, the hatred of the party chief had erupted in the expulsion of 12 militants found reading the *Semana Cómica* in the party headquarters. These individuals had already been warned about the anticommunist nature of their sexual behavior. In a plenum of the Central Committee, Altamirano had demanded sexual abstinence. The official line of the Communists was one with the official line of the church: sex was for procreation only.

The *Avance* text, published inside the *Semana Cómica*, read virtually as a parody of a vintage *Prensa* article against "Sandinista Communism," cliché-ridden bombast rank with vulgar insults. The *Semana Cómica* was guilty of "'promoting vile passions," "false, poisonous, depraved, criminal," guilty of "trafficking in prejudice and vices" that "capitalism [the *Prensa* would have substituted communism] has succeeded in inoculating in our people over long years, plunging us into not only economic prostration but also spiritual humiliation." And like the *Prensa* on the right, *Avance* on the far left resented the government's favoritism toward (i.e., its not punishing) a paper "which saves its [the government's] global interests." For *Avance*, the *Semana Cómica* was as clearly anti-Marxist as it was anticommunist. It condemned itself by professing Sandinism, an aberration from the Marxism of which the Nicaraguan Communists were the sole repository.

SEX AND THE CONDITION OF WOMEN: THE AMNLAE ATTACK

Revolutionary Nicaragua was a dynamic though war-torn country, with the highest population growth rate in the Western Hemisphere (a rate enhanced by improved medical care under the Sandinistas) and half its population under 15. Population growth was not in itself considered a cause for concern—far from it, for unlike many Third World countries Nicaragua considered itself underpopulated and there was little demographic justification for an officially encouraged program of birth control (which scarcely ever existed). But the creative realm of Róger, who personally engendered—by choice he said—only one child in 10 years of marriage, excluded children. For Róger sex was self-sufficient and reproductive, in the first instance, of simple pleasure, with significant by-products of the less simple pleasures of rivalry, conflict, violence, and humiliation. Sex was not procreative, but extramarital, extra-family. I have found only two instances of the inclusion of children in the cartoons, one presented very expressively as the spoiler of marital pleasure, the other the accidental result of, and named, Coitus Interruptus. Pregnancy is a mistake ("I flunked sex-education" [no. 310]), and the "rhythm" method is liable to miss a beat (no. 338). That other notorious prophylactic, TV, also fails to fill its distractive function.

By separating sex from family and household, Róger might appear to be aligning himself with an old and very Nicaraguan machista tradition that condoned men's abandoning women, wives and concubines, and the children they had fathered. The level of desertion, migration, and polygyny left many women as the sole source of financial support for their families. In 1986, 34 percent of all Nicaraguan households (in Managua 60 percent) were headed by women (Molyneux, 1986: 479; Power, 1987: 14). To alleviate this situation the Sandinista government did much to compel men to pay child support and discussed and even implemented other means to alleviate the dreadful plight of women that was inherited from the past.

I believe that the lack of children in Róger's cartoons, like the lack of reference to household, domesticity, and conventional marital relations in general, is to be viewed not as establishing a norm, much less an ideal, but rather as a tactical humorous convenience: by clearly demarcating and limiting the arena of debate, Róger was saying not that there were no others but only that this, sexual rivalry between genders rather than spouses, was important enough to be treated separately and could serve to vent deep-seated social malaise.

At the same time, one would assume that Róger's was very much a male view intended for a male audience, as any exclusive concern with sex tends to be. Yet the amazing figure of 71.7 percent of all girls becoming sexually active between the ages of 9 and 14 constitutes surely another potential adolescent audience: for them and the 6 percent of the readership identified as housemaids (the only gendered audience statistic available), Róger's cartoons may have been positively encouraging, instructive, and in terms of pregnancy (which figures, by omission, as a virtually nonexistent risk), dangerously misleading. From questioning Nicaraguan adult women (Randall, 1993: 112) it emerges that many found his cartoons, when they were aware of them at all, objectionable; but many women would find any kind of sexual humor objectionable, unfunny, and/or at best irrelevant. The contemplation of sex as such, unpalliated by ideas of love and commitment, is not today generally considered liberating for women; nor is pornography—a word used, mistakenly I believe, by some Nicaraguan women for Róger's erotic humor.[6] How far women see sex as a weapon to be used in a liberating struggle (from/against men) is another matter.

The Sandinista government made some efforts on behalf of women, notably by the creation of the National Executive Committee of the Association of Nicaraguan Women (AMNLAE), the national women's organization named after Luisa Amanda Espinoza. She was the first female Sandinista to die in combat, murdered by the *Guardia* at 21. Her mother's experience had been typically burdensome: she had had 21 children, of whom 6 lived, and she had been abandoned by her husband (Randall, 1981: 24). Women played a very essential military and support role in the insurrection and afterwards in regular army militia and self-defense units. AMNLAE had a seat on the Council of State and had 60,000 members and subsidiary offices nationwide. It successfully lobbied for legal reforms; the Law on Nurture called on all family members, including male wage earners, to contribute to household tasks (Harris and Vilas, 1985: 112).

But this was not enough. Many women felt betrayed by the revolution, deplored the lack of a truly autonomous women's movement, saw AMNLAE as a creature of the male-dominated FSLN party, and were horrified by the macho style of Daniel Ortega and the FSLN leadership in the election campaign of 1990. There were acts of personal repression that appeared highly hypocritical given the FSLN leaders' own free sexual mores. Vice Minister of Culture Daisy Zamora was severely punished, suffering professional ostracization for leaving a dead marriage for a better relationship, and dismissal from her post for refusing to sleep with a powerful male government figure (Ranch, 1993: xiii, 108-110, 179; Criquillón, 1995: 227).

But AMNLAE failed signally in one endeavor: to have the right to abortion written into the constitution. By the early 1990s illegally induced abortions were the leading cause of maternal mortality in hospitals (Randall, 1993: 112). The Sandinista party hierarchy was immovably opposed to abortion, and AMNLAE had to conform. For Tómas Borge, speaking on TV, the issue of abortion and family planning was "intellectual claptrap" (Randall' 1993: 57). The Sandinista media, including (especially) the popular Catholic weekly, *Tayacán*, treated such charged topics, if at all, very gingerly indeed. Róger himself called abortion, in an interview, "too big and complex" to deal with, but deal with it (in conjunction with family planning) he did—once, to his cost. Catholic tradition, of course, and presumably many Catholics sympathetic to the revolution disapprove of contraception, let alone abortion. Yet now 22 percent of all births are to women between the ages of 15 and 19 (*Barricada Internacional*, August 1993, 22).

In a 1982 speech to AMNLAE called "Woman and the Nicaraguan Revolution," Borge admitted that the Sandinistas had not confronted the struggle for women's liberation with the same courage and decisiveness as they undertook social and economic transformation and that women continued to bear the main burden of reproduction, child care, and housework, and to suffer exploitation. Borge complained that many men were "revolutionaries in the street, in their workplaces, in their militia battalions – everywhere—but feudal lords in the home" (Rosset and Vandermeer, 1986: 475). Borge spoke admiringly of the women "who have blazed a path of fire and tenderness that has given life and color to this revolution" and who "leave the fragrance of flowers for the fragrance of gunpowder—women who are as fertile in their womb as they are in revolutionary consciousness."

The parallel is revealing indeed and amounts to an injunction: bear children as you bear arms. At a forum (September 26,1987) in which women demanded that abortion and sterilization without the husband's approval be legalized and that birth control and sex education programs be expanded, President Daniel Ortega (father of seven children) spoke against such reforms

on the grounds that the population of Nicaragua needed to increase, not decrease: It was in response to this or a similar speech that Róger Sánchez published in the *Semana Cómica* a "Poster AMNLAE" (October 6–12,1987), a
full-page photograph (presumably a montage) of five women in an advanced
state of pregnancy sitting naked on a bench, identically posed—part, as it
were, of a state-sanctioned (or state-controlled) reproduction machine—and
proclaiming in mock pride, "We are AMNLAE."

This boldly repudiated Ortega's position and deplored AMNLAE's own division of counsel on the subject, its failure to push reforms wholeheartedly
against the (male) Sandinista officials. By humorously attributing the poster
to AMNLAE, Róger risked the accusation that he was ridiculing the organization itself when the opposite was true.

In late 1987 and early 1988, in the midst of an economic crisis that halved
the size of the paper (to eight pages) while the price increased from 10 to
1,000 *cordobas* (to keep pace with inflation), Róger began inserting the occasional mild, nongenital *Playboy*-type photograph, with a humorous caption
added relating it to a news item. The novelty was defended by a translation
from a *Playboy* (January 1988) interview with the Canadian physician and
philosopher F. M. Christensen, explaining the concept of "pornography," his-
torizing it, and justifying its *reading* existence.

Figure 18.1 The "AMNLAE" poster. (*Semana Cómica*, no. 353)

CLOSURE BY THE GOVERNMENT

The addition of erotic photographs of women to the repertoire of the *Semana Cómica* fueled the fire of a leading AMNLAE faction already angry about the "AMNLAE" poster. They soon found, and Róger conveniently offered, a provocation sufficient to have the magazine closed down. Lea Guido, secretary general of the organization, in the name of the "mothers of heroes and martyrs, peasant and working women, and intellectuals who participated in the struggle to form a new Nicaragua," appealed to Tómas Borge to punish the magazine. They alleged violation of the General Media Law forbidding the exploitation of women as sexual or commercial objects and intent to ridicule the celebration of International Women's Day and, generally, to attack the dignity of women. The particular offense was having published (no. 373, March 1988), under a photograph (actually taken from a Japanese magazine) small and of poor quality even by *Semana Cómica* standards, a semireclining woman on a bed with knees raised, wearing only bra and panties, which she pulls at with one hand as if to inspect her pubic area. The genitals are lost in murky shadow, as was usually the case in such photographs. This Róger might have got away with but for the caption, headed "Women Preparing" and continuing "Apparently this March 8, International Women's Day, is going to be celebrated by all legal means, since from now on the most representative of Nicaraguan women is preparing and sprucing up . . . In the photograph an activist preparing for the event." The apparent ridicule of *the* national revolutionary festival compounded the provocation; the radio talk shows buzzed with complaints, which assumed that the woman in the photograph was a prostitute.

The magazine was ordered suspended for five issues, the sort of heavy penalty hitherto meted out, for very different reasons, to the *Prensa*. The *Semana Cómica* in fact did penance for only two weeks. But the independent Sandinista *Nuevo Diario*, never averse to the juicy tidbit, also suffered a suspension (of two days) for carrying the story, complete with photograph and caption, with the question attached: "Is this pornography? Unhealthy? Lack of respect? You tell us." The reappearance of the newspaper (March 9) was the occasion for a front-page diatribe against actions that silenced Sandinista organs and left the *Prensa*, "published in Washington," to continue unmolested in its foul, lying rightist ways. Róger's only crime was "poor taste" (to which he himself admitted in a private interview).

Róger did not change his editorial policy as a result of the sanction. Far from it; he introduced a new feature (from April 1988), the *Sádico Ilustrado*, "Yellow Supplement for Reds," "tabloid of sexual opposition," which "strips revolutionaries naked" with the regular "Diary of a Penis"—and of course the erotic photographs. These now increased in number, size, and explicitness, playing sex against politics by means of captions that purported to give the subject's political views but without particular reference to Sandinista organ-izations. These ironic, allusive, lightly self-mocking texts are a study in them-selves and seem to parody the pathetic utterances of contestants in beauty competitions such as the Sandinista Youth were beginning to organize ("Beauty Contest," 1988), utterances claiming serious ambitions, intellectual-ity, political savvy. (Eliette Elhers, head of the AMNLAE media commission and a member of its executive committee, was expelled for having gone on ra-dio to oppose the national beauty contest [Criquillón, 1995: 227].) To cap the fun, Róger's photographs, so obviously of foreign origin, were often attributed to notable Nicaraguans. The captions, whether they undermined the sexual objectification or merely underlined it, certainly succeeded in slipping the venture under the guard of certain prominent feminist critics such as Sofía Montenegro and Gioconda Belli, the latter the author of Nicaragua's first, and scandalous, erotic poetry. Both sprang to Róger's defense (Montenegro, 1990).[7] Since the photographs were so obviously drawn from capitalist sources and showed blonde North American-looking women, Róger undercut the ac-cusation that he was exploiting Nicaraguan women (to make original photo-graphs of whom would also have simply been more expensive) and added credibility to his claim that he was mocking foreign cultural values. He also quite early on introduced male nudes (which actually preceded the wave of female cheesecake), penis and all.

The controversy stimulated a sophisticated debate between Róger Sánchez, who admitted only to "bad taste"; Marta Mungía of AMNLAE's executive secretariat, who argued that the depiction was a clear "violation of the law and the principles that we established with the revolution"; and Sofía Mon-tenegro, who found the position of the *Semana Cómica* politically "indefensi-ble" but considered censorship a mistake and counterproductive (Lancaster, 1992: 95). Lancaster offers a valuable contextualization of the incident ac-cording to the local conditions and broad theories of pornography, censorship, and civil liberties. His analysis, as delicate and complex as the issues involved, lacks one important context (could we call it a "control group?"), which is our primary focus here: that of Róger's *Humor Erótico* cartoons themselves, which are so much more interesting and important than the reproductions of and captions to the *Playboy*-type photographs presented, editorially (by contrast), as low-grade, trivial, throw-away material. Nor does Lancaster consider the "super-cartoon" of the double-page "Somos AMNLAE" poster, ridiculing (as noted) the organization for its failure to press the legalization of abortion, in the light of Montenegro's comment that abortion is the country's second cause of death, a situation "much more obscene than that photo."

As long as we are criticizing Lancaster, let us point to two significant fac-tual errors: there is nothing "scatological" about Róger's humor; feces never appear, nor does the related bodily function. His drawings are never "obscene" by any contemporary application of the term. To dismiss them as "adolescent" is to deny the complexities and sophistication we discover here. It is not true to say that Róger after the sanction "continued to inflame AMNLAE sensibilities with similar photographs and captions" (my stress). Organizationally, AMNLAE was thereafter left alone. This may have been, in part, because it was no longer deemed a worthy target: its action against the Semana Cómica came at a time when it was widely perceived as having betrayed essential women's causes and lost its militance and much of its influence. Thus Róger did it a favor, so to speak, by giving it a pretext for an appearance of aggressive intervention.

THE CARTOONS: SEX, WORK, AND SPORT

The Semana Cómica with its Humor Erótico is a thesaurus on sexual economy. Sex should be pleasure; it often resembles work, and the aura and traumas of work and workplace often hang over the bedroom like a pall. There are the overproducers (of lovers, orgasms), mostly women, who contrast with those, mostly men, who underproduce, who fail to meet minimal norms. Workplace notices in the bedroom state hours, explain stoppages, warn defaulters. Like all forms of productive labor under capitalism and under a competitive semisocialism like Nicaragua's, sex is subject to the familiar methods and devices of measurement and evaluation, such as graphs, timers, odometers, and filing and accounting procedures, as well as comparisons, competition, and demands for improvement. Here is a reversal of roles, from those Engels saw as characterizing the bourgeois family: husband as mini-boss, wife as proletarian worker. In Róger, the female is cast in the role of the boss, the male in that of the worker, although this is never explicit. The result is that sex becomes stressful, like any form of subjugated labor, and the positive rewards and prizes are too few.

But sex is also a sport that does not discriminate against women. It invites them to the quintessential sporting spirit of competition and physical thrills: "Let's see your slider" (no. 318), but "don't hit and run." Baseball is the Nicaraguan national sport; with Róger, coitus rivals and penetrates it as such. Scores are kept; winners, fouls, and penalties are declared. The sexual imagination runs wild, to violence and excess, the seismological, the primal scream, the exploding condom, the conflagration. Sex is perilous, contortionist, acrobatic, inextricable (e.g., Sánchez, 1986: 12), labyrinthine and (less often) technological, requiring bizarre hooks and winches. This is of course perversion. To a letter in Róger's comic sex-advice column (Consultorio Seximental, no. 360) asking "what is unnatural sex," the editor responded "when technology is used."

NICARAGUAN POSITIONS, BUREAUCRATIC BINDS

Much of this sounds familiar. What seems specifically Nicaraguan in this humorous, fantastic sex economy, what emerges from the particular situation of a country struggling toward socialism, is the way man (foremost, the male) becomes the victim of a political bureaucratization of sex in which the female, no longer the manager setting norms of production, is cast as worker-consumer. Bureaucracy is a rich subject for humor anywhere, but especially in societies where direct and personal attacks on government are not desirable or possible, where old (bourgeois) apparatuses resist the new (socialist) mandates and continue to operate with recalcitrant mentalities and structures. Róger sees the recalcitrance as also that of a sexuality inadequate to the new demands of emancipated women. If only she would return to being a sex object, "just for ten minutes!" (no. 298). But the problem has a clear political analog. The spontaneous flow of sexual feeling is blocked like "spontaneous" (i.e., intuitive) political action by procedural anxieties and lack of independent initiative. The male awaits orders from above (no. 302), instructions from the manual on how to, whether to act, what position to adopt. Neither the manual of sexual positions, the Kama Sutra, nor the manual of political positions, (Lenin's) *What Is To Be Done?* is the answer.

Nor is a straight political harangue, delivered at the bedside from a lectern into microphones, likely to help.

Figure 18.2 **"Don't tell me you were the type that copied from others in the exams . . ."** (Sánchez, 1986: 51)

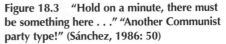

Figure 18.3   "Hold on a minute, there must be something here . . ." "Another Communist party type!" (Sánchez, 1986: 50)

In the bed, that familiar gap between theory and practice yawns like a chasm. And the yawn is detumescent.

This is of course political as well as sexual satire. The confluence of the two is facilitated by a verbal overlap in the word "position." In a highly politicized society like Nicaragua's, it is hard (or should one say soft) not to take positions. New ones are invented, old ones superseded, the spectrum enlarged. "Experiment" is the watchword. Positions are subject to scrutiny, debate, evaluation. Róger proposes that this is also true of positions in the sexual revolution. When Somoza and a narrow Catholic morality ruled, only one position was allowed (bourgeois/man on top); now any position is possible, though some end in confusion and paralysis.

"What starts on top may end up below," Róger roguishly reminds a lady *Pluralista* who wrote to his sex-advice column (*Consultorio Seximental*, no. 317). And (male) political defeat is turned to (female) sexual advantage: "You and your governing from below," she says, delighted to be on top, in allusion to the Sandinista vow after their defeat at the polls in February 1990 (no. 470).

In the liberated territory of the bedroom pluralism is the most desirable state of the sexual constitution, and "democratic openings" are to be sought wherever possible. Sandinista Nicaragua was, *pace* Reagan and his minions, relatively pluralist and relatively democratic, and Róger's relative freedom to critique his own party's shortcomings is to its credit. Nicaragua was certainly no orthodox Marxist or communist state and had more political pluralism than any other country calling itself socialist (60 percent of the economy was still in private hands, seven parties were represented in the National Assembly, six in opposition). In the bedroom marked (in the revolutionary slogan of Paris, May 1968) "Prohibido Prohibir" (no. 293), nothing is forbidden. To be addicted to a single position is to be "sectarian." But a revolution in the outside world cannot survive on pluralism and eclecticism alone.

WOMEN ON TOP

Like the lower classes, women the world over demand access to the top, or a position of equality with men. To the entrenched male, the very concept of equality is alarming; it is like discarding the mattress and doing it standing up: not at all comfortable ("None of this above or below, I want it on equal terms," she ordains) or procreative, for that matter.

Having enjoyed supremacy for so long, the male has difficulty in conceiving anything but a reversal of roles that has haunted the comic media for centuries. Like the bourgeoisie, there are men who would rather self-destruct or quit than share or work for "simultaneity."

We may put to Róger's cartoons the question we put to the sex humor of any society ridden with class conflict (i.e., everywhere). Is the struggle in bed, between the sexes, a substitute or a sublimation or a continuation of the class struggle? Or is it, at most, an analog, a metaphor? Answer: none of the above, *overtly*. For all Róger's politicization of sex, he never explic-

Figure 18.4   "None of this above or below, I want it on equal terms." (Sánchez, 1986: 103)

itly couches it in the classical terms of class struggle, bourgeois versus worker, much less U.S. imperialist versus Nicaraguan nationalist, as he does consistently and necessarily in his straight political cartoons for *Barricada.* To do so would be to cast the two sexes as irreconcilable enemies. The struggle is ideological, simultaneously "for unity and of contraries" (as she puts it, from on top [no. 355]). The struggle in the bed is *within* a class, a Sandinista class split into two gender factions. An apparent exception confirms this rule: the female compares her male companion's sexual inertia to the political impotence of the class enemy

To fail thus, at the very moment when the Nicaraguan people are celebrating their triumph of July 19, 1979! Yet, his failure may only be a momentary one due to excessive patriotic libations forgivable on such occasions. The joke is exemplary, if not typical.[8] No man was ever called a *contra* by his lover, even if, foolish enough to read a list of demands from the bedside, he is castigated as "Oh, God, another rightist" (no. 354).

But there is female cruelty enough without this politically defamatory edge. This too is familiar: efforts at female emancipation in the United States have been met with a backlash of misogyny—male fears and fantasies about cruel or dominant women that show up in all the media at all levels from elite to popular. The stereotype of the devouring, castrating female is as old as the Old Testament; its resurgence in literature, art, and folklore at various times and in various places has presumably always to do with real (if often small or even imagined) shifts in the balance of power in favor of women.

Figure 18.5 "What a contradiction. Every July 19 night I have to compare you to the bourgeoisie." (Sánchez, 1986: 172)

The "castrating female" theme in Róger, while it never reaches the demonic heights (or depths) of its equivalent in U.S. culture, is a minor but insidious presence. It is not my purpose to "justify" this presence or to enter into the old debate whether it is not useful and therapeutic—"liberating"—for men to confront, whether in laughter or not, their worst fears vis-à-vis women.

I once wrote Virgil Partch objecting to a cartoon in which he seemed to make fun of (or least make light of) the torturing of political prisoners, to whose screams he likened the much amplified sound of a rock band. He drew and wrote me back that he was only making fun of the amplified-music buffs. He was, of course, using a metaphor—a tasteless one, perhaps. Róger, too, like all artists, worked with metaphor; his female sexual violence, especially when fantastic or exotic, was a (male) metaphor for the liberating of the (female) sexual imagination.

At the same time, I do not wish to let Róger off the hook. The male imagining of female violence against men is all too often the guilty, even paranoid reaction to a historic pattern, imagined in art and acted out in real life, of male violence against women[9] fueled by fear of sociogender revolution: any moment the world may turn upside down, the abused may seek revenge. Viewed as acting out "female revenge," Róger's cruel or reckless female stands revealed in an unattractive, even deplorable role, one capable of justifying male preemptive violence or at least dominance. But this is only a small aspect, perhaps the extreme edge of Róger's work, and any discussion of the relation of Art and Reality threatens to bog down in uncertainties.

It could be that too many Sandinista Nicaraguans were more concerned about erections than elections, the popular political tribunal that, in the case of Nicaragua in 1990, was manipulated in cunning foreplay by the United States—some would call it rape, with the knife of contra war held at the throat of a starving, bleeding country. A totally unexpected catastrophe to many Sandinistas, the electoral defeat did not break the stride of the *Semana Cómica*. Róger, one of those who foresaw defeat, seemed to distance himself from the FSLN when it lost, having compromised itself with the right not the least by conducting a vulgar, blatantly sexist U.S.-style electoral campaign. Róger seemed to prefer his readers' idea for the formation of a new, independent "Semana Cómica party." Was he aware of the semiexistence of the "Party of the Erotic Left," founded by a group of feminists outside the FSLN (Randall, 1993: 181)?

After the electoral defeat, major articles on the artist and his magazine, without reference to his tremendous record and continuing work as political cartoonist for *Barricada,* put a triumphal wreath on the brow of probably the most popular—certainly the funniest—dissident voice of Sandinism, engaged no longer in a fight with friends but "to the death, everybody against everybody" (*Barricada Internacional*, April 1997, 7). In an ever-worsening economy, with rocketing unemployment, circulation plummeted to 12,000, compensated by an infusion of advertisements. The nudes went full page. Attacks on the church increased, especially for its anticondom and procontra stance, and of course the government was now a legitimate and easy target.

Then in November 1990 Róger Sánchez Flores died of stomach cancer at 30. A last-minute medical visit to Cuba, where he had been honored as one of the world's great progressive cartoonists, failed to save him. Nor could the *Semana Cómica* itself be saved for long. At the time of Róger's death it cost 1 million cordovas a copy. The Nicaraguan love affair was with the art of Róger, personally. There has been no replacement, nor can there be.

NOTES

1. A third collection appeared under the title *Dos de cal, una de arena* (n.d.).

2. Henceforth, "no." refers to *Semana Cómica* issues (which are often undated; an approximate date is given only when germane). Page numbers refer to the *Humor Erótico* anthology (1986).

3. Down to but not including crocodiles (see no. 158), with a particular fondness for dogs.

4. A poll taken after Róger's death in June 1991 broke down the readership as follows: students 23 percent, technicians 14 percent, workers 13 percent, unemployed 11 percent, professionals 10 percent, tradespeople 9 percent, housemaids 6 percent, other 14 percent (interview with Noel Irías, July 1991). There was, unfortunately, no gender breakdown, apart from the housemaids. Lancaster (1992: 100) assumes the core readership to be male adolescents.

5. *Jodarría* has no equivalent in English.

6. For a broadly hostile view of pornography, see MacKinnon (1981: 20). See also Dworkin (1987).

7. Montenegro's thoughtful reaction to issues sensed to be difficult to be dealt with summarily, much less censoriously, is analyzed by Roger Lancaster (1992: 95–96) on the basis of the interview printed in an article by Nick Cooke and Mariuca Lomba (1988). A stereotypical blanked condemnation of Róger's sex humor generally may be found in Collinson (1990: 169) where Róger is criticized for "trivializing and stereotyping women," and "lean[ing] heavily on the whores/nymphomaniac/frigid bitched school of humor."

8. It is, however, assigned a special position in the *Humor Erótico* album (arranged by the publisher, not Róger), introducing the section headed "Criticism, O.K., but of a constructive kind." The woman in the cartoon is clearly not giving constructive criticism.

9. "The rape of women and children . . . has increased by 650 percent in the past three years" (*Barricada Internacional*, April 1997, 7).

REFERENCES

Alemán, Verónica
1993 "Sexist laws scorched." *Barricada Internacional,* March 19.
"Anti-Condom Crusade"
1994 "Anti-condom crusade," *Barricada Internacional,* February 26.
"Beauty contest"
1988 "Beauty contest irks activists." *Guardian,* December 14.
"Censorship unmasked"
1991 "Censorship unmasked." *Barricada Internacional,* September, 35.
Clark, Christian
1990 "Cartoonist Róger . . ." Guardian, December 19.
Collinson, Helen
1990 *Women and Revolution in Nicaragua.* London: Zed Books.
Cooke, Nick and Mariuca Lomba
1988 "The Pandora's box of sexism and machismo has to be opened up." *Pensamiento Propio,* April-May.
Criquillón, Ana
1995 "The Nicaraguan women's movement . . ." in Minor Sinclair (ed.), *The New Politics of Survival: Grassroots Movements in Central America.* New York: Monthly Review Press.
Dworkin, Andrea
1987 *Pornography: Men Possessing Women.* New York: Dutton.
Harris, Richard and Carlos Vilas (eds.)
1985 *Nicaragua: A Revolution under Siege.* London: Zed Books.
Kunzle, David
1984 "Nicaragua's La Prensa: Capitalist thorn in socialist flesh." *Media, Culture, and Society* 6: 151–176.
1995 *Murals of Revolutionary Nicaragua 1979–1992.* Berkeley and Los Angeles: University of California Press.
Lancaster, Roger
1992 *Life Is Hard: Machismo, Danger, and the Intimacy of Power in Nicaragua.* Berkeley and Los Angeles: University of California Press.
MacKinnon, Catherine
1981 "Feminism, Marxism, method, and the state: An agenda for theory," in Nannerl O. Keohane, Michele Z. Rosaldo, and Barbara C. Gelpi (eds.), *Feminist Theory: A Critique of Ideology.* Chicago: University of Chicago Press.
Molyneux, Maxine
1986 "Women: Activism without liberation?" in Peter Rosset and John Vandermeer (eds.), *Nicaragua: Unfinished Revolution.* New York: Grove Press.
Montenegro, Sofia
1990 "Róger, el sexo y la política." *Gente,* November 9, 4.
Power, Margaret
1987."Decade-old women's group keeps heat on." *Guardian,* December 9, 14.
Quant, Midge
1990 "Nicaragua's feminists . . ." *Guardian,* September 26, 13.

Randall, Margaret
1981 *Sandino's Daughters: Testimonies of Nicaraguan Women in Struggle.* Vancouver and Toronto: New Star.
1992 *Gathering Rage: The Failure of Twentieth-century Revolutions to Develop a Feminist Agenda.* New York: Monthly Review Press.
1993 *Sandino's Daughters Revisited.* New Brunswick: Rutgers University Press.
Rosset, Peter and John Vandermeer (eds.)
1986 *Nicaragua, Unfinished Revolution: The New Nicaraguan Reader.* New York: Grove Press.
Sánchez, Róger
1981 *Muñequitos del pueblo: Dos años en la lucha ideológica.* 2 vols. Managua: FSLN.
1986 *Humor erótico.* Managua: Vanguardia.
n.d. *Dos de cal, una de arena.* Managua: Editorial El Amanecer/Barricada.
"Women in Nicaragua"
1991 "Women in Nicaragua, the Revolution on hold." *Envío* 10 (119): 30–41.

19

Evita: The Globalization of a National Myth

Marta E. Savigliano

Have you seen *Evita* (Parker, 1996a)? Not Eva, not Eva Duarte, not Eva Perón, but a version of her historical/mythical character in the diminutive; not just a foreshortening but a downsizing, right from the beginning, to situate spectators comfortably, to help them take a close look at a tamed Eva, an Eva made familiar. This is not the Evita addressed by her *descamisados*, who used the diminutive as a term of endearment, to evoke a shared past of deprivation—their empathy a product of her refusal to forget her origins.[1] This is a different Evita—another Evita myth that acquaints the audience with a story of a woman who makes her way up to a position of great power not because she is so special (after all, we know many women like her, with her aspirations and her ability to manipulate) but because she was lucky enough to live her life in a wealthy banana republic, one of those places where golden tanks, macho boots, corrupt bureaucrats, and a mysteriously emotional religiosity (based on Catholicism's connections with primitive superstitions) ensure that the people are adoring masses or persecuted victims. A Hollywood-made Evita myth requires no more than these elements to convey a clear image of the engines of history at work in places like Argentina at any given time.

In this *Evita,* Evita's controversial role in history is presented in a dramatically undisturbing way, and it becomes moving because her public, political figure is thoroughly personalized and thus banalized. *Evita* is a melodramatic remythologization, conforming to the narrative conventions of melodrama

---

This chapter first appeared in *Latin American Perspectives* 97, 24:6 (November 1997), pp. 156–172.

identified by Peter Brooks (1980). It tells a tale of a self-made woman who, like many women of her time and place, beds her way up and is sensitive enough to exert grand scale token charity among her people but not sensible enough to restrain herself from indulging in Diors, furs, and jewelry. Finally, she must face the limits of power as she faces the limits of her body; she must renounce the vice presidency, and she must die—like a woman and, more specifically, like the femme fatale of film noir (see Kaplan, 1980; Doane, 1991). The story begins with a glamorous, fascinating woman's death, but the tale continues: She was loved, then and now. Look at those interminable lines of dark faces in sorrow, that tango musical lament and danced mourning: They *must* love her.

But this recent, US$60 million remythologizing of Evita could not be successful without its entangled attempt at also remythologizing Argentina's national history. For that purpose, it is sufficient to present a few glimpses of a virtually mute Perón, some dazzling flashes of mobilized military equipment, street violence and corpses now and then, the masses and a balcony. After all, *Evita* is about Evita, isn't it? Why bother complicating her myth with the nation's history? Familiar snippets are enough to trigger all the appropriate stereotypes, situating the viewer comfortably in the mythical terrain of that kind of nation's history. And, if you don't get it, a Che/narrator will provide the necessary anti-Peronist gossip so that we don't fall prey to Evita's intricate charms as so many of those down there did. This Che, too, is subjected to a careful remythologization. He is not the revolutionary conscience one might expect but the voice of "reason," a sensible Che haunting Evita, warning her and us against any romanticization of Evita's life. What makes his point of view privileged and authoritative is that he speaks from all possible class positions, as a participant and observer of Evita's most eventful interventions in Argentine history. His tone is both accusatory and disdainful, and he brings into question Evita's modus operandi both from a moral point of view and from the perspective of an experienced skeptic who can foresee, from the beginning, her destruction.

This *Evita*, then, is this ubiquitous Che's interpretation of Evita, as myth, and of her role in the making of history, and he is reporting to a transnational audience from a pseudo-liberal, "universally" bourgeois perspective that amounts to an anti-Peronist perspective. His rationalist anti-Peronism is not, however, the self-interested anti-Peronism of the oligarchy responding in confabulatory choruses to Evita's attacks on its property and values. This waiter/ journalist/student/factory worker/bartender/valet/peasant and occasionally tuxedoed Che is a transclass cultural translator whose ideology and interests can only be pinned down in his gender-specificity and heterosexual appetites. No matter how much we learn about Evita's promiscuous sexual adventures, her eroticism is displaced in the form of desire for power.[2] Perón is a fatherly figure or a teammate in a passionate pursuit of power, and the only erotically invested romance seems to be in the realm of Evita's dream, in which she dances a frantic, tangoesque waltz with an attractively defiant Che, who manages, like no one else, to put her in her womanly place. In his arms Evita is sincere. But this is a dream, a fantasy, a delirious moment entered simultaneously by Evita and Che when they meet in a state of lost consciousness (she collapses in a church, he faints after being beaten up in a student demonstration). And it seems as though this moment was what Evita had longed for all along: true romance.

THE MADONNIFICATION OF EVITA

The casting of Madonna as Evita and the presence of tangoesque dance scenes throughout the film contribute to producing a version of Evita's history that engages with a personal politics suitable for globalization. Madonna the superstar shapes the ways in which Evita's image and story reach the film audience. There are obvious reasons for this: Madonna is a star-commodity, a contemporary cultural product that is aggressively circulated in the entertainment market (see Bordo, 1993; McClary, 1991). In addition, and unlike traditional film stars, Madonna offers a surface of high visibility on which it is possible to project a variety of personalities and styles. Film stars usually cultivate a strong presence that pervades all the characters they represent on screen. In contrast, Madonna is called a "superstar" because of her lack of depth. Her flatness is precisely what allows her image to shine brightly as an icon (see Tetzlaff, 1993). Rather than inhabiting or playing different characters, she appropriates them. Her ability to put on whatever suits her at the moment imbues her with an aura of power signaled by success and manipulation. This chameleon-like, superficial versatility, combined with the power accrued by the management of her fame, creates a tense connection between Madonna and Evita. Madonna as an all surface/screen superstar projects an unspecific image of Evita, invading Evita's own strong personality, historical depth, and cultural characteristics with a spectacular blurring of boundaries. She dissipates Evita's national and historical specificities as she renders visible a transcultural Evita in terms of universal woman-ness.

Once Evita is Madonnified as a female superstar, Madonna and Evita seem to become a perfect match in ambition, manipulation, and celebrity. Despite their quite different aims and circumstances, both stand for women with power and thus enter hand-in-hand into the pantheon of femmes fatales. Feminist theorists interested in the visual arts, who often make use of psychoanalytic understandings, insist that "woman" as a concept and woman's body as a construct offer a privileged surface on which to project (male) sexual fantasies and fears (see Doane, 1991; Hart, 1994; Allen, 1983; Dijkstra, 1986; Rose, 1986). By definition, woman is the unknown and unknowable dark continent. Always enigmatic, women are all the same and yet constantly changing. The capacity for multiplicity already mentioned in Madonna's case is replicated in the controversies surrounding Evita's personality while alive and her contrasting mythifications after her death: Evita the saint, the whore, the revolutionary, the powermonger (Taylor, 1979). Evita as depicted through Madonna in this film fits point by point the characteristics of the femme fatale, that dangerous side of femininity always threatening to take over women who step aside from the taming rules of patriarchy: she is determined and aggressive, she manipulates men masterfully, she is childless and narcissistic, self-centered and egoistic. The femme fatale is confirmed as a love object, an object offered for adoration. Narcissism, as an erotic self-investment that defies emotional attachments to men and to the male-centered social world, connects Evita's image to Madonna's contemporary version of femme-fatality, transcending cultural and historical differences.

Madonna and not Evita, however, seems to be the main beneficiary of this universalizing operation. She appropriates Evita's charisma and looks to give depth to her own image. Madonna's Evitism cultivates a conservative femininity of her times: romantic, fragile, caring, wrapped up in delicate fabrics, wearing toned-down makeup, and excelling in costly bourgeois good taste. Evita's own image as a strong, foul-mouthed, independent woman is subdued in Madonna's representation, offering spectators a softened Evita, looking for Perón's approval after every public performance, leaning on his shoulder for protection, smiling gently at the poor as she distributes kitchenware and money, moved by her own words as she addresses the crowds. In Madonna's characterization, Evita is romanticized and unthreatening. Her dangerousness as a femme fatale is contained, and not just by her death (the destiny reserved for fatal women who, in the end, always bring fatality to themselves).

Alan Parker's Evita is interesting to analyze from this point of view, because the film's narrative is saturated with death and destruction. Evita's death opens and closes the narrative, tightly containing her disruptive powers as a warning or moral lesson that serves as a backdrop to any potential seduction exerted by her transgressive doings, even when presented in a tamed version as in this case. Most remarkable is that while Evita actually dies (paying the price for her femme-fatality), Madonna acts out (that is, pretends) Evita's death only to resurrect herself as the star who played the coveted Evita role. Evita gives new thrust to Madonna's career. Evita inaugurates Madonna's metamorphosis from pop idol to mature actress.

Audiences, critics, and Madonna herself work hard at blurring the differences between Evita, the historical figure, and Madonna, the star. They compare their lives and their looks, stressing their parallels from the lurid stories
of rags to riches to the bleaching of their hair (e.g., *Clarín*, 1996; Ayerza, 1996;
Martínez, 1996; Escribano, 1996; *Caras*, 1996). And yet, *Evita*, the film, constantly wrestles with the presence of two main female leads, namely, Madonna
and Evita. The Evita/Madonna juxtaposition amounts to a tense competition
between two spectacular identities in which Evita is awkwardly Madonnified
and Madonna cultivates Evitism. One, Evita, plays the dramatic role engaged
with historicity; the other, Madonna, becomes paramount in the scenes that
provide the film its lyrical, transhistorical component (see Dyer, 1992a).

TANGOIZING ARGENTINE IDENTITY

The dance sequences are precisely the sites where the globalization of Evita
takes place and the Argentine national myth becomes transnationalized.
Madonna portraying a dancing Evita is able to produce an intensely personal,
intimate, and thus universal representation of Evita as a "woman."[3] This is a
place that the real Evita rarely inhabited in her life (see Mayer, 1996). Producing these tangoesque images of Evita, Madonna projects a universal image
of a femme fatale, devoid of specificity except for that frivolous exotic touch
(the tango) that makes femmes fatales fascinating in their difference and yet
recognizable or easy to identify with as generic women with power. The spectacularization of a seemingly banal national cultural trait such as the tango
both expands the stereotypical and erases all other specificities that would
work against easy universalistic assimilations.

In *Tango and the Political Economy of Passion* (1995), I examined the complex
relationship between the tango and Argentine national identity (Savigliano,
1995). There, I argued that the tango was not considered a national dance in
Argentina until after the European elites had so identified it. Even then, the
upper and middle classes in Argentina considered it a poor representation in
both senses of the word: it was a lower-class dance, and it inaccurately represented the nation as a whole. Eventually, however, many Argentines accepted
the European view of Argentina, the tango, and the connection between the
two. The internalization or reproduction of the European point of view is what
I have called "auto-exoticism"—seeing oneself as an exotic Other. These days,
not very many Argentines actually dance the tango, but most would identify
it as a key component of Argentine national identity.

Eva Perón was one of many Argentines who did not dance the tango. In
fact, both she and her compatriot Che Guevara were renowned for their lack

of skill at dancing. For example, Cabrera Alvarez includes the following passage in his biography of Che (1987: 77):

There is a dance that night, and the friends decide to go. It's a bustling crowd, and the couples seem to multiply on the dance floor. Ernesto ["Che" Guevara] approaches his friend and tells him in a low voice, "Runt, listen well. I'm going to dance, but you know . . . " Alberto [Granados] doesn't need any kind of explanation to know that his friend is incapable of distinguishing a military march from a *milonga.* "When they playa tango," Ernesto requests, "kick me, then I'll know what it is. Agreed?" More or less every other piece played by the improvised band is a tango, but for some reason they suddenly play a Brazilian *shoro* entitled "Delicado." Granados remembers the song was popular at the time his friend began to court Chichina, and wishing to remind him of that time, taps him with his foot. Ernesto takes a young woman out to dance. The tempo of the *shoro* is quick, but he doesn't hear it. He dances to the beat of a tango, marking off his steps with mathematical precision.

There are similar stories about Evita's incompetence as a dancer, including an account of why the famous actress and tango singer Libertad Lamarque slapped the lesser-known Evita during the filming of *La Cabalgata del Circo.*[4] Alicia Dujovne Ortiz writes (1995: 87):

According to the testimony of Sergia Machinandearena, the scene of the slap, or of the heated discussion between the real star and the starlet with "clout," took place during the rehearsal of a *pericón,* a folkloric dance that requires no special talent and that all Argentine schoolchildren can do. But despite her fine and delicate feet, Evita did not manage to adapt them to the demands of the rhythm. And Libertad, who danced very well, finally reacted. According to her own testimony, she did not slap Evita on the cheek, but she did tell her off completely—how she was fed up with Evita's absurd hours and had it up to here with the aforementioned *pericón,* for which they had had to hire a dance professor to try to untangle Evita's feet.

Evita and Che, however, dance in several scenes in *Evita,* following the conventions of Broadway and Hollywood musicals. In fact, Evita dances significantly more in Alan Parker's film than she did in the stage versions of the musical, where tangos performed by professional dancers appeared almost entirely as a backdrop providing the Argentine "cultural ambiance." The filmed *Evita*'s extra dancing is a reflection of Madonna's presence as a music-video diva, taking over the centrality of the historical character. The Madonnification of Evita spectacularizes the female body and its desires, engaged in recognizably stylized movements that reveal its enigma in the form of a "natural" code. Madonna/Evita's tangoesque dances, as such, are a lyrical relief in which the corporeal and the emotional invite spectators to abandon the pursuit of intellectual appraisals of Evita's life. The dancing moments appeal to the logic of the senses, a logic that allows for gaps, contradictions, and fragmentation to

run smoothly on a totalizing register in which specificities become mere formal details. From a cinematic point of view, dancing familiarizes Evita as it focuses on her generic femininity while it diverts attention from her politics.
The tango dances are coded in either tropical, Hispanic, or waltzed styles, providing a mere "cultural" reference to be interpreted according to stereotypes
attributed to more familiar dance genres. Thus, Evita's tango-rumba—performed on a crowded city bus in the midst of her first arrival in Buenos
Aires—announces the contagious, irresistible excitement that promises to
turn the metropolis into her territory/dance floor. Her first incursion into a
rowdy bar is signaled by a couple performing a tango-flamenco, announcing
the dark, alcohol—and smoke—ridden underworld into which she will im-
merse herself, paying the price for her ambition. The tango-waltzes she dances
in the arms of Che and Perón show her classy, conflicted arrivals at the pin-
nacle of power. Madonna/Evita's most tango-like tangos, of which glimpses are
offered, stand for her most debased stages of prostitution, dancing in close embrace with rough-looking Latin men in dusty dance halls. The tango's allusion
to excessive eroticism has frequently been coupled in filmic uses with destructive, antisocial appetites for power—the tango as a fascist dance. Parker's Evita
makes use of these resonances, politicizing Evita's personal desires and neu-
tralizing the politics at play in the configuration of national, cultural stereotypes. Indeed, one of the most important ways in which the film marks
Madonna's Evita as Argentine is by showing her dancing the tango. Evita tan-
goizes Argentina as a nation and Evita as a national myth, drawing on a familiarly exotic cultural reference laden with political implications that pack-
ages Argentine "otherness" for global consumption.

Madonna/Evita dances both the most gruesome and sublime landmarks of
her biography, and her dances always indicate some kind of social mobility.
She dances her arrival in Buenos Aires, fleeing from the prospects of a dull future in Junín, a small town where her fate as a bastard is insurmountable. She
dances, night after night, in sleazy bars and dance halls, in the arms of older
working-class or ruffianesque Latin men. (These professional Argentine tango
dancers are not mentioned by name either in the film credits or in the captions of Parker's book The Making of Evita [1996b]. They are Pedro Mon-
teleone, Guillermo Cunha Ferre, and Luis Salinas.) These shady tangos, recognizable by the inclusion of ganchos and other paradigmatic figuras such as
ochos and cepilladas, mark Evita/Madonna's shameful but obstinate path to the
top by manipulating machismo (associated with the tango). These tangos
stand for sexual favors, and the tango dance halls become fancier and her
dancing partners whiter and better-dressed as she endures this tangoesque rite
of passage from destitute prostitution to a more rewarding and even legitimate
prostitution in the arms of Perón.

Madonna/Evita's dance scenes with Perón signal their first encounter: a brief, slow dance in which the shots focus on their faces, studying each other, culminating in a striptease with her gloves (reminiscent of Rita Hayworth's *Gilda*,[5] another woman in Buenos Aires trying to escape her past). A dance also marks Evita's triumphal entrance, after her wedding to Perón, into the circles of political power. Like a queen, all in white, Evita/Madonna climbs the stairs of a monumental palace-like building, waltzes with old generals, diplomats, and public figures, and leaves the scene in Perón's arms, always dancing, in graceful transition to her prominent (yet inexplicable) place in history.

The dances of sorrow, the slow-paced tango laments performed by somber Argentines in dimly lit indoor and outdoor settings, zooming in on grave Latin faces of all ages, indicate Evita's passage from life to death to immortality. The death-dance scenes, prominently featuring María and Roberto (a well-known professional tango couple also ignored in the film credits), open and close the film narrative, making the tango an exotic, ritualistic dance of mourning associated with a strange religiosity. Thus, the Argentine tango, a national symbol of Argentineness, confers an aura of primitiveness and alterity on Evita's mythification and on the mores and customs of Argentines. Evita and her people are carefully exoticized to establish the distance necessary to generate fascination in the global spectator. At the same time, and in tense contradiction with this exoticizing thrust, Evita's doings and, especially, her personal motives and psychological traits are presented in terms that are familiar enough to elicit a transnational audience's identification.

THE BANALIZATION OF THE POLITICAL

Popular psychoanalytic interpretations (what Freud might have called "wild psychoanalysis") slip into this *Evita*. Beyond historical-political-social circumstances, what seems to be important for the audience to know is that this very special woman's life story can only be understood from the point of view of the psychic consequences of a sad and wounded child's development. The lack of a legitimate father and the presence of a morally corrupt mother combined to produce a female subject obsessed with compensating for the degrading status of being a bastard. Her beauty, determination, and aggressive personality allowed her to manipulate her way to the top, but she could not come to terms with her success; she felt either undeserving or unsatisfied or both, and therefore she worked too hard and wanted too much until she reached her own bodily limits. She had to pay the price; she died.

"Don't cry for me, Argentina." Don't cry for me, because I got what I deserved, because my death makes perfect sense—and also because I lived my life this way so that I would be remembered, don't you see? I plotted my own mythologization! This is where the audience is led by this highly personalized and psychological version of Evita's life. Politics and historico-social background are there (not very carefully researched or concerned with accuracy, but that is another story), spectacularized in dazzling shots that convey this movement of starting from the surface, the appearances, the muddled noise of contextual information, in order to reach the depth, the kernel, the dark continent of Evita's unconscious. The result is both convincing and undisturbing. A grand story, but a sad one—an exhausting career and a spectacular end. Adored and hated, forever, she got away with it, and we are left wondering if this is the fate of women who engage fully in the world of politics.

Attending primarily to the personal, as this *Evita* encourages audiences to do, we are immersed in a moral riddle, trying to figure out how to deal with justified or unjustified causes, means and ends. Did the causes justify her means? (That is, did her illegitimacy justify her defiant and aggressive behavior toward the dominant classes?) Or did her ends justify her means? (That is, did her pursuit of social justice justify her authoritarianism and her fanaticism?) Or did her causes justify her ends, whatever her means? (That is, did her early experiences of deprivation justify her hunger for power, regardless of the personal and social costs?) Or were her means unjustified no matter what causes and no matter what ends? (That is, no matter what traumatic experiences struck her in the beginning, no matter what egotistical or noble social concerns moved her to act, her demagogic and calculating manipulations in the political arena wronged others and Argentina's history.) This *Evita* does not produce the elements necessary for an informed assessment because of its uneven treatment of the persona/psychological story vis-à-vis the political and sociohistorical context. Not only is there not enough context but the context provided is not complex enough, not blurred enough, creating the impression that it is simply a frame for the personal picture of a historical and mythical political figure.

Like a modern fable, a soap-operatic moral tale, this *Evita* offers a universally applicable lesson beyond place and time. Looked at from the point of view of the projection of a femme fatale image onto Evita, it seems as if Parker's *Evita* would code all political and historical information as a series of catastrophes (earthquakes, social upheavals, political repression) unknowingly brought about by the mere presence of Evita.

This *Evita* fails to construct a public persona, either mythical or historical. The aesthetic treatment of the political scenario, carried out mainly through images of great visual impact but of little explanatory power, and the treatment of Evita's personal motives and desires, addressed insistently through the lyrics, generate the effect of two parallel, contrasting scores that never amount to a syncopated rendering. In this *Evita*, the political happens and the personal speaks or, rather, sings, even when it talks politics. In addition, the musicality of the words, regardless of their content, creates a climax of intimacy and a transcendental, intersubjective bridge, prompting a rush across cultures, nations, and history (see Dolar, 1996).

The singing voice is dangerously powerful in that it appeals to emotions that provide synthetic judgments not readily accessible to criticism. The voice beyond the words, like the stylized movement of the dancing body (beyond necessary pragmatic activity), is taken for a senseless play of sensuality. These are fascinating forces, pregnant with excessively moving and intricate meanings, and yet in themselves are considered empty and frivolous. I tentatively suggest that, at least in contemporary Western and Westernized cultures, the singing voice and the dancing body exhibit a dimension that runs counter to self-transparency and to sensibility, as if their pleasurable corporeality operated against the logos and the physicality associated with labor and the production of meaning—singing and dancing being the "other" of production, its radical alterity. And yet, music, song, and dance constitute powerful discursive registers that operate, in conjunction with the image, in the production of signification. They allocate points of view, points of hearing, and points of kinesthetic identification that alternately reproduce and challenge hegemonic perspectives (see Shohat and Stam, 1994).

Alan Parker, in The Making of Evita, recognizes the challenges posed by the filming of a historical account in which all the words are sung. He declares his intention of producing an "objective," "balanced" account of Evita's controversial life at the same time that he acknowledges that the screenplay is based on the libretto of the 1970s British musical "Evita" (which was probably inspired by Perón's return to Argentina after 18 years of exile). The lyrics belong to Tim Rice, as in the stage version. They are based on a book by María Flores (1952), The Woman with the Whip. María Flores was the nom de plume of Mary Main, an Anglo-Argentine historical novelist who returned to Argentina in the early 1950s, at the height of Evita's interventions into politics. The book was published in New York in 1952 and was translated into Spanish and published in Buenos Aires only in 1955, after Perón's ouster. It provided a magnificent collection of elaborate anti-Peronist gossip (Fraser and Navarro, 1996: 199 n. 11). Parker's Evita tries to compensate with images for some of the historical background missing from the stage version, but the lyrics (being roughly the same) bend all the complex information toward a seamless narrative of oppositional politics coded as an analysis of a personality type: Evita as the woman with the whip, resentful, power-hungry, and so on. As Evita's "problematic" personality becomes more and more paramount, the ideological and political motives that guided her behavior (such as the redistribution of wealth) become less and less relevant. We are being taught a lesson about a woman who misbehaved—a universally applicable lesson. The fact that she misbehaved with Peronist goals in mind and that her misbehavior contributed to Peronist political ends becomes superficial.

THE POLITICS OF APOLITICAL MYTH-MAKING

Parker's Evita's final scenes clearly direct attention away from historical specificities and beyond ideological considerations. At the majestic site of Evita's wake, countless sorrowful Argentines, one by one, slowly approach the glass-topped coffin. Perón watches gloomily, standing by the corpse that seems to symbolize the death of his source of power. The presence of Che by the coffin suddenly catches Perón's and our attention. Che defiantly places a last kiss on Evita as he directs an intense look in Perón's direction. Perón returns the look, puzzled at first and then with growing suspicion. Above the woman's dead body, two powerful men exchange menacing looks. Blackout, the end. It all comes down to another exemplary story of machismo. The audience is prompted to wonder: What would have happened if Evita had ever met and fallen in love with Che? The suggested response in the film is romantically apolitical: Perón would have been jealous. Either in Che's or in Perón's arms, Evita would have been no more (or less) than a woman whose passionate doings unfailingly nurtured rivalry among men—a drive stronger than history, stronger than politics. Evita's ending seems to imply that, as a matter of fact, sexual politics would supply us a universally applicable answer to the question of what politics is—a masterfully depoliticizing take on politics.

This is in fact a remarkably effective political move, given that it projects all the stereotypical knowledge about the political atmosphere that surrounded Evita's Argentina onto the Argentina of today. Evita and especially Perón and Peronism were matters of great international attention and political concern toward the end of World War II. The international press reported on Perón's and other military officers' sympathies if not connections with Franco, Hitler, and Mussolini; Peronism's alleged resemblances to Nazism and fascism; and stories about corrupt dealings with officers from these totalitarian and genocidal regimes who sought asylum in the vast pampas. The truth of these reports is still being debated in international scholarly circles. The association between Peronism and fascism or, for the more prudent, between Peronism and totalitarian-nationalist-populist-demagog personalistic regimes that respond to antidemocratic ideological inclinations is accepted, in general, as a given. When one adds to this a superficial knowledge of the successive military dictatorships of the 1960s and the 1970s, equally subsumed under the rubric of fascism, one has a picture of sorrowful victims and victimizers who could never learn the lessons of democracy. The intervention of the United States in Latin American affairs during these decades, seeking either to overthrow or to consolidate these regimes, is frequently left out or underestimated. The impressions left by this fragmentary information do their work as they remain unaddressed on the screen.

It could be argued that this *Evita* is a spectacle. I agree, so long as by "spectacle" we mean an artistic, creative rendering of a story that in providing a synthetic, condensed view of a complex and often puzzling historical phenomenon fully engages the political and ideological terrains (see Dyer, 1992a, 1992b; Nichols, 1981). Spectacles that address the interstices between a nation's history and its myths, produced for a transnational audience, effectively do political work. As the artist (in this case the director) chooses what to keep and what to discard, what to stress in the plot, what connections to establish and what to leave out, an aesthetic rendering comes to life that is not very different from myth in its symbolic power.

Myths are beliefs, not specifically true or untrue, certainly invested with the power of representing something worth knowing. They are particularly interesting in that they effect representations between the real thing and its interpretations, between the historical and the historiographic. An artistic production of this kind, a cinematographic spectacle, is also in-between, neither documentary nor fictional narrative. Spectators, especially when not well-informed, are left either skeptical or enraptured or both. This one masterfully crafted impressionistic interpretation is the only information that most viewers will ever have the time or interest to get about Evita. Evita thus enters the transnational scene through a powerful medium that generates a new myth capable of reproducing old myths about Latin American history, reinforcing universalistic connections via subjective identifications, reinstating the morality of fear and fascination surrounding the explosive woman-power equation, and generating a whole new global package of "Evitist" commodities including Evita fashion, jewelry, cosmetics, coffee-table and academic books, and even US$1,500, seven-day Evita tours (e.g., Chacón, 1996; *Vogue*, 1996; *Honolulu Advertiser*; 1997).

THE MENEMIZATION OF EVITA

"Have you seen *Evita*?" I am repeatedly asked, and then "What do you think?" And it takes me some time to sort out and choose a referent (what I think about Evita, the historical figure, pleading with or agitating the masses on the balcony, or the peripatetic embalmed corpse now locked up in a mausoleum in *La Recoleta*; about Evita as portrayed in other recent films; about Madonna's performance of Evita; or about the film, *Evita,* directed by Alan Parker, as a whole, a work of cinematic art or a piece of entertainment?) And how should I respond? As a cinema buff, a cultural translator, a responsible scholar, or a representative of the Argentines (and, if the latter, of which ones? the Peronists or the anti-Peronists? the right- or the left-wing Peronists? the nationalist or liberal [Menemist] Peronists? or the ones above and beyond these disputes, who welcome any representation of Argentines in a Hollywood production, calculating that it is better to be there, identified even if misrepresented in global culture, than totally erased and ignored?)? Who or what is Evita, and who/what do I represent when I talk/write about Evita?[6]

None of my colleagues or friends have the time, interest, or patience to let me go carefully through this entangled checklist before I respond. Therefore I have come up with an answer that gives me some room to complicate things: "Yes, I've seen both of them." The initial surprise at this doubling of Evita allows me some time to assemble a combination of responses, trying to address all these issues, synthetically, at once. This is my opportunity to protest the Evita question and to attempt to unravel and reweave what seems to be a simple, straightforward question. In order to focus my thoughts somewhat, I have addressed the present remythologizing of Evita, the historical figure and the myth, through the intervention of the Hollywood filmmaking apparatus. My intention has been to relate this cinematic production to the transnational spectacularization of Third World historical figures and to the global circulation of Latin American national myths. I would like to conclude with some reflections on Argentine responses to the decision to produce a Hollywood version of *Evita* (not to the film itself, because it had not yet been shown in Argentina when I was last there). These early responses are, in one way or another, concerned with issues of cultural imperialism.

It has been widely argued that "culture," especially "popular culture"—including not only music or dance but also myths—now circulates globally, despite its obviously local/national original production. But discussions have engaged more fully with the mechanisms of transnationalization than with the politics of cultural piracy or appropriation. The local Argentine reactions to the Hollywood production of *Evita*—culminating in an Argentine filmic counterversion (*Eva Perón,* directed by Juan Carlos Desanzo, screenplay by José Pablo Feinman, starring Esther Goris as Eva Perón and Victor Laplace as Perón, Aleph Producciones, 1996) with at least two more films planned (*La Maga,* 1996a)—fully engage the political dimension of these transnational undertakings and demonstrate resistance not only to what is perceived as the unethical or irresponsible use of national symbols or icons but also to the persistence of unequal relations of power between nations and constituencies in the course of so-called globalization and transnationalism.

Whose perspective on Evita is more likely to achieve the status of a globally circulated myth? Argentines have a clear, consistent opinion on this despite the differences among them that have produced competing histories of Evita and contrasting Evita myths (see the contributions of Marcos Mayer, Pablo Chacón, Gabriela Bolognese, Horacio González, and Antonio Cafiero in *El Nuevo Porteño*, 1996). No one seems to doubt that the Evita that Argentine children will know will be the one represented by Madonna in Alan Parker's Hollywood film, and they resent it. *"Evita hay una sola, y es nuestra"* (There is only one Evita, and she is ours) proclaimed the posters plastered across Buenos Aires on the international film crew's arrival. This is, of course, wishful thinking (see the contributions of Juan Pablo Feinmann, María Saenz Quesada, Alicia Dujovne Ortiz, Abel Posse, and Marysa Navarro in *La Maga*, 1996b).

There have been many myths of Evita in and outside of Argentina, but this time something different seems to be at stake. The Hollywood remythification of Evita fits almost too well the trend of spectacular politics introduced by the current Peronist government under Menem. Menemism, as critics of the social costs embedded in this government's free market policies brand this refashioning of Peronism, has retained nothing but the memory of what once moved hopeful masses of Argentines—the ideals of social justice, economic independence, and political self-determination. Hollywood's *Evita*—spectacular, frivolous, depoliticized—evokes precisely Menem's understanding of a Peronism suited to our times. The film recalls the past glories of Peronism and reveals its unviable utopianism. The memory of Evita's willingness to give up her life for the cause of her *descamisados* still helps win elections in the midst of a generalized confusion brought about by Menem's use of Peronist slogans and symbols to implement neoliberal policies.

Argentines have no doubt that this Hollywood remake of Evita's myth will have a global impact on the representation and interpretation of Argentine history, an impact that some welcome and others resist. Globalization is well under way, and the new empire is one in which very few Argentines will have a say about the history or the myths that will explain our past and guide our future. Antonio Negri (1996), an Italian Marxist political philosopher, suggests that at this point we would do better to move beyond the problem of how to resist global imperialism and focus instead on what kind of empire we want.

NOTES

1. Evita's origins, marked by her birth out of wedlock as well as by the class ascription of her maternal family, have been a matter of much debate. Her own attempts at manipulating information on her birth and her family's status have been extensively

discussed by Fraser and Navarro (1996) and Dujovne Ortiz (1995). In a recent presentation at the UCLA Center for Latin American Studies (April 1997), Tulio Halperin Donghi observed that it is false to consider Evita's maternal family as lower-class, given that both her sisters married Argentine professionals (a lawyer and a military officer). Thus, Evita's alignment with the *descamisados* seems to have been more of an ideological choice on her part. This observation opens up space for a political rather than a psychological analysis of her historical figure.

2. On the desexualized image of Evita and its resexualizing moments, when Madonna, the star, takes the leading role in the film, particularly in the dance scenes, I have been following Richard Dyer's (1992a) analysis of the ideological/cultural functions of star images and their relations to the construction of film narratives, characters, and so on.

3. Linda Williams (1989) argues that pornographic films as well as musicals strive to represent that which cannot be directly seen or that which has been previously invisible. Women's desires, motives, and impulses thus figure prominently in these genres. I suggest that dancing provides the opportunity within the film narrative for historicity and cultural specificity to be subsumed under a generalizable imaging of "expressions" and "true feelings." Dancing as a shorthand for accessing the essence of the plot acquires an explanatory power that usurps the relevance of other complex information.

4. Directed by Mario Sofficci, screenplay by Francisco Madrid and Mario Sofficci, starring Hugo del Carril, Libertad Lamarque, and Eva Duarte (Argentina, 1945).

5. Directed by Charles Vidor, screenplay by Marion Parsonnet, starring Rita Hayworth as Gilda, Glenn Ford as Johnny Farrell, and George MacReady as Ballin Mundson (Columbia Pictures, United States, 1946).

6. Similar questions have been confronted, directly or indirectly, by Argentine fiction writers and playwrights such as Tomás Eloy Martínez (1995), Rodolfo Walsh (1986), Luisa Valenzuela (1983), Néstor Perlongher (1986), Copi (1970), and Leónidas Lamborghini (1972). Issues of power and sexuality surrounding the erotics of nationalism are at the center of these works. The analysis of their strategies of representation and self-representation is beyond the scope of this article.

REFERENCES

Allen, Virginia
    1983 *The Femme Fatale: Erotic Icon.* Troy, NY: Whitston.
Ayerza, Laura
    1996 "Cara a cara con Madonna." *Gente,* February 1, 22–34.
Bordo, Susan
    1993 "'Material Girl': The effacement of postmodern culture," pp. 265–290 in Cathy Schwichtenberg (ed.), *The Madonna Connection: Representational Politics, Subcultural Identities, and Cultural Theory.* Boulder, CO: Westview Press.
Brooks, Peter
    1980 "The mark of the beast: Prostitution, melodrama, and narrative," pp. 125–140 in D. Gerould (ed.), *Melodrama.* New York: New York Literary Forum.
Cabrera Alvarez, Guillermo
    1987 *Memories of Ché,* translated by J. Fried. Secaucus, NJ: Lyle Stuart.

Caras
1996 "Madonna: 'Soy igual que Evita.'" January 24.
Chacón, Pablo E.
1996 "Evita fashion." *Nuevo Porteño* 1(4): 38–39.
Clarín
1996 "Dos mujeres, dos destinos." January 28, 41.
Copi (Raul Damonte Taborda)
1970 "Eva Perón." Manuscript.
Dijkstra, Bram
1986 *Idols of Perversity: Fantasies of Feminine Evil in the Fin-de-Siécle Culture.* New York: Oxford University Press.
Doane, Mary Ann
1991 *Femme Fatales: Feminism, Film Theory, Psychoanalysis.* New York: Routledge.
Dolar, Mdlar
1996 "The object voice," pp. 7–31 in Renata Salecl and Slavoj Zizek (eds.), *Gaze and Voice as Love Objects.* Durham, NC: Duke University Press.
Dujovne Ortiz, Alicia
1995 *Eva Perón: La biografía.* Buenos Aires: Aguilar.
Dyer, Richard
1992a "Entertainment and utopia," pp. 18–34 in *Only Entertainment.* London: Routledge.
1992b "Four films of Lana Turner," pp. 65–98 in *Only Entertainment.* London: Routledge.
Escribano, José Claudio
1996 "Procura la actriz mimetizarse con Eva." *La Nación*, January 23, 5.
Flores, María [Mary Main]
1952 *The Woman with the Whip.* Garden City, NY: Doubleday.
Fraser, Nicholas and Marysa Navarro
1996 *Evita: The Real Life of Eva Perón.* New York: W.W. Norton.
Hart, Linda
1994 *Fatal Women: Lesbian Sexuality and the Mark of Aggression.* Princeton: Princeton University Press.
Honolulu Advertiser
1997 "Buenos Aires: The city of Evita." *Honolulu Advertiser*, January 5.
Kaplan, E. Ann (ed.)
1980 *Women in Film Noir.* London: British Film Institute.
Lamborghini, Leónidas
1972 "Eva Perón en la hoguera." *Partitas.*
La Maga
1996a "Tres películas en marcha y otros dos proyectos en duda." January 31, 5.
1996b "Tema: Santa o hereje: ¿Quién fue Evita?" January 31, 1–7.
Martínez, Tomás E.
1995 *Santa Evita.* New York: Vintage Español.
1996 "Lo que no se perdona" *Página/12*, February 7, 3.
Mayer, Marcos
1996 "Planeta Evita." *El Nuevo Porteño* 1(4): 36–45.
McClary, Susan
1991 "Living to tell: Madonna's resurrection of the fleshly," pp. 148–166 in *Feminine Endings: Music, Gender, and Sexuality.* Minnesota: University of Minnesota Press.

Negri, Antonio
    1996 "Después de la globalización, el imperio." *El Nuevo Porteño* 1(4): 85.
Nichols, Bill
    1981 *Ideology and the Image: Social Representations in the Cinema and Other Media.*
    Bloomington: Indiana University Press.
El Nuevo Porteño
    1996 "Dossier: Si Evita viviera." December, 35–53.
Parker, Alan
    1996a *Evita* (Alan Parker and Oliver Stone, screenplay; Tim Rice, lyrics; Andrew
    Lloyd Webber, music; starring Madonna [Evita], Antonio Banderas [Che], and
    Jonathan Pryce [Perón]). Hollywood Productions.
    1996b *The Making of Evita.* New York: Harper Collins.
Perlongher, Néstor
    1986 "Evita vive (en cada hotel organizado)." *Cerdos y Peces.*
Rose, Jacqueline
    1986 *Sexuality in the Field of Vision.* London: Verso.
Savigliano, Marta E.
    1995 *Tango and the Political Economy of Passion.* Boulder, CO: Westview Press.
Shohat, Ella and Robert Stam.
    1994 "Stereotype, realism, and the struggle over representation," pp. 178–219 in *Un-
    thinking Eurocentrism: Multiculturalism and the Media.* London: Routledge.
Taylor, Julie M.
    1979 *Eva Perón: The Myths of a Woman.* Chicago: University of Chicago Press.
Tetzlaff, David
    1993 "Metatextual girl: Patriarchy-postmodernism-power-money-Madonna," pp.
    239–263 in Cathy Schwichtenberg (ed.), *The Madonna Connection: Representational
    Politics, Subcultural Identities, and Cultural Theory.* Boulder, CO: Westview Press.
Valenzuela, Luisa
    1983 *Cola de lagartija.* Buenos Aires: Bruguera.
Vogue
    1996 "Madonna's moment as Evita, mother, and fashion force." October.
Walsh, Rodolfo
    1986 "Esa mujer," pp. 9–19 in *Los oficios terrestres.* Buenos Aires: Ediciones de la Flor.
Williams, Linda
    1989 *Hard Core: Power, Pleasure, and the "Frenzy of the Visible."* Berkeley: University of
    California Press.

Annotated Index of Articles on Women and Gender in *Latin American Perspectives*

Title/Description	Author	Issue/Vol./No.	Date	Pages
"Facing Destruction, Rebuilding Life: Gender and the Internally Displaced in Colombia" Examines the dynamics of violence in Colombia and the gender-differentiated effects of displacement, especially the dual process of the destruction and the reconstruction of lives and homes.	Meertens, Donny	116/28/1	January 2001	132–148
"Gender, Race, and the Struggle for Social Justice in Brazil" Considers the effects of race, class, and gender discrimination in the labor market and specifically on the ability to access better paying jobs in the urban center of São Paulo.	Lovell, Peggy	115/27/6	November 2000	85–103
"Caribbean Transnationalism as a Gendered Process" Within a political economic analysis of globalization, examines the gendered process of transmigration, with special emphasis on the human dimensions.	Ho, Christine G. T.	108/26/5	September 1999	34–54
"Seeking Our Own Food: Indigenous Women's Power and Autonomy in San Pedro Chenalhó, Chiapas (1980–1998)" A close-up look at the lives of indigenous women and their perceptions and visions of their roles in social movements, democratization, and sustainable development.	Eber, Christine E.	106/26/3	May 1999	6–36
"Bodies, Faith, and Inner Landscapes: Rethinking Change from the Very Local" Considers urban women in a Guadalajara neighborhood and the gender dimensions of economic restructuring; emphasizes the ways in which economic crisis leads to new possibilities for negotiating power relations.	Price, Patricia	106/26/3	May 1999	37–59

Title	Author	Issue	Date	Pages
"*Odyssey: Negotiating the Subjectivity of Mulata Identity in Brazil*!" Explores mulata identity in Brazil from the critical perspectives of black women from the United States, with a focus on the intersections of gender and class.	Gilliam, Angela and Onik'a Gilliam	106/26/3	May 1999	60–84
"*Gendered Revolutionary Bridges: Women in the Salvadoran Resistance Movement (1979–1992)*" A look at women's role in closing the gap between the guerrillas and the masses during the civil war in El Salvador.	Shayne, Julia Denise	106/26/3	May 1999	85–102
"*The Adverse Effects of Structural Adjustment on Working Women in Mexico*" Considers the destructive effects on women of structural adjustment and women's roles as "shock absorbers" of neoliberal fallout.	Alarcón-González, Diana and Terry McKinley	106/26/3	May 1999	103–117
"*Gender Equality in the Salvadoran Transition*" Examines questions of women's representation and gender equality in the transition of the FMLN from a guerrilla movement into a political party.	Luciak, Ilja	105/26/2	March 1999	43–67
"*Róger Sánchez's 'Humor Erótico' and the Semana Cómica: A Sexual Revolution in Sandinista Nicaragua?*" A look at the contributions of the talented and controversial political cartoonist during the Sandinista years in Nicaragua.	Kunzle, David	101/25/4	July 1998	89–120
"*Transferring Risks, Microproduction, and Subcontracting in the Footwear and Garment Industries of Lima, Peru*" Examines the deteriorating work conditions for women in the footwear production process, with a special focus on the linkages between the large-scale and small-scale sectors.	Ypeij, Annelou	99/25/2	March 1998	84–103

Title/Description	Author	Issue/Vol./No.	Date	Pages
"Approaches to Understanding the Position of Women Workers in the Informal Sector" Argues that poor women, as part of the "disguised proletariat" in their work as garbage pickers, recyclers, and other "informal" jobs, contribute to the profit-making capacities of the capitalist system.	Wilson, Tamar Diana	99/25/2	March 1998	105–119
"Gender Ideologies and the Informal Economy: Reproduction and the 'Grapes-of-Wrath Effect' in Mata Chico, Peru" Examines the commodification of domestic labor, as women come to consider their domestic products or services as exchangeable, and the subsequent dependence on commodity exchange by the peasant household.	Vincent, Susan	99/25/2	March 1998	120–139
"Evita: The Globalization of a National Myth" Argues that the popular Hollywood-made *Evita* myth necessarily remythologizes and distorts Argentine national history.	Savigliano, Marta E.	97/24/6	November 1997	156–172
"Women's Multiple Roles in Economic Crisis: Constraints and Adaptation" In the context of structural adjustment policies, considers women's roles during macroeconomic crisis through a case study of a low-income housing project in Quito.	Pitkin, Kathryn and Ritha Bedoya	95/24/4	July 1997	34–49
"Story without Words: Women and the Reaction of a Mestizo People in Guayaquil, 1820–1835" Explores the gender specificity of the concept of *mestizaje* by telling the story of women living along the River Guayas who chose to establish relationships with partners from outside their groups.	Townsend, Camilla	95/24/4	July 1997	50–67

Title / Description	Author(s)	Issue	Date	Pages
"Trapped between Civilization and Barbarism: José de la Cuadra's The Tigress" Critically evaluates the characterization of the Tigress as interpreted in the 1990 Luzuriaga film and argues that it is inconsistent with the original portrayal in Cuadra's 1935 story, a noteworthy piece of Ecuadorian literature.	Handelsman, Michael	95/24/4	July 1997	69–80
"'Out of Place': Ecuadorian Women in Science and Engineering Programs" Explores the changes in Ecuadorian gender relationships as they are reflected in significant increases in the numbers of women students in universities, especially in the science and engineering fields.	Muñoz, Estela Altuna and Frederick Weaver	95/24/4	July 1997	81–89
"Women in Argentina during the 1960s" Examines the neofeminist movement as it was affected by changes and continuities in attitudes and values with respect to daily life that influenced women's behavior and self-images.	Feijoó, María del Carmen and Marcela M. A. Nari	88/23/1	Winter 1996	7–26
"After the Revolution: Neoliberal Policy and Gender in Nicaragua" Considers the consequences of structural adjustment policies for Third World women and men and the particular effects as they play out in the capital city of Managua.	Babb, Florence E.	88/23/1	Winter 1996	27–48
"The Disruptions of Adjustment: Women in Nicaragua" Discusses the daily lives of poor Nicaraguan women as they are affected by the implementation of an economic "stabilization" program.	Fernández Poncela, Anna M.	88/23/1	Winter 1996	49–66
"The Mother of the Nicaraguans: Doña Violeta and the UNO's Gender Agenda" Explores debates over Nicaraguan gender relations from the 1990 election through the end of 1992.	Kampwirth, Karen	88/23/1	Winter 1996	67–86

Title/Description	Author	Issue/Vol./No.	Date	Pages
"The Sociodemographic and Reproductive Characteristics of Cuban Women" Considers the relationship between the social, educational, and economic participation of women since the revolution and the process of reproduction of the Cuban population.	Catasús Cervera, Sonia I.	88/23/1	Winter 1996	87–98
"The Color of Love: Young Interracial Couples in Cuba" Examines the situation of interracial couples and continued discrimination, as a way to understand contemporary race relations in Cuba.	Fernández, Nadine T.	88/23/1	Winter 1996	99–117
"Modernization, Adjustment, and Peasant Production: A Gender Analysis" Examines the effects of agricultural modernization on peasant families in Mexico, with an emphasis on the relational impact of gender inequality.	Zapata Martelo, Emma	88/23/1	Winter 1996	118–130
"Constructing and Negotiating Gender in Women's Police Stations in Brazil" Examines the evolution of all-female police stations, the political issues involved in their operation, and theoretical implications.	Nelson, Sara	88/23/1	Winter 1996	131–148
"Close Encounters of the Third World Kind: Rigoberta Menchú and Elisabeth Burgos' Me llamo Rigoberta Menchú" Reflects on the multiple voices of Rigoberta, arguing that she speaks not only for herself, but for the communities to which she belongs.	Brittin, Alice A.	87/22/4	Fall 1995	100–114
"The Urban Family and Poverty in Latin America" Examines the outcomes of neoliberal policies for women and families, focusing on the rise of urban poverty during the 1980s and on the families of urban workers.	González de la Rocha, Mercedes	85/22/2	Spring 1995	12–31

Title	Author			
"Economic Restructuring and Gender Subordination" Considers the effects of economic crisis, restructuring, and the expanded participation of women in wage labor in Cuba, the Dominican Republic, and Puerto Rico and whether such participation has led to an increase in women's consciousness or autonomy.	Safa, Helen I.	85/22/2	Spring 1995	32–50
"Planned Development and Women's Relative Power: Steel and Forestry in Venezuela" Explores the factors that contribute to women's relative power (control over their decisions and influence on others) in a comparative study of different industrial sectors.	Rakowski, Cathy A.	85/22/2	Spring 1995	51–75
"Gender, Class, and Water: Women and the Politics of Water Service in Monterrey, Mexico" Analyzes the strategies and results of women's protests and collective actions in the context of national and local water policies and politics.	Bennett, Vivienne	85/22/2	Spring 1995	76–99
"Reading between the Lines: Women, the State, and Rectification in Cuba" Using feminist assumptions, locates women and gender in the full spectrum of Cuban socialism, including the relationship of Cuban women to the official strategy for their liberation, with a focus on the mid-1980 to mid-1990 period.	Lutjens, Sheryl L.	85/22/2	Spring 1995	100–124
"Chilean Women's Organizations" Examines the ways women organized against the dictatorship, with an emphasis on the increase in women's level of awareness and public participation.	Cañadell, Rosa M.	79/20/4	Fall 1993	43–60

Title/Description	Author	Issue/Vol./No.	Date	Pages
"Women in Mexico's Popular Movements: Survival Strategies against Ecological and Economic Impoverishment" Considers the gender division of labor that gives women the primary responsibility for reproducing labor-power with extremely limited resources and whether this has resulted in changes in traditional roles or an increase in women's power in the household.	Stephen, Lynn	72/19/1	Winter 1992	73–96
"Rigoberta's Secrets" Considers the multiple meanings behind what *isn't* being said by Rigoberta Menchú in her widely-read testimonial.	Sommer, Doris	70/18/3	Summer 1991	32–50
"Remembering the Dead: Latin American Women's 'Testimonial' Discourse" Considers the meanings of women's discourse and testimonial literature and explores the related questions of oral history as a means by which to obtain a narrative, female sexual slavery as the cause of *testimonio*, and the personal as the political.	Sternbach, Nancy Saporta	70/18/3	Summer 1991	91–102
"Reclaiming Voices: Notes on a New Female Practice in Journalism" Explores the liberating possibilities offered by the first-person narrative, testimony, or oral history when compared to the *"impartial"* news stories found in the popular press.	Randall, Margaret	70/18/3	Summer 1991	103–113
"The Myth of Being 'Like a Daughter'" Discusses efforts to organize servants in Lima, Peru and the challenges posed by macroeconomic forces that keep domestic servants in a marginal position.	Young, Grace Esther	54/14/3	Summer 1987	365–380

"Brazilian Women in Exile: The Quest for an Identity" Argues that the period of exile has exercised a fundamental influence on building the identity of the Brazilian women who lived in exile either by force or choice during the period of military rule, with significant discussion of the feminist organizations developed by women in exile.	Neves-Xavier de Brito, Angela	49/13/2	Spring 1986	58–80
"Gender and Class in the Transition to Capitalism: Household and Mode of Production in Central Peru" Analyzes the intersection of patriarchy and mode of production during the capitalist transition in central Peru, with emphasis on the survival of the peasant household economy and production.	Mallon, Florencia E.	48/13/1	Winter 1986	147–174
"From Calpixqui to Corregidor: Appropriation of Women's Cotton Textile Production in Early Colonial Mexico" Analyzes continuity and transformation of domestic relations of production, focusing on the ways indigenous women's cotton textile production within their own households was an integral part of the colonial socio-economic structure.	Villanueva, Margaret A.	44/12/1	Winter 1985	17–40
"Women and Slavery in the Caribbean: A Feminist Perspective" Reinterprets the history of slavery in the Caribbean to expose some of the ideology that conceals material oppression and challenges the myth that associates plantation field labor with a male slave labor force.	Reddock, Rhoda E.	44/12/1	Winter 1985	63–80
"Honor Ideology, Marriage Negotiation, and Class-Gender Domination in New Mexico, 1690–1846" Studies the key role that control over marriage choice played in the maintenance of social inequality, focusing on changes in the mode of marriage formation and how parents and children negotiated their behavior and disparities of power.	Gutiérrez, Ramón A.	44/12/1	Winter 1985	81–104

Title/Description	Author	Issue/Vol./No.	Date	Pages
"Guatemala: Women in the Revolution" Considers the importance of the progressive church in raising the consciousness of the poor of Central America and reveals the increasing degree to which women's emancipation has been incorporated into the revolutionary struggle.	Statements by two women involved in revolutionary struggle	36/10/1	Winter 1983	103–108
"Paid Domestic Service in Brazil" Establishes links between the process of industrialization in Brazil and the extensive use of paid domestic workers, with emphasis on the ways domestic work reproduces the sexual division of labor.	Filet-Abreu de Souza, Julia	24/VII/1	Winter 1980	35–63
"Testimonies of Guatemalan Women" Statements by women of different backgrounds who "opt to side with the majority of the people" in the civil war in Guatemala.	Herrera, Luz Alicia	25&26/VII/ 2&3	Spring/ Summer 1980	160–168
"El Comité de Amas de Casa de Siglo XX: An Organizational Experience of Bolivian Women" Focuses on the work of women from the Bolivian tin mines in a housewives' organization: How it began, forms of organization and struggle, difficulties and possibilities encountered, and theoretical contributions.	Viezzer, Moema	22/VI/3	Summer 1979	80–86
"Mobilizing Women: Revolution in the Revolution" Summarizes the theory and practice of socialist movements with regard to the participation of women and all the components of "the woman question," including how women can be mobilized on behalf of or as part of the working class and on behalf of their own liberation in ways that also advance the movement for socialism.	Chinchilla, Norma Stoltz	15/IV/4	Fall 1977	83–102

Title / Description	Author	Volume	Date	Pages
"El Poder Feminino: *The Mobilization of Women against Socialism in Chile*" — Addresses the class nature, motivation, and impact of the women's opposition movement during the 1970–1973 Allende period.	de los Angeles Crummett, María	15/IV/4	Fall 1977	103–113
"*Women in Contemporary Argentina*" — Explores through personal accounts the ways women participate in and are affected by the class struggle and ideological warfare waged in the late 1970s during the period of military dictatorship.	Marini, Ana María	15/IV/4	Fall 1977	114–120
"*The Chilean Women: Reaction and Resistance*" — Reflects on the need for a movement built around true revolutionary principles that, whether under progressive governments such as the *Unidad Popular* or military dictatorship, affirm the right of women to organize their own forces and define their own roles.	Andreas, Carol	15/IV/4	Fall 1977	121–125
"*The Changing Class Composition of the Female Labor Force in Latin America*" — Examines the changes in patterns of female labor force participation and new divisions of labor as a result of the development of industrial capitalism in Latin America.	Safa, Helen Icken	15/IV/4	Fall 1977	126–136
"*Women, Development, and Anthropological Facts and Fictions*" — Exposes the ways development theories in the imperialist context ignore the precedent of egalitarian society and undermine women's autonomy and the privatization of their social and economic roles.	Leacock, Eleanor	12&13/IV/1&2	Winter/Spring 1977	8–17
"*In Dubious Sisterhood: Race and Class in Spanish Colonial South America*" — Confronts the assumption that sex is as important a force in the historical process as class; examines the experiences of white, black, Indian, and *mestiza* women in the context of a colonial situation in a pre-industrial setting.	Burkett, Elinor C.	12&13/IV/1&2	Winter/Spring 1977	18–26

Title/Description	Author	Issue/Vol./No.	Date	Pages
"Women, Mode of Production, and Social Formations" Examines the specific problem of women within social formations where the capitalist mode of production is dominant, arguing that the limits of women's liberation are to be found in the active existence of capital.	Saffioti, Heleieth I. B.	12&13/IV/ 1&2	Winter/Spring 1977	27–37
"Women in Changing Modes of Production" Uses the work of Engels to highlight the linkages between the material basis of women's oppression and the particular mode of production at given points in history.	Fee, Terry and Rosalinda González	12&13/IV/ 1&2	Winter/Spring 1977	38–47
"Changing Social Relations of Production and Peruvian Peasant Women's Work" Argues that the development of the productive forces under the transition from servile to capitalist relations of production is progressive, but the development of capitalism has contradictory effects on different groups of rural women, depending on their relation to the means of production.	Deere, Carmen Diana	12&13/IV/ 1&2	Winter/Spring 1977	48–69
"The Chicana Woman: An Historical Materialist Perspective" Looks as the relation between the development of private productive property in the U.S. Southwest, the subsequent requirement for labor power, and the nature of the subjugation of women under feudalism and capitalism in order to analyze the role of the Chicana in historical development.	Apodaca, Maria Linda	12&13/IV/ 1&2	Winter/Spring 1977	70–89
"Monopoly Capitalism and Women's Work during the Porfiriato" Analyzes, through the use of historical and statistical data, how and why Mexican women were initially incorporated into the work force, and how and why their employment became subjugated to the needs	Towner, Margaret	12&13/IV/ 1&2	Winter/Spring 1977	90–105

of monopoly capitalism, with a focus on the politicization of women and their role in political movements, especially the national crisis of 1907.

King, Marjorie
"*Cuba's Attack on Women's Second Shift, 1974–1976*"
Looks at what happened following the adoption of the Family Code, including the average male's response and changes in rates of women joining the forces of production, and evaluates how Cuba is tackling the basic obstacle to women's incorporation into productive work: the second shift.
12&13/IV/ 1&2 — Winter/Spring 1977 — 106–119

Fee, Terry and Rosalinda González
"*Imperialism, the State and Political Implications for the Liberation of Women*"
Looks at the nature of imperialism, the role of the state, and the contemporary roots of women's oppression to draw out theoretical and practical implications for women's liberation.
12&13/IV/ 1&2 — Winter/Spring 1977 — 120–134

Vaughan, Mary K.
"*Women, Class, and Education in Mexico, 1800–1928*"
Looks at the expansion of public schooling and extension of other social services by the state, functions once performed by the family, and argues that women "reformers" employed by the state sought to develop and strengthen the subordinate role of working class women in reaction to the mobilization of peasants and workers in the Mexican Revolution.
12&13/IV/ 1&2 — Winter/Spring 1977 — 135–152

Schmink, Marianne
"*Dependent Development and the Division of Labor by Sex: Venezuela*"
Argues that, within a context of dependent capitalist development, the expected automatic increase in women's participation rates and female status may never come about, with specific focus on the Venezuelan case.
12&13/IV/ 1&2 — Winter/Spring 1977 — 153–179

Title/Description	Author	Issue/Vol./No.	Date	Pages
"Women Workers and the Class Struggle: The Case of Argentina" Links the roles women play in class society to women's potential to participate directly in class struggle, arguing that when the forms of struggle change, so too does the nature of women's involvement.	Hollander, Nancy Caro	12&13/IV/ 1&2	Winter/Spring 1977	180–193
"Guatemalan Working Women in the Labor Movement" Responds to the appeal, "Equality, Development, and Peace" made by the International Women's Year and asks, What women? in the context of the social and economic realities and struggles of the working women of Guatemala.	Irías de Rivera, María Amalia and Irma Violeta Alfaro de Carpio	12&13/IV/ 1&2	Winter/Spring 1977	194–202
"American Mother" Poem on birth and womanhood.	Metzger, Deena	4/II/1	Spring 1975	67–68
"The Mobilization of Women during the PU Government" Responds to a *Los Angeles Times* article, which implies that active women supported only right-wing forces and dispels the "myth of the valiant Chilean woman."	Garrett-Schensch, Pat	4/II/1	Spring 1975	101–103
"We Need a Government of Men and Women" Reports on the second National Congress of the Federation of Cuban Women and critically and sympathetically analyzes the weaknesses and strengths of the process.	Randall, Margaret	4/II/4	Supplement 1975	111–117
"Si Evita Viviera" Studies the contemporary appeal of the Peronist movement and the importance that women were able to assume within the movement and the class contradictions symbolized by Isabel (right) and Evita (left).	Hollander, Nancy Caro	1/3	Fall 1974	42–57

Index

abortion, 147–48, 188, 190, 216, 227n4, 331
abuse of women, 104–5. *See also* violence against women
Acevedo, Luz del Alba, 30–31
Acosta-Belén, Edna, 31
Afro-Latin Americans, 257–58
agriculture, 94–95, 97–98, 100–102, 147
Agroindustrial Units for Women (UAIMs), 101–2, 105
alcohol use, 236
Alegría, Claribel, 313–14, 318
Alemeida, Carlinda de, 203, 208, 210n7
Allende, Salvador, 158–59, 294, 299
Altamirano, Eli, 328
Alvarez, Cabrera, 349
Alvarez, Sonia, 180, 190, 191n1, 250
Amas de Casa Populares, 34
AMNLAE. *See* Association of Nicaraguan Women (AMNLAE)
Anderson, Jeanine, 83
anti-Peronism, 345–46
antifeminism: FMC, 215, 227n3; success of policies, 186–90, 192n8
antifeminist policies, 179–80, 191n1
antigay legislation, 188, 189
Appadurai, Arjun, 267
appliances, 74n13
Aranda, Josefina, 97

Argentina, 140, 167; as depicted in *Evita*, 354–55; emergence of feminism, 267–68; national identity, 348–51; unemployment, 74n11; women in labor force, 73n10; women in politics, 138
Arizpe, Lourdes, 97
Arrom, Sylvia, 292n6
artisanal workshops, 163–64
Assessoria Especial das DDMs, 203
Association of Nicaraguan Women (AMNLAE), 193n13, 329–32, 333–35
Autonomous Feminist Tendency, Chile, 166
autonomous socialist women's movement, 133–34
Avance, 328–29

Bahamas, 140
Banco Sol, 30
barkeepers, 286–88, 292n3
Barnet, Miguel, 317
Barrett, Michèle, 5
Barricada, 324–25, 327, 340–41
barrios, 162, 163
beauty, Cuban views of, 221–22
bed, as setting for sexual humor, 326
Belli, Gioconda, 334
Benería, Lourdes, 96
Bertaux, Daniel, 300

bestiality, 325, 341n3
biologism, 219
birth control, 3
Bisseret, Noelle, 297
Blay, Eva, 201
Blumberg, Rhoda Lois, 143
Bohemia, 219
Bolivia, 29, 30, 68, 140, 172–78
Bolivian Workers Union, 173–74
Bonafini, Hebe de, 313–14, 317, 319n9, 320n22
Borge, Tómas, 331, 333
Bose, Christine E., 31
Boserup, Ester, 32
Bourdieu, Pierre, 208–9
Bourgeois: democratic revolution and, 134–35; feminism and, 215; sexual cartoons and, 325–26
Boyle, Catherine M., 249, 266
Brazil, 74n11, 140; description of first DDM, 198–99; exodus from political activities by women, 294; female-headed households, 73n10; gender consciousness and, 190; income distribution, 73n7; Landless Peasant Movement, 150; leadership of, 149–50; poverty, 34; protection of threatened peoples, 257–58; textile industry, 50
Brazilian Left, 295–96, 305, 308n1
Brazilians: exiled in Chile, 298–300; exiled in Europe, 300–303; exiled in Latin America, 297–98
bride service, 235, 236
Brooks, Peter, 345
Bunster-Burotto, Ximena, 315, 319nn16–17
Burgos, Elizabeth, 265
Burkett, Elinor, 281

Cabezas, Omar, 317
Campanha, 304, 308n4
Campioni, Mia, 226n1
Canada, 123, 125n1
Cañadell, Rosa M., 144, 157–71
Candido, Antonio, 297
Cantro Flora Tristan, Lima, 269

capitalism, 5, 116, 118; agriculture and, 94–95; assembly work and, 119; Caribbean, 117; gender neutrality of, 20; globalization and, 35; hardships for women and, 91–92; mining women and, 176–78; women's work and, 32
Caranza, Venustiano, 252
Cárdenas, Cuáhtemoc, 139
Cárdenas, Lázaro, 94
cargos, 235–37, 240–41
Caribbean Basin Initiative, 46
Carpentier, Alejo, 319n16
cartoons, 324–43
Cartoons of the People, 324
Carvallo, Bismark, 325
Casa de la Mujer La Morada, Santiago, 269
casa-calle distinction, 56, 57, 58
casas de le mujer, 217, 219
Castilho, Lindomar, 200
castrating female, 339, 340
Castro, Fidel, 223, 227n7
Castro, Mary Garcia, 150
Castro, Raúl, 214
Catholic Church, 147, 189; family planning, 331; family structure, 259; Mexico, 236; sexual humor and, 325; Virgin Mary and, 182
CECF. *See* State Council on the Status of Women (CECF)
cemetery, 314, 319nn8–9
censorship, 333–35
census, 80–81, 88n1, 282–83
Central America, 140, 270
Central American Historical Institute, 192n7
Central Obrera Boliviana, 173–74
Centro de Investigacion para la Acción Femenina, 47
Chamorro, Pedro Joaquín, 180–81, 191n3
Chamorro, Violeta de, 138, 179, 180–83, 186, 191n3, 192n9, 324
Chaney, Elsa, 140–41, 149
Chevigny, Bell Gale, 320n25
Chiapas, Mexico, 231–42
child care, 54, 114, 118, 255, 286; Canada, 123; Cuba, 225; transnational families, 122–23; as women's function, 216

children: assisting with workloads, 65, 74n12; child support, 187, 188–89, 192n11, 218; in labor force, 34; mother-child bond, 114; parent-child relationships, 124, 216; portrayal of in sexual cartoons, 329–30; resources distribution and, 69; testimonials and, 217–18, 320n26; of uneducated mothers, 252

Chile, 294, 307; abortion and, 148; Brazilian exiles and, 298–300; education, 251; emergence of feminism, 267–68; food consumption, 66; gay and lesbian rights, 259; income distribution, 73n7; poverty, 34; power in (1973–1989), 159–60; textile industry, 50; women in labor force, 25; women in politics, 140

Chilean Left, 299

Chinchilla, Norma Stoltz, 132–41

chinganeras, 286–88, 292n5

Christensen, F. M., 332

Christianity, 325

Chungara, Domitila de, 172, 263, 269

church and state, 81

Circle of Brazilian Women, 295, 303–6

Circulo de Mulheres Brasileiras, 295, 303–6

citizenship, 146

class conflicts, 8, 91, 253

class consciousness, 163

class mobility, 125

class struggles, 177, 269, 296

CNPA. *See* Plan de Ayala National Council (CNPA)

co-optation of labor, 48

Colectivo de Encuentro entre Mujeres, 239

Colombia, 74n11, 140, 257–58

combatants, 141, 142–43, 233, 296–97, 330

Comisión Económica para America Latina y el Caribe, 64

Comité de Amas de Casa de Siglo XX, 172–78

Comité en Defensa de la Economia Popular, 103

Commission on Human Rights, 164, 168

Committee of Housewives of *Siglo XX*, 172–78

common-law marriage, 68

communal workshops, 162–63

Communist Party of Nicaragua, 328–29

community service, 235–36

CONAMPU. *See* National Council of the Urban Popular Movement (CONAMPU)

Confederation of Cuban Workers, 49

Confederation de Trabajadores Cubanos, 49

conjugal relationships, 114–15

Conselho Estadual da Condição Feminina, 201–3, 210n4

consumer goods, 66–67, 74n13

consumer prices, 63

consumption, 66–67, 69, 74nn13–14, 93

contribución, 281–82

Convention on the Elimination of Discrimination against Women, 146–47

Cooke, Nick, 341n7

Coordinadora Nacional del Movimiento Urbano Popular, 99–100, 104–5

Coordinadora Nacional "Plan de Ayala", 102–4

Coordinator of Social Organizations, Chile, 166

Corominas, Joan, 318n3

Correa, Rosmary, 203

Costa, Albertina Oliveira da, 294–95

Costa Rica, 65, 73nn9–10, 140

Craske, Nikki, 145

crimes, 187–90, 193nn15–16, 199, 239, 288; fines for, 290, 292n5

cross-border movements, 149

Cruz, Petrona de la Cruz, 239

Cuba, 294, 298; differences among women in, 220–21; division of labor, 133; female-headed households, 55; FMC, 214–23, 227nn3–4; impact of household economy on women, 53–55; occupational segregation, 51; socialist state and, 213–19; state policies, 49, 146; women in politics, 138; women's access to resources and, 49–52; worker's rights, 50

Cuban Revolution, 298

Cuenca, Laura Mendez de, 252–53

cult of virility, 136–37
culture: definition, 249; feminism and, 5; global cultural economy, 250; identity and, 256; overview of research perspectives, 249–51; transnational scope of, 356
Cunningham, Mirna, 182, 190

Dagnino, Evelina, 250
dancing, 348–51, 358n3
day laborers, 257, 279, 290
DDMs. See *delegacias de defesa da mulher* (DDMs)
de Brito, Angela Xavier, 269, 294–310
de Janvry, Alain, 62
Debate group, 302, 308n3
defense of honor, 200–201
delegacias de defesa da mulher (DDMs), 197–98, 201–8
democracies, 131–32, 136–41
demographics, 2–3; 1950 to 1980, 43; African-ancestry population, 257; age of women who migrate, 89n5; female-headed households, 55; Mexico City, 292n6; population of urban areas, 282–83; poverty, 72n1; women in labor force, 23
depeasantization, 95
descamisados, 344, 357–58n1
development, 21–22, 30–33
Díaz, Nidia, 142
dictatorships, 9
diets, 66, 74n15
Dietz, James, 172–78
Distribuidora Conasup, 101
Distributor for National Food Program, 101
division of labor, 235; Caribbean, 119; Cuba, 132–33; gendered, 32, 35, 92; patron families and, 83–84
Dixon, Marlene, 135
domestic abuse, 104–5
domestic structures, 67–68
domestic violence, 199, 237
domestic work and workers, 25, 27, 74n12, 89n6; age, 82, 89n5; Bolivia, 177; Canada, 126n1; Caribbean, 117;

characteristics demanded of, 85–87; from family of origin to patron family, 79–84, 88–89n2; Guayaquil, 286; marginalization of, 79–84, 87; organizing of, 78; vs. vending, 85–87; wages, 85–86, 87
Dominican Republic, 46, 48–55, 140
Donghi, Tulio Halperin, 357–58n1
Dore, Elizabeth, 137, 146
dress, holiday, 290
Dujovne Ortiz, Alicia, 349, 357–58n1
Dyer, Richard, 358n2

Eber, Christine E., 149, 231–45
economic aid, 185, 192n7
economics: Chile, 8, 23–24, 159–60; cost-saving mechanisms, 74n14; crisis of 1980's, 44–45; effect on urban households, 61–62, 72–73n3; gender index measures, 35; impact of household economy on women, 52–55; Mexico, 93–95; women as mothers and workers, 116–19; Ecuador, 34, 140, 257, 278–91
education, 2, 43; abuse victims, 208; Chile, 251; fields of study, 25; gendered policies of, 183–84; home-based trades, 253; labor force and, 23–24, 64; Mexico, 233–34, 242n2, 251–60; theoretical-practical training, 252–53; vocational training, 253; women soldiers, 233
Einhorn, Barbara, 213–14, 226n2
Ejército Zapatista de Liberación Nacional, 233, 240, 242n2
ejidos, 94–95, 100–102, 103, 105
El Salvador, 141, 142–43
elections, Nicaragua, 140, 180–83, 327
employment, 2; Costa Rica, 73n9; Cuba, 49, 213–15; gendered policies of, 49, 184–85, 192n7; urban population, 63, 73n9; wage-labor of working-age groups, 61, 72n2. See also labor force
encuentros, 269–70
entertainers, 287
environmental issues, Mexico, 93–94
EPZs. See export processing zones (EPZs)

Erikson, Erik H., 297
Erundina, Luis, 139
Escobar, Arturo, 250
Espín, Vilma, 214–19, 227n3
Espinosa, Isabel Juarez, 239
Espinoso, Manuel, 280
Espinoza, Luisa Amanda, 193n13, 329–32, 333–35
essentialism, 4, 207
estado límite, 315, 316, 317, 319n15
Esteva Febregat, Claudio, 280
ethnicity, differences in, 256–57
ethnography, indigenous women in Mexico, 233–42
Evita, 266, 344–60
export processing zones (EPZs), 28, 48, 117
export-led industries, 44, 50–52, 58, 97–98
extended families, 54–55, 65, 67, 74nn16–17; economic production and, 117–18; flexibility of, 74–75n20; increase in number of, 85
EZLN. *See* Zapatista Army of National Liberation (EZLN)

Faber, Daniel, 91
Family Code, Cuba, 49, 55, 56–57, 133, 216
family and families; Cuba, 216, 222, 223, 224–25; importance of, 56–57; Nicaragua, 183, 191n5; nuclear family, 114; private vs. public spheres of, 79–84, 88–89n2; testimonials and, 317–18, 320n26; two-wage earners, 45; wages, 118; working-class, 253–54. *See also* child care; extended families
family planning, 227n4, 302, 331
Farabundo Martí National Liberal Front (FMLN), 142–43
Federacion de Mujeres Cubanas, 48, 49, 214–23, 227nn3–4
Federation of Cuban Women, 48, 49, 214–23, 227nn3–4
fem, Debate Feminista, Ventanas, Géneros, Estudos Feministas, Feminaria, 269
female consciousness, 98
female sexual slavery, 315–16, 319nn16–18

female-headed households, 3, 27, 43, 72–73n3; Brazil, 73n10; financial status and, 53–54; as garbage pickers, 29–30; percentage of, 55; resource distribution in, 68–70
feminine perspectives, 8
feminism, 261; Brazilian exiles and, 302–7, 309n6; Cuba, 224–25; culture and, 5; Jaquette's view and, 8–9; state policy and, 209; Third World, 7–10; transformation of in Latin America, 251; transnational, 267–70; women's narratives and, 263
Feminisms and Internationalism, 270
feminist theory, 4–6, 131–32, 267–68
Ferreira, Izilda Aparecida Carvalho, 198–99, 209, 210n7
fertility rates, 2–3, 23–24
feudal laws and customs, 134
fiesta leaders, 235–36
Flakoll, Darwin, 313
Flores, María, 353
FMLN. *See* Farabundo Marti National Liberal Front (FMLN)
food production, 94
food programs, 221
Foreign Report, 227n7
formal sector workers, 25, 28, 32
Fortaleza de la Mujer Maya, 239
Fortuna, Juan Carlos, 73n8
Foster, Cecil, 124–25
France, 303–7
Franco, Jean, 147–48, 262–63, 269, 320n23
Franko, Patrice, 29
Fraser, Nicholas, 357–58n1
Frente Farabundo Martí para la Liberación Nacional, 142–43
Frente Nacional en Defensa del Salario y Contra la Austeridad y la Carestía Nacional, 103
Frente Sandinista de Liberación Nacional, 180–81, 190, 193n15, 324, 327, 331, 340
Freyermuth Enciso, Graciela, 237
FSLN. *See* Sandinista National Liberation Front (FSLN)

"fulana," 215
Fundaçao Carlos Chaga, Sao Paulo, 269

Galeano, Eduardo, 172
Galvão, Patricia, 137
gambling, 287
garbage pickers, 29–30
Garcia, Brigida, 64
garment and textile industries, 47–48,
    50–51
gays and lesbians, 188, 189, 193n13,
    193n15, 259
gender, 4, 6–7, 20, 209, 240; ascribed roles
    of, 186–87; discrimination in El
    Salvador, 141, 142–43; division of in
    labor force, 25–29, 32, 35; equality of,
    49, 56, 134; gender-specific violence,
    203, 205–6; globalization and, 33–35;
    impact of education on gender
    relations, 183–84; index of articles on,
    361–74; inequality of, 115–16, 144;
    militarist groups and, 296–97;
    Nicaragua, 179–80, 183–85, 192n6;
    protest movements and gender
    interests, 143–45; sex cartoons and,
    329–32; sex-crime legislation, 187–90,
    193nn15–16; sexual slavery,
    319nn16–18; Siglo XX housewives
    committee, 174–75; state policies and,
    145–48
gender complementarity, 235–36
gender ideology, 55–57, 234, 242n3
gender interests, 220
globalization, 3; capitalism and, 35; gender
    and, 6–7, 33–35; labor markets and,
    33–35; transnational social systems,
    120–25; women in labor force and, 58,
    119–20
Goldberg, Anette, 306
González de la Rocha, Mercedes, 34,
    61–75
González-Echeverria, Roberto, 319n19
Gordon, Pamela, 138
Gotkowitz, Laura, 219
government and bureaucracy: ministries,
    145; police in Brazil, 206–8; reaction to
    women's movements, 175; reduction of

employment in, 185, 192n7; response
    to changes in Caribbean, 112–13; as
    subject of cartoons, 336–38
Granados, Alberto, 349
Granma, 219
Grosz, Elizabeth, 226n1
Grupo de Mujeres, 239
Guadalajara, Mexico, 65
Guatemala, 263, 264–65
Guayaquil, Ecuador, 257, 278–91
guayaquileños, 279, 280
Gueller, Laura, 138
guerillero, 301
Guevara, Che, 296, 348–50, 354
Guido, Lea, 333
Guy, Donna J., 270
Guyana, 140

Hahner, June E., 260
Hall, Stuart, 209
Hamilton, Nora, 192n9
Hamington, Maurice, 182
Haug, Frigga, 213
heads of households: hours worked by, 64;
    income, 69; poverty and, 69, 283–84,
    292n3; unemployment of, 74n11. See
    also female-headed households; male-
    headed households
health, agricultural laborers, 97–98
Helg, Aline, 257
Hendrickson, Carol, 266
Henry, Frances, 123
higglers, 117
History of Latin America, 281
Ho, Christine G. T., 35, 112–28
homosexuality, 259
households: at-risk groups, 71; changes in
    composition of, 67–68; effect of
    economic conditions on, 52–55, 61–62,
    72–73n3; income of, 64–65;
    inequalities of chores, 215–26;
    networks of mutual assistance, 68;
    three-generation households, 55;
    transformation of, 63
housewifization, 32
housewives, Bolivia, 172–78
housing, 54, 162, 278, 282

Human Development Report, 1995, 19
human rights: abuses of in Chiapas, 237–38; women's organizations and, 164
Humor Erótico, 324–25, 341n8; Communist Party and, 328–29; criticism of, 334–35, 341n7; description of cartoons, 335; plight of women and, 329–32; portrayal of children in, 329–30; readership, 327, 341n4; stage setting for, 325–26; supremacy of women and, 338–41
hygiene, 254–55

I, Rigoberta Menchú, 264–66
ideascape, 267, 270
identity, 295, 297; Brazilian exiles, 305–7, 308–9n5; Cuban women, 221–22; culture and, 256; *mestizo* society, 257, 279–91; nationalism and, 259–60; political activists, 298–99; sexual, 259; shared regional feminist, 269; social, 297; tango and Argentine national identity relationship, 348–51
immigration, 123, 256, 257
import substitution, 44, 94
income: decline in, 65; earned by members of households, 64; heads of households, 69, 74n19; inequality of, 62, 73n7; sources of, 64–65, 118–19
income distribution, 62, 73n7
India, 134
industrial home work, 96–98
industrial workers, 47
infant mortality, 3
informal sector, 28–29; growth of employment in, 64; Mexico, 93–96. *See also* domestic work and workers
Instituto Nicaragüense de Seguridad Social y Bienestar, 184
Inter-American Commission of Women, 137
Inter-American Foundation, 105
intermediario, 313
International Labor Organization, 25
International Ladies' Garment Workers' Union, 51

International Monetary Fund, 44
interracial relationships, 283

Jackson, Stevi, 4
Jagan, Janer, 138
Jaquette, Jane, 8–9
Jara, René, 312, 317
Jelin, Elizabeth, 104, 148
Jofre, Manuel, 317
Johnson-Odim, Cheryl, 8
jornaleras, 279
journalism, 260, 261–62
Juventud Rebelde, 222

Kampwirth, Karen, 140, 179–96
Kaplan, Temma, 98
kinship, Caribbean, 113–15
Kirkwood, Julieta, 159
Klatch, Rebecca, 180, 186
Kunzle, David, 259, 323–43

La Cabalgata del Circo, 349
La Delegada, 222
La Palabra de Dios, 236
La Paz, Bolivia, 68
labor: concepts of, 32; globalization and, 33–35
labor force, 23–27, 34, 44, 64, 117; 1950–1980, 43; Cuba, 46–48; day laborers, 257, 279, 290; Dominican Republic, 46–48; female-heads of households and, 73n10; formal sector, 25, 28, 32; garbage pickers, 29–30; gender division of, 25–29; globalization impact on women, 119–20; informal sector, 28–29, 64, 93–96; intensification of work in, 64–65, 70; marginalization of women's participation in, 253; occupational segregation, 50–52; service sector, 28, 43, 79–84; survival strategies related to, 92, 107n2; tertiary sector, 48–49; vendor sector, 85–87; wage labor, 46–49; women as mothers and workers, 116–19, 135, 213–15. *See also* domestic work and workers; employment; unemployment

Lacayo, Antonio, 189
Laclau, Ernesto, 209
laissez-faire conservatives, 186–88, 193n16
Lancaster, Roger, 334, 341n4, 341n7
land invasions, 162, 164
land reform, 94
land rights, 102
Landless Peasant Movement, Brazil, 150
Larrios, Luisa del Carmen, 187
Latin American Left, 299
Latin American Perspectives, 8, 10, 263; index
    of articles on women and gender, 361–74
Lavrin, Asuncion, 9, 259, 267–70
Lazaro Cardenas Union of *Ejidos* (UELC),
    100–102, 105
Le Recoleta, 355
Leacock, Eleanor, 20–29
Lebsock, Suzanne, 292n3
legal rights, 239
Let Me Speak, 172–78
liberation movements, 133, 136, 177
life expectancy, 2
Lima, Peru, 85, 86
L'information des femmes, 304–5
lo maravilloso, 319n15
Lomba, Mariuca, 341n7
López, Beatriz, 287
Los Angeles Times, 97
lower class: feminist groups, 165; low class
    consciousness, 135
Luciak, Ilja A., 141, 142–43
Lutjens, Sheryl L., 146, 213–30

McAllister, Carlota, 266
Machinandearena, Sergia, 349
machismo, 9
Madonna, 346–48, 350–51, 355–56, 357,
    358n2
Main, Mary, 353
The Making of Evita, 353
male-headed households, 68–70, 72–73n3
Mallon, Florence, 280
malnutrition, 69
maquila production, 28
maquiladora, 44, 97
marginalization; of domestic workers,
    79–84, 87; oral histories and, 316,

319n19; of urban women, 96; of
    women in labor force, 253; of women's
    police stations, 210n3
Marginalized Women, 231
marianismo, 9, 137
marriage: collapse of, 123–24; common-
    law, 68; impact of household economy
    on, 53–54, 58; interracial, 28; legal vs.
    nonlegal unions, 114–15; Mexico, 235;
    state policies and, 259
Martinez, Ana Guadalupe, 142
Marxism, 5, 6–7, 8–9, 327
masculinity, 136–37
maternal deaths, 237
matrifocal family structure, 113–15
Matthei, Evelyn, 145
mediation, women and state, 219–20
medical care, 285–86
Medin, Tzvi, 221
Menchú Tum, Rigoberta, 263, 264–66,
    314, 320n21
Menemism, 355–57
mestizo society, 234, 242n3, 257, 279–91
Mexican Alimentation System, 94
Mexico, 65, 93; abortion and, 148;
    Brazilian exiles, 298; diet, 66–67;
    economic crisis, 93–95; environmental
    issues, 93–94; leadership of, 149–50;
    networks of mutual assistance, 68;
    poverty, 73n5; power and women in,
    148; violence in, 74n18; women in
    politics, 138–39, 140
Mexico City, Mexico, 93, 149–50, 292n3,
    292n6
Meyer, Doris, 319n13
microenterprises, 30
middle class, 62; Brazilian exiles, 300;
    domestic workers and, 80–83, 85;
    economic crisis and, 62, 73n5; feminist
    groups and, 165; SOS-Mulher, 200;
    women's groups and, 163
migrants and migration, 43; age of, 89n5;
    domestic workers, 85; from Mexico, 93;
    to Canada, 123–24, 126n2; to Caribbean
    area, 112–13; to Guayaquil, 281–82; to
    Peru, 86; women as part of, 94–95
militarist groups, 296–97, 308n1

military: military rule, 141; training, 296;
women soldiers, 233; Miller, Francesca,
267, 269
Millikan, Brent H., 91
mining women, 172–78
Minority Rights Group, 256–57
Mistral, Chilena Gabriela, 260
Mittelman, James H., 33
Mohanty, Chandra, 8, 207
Molyneux, Maxine, 145, 146, 214, 220,
226–27nn2–3
Montejo, Esteban, 317
Montenegro, Sofia, 334, 341n7
Montoro, Andre Franco, 201
moral education, 254–55
Mörnei, Magnus, 281
Moscoso, Mireya, 138
Moser, Caroline, 70
mother-child bond, 114
motherhood, 181, 259, 317; Caribbean,
113–16; wife-mothers, 135; women as
mothers and workers, 116–19, 213–15
Mothers of the Plaza de Mayo, Argentina,
263
Mouffe, Chantal, 209
Mouvement pour la liberation de l'avortement
et la contraception, 302, 308n2
Movement for the Freedom of Abortion
and Contraception, 302, 308n2
Movement of Militant Mothers for
Education, 215
Movimento de Emancipacao do Proletariado,
204, 308n4
Mujeres, 218
Mujeres Marginadas, 231
Munck, Ronald, 7
Munequitos del Pueblo, 324
murder trials, Brazil, 199–200

narratives. See oral histories; testimonial
journalism
Nash, June, 8
National Committee for the Defense of
the Popular Economy, 103
National Council of the Urban Popular
Movement (CONAMPU), 99–100,
104–5

National Family Group, Cuba, 216
National Front in Defense of Wages
against Austerity and the High Cost of
Living, 103
National Liberation Zapatista Army, 74n18
National Study of the Budgeting of Time,
215–16
nationalism, 227n8, 259–60, 268, 358n6
Navarro, Marysa, 357–58n1
Negri, Antonio, 357
Nelson, Sara, 147, 197–212
neoliberalism, 33
networks of mutual assistance, 68
New Brazilian Republic, 200
New Left movements, 4–5
NGOs. See nongovernmental organizations
(NGOs)
Nicaragua, 140; Communist Party, 328–29;
contested gender relations, 179–80;
elections, 327; plight of women in,
329–32; poverty, 34; presidential
campaign, 180–83; protection of
threatened peoples, 257–58; textile
industry, 50
Nicaraguan Institute of Social Security
and Welfare, 184
nongovernmental organizations (NGOs),
145, 148–49
nonmilitarists, 308n1
Nos Mulheros, 269
nuclear family, 114–15
Nuevo Diario, 328, 333

Obando y Bravo, Miguel, 189
occupational categories, 25–27
occupational segregation, 50–52
oil reserves, 94
Olea, Raquel, 270
Oliveira, Orlandina, 64
Operation Bootstrap, 46
Oppression: of Brazilian exiles, 300,
303–5; gender and, 240; Third World
women, 21–22; total-oppression
stereotype, 233–35; women's
movement and, 168
oral histories, 260, 261–63, 313–14,
318nn5–7, 319n13; Brazilian women in

exile, 294–95; female sexual slavery,
315–16, 319nn16–18; male narrators,
315–17, 319nn14–15; personal and
political, 316–18, 320nn25–26. See also
testimonial journalism
Organization of American States, 257
Ortega, Eugenio, 74n14
Ortego, Daniel, 183, 331–32
Özler, Süle, 35

Pagotto, Carmen Silvia, 65
Palavicini, Felix F., 252
Pan-Americanism, 267
Pan-Mayan movement, 258
Panama, 29, 140
Paraguay, 138
parent-child relationships, 124, 216
Paris, France, 303–6
Parker, Alan, 347, 349, 352, 353, 357
Partch, Virgil, 340
Partido dos Trabalhadores, 202
Partido Movimento Democrático Brasileira,
201
Partoy, Alicia, 320n21
Party of the Brazilian Democratic
Movement, 201
Pastore, José, 65
paternalism, 82, 88, 223
patriarchy, 5, 56, 116, 118
patriotism, 254
patron families, 79–84, 85–86, 88
peasant organizations, 102–3
peddlers, 286
Peña, Lorena, 142
pericón, 349
Permanent Commission on Women,
Children, Youth, and the Family,
186–88, 192n10
Perón, Evita, 137; eroticism of, 346,
358n2; Madonnification of, 346–48;
myth-making and, 354–57; origins,
344, 357–58n1; remythologization of,
344–45; tango dancing, 350–51;
transnationalization of, 348–51,
358n3
Perón, Juan, 351, 353, 354
Peronism, 357

Peru, 140, 167; abortion and, 148; census
information, 80–81, 88n1; poverty, 34;
service sector employment in, 80–82;
vending vs. domestic service, 85–86
Petras, James, 132, 150, 167
Pettman, Jan Jindy, 145–46
phallocentrism, 226n1
photography, erotic, 326, 332, 333–35
PIDER. See Program for Investment in
Rural Development (PIDER)
Pinochet, Augusto, 157
Pinto, Delmi Marcela, 237
Pitanguy, Jacqueline, 205
Plan de Ayala National Council (CNPA),
102–4
plantations, 282
Playboy, 326, 332, 334
Plazarte, Vidala, 288
pluralism, 182n8, 337–38
Pluralista, 337
police academy, 202, 204, 208, 210n4
police stations, Brazil, 197–208
political cartoons, 324–25, 327–28
political economy, gendering of, 6–7, 19,
36n1
political patronage, 113
politics, 4–5, 186, 209, 237–38, 298; activists
exiled from Brazil, 294, 301–2;
advantages of, 319n14; Chamorro's
campaign, 180–83; Cuba, 221; *Evita* story
and, 351–55; exit polls, 183, 191n4;
gendered policies of Chamorro
administration, 183–85; Guayaquil, 290;
impact of state policy on women, 145–48;
mass action, 295–96, 308n1; political
organizations, 298–301, 306; portrayal of
in cartoons, 336–38; protest movements
and, 144–45; reduction of women's role
in, 169; sexually explicit material and,
333–34; symbolism of in campaigns, 182,
183, 192n9; women's participation in,
104, 131–32, 136–41, 149, 163, 166–68
pollution, 93–94
polygamy, 115
popular movements, 98–106
Popular Unity, Chile, 158–59
pornography, 333, 358n3

Post, Ken, 6–7
poverty, 3, 33–34, 71, 72n1; Caribbean, 119;
    economic crisis of 1980s and, 44;
    employment opportunities and, 81;
    hardships on women, 91–92; heads of
    households and, 69, 283–84, 292n3;
    Mexico, 73n5; urban poor, 62, 73nn5–7;
    women's organizing efforts and, 104–6
power, 148–50, 159–60
Prates, Suzana, 73n8
pregnancy, 54
Prensa, 180–81, 329, 333
Price, Marilyn, 120–22
production, 6
Program for Investment in Rural
    Development (PIDER), 100–102
*Programa para Inversiones en Desarollo
    Rural*, 100–102
prohibition movement, 236
proletarianization, 95
prostitution, 222–23, 239
protest movements, 143–45, 148, 225,
    227n7
Protestant religion, 236
psychologists, 204, 210n5
Puerto Rico, 46, 48–55
puestos preferentes, 49

Quiroz, Ana Fidelia, 221
quota laws, 140

race, differences in, 256–57
race relations, 125–26, 257, 283
Radcliffe, Sarah A., 148
Radio Tierra, 269
raft houses, 278, 282
Randall, Margaret, 260, 261–63
Rapp, Rayna, 80
Rayas, Lucia, 147–48
Red Mask, 237–38
redemocratization, 131–32, 145
relationships, forms of, 289, 297
repression, Chile, 161
reproductive health of women, 216
reproductive work, 97, 107n2, 118
resources: access to, 49–52; unequal
    distribution of, 68–70

"The Revolutionary Women's Law,"
    239–40
revolutions, 141; Mozambique, 133;
    Nicaragua, 180, 191n2; women's
    participation in, 316, 316n24,
    320nn21–22
Rice, Tim, 353
Rios, Carbajal, 103
Rocha Lima, Valentina, 295
Rodríguez, Carlos Rafael, 213
Roldán, Martha, 96
Rubbo, Anna, 88–89n2
rural population, 96–97, 98, 220–21, 282
Rus, Jan, 263, 264–70

Sacks, Karen, 80
Sádico Ilustrado, 333
Sadoulet, Elisabeth, 62
Safa, Helen I., 43–60, 119
Salinas de Gortari, Carlos, 100, 101–2
San Pedro, Mexico, 231–42
Sánchez, Róger, 313, 323–43
Sandinista National Liberation Front
    (FSLN), 180–81, 190, 193n15, 324,
    327, 331, 340
São Paulo, Brazil, 198–99, 200–201
Savigliano, Marta E., 266, 344–60
Scheper-Hughes, Nancy, 259
Schild, Veronica, 149
Schkolnik, Mariana, 74n14
Scott, Alison MacEwen, 88–89n2
Scott, Joan, 4
Second Wave Feminism, 4
Segal, Lynne, 9–10
Semana Cómica, 323, 325, 326–27,
    333–35, 340
*Semanario de Humor, Marxismo, Sexo y
    Violencia*, 327
Semanario de la Jodarria Nicaragüense, 327
service sector workers, 28, 43, 79–84
sex crimes, 187–90, 193nn15–16, 199, 239
sex education, 216–17
sexual morality, 217
sexual relations: age of participants, 330;
    female sexual slavery, 315–16,
    319nn16–18; political leaders, 331;
    research in, 259. *See also Humor Erotico*

shamans, 235–36
Siglo XX, 172–78
Silva, Benedita da, 258
Singer, Pavl, 74n13
single mothers, 54–55
Sinha, Mrinalini, 270
Sirias, Adilia, 187
Sistema Alimentaria Mexicana, 94
slave trade, 256
slavery, 282, 286; female sexual slavery,
    315–16, 319nn16–18; fugitive, 290;
    inheritance and, 288
Sleep On, Beloved, 124
social class, 133, 166, 167, 300; impact of
    crisis on, 157–59; Peru, 80–82,
    88–89n2
social conservatives, 186–87
social movements, 98–106, 134, 158,
    167–68, 300
social services, 63, 73n8, 184
social workers, 204, 210n5
socialism, 132, 136, 178
socialist feminism, 269–70
socialist movements, 134
socialist states, resilience of, 225–26,
    227n8
socialization: Chiapas, 236–37; domestic
    workers, 79–84; transformation of,
    132–36
Socolow, Susan Migden, 27
sodomy, 188
Solórzano, Elida, 184
SOS-Mulher, 200–201
soup kitchens, 162
South America, 140
Southern Cone feminism, 9
sovereignty, power and, 148–50
squatter encampments, 162, 164
Stabile, Carol A., 270
Standing, Guy, 58
Stanley, Charlotte, 294–310
State Council on the Status of Women
    (CECF), 201–3, 219n4
state policies: Cuba, 213–19; impact on
    status of women, 48–49; marriage and,
    259; political power and, 145–48; racial,
    257; women and, 145–48, 213–33

status of women, 20; Brazil, 201–3, 210n4;
    domestic vs. public spheres, 79–84,
    88–89n2; impact of access to resources
    on, 49–52; impact of gender ideology
    on, 55–57; impact of household income
    on, 52–55; impact of state policies on,
    48–49; paid labor and, 45, 46–48
Stearns, Jill, 6
Stephen, Lynn, 34, 91–111
Sternbach, Nancy Saporta, 263, 311–22
Stevens, Evelyn P., 136–37
Stolcke, Verena, 57
Stoll, David, 263, 264–65
Storni, Alfonsina, 260
Strength of the Mayan Women, 239
Strobel, Margaret, 8
structural adjustment policies, 44, 45, 48,
    63
subsidies, 63, 100
suffrage, 137–38
supermadre, 140, 149

tango, 348–51, 358n3
Tango and the Political Economy of Passion,
    348
Taussig, Michael, 88–89n2
Tayacán, 331
technology, 250
teenage pregnancy, 54
Teitelboim, Berta, 74n14
Terner, Michel, 202
terrorism, 160
tertiary sector workers, 48, 49
testigo, 312, 318n3
testimonial journalism, 260, 261–62;
    Menchu's story, 263, 264–65; overview,
    311–13. See also oral histories
testimonio, 312, 313, 314, 316, 317
Third World feminism, 7–10
Third World nations, development of,
    21–22
three-generation households, 55
Tiano, Susan, 29
Tijerino, Doris, 188, 193n13
Timerman, Jacobo, 317, 319n14
Tironi, Ernesto, 74n14
total-oppression stereotypes, 233–35

Townsend, Camilla, 257, 278–93
Townsend, Janet Gabriel, 148
trade, 250
transfer payments, 51, 58
travel literature, 260
tropical diseases, 285
Tsobol Antzetik, 231
Tuchman, Paula, 172–78
Turits, Richard, 219
two-wage-earner families, 45
Tzotzil cargo, 235

UAIMs. *See* Agroindustrial Units for
  Women (UAIMs)
UELC. *See* Lazaro Cardenas Union of
  Ejidos (UELC)
Uggen, John F, 157–71
unemployment, 25–27, 44, 48; Caribbean,
  119; economics of, 63–64; heads of
  households, 64, 74n11
Unidad Popular, 298
Unidades Agroindustrias de la Mujer, 101–2,
  105
Union de Ejidos "Lázaro Cárdenas",
  100–102, 105
Union Nacional Opositora (UNO), 180,
  183–90, 192n6
Unions: garment industry, 51–52;
  organization of, 172–78
United Nations, women's share of
  economic activity rates, 23, 36n2
United States: Agency for International
  Development, 183–84; economic aid to
  Chamorro administration, 185, 192n7;
  foreign relations, 261; policy toward
  Cuba, 224; politics, 186; role in
  garment industry, 52
Universidad Popular, 252–53
University of Havana, 219
UNO. *See* Union Nacional Opositora
  (UNO)
unwaged work, 19
upper class, women's organizations and,
  161
urban population, 282–83; character of, 65;
  Cuba, 220–21; decline in real wages of,
  62; employment, 63, 73n9; female

consciousness and, 98; marginalization of
  women in, 96; Mexico, 93; poverty of,
  62, 73nn5–7; sources of income, 64–65;
  wage-labor force, 96
urbanization, 23–24
Urbina, María, 288
Uruguay, 65, 267–68, 294, 298

Van Young, Eric, 292n6
Varela, Maria Elena Diaz, 225
Vaughan, Mary K., 251–60
Vazquez, Ana, 300–301, 306
vendor sector, 85–87, 117
venereal diseases, 286, 292n4
Venezuela, 65, 74n11, 139, 140
Viezzer, Moema, 141, 172–78
violence against women, 340, 341n9;
  CECF role, 202; Chiapas, 239–40;
  discrimination in judicial systems,
  199–201; Guayaquil, 289; prosecution
  of, 197, 204–5; reports of, 205
violent emotion defense, 199–200
Virgin Mary, 182
voter profiles, 183

wages, 25, 45, 62, 118; agricultural
  laborers, 97–98; domestic workers, 84,
  85–86, 87, 89n6; garbage pickers, 30;
  home-based industries, 97; impact on
  women's status, 46–49; income
  inequality, 62, 73n7; labor statistics,
  117; *maquila* production, 28; Mexico,
  237; mine workers, 177; minimum
  wage, 48, 87, 93; occupational
  segregation and, 50; significance to
  women, 71; state policy and, 49; type
  of work and, 119
weaving cooperatives, Mexico, 231–42
Weekly of Nicaraguan Fun, 327
West, Guida, 143
Westwood, Sallie, 148
widowhood, 180–82
Wieringa, Saskia, 148, 267, 269
Williams, Linda, 358n3
Wilson, Tamar Diana, 29–35
Wives: functions of, 254; as political
  candidates, 180–83; wife-mothers, 135

The Woman with the Whip, 353
womanhood, 182–83
Woman's Role in Economic Development, 32
Women for Democracy, 168
Women United, 231
Women's Group, 239–40
women's interests, 220
women's movements, 133–34, 192n8;
    challenge to sex-crime legislation,
    189–90; Chile, 161–65; divisions within,
    168–69; France, 302; Nicaragua,
    187–90; politics and, 169; response to
    violence against women, 199–200;
    reversals for, 166–68; women's police
    stations and, 197, 201–4
women's organizations, 165, 191n1, 200,
    240; Afro-Latin American, 258;
    AMNLAE, 193, 329–32, 333–35;
    autonomy of, 214, 219, 226n1, 240,
    303; Bolivia, 172–78; Chiapas, 239–40;
    Chile, 161–65; Circulo, 303–6;
    contribution to struggle theory, 176–78;
    FMC, 214–23, 227nn3–4;
    generalizations derived from, 175–76;
    Mexico, 97–106; mobilization of, 180;
    participation in, 218; political forces
    and, 166, 167–68; recognition of,
    269–70; trends in, 267–68
women's police stations, 197, 201–4
Women's Reconciliation, Chile, 166, 169

women's rights, 105, 147, 149, 203,
    239–40, 289
women's studies, 217, 269
women's work, 19–20, 23–27
Woollacott, Angela, 270
The Word of God, 236
Workers' Party, 202
workers' rights, Cuba, 50
workers' solidarity, 51–52
working conditions, 103; domestic
    workers, 87; garment industry, 51–52;
    poor women, 96–98
workshops, 162–64
World Bank, 44

Yagual, Ana, 287
Young, Grace Esther, 27, 78–90
Young, Linda Wilcox, 62
Yúdice, George, 250

zambo, 283
Zamora, Daisy, 331
Zapatista, 237–40
Zapatista Army of National Liberation
    (EZLN), 233, 240, 242n2
Zapatista movement, 149
Zapatista Revolutionary Law for Women,
    149
Zapatistas, 231–32
Zylberstagn, Helio, 65

About the Contributors

Jennifer Abbassi received her Ph.D. in political science from the University of California, Riverside, in 1994. She is associate professor of political science and chair of the international studies program at Randolph-Macon Woman's College. She teaches courses on global issues, international law, and Latin American political economy. Her research interests include new developments in international human rights law, the Cuban revolution, and feminist pedagogies. Her publications include articles on agricultural markets in Cuba and on process-oriented teaching and learning.

Rosa Cañadell is a psychologist and Ph.D. candidate in anthropology. She teaches in Pedraforca National Institute of Professional Development in Barcelona and lectures at the University of Barcelona. Her research focuses on social movements, women's movements in Latin America, cultural diversity, and critical pedagogy. She has published in the United States, Spain, Argentina, Mexico, and Chile, and is currently a member of the Comité de Apoyo of the Movimiento Sin Tierra (Brazil), USTEC (the Union of Educators, Catalonia), and the National Council of the United Left Party in Catalonia (Esquerra Unida i Alternativa).

Norma Stoltz Chinchilla is professor of sociology and women's studies at California State University, Long Beach. She has published articles on women's movements in Latin America, feminism and nationalism, and gender and immigration among Central American immigrants in Los Angeles. Her works include *Nuestras Utopias: Mujeres Guatemaltecas en el Siglo XX* (1998) and, with Nora Hamilton, *Seeking Community in a Global City: Guatemalans and Salvadorans in Los Angeles* (2001).

Christine E. Eber is assistant professor of anthropology at New Mexico State University. She is author of "Buscando una nueva vida: Liberation through Autonomy in San Pedro Chenalhó, 1970–1998," in *Latin American Perspectives* and, with Janet Tanski, of "Obstacles to Women's Grassroots Development Strategies in Mexico" in *The Review of Radical Political Economics*.

Mercedes González de la Rocha is senior researcher of social anthropology at the Centro de Investigactiones y Estudios Superiores in Guadalajara, Mexico. As part of her recent consultant work with the U.N. Development Program, she published "Private Adjustments: Household Responses to the Erosion of Work" (2000) and, with Alejandro Grinspun, "Private Adjustments: Households, Crises, and Work," in *Choices for the Poor* (2001).

Christine G. T. Ho is visiting associate professor of African and Latin American studies at Colgate University. Her recent work on Caribbean popular culture includes "Popular Culture and the Aestheticization of Politics: Hegemonic Struggle and Post-Colonial Nationalism in the Trinidad Carnival" in *Transforming Anthropology*, and "Globalization and the Diaspora-ization of Caribbean Peoples and Popular Culture," in a forthcoming issue of *Journal of the Caribbean and Its Diaspora*.

Karen Kampwirth is associate professor of political science at Knox College. She is coeditor, with Victoria Gonzalez, of *Radical Women in Latin America: Left and Right* (2001). She is also the author of *Revolution in the Real World: Women and Guerrillas in Latin America* (forthcoming).

David Kunzle is professor of art history at the University of California, Los Angeles. His most recent publication on Latin American art is *Che Guevara: Icon, Myth and Message* (1997).

Eleanor Leacock (1922-1987) was chair and professor of anthropology at the City College of New York. Her numerous publications include, with Mona Etienne, *Women and Colonization* (1980), *Myths of Male Dominance* (1981), *Visibility and Power: Essays on Women in Society and Development* (1986) and, with Helen Safa, *Women's Work* (1986).

Ilja A. Luciak is associate professor of political science at Virginia Polytechnic Institute and State University. His latest publication is *After the Revolution: Gender and Democracy in El Salvador, Nicaragua and Guatemala* (2001). He is currently working on a project for the European Commission on "Gender Equality and Democratization in Central America and Cuba" while a guest researcher at the Institute of Latin American Studies in Vienna, Austria.

Sheryl L. Lutjens received her Ph.D. in political science from the University of California, Berkeley, in 1987. She is professor of political science at Northern Arizona University, where she has taught courses in women, politics, and power; women in Latin America; Latin American politics; development; comparative politics; and public administration, among others. Her research interests include feminist theory, democracy, and the state, and her publications include *The State, Bureaucracy, and the Cuban Schools: Power and Participation* (2000) and other writings on Cuba.

Sara Nelson returned to São Paulo in 1994 to conduct her dissertation fieldwork on women's police stations. She completed her doctorate in cultural anthropology from the University of Washington in 1997 where she lectured in the departments of anthropology and women studies for two years. She currently lives in Seattle and is involved in grassroots antiviolence work.

Margaret Randall lives in Albuquerque, New Mexico. Her books on gender in Latin America include *Sandino's Daughters* (1995), *Sandino's Daughters Revisited* (1994), *Gathering Rage: The Failure of Twentieth-Century Revolutions to Develop a Feminist Agenda* (1992) and *Our Voices/Our Lives: Stories of Women from Central America and the Caribbean* (1995). Her forthcoming works include *Coming Up for Air*, a compilation of poetry, memoir, essay and photographic portfolio, and *Where They Left You for Dead*, a collection of poems.

Jan Rus is codirector, with Diane L. Rus, of the Native Language Publishing Project (Taller Tzotzil), Instituto de Asesoría Antropológica para la Región Maya, San Cristóbal. He is also affiliated with the department of anthropology at the University of California, Riverside. His recent work includes, with Aída Hernández and Shannan Mattiace, *Land, Liberty and Autonomy: The Indigenous Peoples of Chiapas and the Zapatista Movement* (forthcoming) and, in Spanish, *Tierra, libertad y autonomía: Respuestas regionales al Zapatismo en Chiapas* (forthcoming).

Helen I. Safa is professor emerita of anthropology and Latin American studies at the University of Florida. She is author of *The Myth of the Male Breadwinner: Women and Industrialization in the Caribbean* (1995) and numerous articles on Dominican women in export manufacturing and on women and work more broadly, including "Female-headed Households in the Caribbean and the Diaspora: Deviant or Alternative form of Family Organization?" *Latino(a) Research Review*.

Nancy Saporta Sternbach is professor of Spanish at Smith College. She is coeditor, with Alberto Sandoval, of an anthology of U.S. Latina plays, titled

Puro Teatro: A Latina Anthology (2000) and *Stages of Life: Transcultural Performance and Identity Formation in U.S. Latina Theatre* (forthcoming).

Marta E. Savigliano is professor of culture and performance studies at the University of California, Los Angeles. She is the author of *Tango and the Political Economy of Passion* (1995) and *The Case of Angora Matta: Tangophilia, Ethnographitis, and Other Translingual Outbursts of North-South Consciousness* (forthcoming), a mixed-genre book containing scholarly essays and critical fiction, and other publications on the historical, ethnographic, and cinematographic dimensions of popular dance in Latin America and its representations abroad.

Lynn Stephen is professor of anthropology at the University of Oregon. Her publications include *Zapotec Women* (1991), with María Teresa Tula, *Hear My Testimony: María Teresa Tula, Human Rights Activist of El Salvador* (1994), *Women and Social Movements in Latin America: Power from Below* (1997), and *Zapata Lives: Histories and Political Cultures in Southern Mexico* (2001).

Camilla Townsend is associate professor of history at Colgate University. She is author of *Tales of Two Cities: Race and Economic Culture in Early Republican North and South America* (2000) and numerous articles on women and gender issues.

Mary Kay Vaughan is professor of history at the University of Maryland. She is coeditor, with Heather Fowler Salamini, of *Creating Spaces, Shaping Transitions: Women of the Mexican Countryside, 1850–1990* (1994). She is also the author of *Cultural Politics in Revolution: Teachers, Peasants, and Schools in Mexico, 1930–1940* (1997) and numerous articles on women, gender, and education.

Moema Viezzer is a member of the executive committee of the Instituto de Comunicação Solidária in the Brazilian state of Paraná. Following the publication of this article, she returned to Brazil after seven years in exile and founded Rede Mulher de Educação (Women's Network on Popular Education). Her areas of interest include gender equity and transformative learning for transformative leadership from a feminist perspective.

Tamar Diana Wilson is a research affiliate in the department of anthropology, University of Missouri, St. Louis. Her numerous publications include a forthcoming article on the masculinization of the maquiladoras (*Review of Radical Political Economics*) and a coedited book, with Judith E. Martí, on women in the informal sector.

Angela Xavier de Brito is a researcher at the CERLIS (Research Center on Social Relations), a research team from the University of Paris V associated with the National Center of Scientific Research. Her work focuses on the realities and experiences of foreign persons in all their forms (exiles, migrants, students) in the countries of reception. Her many works include "Circe or Penelope? Latin-American Women in Exile," in D. Joly's *Exclusion and Integration of Minorities in Europe* (1998) and "Les étudiants étrangers: des personnes en déplacement," in H. Malewska et al., *Identités, altérités, acculturation* (forthcoming).

Grace Esther Young is assistant professor of sociology at Adams State College. Her dissertation explored the survival strategies of low income, rural Quebec mothers. As board president of the San Luis Valley Welfare Advocates, she works to alter local dynamics of power by educating, training, and organizing low-income families as a way to enhance their self-worth and quality of life.